THE ORGANIZATION OF ACTION
A NEW SYNTHESIS

THE ORGANIZATION OF ACTION:
A NEW SYNTHESIS

C. R. GALLISTEL
University of Pennsylvania

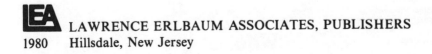 LAWRENCE ERLBAUM ASSOCIATES, PUBLISHERS
1980   Hillsdale, New Jersey

DISTRIBUTED BY THE HALSTED PRESS DIVISION OF
JOHN WILEY & SONS
New York   Toronto   London   Sydney

Original Illustrations by John Woolsey.

Lawrence Erlbaum Associates, Inc., Publishers
365 Broadway
Hillsdale, New Jersey 07642
Distributed solely by Halsted Press Division
John Wiley & Sons, Inc., New York

Library of Congress Cataloging in Publication Data

Gallistel, C. R. 1941–
  The organization of action.

  Bibliography: p.
  Includes indexes.
  1. Animal mechanics.   2. Efferent pathways.
3. Reflexes.   4. Motivation (Psychology)   I. Title.
QP303.G28   591.1'852   79-22565
ISBN 0-470-26912-x

Printed in the United States of America

To the women in my life—
Mabel, Betty, and Rochel

Contents

Preface

This book is plagiarism on a grand scale. It constructs a thesis about the organization of action, making extensive use of other men's words. The plagiarism is not an act of theft, but an act of homage. Most psychologists are insufficiently aware of the rich empirical and conceptual contributions that "my" authors have made to our understanding of how animal action is generated.

My hopes for this book are twofold: (1) to convince psychologists and behavioral neurobiologists that the conceptual gap between muscles and motivation is not the yawning chasm most of us imagine. We actually understand much about how such abstractions as a "hunger signal" get translated into the lengthy, variable, and complex pattern of muscular contractions that constitute the behavior of seeking and eating food; (2) to bring to the attention of the psychologists the work that has produced this understanding, work that for various reasons is not as well known to psychologists as it should be.

The original impetus for this book arose from my research and teaching on the physiological and neurophysiological bases of motivation. Like most phyisological psychologists, I conceive of motivation in terms of central motive states, processes in the central nervous system that dispose animals to behave in certain ways and not others, to copulate and not to drink, or vice versa. In the first edition of his *Theory of Motivation,* Bolles (1967) summarizes this approach as follows:

> the neural and hormonal bases of the state are discovered, their effects upon behavior noted, and the controlling antecedent conditions are hunted down.

> Explanations of specific behavior result that may quite legitimately be considered to constitute a theory of motivation. The physiologist's concern here is ordinarily, however, not with explaining behavior but rather with elucidating the nature of the central state. The consequent linkages to behavior are often considered as more properly of concern to the psychologist. Thus, it has been fairly common to . . . speak of hunger and thirst as the "urges" to eat and drink [p. 114].

Physiological psychologists, in other words, generally end their analysis of motivation with a grand wave of the hand. The motivational signals exit from the diagrams along some mysterious arrow called "the final common path to behavior." After some years of teaching, the urge to venture down that path became irresistible; and so I began to delve into the literature on basic motor mechanisms.

The second and decisive impetus for this book came some years later in a conversation with George Mandler. He remarked that what modern cognitive psychology most lacked was any sort of theory of action. By then, my delving in the literature on motor mechanisms had persuaded me that there was within this literature a view of action that would be congenial to modern cognitive psychologists, if only they were aware of it. The view emphasizes internal structure and above all hierarchical structure. Surely that would be congenial to modern psychology. Furthermore, the view was grounded in detailed behavioral observations, observations that served to illuminate and particularize ideas that sometimes seem dark and vague when they appear in general abstract discussions of how behavior is organized. I set out more or less on the spot to bring this diverse material together in a way that would make it both accessible to and digestible by modern students of psychology.

I believe that even at the introductory level, students should read as much as possible of the original literature. I also believe that they ought, in general, to read classic papers, rather than "the latest word." If students read only the papers of the last 10 years, they have no idea where the concepts in those papers came from. The papers reprinted here represent very early and unusually lucid statements of many of the concepts that are, or should be, central to modern analysis of animal action. Much of the text that I have written is designed to help students understand the conceptual essence of these papers. To the same end, there is a Glossary and Index at the end of the book, where students will find definitions of technical terms and references to other places in the text where a given concept is explained. I have used these readings in an introductory course in physiological psychology, with considerable success. I very much hope that they will be used by other teachers in similar courses.

I was greatly aided by George Mandler and Jeffrey Wine, who critically read the entire first draft, and by Robert Bolles, who gave a detailed critical reading of the first nine chapters, and to Renée Baillargeon who did the same for the first four chapters. I am grateful to them. I am also grateful to graduate and undergraduate students too numerous to mention, who have made a variety of valuable comments on the early drafts. John Woolsey, the illustrator for the book, provided innumerable valuable suggestions for improving the communicative force of the illustrations. Finally, without my wife, Rochel Gelman, I would not have enjoyed the peace of mind required to complete this project. The project proved considerably more arduous than I anticipated.

C. R. Gallistel
Philadelphia

THE ORGANIZATION OF ACTION: A NEW SYNTHESIS

1 Introduction and Overview: De Anima and Animals

The windmill stands on a plain, moving only when acted upon by a palpable external force, the wind. Its movements are relatively simple, extremely stereotyped, and obviously molded by the structure of the mechanism.

Beneath one of the footings, a wild rat digs a burrow. There does not seem to be any external force that initiates the rat's movements. Its movements are bafflingly complex and not at all stereotyped. The precise form of these movements varies constantly. These variations are not random. They are almost always functionally appropriate. The variations enable the rat to overcome obstacles to its continued tunneling. They adapt the digging pattern to the fluctuating conditions with which it must cope. Finally, it is not at all clear how, or even if, the observable structure of the rat determines any but the outermost limits on the form of its movements.

The movements of animals differ so strikingly from the movements of inanimate objects that throughout most of the history of analytic thought about natural phenomena it was taken virtually for granted that these movements betrayed the presence of processes of a nonphysical nature. The very term animal derives from the Greek word animos, by way of the Latin *anima*. The original Greek meaning was "wind." Greek and Latin philosophers used the word to refer to some active but insubstantial principle or aspect of reality that was present in "animals" but absent from the ordinary objects of the physical world. This concept of anima was transmuted into the concept of a soul as Hellenic thought fused with Hebraic thought. The presence of anima was invoked in order to explain the phenomena of organismic movements. So great was the apparent discrepancy between the movements of animals and the movements of ordinary physical objects that a special constituent seemed clearly called for.

1

In the late Renaissance, analytic thinkers first confronted man made machines that made intricate lifelike movements in the absence of any apparent external forces. These animated machines were the fancy clocks and mechanical dolls that were a by product of the Renaissance explosion in man's mechanical ingenuity (see Fig. 1.1). These clockwork animals and statues suggested to Descartes that at least some aspects of animal movement might be explainable on purely physical principles. One could explain some animal movement in exactly the same way as one would explain the actions of a machine, that is, by describing the structure of the inner mechanism and invoking one or another kind of physical causality.

But the behavior of the animated statues of Descartes' time was only superficially lifelike. Upon close examination, it lacked intelligence. There was no indication that thought or thoughtlike processes played a role in patterning the movements of these machines. The movements of these machines did not adapt in an intelligent way when circumstances were altered so as to render the normal pattern of movement nonfunctional.

As a philosopher engaged in writing out a philosophical essay, Descartes was intensely aware of the role that thought plays in patterning some kinds of human action. He did not think that the more intelligent actions, the ones shaped by thought, could be explained in the same way one would explain the actions of a machine. In his famous dictum, "I think, therefore I am," the "I" refers to a special nonphysical constituent of Descartes, the thinking constituent. This constituent is the sovereign soul. Its deliberations initiate and direct our more intelligent actions, as for example, the actions we perform when we play chess, write out the proof of a theorem, or write out a philosophical essay. This soul is by definition free of the dictates of physical determinism. "*Cogito ergo sum*" is an *ad hominem* argument for the existence of this nonphysical constituent, supposedly directing the movements of the hand that holds the philosopher's pen.

It seemed to Descartes—and it still seems to most of us—that one could never build a machine capable of composing philosophical essays. Nor did it seem that this was for want of small enough or precise enough gears, nor any other such trivial reason. Rather it seemed that the processes underlying man's more thought-filled actions must be such that they could not *in principle* be embodied in the workings of a machine. These principles, however vague we may be about what exactly they are, seem to possess a subtlety and refinement that precludes their realization in anything subject to the gross constraints of the physical world. Our intuition fairly screams that the principles governing our more intelligent actions require for their realization a domain free of the constraints of space and time, mass and energy—the constraints that fetter operations in the physical domain. Our thoughts require, in short, a *mental* domain, the domain of intelligence.

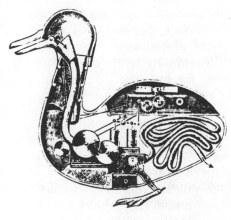

a   b

FIG. 1.1. The 17th and 18th centuries saw the construction of the first lifelike automatons, culminating in: (*a*) Jaques Vaucanson's duck, which swam, flapped its wings, preened itself, ate food and excreted the feces-like results of its 'digestion'. (*b*) Pierre Jacquet-Droz's 'scrivener,' a doll that wrote out the words "Welcome to Neuchâtel" after dipping its pen in an ink well and shaking it twice. Later Droz, in collaboration with his son, constructed a 'draughtsman' whose movements were so lifelike that the elder Droz was tried for sorcery. [Reproduced from: Eco, U., & Zorzoli, G. B. *The picture history of inventions*. New York: Macmillan, 1963].

One of the characteristics of human action that seems to betray the presence of some nonphysical "intelligence," is the extraordinary flexibility manifest in human action. Bruner (1970) comments with bemused chagrin on the motor flexibility displayed by his stepson, who, it appears, employs this flexibility to humble his distinguished father on the squash court.

> My stepson who, I assure you, is not so stylish a squash player as I am but a cleverer one, has beaten me all too regularly by such feats as hitting a return beneath a raised leg when caught facing the rear wall of the court! When humans can do this type of substitution in real time, we say they are good athletes; there are situations not so constrained by timing where we would be more likely to say that the performer who showed a flair for appropriate substitutions was "clever" rather than a good athlete [p. 66].

What is remarkable about the movements of skilled athletes is not only the wide variety of actions used to achieve the same general end but also the rapidity with which the particular actions are altered in order to cope with changes in circumstance. The flexible and rapid adoption of new action sequences in response to changes in circumstance is so closely allied to our intuitions about intelligence itself that Bartlett (1958) begins his influential book on thinking with a lengthy discussion of the characteristics of skilled action. *If, therefore, one can describe the kinds of neural circuitry and organizational principles that enable animals to make rapid but functionally appropriate modifications of ongoing patterns of movement, one has begun to describe the physical basis of intelligence.*

PHYSICAL REALIZABILITY

In this book, I assume that we are allowed no recourse to physically unrealizable principles and processes in order to explain what underlies the organization of action, no matter how intelligent that action appears. I reject, in other words, the distinction between "intelligent" actions and machine actions. I assume that the intelligence of animal action is simply a consequence of the intricacy and subtlety of construction in the machine that generates that action, namely, the central nervous system of the animal. Since an orderly temporal sequence of muscular contractions underlies any animal action, a scientific analysis of the organization of this action is concerned with specifying the types of physically realizable processes that underlie the generation of orderly temporal sequences of commands to the muscles of the body. Thus, one constraint imposed on the discussion at the outset is that we consider only processes that can be specified in sufficient detail so that an embodiment or physical realization of the process (i.e., a working model) can be built.

Such a commitment does not imply the metaphysical belief that physical reality is the only reality. Computer programs are certainly real. To believe otherwise would be to believe that IBM invests vast sums of money every year to develop and copyright unrealities. Yet computer programs are not physical entities. A computer program is a sequence of instructions causing the computer to do first this, then that, and so on. In order for instructions to be executed by a computer, they must be embodied in some physical form, such as a set of holes in a paper card, or a sequence of magnetized spots on a tape. But IBM does not copyright any physical embodiment of the sequence of instructions. A sequence of instructions is an abstraction. It has no weight, no energy, no position in space and time. In short, it has none of the attributes that physical things have. Computer programs are, in fact, an illustration of the fact that conceptions are real; where by conceptions I mean coherent sets of principles. And by principles I mean explicit rules or laws that determine how something will behave, as, for example, the instructions in a computer program determine how the computer will behave. In the final analysis, what this book is about are the conceptions by which we may understand the generation of animal action. However, these are required to be conceptions of a particular kind, namely conceptions that may be embodied in the structure of a machine.

In practice, the commitment to physically realizable conceptions means largely that I hope to use only precise and explicit conceptions rather than vague and implicit ones. An excellent test of the precision and explicitness of a conception is to build a physical embodiment of it, or to find one that is already built. Thus, for example, in Chapter 6, one can convince oneself of the precision and explicitness of the concept of a tropotaxis simply by noting that the Sidewinder missile constitutes a physical embodiment of this concept. It is in this spirit, that I occasionally illustrate the conceptions presented in this book by reference to electronic (e.g., p. 57) or mechanical embodiments of them.

One of the odd characteristics of the mental versus physical dualism that has been a central feature of Western thought for several centuries, is that precise and explicit principles that were necessarily mental (in the sense of not physically realizable) have very seldom been put forward. The principles that many firm dualists have put forward in order to explain events supposedly occurring in the mental domain have been physically realizable, at least insofar as the principles were precise and explicit. For example, the laws of association formulated by 18th and 19th Century English philosophers, all of whom were dualists, are easily given a physical realization. It is easy to construct a machine that exemplifies the law of contiguity, which states that the more often two inputs have occurred together, the more readily the occurrence of one input will activate the record of the other. Other laws of association, insofar as they are explicit and unambiguous, are readily simulated on a computer. Since a belief in dualism generally rests on an intuition that the actions of the mind are inexplicable by physically realizable principles, it is curious that the laws of the mind formulated by dualist philosophers should be of a kind that are easily given a physical embodiment. If one constructed a machine that operated exactly in accord with the laws that determine the operation of the mind, in what sense could one claim that the machine did not have a mind?

It might be objected here that any and all precisely formulated principles may be given a physical realization. I believe, however, that a principle or a conception may be precise and explicit and yet not be physically realizable. Higher mathematics seems to be full of such conceptions. I say seems to be, because some bizarre mathematical conceptions, such as non-Euclidian geometries, have a disconcerting tendency to be the best representations of physical reality, when physical reality is probed deeply enough. Nonetheless, certain mathematical conceptions—such as the function that is 1 for all rational values of its argument and 0 for all irrational values—cannot have a physical realization, despite their mathematical precision and explicitness. That is to say, the relation described by this precise but bizarre function could not hold between any physical variables. This function could not describe, for example, the relation between time and the velocity, mass, energy, and so on, of any physical entity. Nor could a computer print any finite segment of this function in any finite amount of time. Thus, it is possible to have principles of the kind to be treasured in any dualistic account of action, that is, in any account where action is thought to be determined by physically unrealizable principles. A commitment to physically realizable principles does exclude certain principles that *could* be thought to determine action.

Some parapsychologists seem to believe that one mind may influence the action of another without the expenditure of any energy in the physical sense of energy. If this belief should prove true, then there are indeed physically unrealizable principles determining human behavior. However, believers in the occult do not seem inclined to formulate those physically unrealizable principles in a precise way. They seem content merely to emphasize their nonphysicalness. So, to repeat, in practice the commitment to physically realizable conceptions is a commitment to precise and explicit conceptions.

A further constraint, honored strongly during the early part of the book and less strongly later on, is that there be compelling experimental demonstrations that processes of a suggested type really are at work in determining the temporal ordering of muscle commands in a living organism. This commitment reflects my scientific upbringing. I am a physiological psychologist. I am concerned not only with the conceptions by which we may understand the generation of animal action, but also the way in which those conceptions are embodied in the organ of that action, namely the central nervous system. In so far as possible, I want to indicate in this book how various principles are, or at least might be, embodied by neural circuits, functioning in accord with known principles of neurophysiology.

In short, I cannot resist the temptation to neurologize. In some cases, the existence of neural circuits of the kind posited by the neurologizing is supported by experimental observations at the neurophysiological level. In most cases, the neurophysiological evidence for the proposed circuits is at best suggestive. In some cases, the proposed circuits are rank speculation. In all cases, however, the proposed circuits do at least function in accord with experimentally demonstrated principles of neurophysiology. The purpose in suggesting specific circuits is only to show, where possible, that a neurophysiological embodiment of a given conception may readily be imagined.

The danger in proposing neurophysiological embodiments is that the reader may mistake the embodiment for the conception itself. In the hope of forestalling this, I aver here and now that most of the neural circuits proposed in the chapters that follow will no doubt prove to be wrong, in details if not in toto. The conceptions they embody will, however, prove to be correct; or so I hope. That is, when we have an experimentally documented picture of the neural circuit mediating a particular behavioral function, it is to be hoped that that circuit will be a recognizable embodiment of the conception by which that function was "explained" in these pages.

THE INTELLIGENT COCKROACH

In attempting to demonstrate that the kinds of processes invoked to explain the organization of action are physically realized in living organisms, I frequently consider experimental work on organisms as lowly as the snail and the cockroach. Descartes was willing to consign the motions of nonhuman animals to the domain of phenomena that might be explainable on purely physical principles. Had he been aware of the intelligence that is manifest in the movements of such lowly animals, he would perhaps have been less willing to strip animals of their anima.

The cockroach, unlike man, has not two but six legs that must be moved in an orderly sequence in order for the roach to progress out of the light and into the dark, hidden areas where it quite justifiably feels safest. The roach that one sees scurrying out of some suddenly illuminated area is moving his six legs in a sequence that would please the most fastidious engineer. At any moment, three of the legs—the front and back legs on one side and the middle leg on the other side—are planted on the ground to form a tripodal support, while the other three legs are being lifted and moved forward. When one triplet of legs has been lifted and advanced, it then supports the body while the other triplet is lifted and advanced. Thus, the sequence of leg movements of the scurrying roach is organized in such a way that at every moment of the sequence the body is held up by a stable tripod. The tripod is stable because the triangle formed by the triplet of planted legs encloses the vertical axis (the center of gravity) of the roach's body.

Our appreciation for the complexity of the organizing principles underlying the roach's leg movements is heightened when we consider the number of individual components (muscles) that must be suitably ordered into action for the legs to exhibit the alternating tripod sequence of the rapidly running roach. Oversimplifying somewhat, the motion of *each* leg is controlled by the contraction and relaxation of six muscles. In order for the six legs of the roach to be moved in an orderly tripodal sequence, $6 \times 6 = 36$ muscles must be contracted and relaxed in an orderly sequence.

If the alternating-tripods sequence were the only sequence that the cockroach used in forward progression, we might be impressed by the intricacy of the processes that could organize the activity of 36 muscles, but such intricacy would be clearly within the design capabilities of even a Renaissance clockwork mechanician. The Renaissance clockmaker would be more severely taxed, however, if we asked him to make a machine that exhibited all of the leg movement sequences exhibited by the cockroach in forward progression. The alternating tripod gait is characteristic only of the rapidly running cockroach that the amateur observer is most likely to encounter. The more patient observer, who looks at forward progression in the cockroach and/or other insects under less pressing circumstances, finds that the roach uses many leg movements other than the alternating-tripods sequence. In fact, insects have been observed to use most of the sequences that leave at all times a stable configuration of planted feet, and *none* of the sequences that result at some point in an unstable configuration—a configuration in which the planted feet failed to enclose the body's center of gravity.

At this point our respect for the complexity of the underlying organizing mechanism should be considerable. The mechanism generates a variety of leg movement sequences, each sequence requiring an appropriately timed activation of 36 different muscles. The mechanism is so designed that it does *not* generate any inappropriate (unstable, nonfunctional) sequences. Nonetheless, we seem still to be dealing with a mechanism that must exhibit only an impressively large number of "stereotyped" output patterns—nothing more impressive than a player piano with a large number of roles. There is still no sign here of those sudden adaptations to altered circumstances that are a striking aspect of the movements of higher animals, and that seem to bespeak the presence of intelligence.

One may, however, test how like a player piano the mechanism is that generates the tripodal gait of the scurrying roach. One need only trap the roach and, using a fine pair of scissors, amputate the middle leg on each side, then release the roach to scurry on its way. If the organizing machinery underlying the roach's leg movements activates the muscles according to the same patterns as before the operation, then the roach's scurrying should be severely hampered by the amputation. In the tripodal gait, the left front and the left rear legs are lifted off the ground in phase, that is, at the same time (and likewise for the right side). This causes no difficulty in the intact roach, since the middle leg holds up a side during the phase when the front leg and rear leg are simultaneously lifted. But in the roach with both middle legs amputated there is nothing to support the side if the front leg and rear leg are lifted simultaneously.

The sudden failure of the old pattern to be functional under the new circumstances would not alter the output of a player piano. The player piano would persist in simultaneously ordering the lifting of the ipsilateral ('same-sided') front and the rear leg, thereby removing all support on that side. A player piano cannot be expected to compensate for the alterations produced by the experimental scientist. But this is not asking too much of the machinery that controls the gait of the frightened roach; the post-operative roach immediately runs off with the ipsilateral front and rear legs being lifted and set down in alternation rather than simultaneously. Now the roach lifts its *left front* and *right rear* legs simultaneously, leaving the left rear and right front legs planted to provide bilateral support for the body. When the left front and right rear legs have been advanced and planted, the right front and left rear legs are lifted. Thus, before the amputation the motor commands to the left front and left rear legs were sent out *in phase* (at the same point in the stepping cycle). After the amputation, the commands are sent out 180° *out of phase* (i.e., at opposite points in the stepping cycle). Conversely, before the amputation the commands to the left front and right rear legs were 180° out of phase; after the amputation they are in phase. The happy result of this change in the relative timing of commands to the front and rear legs is that at no point in the roach's leg movement cycle are both legs on the same side off the ground at the same time!

This happy coincidence between the coordinating machinery's response to changes in circumstances and the beneficent consequences of that response from the standpoint of the roach's forward progression is the sort of intelligence that makes the organization of action a fascinating field of study. This introductory look at leg coordination in the cockroach is intended to justify the extensive use of experimental data from "lower" animals in our attempt to understand the processes underlying the organization of action. The roach clearly displays at least to some extent what Bartlett (1958) regarded as the essence of skilled action (a precursor of intelligence):

> ...all forms of skill, expertly carried out, possess an outstanding character of rapid adaptation. For items within the series have, within wide limits, a fluid

order of occurrence and varying qualities. So what is called the same operation [e.g., forward progression] is done now in one way and now in another, but each way is, we say, 'fitted to the occasion' [p. 14—phrase in brackets mine].

Thus, the neural machinery that organizes the sequences of stepping movements in the cockroach already manifests some elementary properties of intelligence. We will see that the machinery underlying this manifestation of intelligence in action represents an intermediate level of organization in a hierarchically structured system. The machinery that generates the stepping patterns of forward locomotion constitutes a prepackaged unit of intelligent action. This "package" may be called upon, along with other such intermediate packages, by the highest levels of the central nervous system in order to create still more intelligent and purposeful patterns of action. It is one purpose of this book to trace the construction of these intermediate units of behavior from the elementary units of behavior that directly control the muscles themselves. A second purpose is to show that the properties of behavior discussed under the heads of motivation, intent, purpose, and intelligence emerge from the hierarchical synthesis of the intermediate units. Thus, an overarching purpose of the book is to bridge the conceptual gap between motivation and muscles, between brains and brawn.

OVERVIEW

Elementary Units of Behavior.   The dominating idea in this book and the one that governs its organization is the idea that behavior is produced by a hierarchically structured mechanism. At the bottom of this hierarchy are elementary units of behavior. The elementary units of behavior are like the elements of chemistry: All behavior is a compound of elementary units of behavior, just as all chemicals are compounds of the 96 chemical elements. A chemical element is irreducible in the sense that it cannot be analyzed into anything else that qualifies as a chemical substance. An elementary unit of behavior is irreducible in the sense that anything less than that cannot explain a naturally occurring movement. In order to explain a naturally occuring movement you need: (1) one or more muscles, whose contraction is the mechanical cause of the movement; (2) an element that delivers a contraction initiating signal to the muscles; and (3), an element in which neural signals arise, either spontaneously or in response to a naturally occuring stimulus. In single-celled organisms, these three elements—the contractor, the conductor, and the originator—are one and the same. In multicelled animals, they are usually distinct.

There are only a few kinds of elementary units of behavior. Chapters 2, 4, and 6 introduce three of the most important kinds—the reflex, the oscillator, and the servomechanism. In a reflex, the signals that initiate contraction originate in sensory receptors. Although the reflex movement may affect the sensory receptors, one does not have to consider this "feedback" effect in formulating the principles that determine a reflex movement. In an oscillatory unit of behavior, the muscle contractions repeat in rhythmic fashion. The contraction-triggering signals originate in a central neural oscillator, a neuron or neural circuit that puts out rhythmically patterned signals—a sort of neural metronome. In a servomechanism, the signals that initiate contraction originate from a discrepancy between two input signals. At least one of the input signals originates at a sensory receptor. The other input signal may originate at a receptor or it may be a signal of complex central origin. When there is a discrepancy between the two input signals, a third signal arises, called the error signal. The error signal initiates or controls muscular action. The resulting movements tend to reduce the discrepancy between the two inputs, thereby reducing the error signal. This is called negative feedback, for obvious reasons. In servomechanisms the precise character, amount, and timing of this negative feedback are a crucial aspect of the mechanism's functioning.

Chapters 3, 5, and 7 elaborate on the principles governing the interactions between elementary units when those units are catalyzed by signals descending from higher levels of the system. Chapter 3 describes processes, such as reciprocal facilitation, reciprocal inhibition, and chaining, that are observed in the interaction between reflexes. Chapter 5 describes the processes of superimposition and phase-dependent acceleration/deceleration that are observed when oscillators interact. Chapter 7 describes the processes of corollary discharge and efference copy that may be observed whenever feedback effects (reafferent signals) are important in the interactions between elementary units.

Some of these functional units and some of the interaction principles are well known to psychologists. The reflex, for example, and the principle of reflex chaining have been central concepts in psychological thought throughout this century. On the other hand, oscillators and the principle of phase-dependent acceleration or deceleration are not familiar to most psychologists, despite the fact that this elementary unit of behavior and its associated interaction principles were experimentally delineated by von Holst some forty years ago. Taxic orienting mechanisms—the type of servomechanisms described in Chapter 6—are familiar to many psychologists, but they have played only a minor role in psychological thought. Concepts of reafference and efference copy have held an even more peripheral place in psychological explanations of behavior. The first seven chapters gather together in one place classic descriptions of these elmentary units of behavior and principles of interaction.

Complex Units of Behavior (Central Programs).   The presentation of the hierarchical structure begins in Chapter 8, in which is reprinted an edited version of a paper by Paul Weiss. This paper develops both the hierarchical conception and the concept of central programs. The paper appeared in 1941, before its time. The concepts of hierarchical structure and central programming were not congenial to the then dominant reflex or S–R school of thought. Now, when central programming and hierarchical structure have become important in the analysis of behavior, the paper has not enjoyed the revival it deserves.

A central program is a complex unit of behavior. It generates complex sequences of movements, whose general pattern does not depend upon the pattern of sensory input during the running off of the program. It is called a central program to indicate that the basic pattern depends on signal patterns arising within the central nervous system rather than upon signal patterns arising from the play of stimuli upon sensory receptors. The program comes from within, not from without. Sensory signals arising during the execution of the program may induce many adaptive variations, however. The cockroach's adaptation to leg amputation will prove to be an example of such a variation. Because of the variations induced by sensory signals, the movements generated by a central program are far from stereotyped. These variations provide instances of intelligent adaptation in the absence of learning. They caution against the long standing psychological tradition of regarding the capacity for intelligent adaptation and the capacity to learn as one and the same thing.

A central program is a *unit* of behavior in the sense that it is called up as a whole. Weiss's experiments show that the central programs for forward and backward walking in the salamander are units in just this sense. The salamander's nervous system can activate one program or the other. It cannot activate half of one and half of the other. A central program is a *complex* unit in that it may be analyzed into simpler units, which may in many cases be further analyzed into yet simpler units of behavior. Again the chemical analogy is instructive. Proteins are a complex unit of biochemistry. They act as functional units in most biochemical processes; yet they may be analyzed into amino acids, which may be further analyzed into rudimentary combinations of elements—carbon rings, amines, etc—and these rudimentary combinations may, finally, be analyzed into the basic elements—carbon, nitrogen, etc.

The Nature of the Hierarchy.   The hierarchical structure of the army is perhaps more suitable than the hierarchical structure of chemistry as an analogy for the structure of the machinery of behavior. In the army, it is authority or control that is hierarchically arranged. The general controls the colonels, the colonels control the majors, the majors the captains, and so on down to the privates, the irreducible elements of military action. Similarly, the circuits that govern complex behavior do so by sending down signals that facilitate or inhibit the activity of circuits that control simpler behavior, and so on down to the elementary units of behavior. These controlling signals create complex behavior by controlling the activity of simpler units of behavior.

The behavioral hierarchy differs from the military in one important respect. In the military hierarchy, a captain is under the command of only one colonel, a colonel under the command of only one general, and so on, up and down the ranks. By contrast, a unit of behavior is subject to control by several different and often antagonistic higher level units. A reflex is facilitated and/or inhibited by several different central programs, and the reflex plays a role in each. The lines of authority in the nervous machinery cross again and again. When the lines of control are represented diagrammatically, they form a lattice-like pattern, which has led me to term the behavioral system a lattice-hierarchy. The concept of a lattice-hierarchy is illustrated at some length at the end of Chapter 8.

The Principle of Selective Potentiation. Chapter 9 further elaborates on the hierarchical conception by pointing out diverse manifestations of hierarchical structure in experiments ranging from brain transections, through operant conditioning to behavior genetics. Chapter 9 also elaborates on the principle of selective potentiation: This principle is central to understanding how basic patterns of action are adapted to a particular momentary circumstances. The central programs do not directly order lower level units into action; rather they selectively potentiate certain subsets of more elementary units, namely, those subsets whose actions would at a given moment be consistent with the general pattern specified by the central program. The subset of selectively potentiated units constitutes a set of "viable options." Which of the viable options is actually exercised on a given occasion depends on prevailing circumstances. Thus, although the general pattern is laid down by commands issuing from high levels of the central nervous system, the realization of these patterns is fitted to prevailing circumstances through the circumstance-dependent exercising of options at ever lower levels of the hierarchy. As the passages from Bruner and Bartlett point out, the flexible and highly adaptable implementation of general patterns of action is what leads us to characterize an action as intelligent. Understanding how the principle of selective potentiation operates within a hierarchical structure enables one to see how intelligent action may be generated by physically realizable structures.

Motivation. Chapter 10 argues that our concept of motivation refers to the operation of the principle of selective potentiation at the highest levels of the action hierarchy. It argues furthermore that many of the principles governing the generation of selectively potentiating signals within upper levels of the hierarchy are the same principles that determine the properties of the elementary units of behavior. Thus, concepts derived from studies of sensorimotor coordination not only bridge the gap between muscles and motivation, they go a long way toward illuminating the processes underlying motivation itself.

Role of Cognition.   Psychologists, however, are bound to be dissatisfied wtih any discussion of motivation that does not make contact wtih another source of organization in action, namely, an organism's cognition of the world around it. In Chapter 11, I interpret cognition to mean the representation of the world stored in memory. I then review some experimental demonstrations that learned representations of the terrain play a central role in controlling goal-directed locomotion in both the rat and the wasp. I focus on these creatures to emphasize that cognitive control of action is in no way peculiar to man and the primates. On the contrary, it may profitably be studied in an organism as simple as the wasp (which is still, of course, a far from simple organism). Having brought cognition within the purview of the behavioral physiologist working on 'simple' organisms, I review Deutsch's (1960) theory of learning, the only cognitive map theory that explicitly specifies physically realizable principles whereby representations of the world may be made to enter into the control of animal action. This theory may point the way toward the final marriage between cognition and action, a marriage that acknowledges the immense contribution that cognitive processes may make to the intelligence of an organism's behavior.

Chapter 12 reviews recent cognitively oriented work on the organization of action, from the perspective of the preceding chapters. The emphasis on hierarchical organization in most recent work is, needless to say, consonant with the classic but little known material presented in the preceding chapters. Greater familiarity with the work represented by the papers reprinted in Chapters 2–8 will enrich the conceptual bases of modern work. The classic work has a particularity and concreteness that clarify certain concepts, which are treated in a general and sometimes vague way in cognitively oriented discussions of action. For example, the analysis of insect walking in Chapter 5 clarifies the manner in which hierarchical organization resolves what Turvey (1977) calls the degrees of freedom problem. Roughly speaking, the degrees of freedom problem boils down to the problem that the higher levels cannot possibly be bothered to instruct the lowest levels exactly how to carry out a required action, such as walking. There are too many slightly different ways of walking, each suited to slightly different circumstances. The higher levels must in some sense issue a simple walk command, leaving it to lower levels to determine exactly how the business of walking shall be carried on from moment to moment. Chapter 5 shows in some detail exactly how this conception is put into practice in the walking of insects. A very similar analysis of walking applies to the cat (Pearson, 1976), so the principles particularized in Chapter 5 appear to be quite general.

In summary, there is a classic literature on the organization of action. The literature ought to be better known to psychologists than it is. This book serves as an introduction to that literature and to the important concepts it contains.

2 The Sherringtonian Reflex

Since our goal is to give an account of the organization of action that rests on experimentally documented mechanisms of the central nervous system, a minimal respect for the history of scientific work on this topic demands that we start with the work of Sir Charles Sherrington. Sherrington's landmark book, *The integrative action of the nervous system,* first published in 1906, set a new standard for the analysis of organized action in terms of neural processes whose nature had been established by careful and extensive behavioral experimentation. Sherrington's analysis of action rested on, and was illumined by, extensive experiments on the reflex actions mediated by the neural machinery in the spinal cord of the monkey, the dog, and the cat. In the opening pages of his book Sherrington summarized his experimental findings on the reflex actions of the spinal cord and the conclusions he drew from these findings. This summary is sufficiently clear and comprehensive to make further introduction superfluous.

Introductory—Coordination of the Simple Reflex*

SIR CHARLES SHERRINGTON

ARGUMENT: The nervous system and the integration of bodily reactions. Characteristics of integration by nervous agency. The unit mechanism in integration by the nervous system is the reflex. Coordination of reflexes one with another. Coordination in the *simple reflex*. Conduction in the reflex-arc. Function of the receptor to lower for its reflex-arc the threshold value of one kind of stimulus and to heighten the threshold value of all other kinds of stimuli for that arc: it thus confers selective excitability on the arc. Differences between conduction in nerve-trunks and in reflex-arcs respectively. These probably largely referable to the intercalation of synaptic membranes in the conductive mechanism of the arc. Latent time of reflexes. Reflex latency inversely proportional to intensity of stimulation. Latency of initial and incremental reflexes. None of the latent interval consumed in establishing connexion between the elements of a resting arc. *After-discharge* a characteristic of reflex reactions. Increase of after-discharge by intensification of the stimulus, or by prolongation of short stimuli. 'Inertia' and 'momentum' of reflex-arc reactions.

Nowhere in physiology does the cell-theory reveal its presence more frequently in the very framework of the argument than at the present time in the study of nervous reactions. The cell-theory at its inception depended for exemplification largely on merely morphological observations; just as these formed originally the almost exclusive tests for the Darwinian doctrine of evolution. But with the progress of natural knowledge, biology has passed beyond the confines of the study of merely visible form, and is turning more and more to the subtler and deeper sciences that are branches of energetics. The cell-theory and the doctrine of evolution find their scope more and more, therefore, in the problems of function, and have become more and more identified with the aims and incorporated among the methods of physiology.

The physiology of nervous reactions can be studied from three main points of view.

---

*Reprinted from: Sherrington, C. S. *The Integrative Action of the Nervous System.* New Haven: Yale University Press, 1947 edition. By permission of Yale University Press.

In the first place, nerve-cells, like all other cells, lead individual lives—they breathe, they assimilate, they dispense their own stores of energy, they repair their own substantial waste; each is, in short, a living unit, with its nutrition more or less centered in itself. Here, then, problems of nutrition, regarding each nerve-cell and regarding the nervous system as a whole, arise comparable with those presented by all other living cells. Although no doubt partly special to this specially differentiated form of cell-life, these problems are in general accessible to the same methods as apply to the study of nutrition in other cells and tissues and in the body as a whole. We owe recently to Verworn and his co-workers advances specially valuable in this field.

Secondly, nervous cells present a feature so characteristically developed in them as to be specially theirs. They have in exceptional measure the power to spatially transmit (conduct) states of excitement (nerve-impulses) generated within them. Since this seems the eminent functional feature of nerve-cells wherever they exist, its intimate nature is a problem coextensive with the existence of nerve-cells, and enters into every question regarding the specific reactions of the nervous system. This field of study may be termed that of *nerve-cell conduction.*

But a third aspect which nervous reactions offer to the physiologist is the *integrative.* In the multicellular animal, especially for those higher reactions which constitute its behavior as a social unit in the natural economy, it is nervous reaction which *par excellence* integrates it, welds it together from its components, and constitutes it from a mere collection of organs an animal individual. This integrative action in virtue of which the nervous system unifies from separate organs an animal possessing solidarity, an individual, is the problem before us in these lectures. Though much in need of data derived from the two previously mentioned lines of study, it must in the meantime be carried forward of itself and for its own sake.

The integration of the animal organism is obviously not the result solely of any single agency at work within it, but of several. Thus, there is the *mechanical* combination of the unit cells of the individual into a single mass. This is effected by fibrous stromata, capsules of organs, connective tissue in general, for example, of the liver, and indeed the fibrous layer of the skin encapsulating the whole body. In muscles this mechanical integration of the organ may arrive at providing a single cord tendon by which the tensile stress of a myriad contractile cells can be additively concentrated upon a single place of application.

Integration also results from *chemical* agency. Thus, reproductive organs, remote one from another, are given solidarity as a system by communication that is of chemical quality; lactation supervenes *post partum* in all the mammary glands of a bitch subsequent to thoracic transection of the spinal cord severing all nervous communication between the pectoral and the inguinal mammae (Goltz). In digestive organs we find chemical agency coordinating the action of separate glands, and thus contributing to the solidarity of function of the digestive glands as a whole. The products of salivary digestion on reaching the pyloric region of the stomach, and the gastric secretion on reaching the mucosa of the duodenum, make there substances which absorbed duly excite heightened secretion of gastric and of pancreatic juice respectively suited to continue the digestion of the substances initiating the reaction (Bayliss & Starling, 1899; Edkins, 1905). Again, there is the integrating action effected by the circulation of the blood. The gaseous exchanges at one limited surface of the body are made serviceable for the life of every living unit in the body. By the blood the excess of heat produced in one set of organs is brought to redress the loss of heat in others; and so on.

But the integrative action of the nervous system is different from these, in that its agent is not mere intercellular material, as in connective tissue, nor the transference of material in mass, as by the circulation; it works through living lines of stationary cells along which it dispatches waves of physicochemical disturbance, and these act as releasing forces in distant organs where they finally impinge. Hence it is not surprising that nervous integration has the feature of relatively high *speed*, a feature peculiarly distinctive of integrative correlation in animals as contrasted with that of plants, the latter having no nervous system in the ordinary sense of the word.

The nervous system is in a certain sense the highest expression of that which French physiologists term the *milieu interne*. With the transition from the unicellular organism to the multicellular a new element enters general physiology. The phenomena of general physiology in the unicellular organism can be divided into two great groups; namely, those occurring within the cell, intracellular, and these occurring at the surface of the cell, in which forces that are associated with surfaces of separation have opportunity for play at the boundary between the organism and its environment. But in the multicellular organism a third great group of phenomena exists in addition; namely, those which are *inter*cellular, occurring in that complex material which the organism deposits in quantity in the intercellular interstices of its mass as a connecting medium between its individual living units.

When the intercellular substance is solid, for example, in many connective tissues, the physiological agencies for which it affords a field of operation are mechanical rather than chemical. The organism obtains from it scaffolding for supporting its weight, levers for application of its forces, etc., and in this degree the intercellular material performs an integrative function. Where the intercellular material is fluid, as in blood, lymph, and tissue juice, it constitutes a field of operation for agencies chemical rather than mechnical. The intricacy of the chemistry of this *milieu interne* is shown by nothing better than by the specificity of the precipitins, etc., the intercellular media for each separate animal species yielding its own particular kinds. The cells of a multicellular organism have therefore in addition to an environmental medium in which the organism as a whole is bathed, and to which they react either directly or through the medium of surface cells, an *internal medium* created by their organism itself, and in many respects specific to itself.

But the internal interconnexion of the multicellular organism is not restricted to intercellular material. Intercellular material is, after all, no living channel of communication, delicately responsive to living changes though it may be. An actually living internal bond is developed. When the animal body reaches some degree of multi-cellular complexity, special cells assume the express office of connecting together other cells. Such cells, since their function is to stretch from one cell to another, are usually elongated; they form protoplasmic threads and they interconnect by conducting nervous impulses. And we find this living bond the one employed where, as said above, speed and nicety of time adjustment are required, as in animal movements, and also where nicety of spatial adjustment is essential, as also in animal movements. It is in view of this interconnecting function of the nervous system that that field of study of nervous reactions which was called at the outset the third or integrative, assumes its due importance. The due activity of the interconnexion resolves itself into the coordination of the parts of the animal mechanism by reflex action.

It is necessary to be clear as to what we understand by the expression 'reflex' action.

In plants and animals occur a number of actions the initiation of which is traceable to events in their environment. The event in the environment is some change which acts on the organism as an exciting *stimulus*. The energy which is imparted to the organism by the stimulus is often far less in quantity than the energy which the organism itself sets free in the movement or other effect which it exhibits in consequence of the application of the stimulus. This excess of energy must be referred to energy potential in the organism itself. The change in the environment evidently acts as a releasing force upon the living machinery of the organism. The source of energy set free is traced to chemical compounds in the organism. These are of high potential value, and in immediate or mediate consequence of the stimulus decompose partly, and so liberate external from internal energy. It is perfectly conceivable, and in many undifferentiated organisms, especially in unicellular, for example, amoeba, is actually the case, that one and the same living structure not only undergoes this physicochemical change at the point at which an external agent is applied, but is subject to spread of that change from particle to particle along it, so that there then ensue in it changes of form, movement. In such a case the initial reaction or *reception* of the stimulus, the spatial transmission or *conduction* of the reaction, and the motor or other *end-effect*, are all processes that occur in one and the same living structure. But in many organisms these separable parts of the reaction are exhibited by separate and specific structures. Suppose an animal turn its head in response to a sudden light. Large fields of its body take part in the reaction, but also large fields of it do not. Some of its musculature contracts, particularly certain pieces of its skeletal musculature. The external stimulus is, so to say, led to them by certain nerves in the altered form of a nervous impulse. If the neck nerves are severed the end-effect is cut out of part of the field; and the nerves themselves cannot exhibit *movement* on application of the stimulus. The optic nerve itself is unable to enter into a heightened phase of its own specific activity on the application of light. Initiation of nervous activity by light is the exclusive (in this instance) function of cells in the retina, that is, retinal receptors. In such cases there exist three separable structures for the three processes—*initiation, conduction* and *end-effect*.

These reactions, in which there follows on an initiating reaction an end-effect reached through the mediation of a conductor, itself incapable either of the end-effect or, under natural conditions, of the inception of the reaction, are 'reflexes.' The conductors are nerve. Usually the spaces and times bridged across by the conductors are quite large, and easily capable of measurement. Now there occur cases, especially within the unicellular organism and the unicellular organ, where the spaces and times bridged are minute. In them spread of response may involve 'conduction' (*Poteriodendron, Vorticella*) in some degree specific. Yet to cases where neither histologically nor physiologically a specific conductor can be detected, it seems better not to apply the term 'reflex.' It seems better to reserve that expression for reactions employing specifically recognizable nerve-processes and morphologically differentiated nerve-cells; the more so because the process of conduction in nerve is probably a specialized one, in which the qualities of speed and freedom from inertia of reaction have been attained to a degree not reached elsewhere since not elsewhere demanded.

The conception of a reflex therefore embraces that of at least three separable structures—an *effector* organ, gland cells or muscle cells; a conducting nervous path or *conductor* leading to that organ; and an initiating organ or *receptor* whence the reaction starts. The conductor consists, in the reactions which we have to study, of at least two nerve-cells—one connected wtih the receptor, the other with the effector. For our purpose the receptor is best included as a part of the nervous system, and so it is convenient to speak of the whole chain of structures—receptor, conductor, and effector—as a *reflex-arc*. All that part of the chain which leads up to but does not include the effector and the nerve-cell attached to this latter, is conveniently distinguished as the *afferent-arc*.

The reflex-arc is the unit mechanism of the nervous system when that system is regarded in its integrative function. *The unit reaction in nervous integration is the reflex*, because every reflex is an integrative reaction and no nervous action short of a reflex is a complete act of integration. The nervous synthesis of an individual from what without it were a mere aggregation of commensal organs resolves itself into coordination by reflex action. But though the unit reaction in the integration is a reflex, not every reflex is a unit reaction, since some reflexes are compounded of simpler reflexes. Coordination, therefore, is in part the compounding of reflexes. In this coordination there are therefore obviously two grades.

THE SIMPLE REFLEX

There is the coordination which a reflex action introduces when it makes an effector organ responsive to excitement of a receptor, all other parts of the organism being supposed indifferent to and indifferent for that reaction. In this grade of coordination the reflex is taken apart, as if separable from all other reflex actions. This is the *simple reflex*. A simple reflex is probably a purely abstract conception, because all parts of the nervous system are connected together and no part of it is probably ever capable of reaction without affecting and being affected by various other parts, and it is a system certainly never absolutely at rest. But the simple reflex is a convenient, if not a probable, fiction. Reflexes are of various degrees of complexity, and it is helpful in analysing complex reflexes to separate from them relfex components which we may consider apart and therefore treat as though they were simple reflexes.

In the simple reflex there is exhibited the first grade of coordination. But it is obvious that if the integration of the animal mechanism is due to coordination by reflex action, reflex actions must themselves be coordinated one with another; for coordination by reflex action there must be coordination of reflex actions. This latter is the second grade of coordination. The outcome of the normal reflex action of the organism is an orderly coadjustment and sequence of reactions. This is very patently expressed by the skeletal musculature. The coordination involves orderly coadjustment of a number of simple reflexes occurring *simultaneously*, that is, a reflex pattern, figure, or 'complication,' if one may warp a psychological term for this use; orderly *succession* involves due supersession of one reflex by another, or of one group of reflexes by another group, that is, orderly change from one reflex pattern or figure to another. For this succession to occur in an orderly manner no component of the previous reflex may remain which would be out of harmony with the new reflex that sets in. When the change from one reflex to another occurs it is therefore usually a far-reaching change spread over a wide range of nervous arcs.

This compounding of reflexes with orderliness of coadjustment and of sequence constitutes coordination, and want of it incoordination. We may therefore in regard to coordination distinguish coordination of reflexes simultaneously proceeding, and coordination of reflexes successively proceeding. The main secret of nervous coordination lies evidently in the compounding of reflexes.

COORDINATION IN THE SIMPLE REFLEX

It is best to clear the way toward the more complex problems of coordination by considering as an earlier step that which was termed above, the first grade of coordination, or that of the simplex reflex. From the point of view of its office as integrator of the animal mechanism, the whole function of the nervous system can be summed up in the one word, *conduction*. In the simple reflex the evidence of coordination is that the outcome of the reflex as expressed by the activity induced in the effector organ is a response appropriate to the stimulus imparted to the receptor. This due propriety of end-effect is largely traceable to the action of the conductor mediating between receptor and affector. Knowledge of the features of this 'conduction' is therefore a prime object of study in this connection.

But we have first to remember that in dealing with reflexes even experimentally we very usually deal with them as reactions for which the reflex-arc as a whole and without any separation into constitutent parts is laid under contribution. The reflex-arc thus taken includes the receptor. It is assuredly as truly a functional part of the arc as any other. But, for analysis of the arc's conduction, it is obvious that by including the receptor we are including a structure which, as its name implies, adaptation has specialized for excitation of a kind different from that obtaining for all the rest of the arc. It is therefore advantageous, as we have to include the receptor in the reflex-arc, to consider what characters its inclusion probably grafts upon the functioning of the arc.

Marshall Hall (1850) drew attention to the greater ease with which reflexes can be elicited from receptive surfaces than from afferent nerve-trunks themselves; and this has often been confirmed (Eckhard, Biedermann). Steinach (1899) has measured the lowering of the threshold value of stimulation when in the frog a reflex is elicited by a mechanical stimulus applied to skin instead of to cutaneous afferent nerve. The lowering is considerable. There are numerous instances in which particular reflexes can be elicited from the receptive surface by particular stimuli only. Goltz (1869) endeavoured in vain to evoke the reflex croak of the female frog by applying to the skin electrical stimuli. Mechanical stimuli of non-nocuous kind were the only stimuli that proved effective. By direct stimulation of the afferent nerve itself the reflex could but rarely be elicited at all. Later Goltz's pupil Gergens (1876) succeeded in provoking the reflex by applying to the skin a mild discharge from an influence machine.

A remarkable reflex (Sherrington, 1905) is obtainable from the *planta* of the hindfoot in the '*spinal*' dog. The movement provoked is a brief strong extension at knee, hip, and ankle. This is the 'extensor-thrust.' It seems obtainable only by a particular kind of mechanical stimulation. I have never succeeded in eliciting it by any form of electrical stimulation, nor by any stimulation applied directly to an afferent nerve-trunk.

Again, a very characteristic reflex in the cat is the pinna-reflex. (Sherrington, 1905) If the tip of the pinna be squeezed, or tickled, or in some cases even touched, the pinna itself is crumpled so that its free end is turned backward, as in Darwin's (1872) picture of a cat prepared to attack. The afferent nerve of this reflex appears to be in part at least not the cranial fifth nerve, but the foremost cervical. The reflex emerges very early from the shock of decerebration and is submerged very late in chloroform narcosis. This reflex, easily elicitable as it is by various mechanical stimuli to the skin, I have never succeeded in provoking by any form of electrical stimulation.

The same sort of difference, though less marked in degree, is exhibited by the scratch-reflex (Goltz, 1881; Haycraft, 1890; Sherrington, 1905; Sherrington, 1904a; Sherrington & Laslett 1903). This reflex is one in which various forms of innocuous mechanical stimulation (rubbing, tickling, tapping) applied to the skin of the back behind the shoulder evoke a rhythmic flexion (scratching movement) of the hind-limb, the foot being brought toward the seat of stimulation. This reflex in the spinal dog, although usually elicitable, varies much under various circumstances in its degree of elicitability. When easily elicitable it can be evoked by various forms of electrical stimulation as well as by mechanical; but when not easily elicitable electrical stimuli altogether fail, while rubbing and other suitable mechanical stimuli still evoke it, though not so readily or vigorously as usual.

A question germane to this is the oft-debated sensitivity of various internal organs. Direct stimulation of various afferent nerves of the visceral system is itself well known to yield reflexes on bloodpressure, etc. But in regard to the sensitivity of the organs themselves we have, on the one hand, the passage of bile-stones, renal calculi, etc., accompanied by intense sensations, and on the other hand the insensitivity of these ducts and various allied visceral parts as noted by Haller (1752) and observed by surgeons working under circumstances favorable for examining the question. The stimulation which excites pain in these internal organs is usually of mechanical kind, e.g., calculus, and the surgeon's knife and needle provide mechanical stimuli, and Haller and his co-workers in their research employed multiform stimuli, many of them mechanical in quality. But though mechnical, the latter are remote in quality from the former; the former are distensile. The action of a calculus can be imitated by injecting fluid of itself innocuous. Marked reflex effects can then be excited (Sherrington, 1899) from the very organs (Fig. 2.1), the cutting and wounding of which remain without effect. For Haller's and the surgical experience to be harmonized with the medical evidence from calculi, etc., all that is necessary is that the mechanical stimulation be *adequate*, and to be adequate it must be of a certain kind. Thus we see that when the mechanical stimulation employed resembles that occurring in the natural accidents that concern medicine, the experimental results fall into line with those observed at the bedside.

Therefore we may infer provisionally—for the facts justify only a guarded judgement—that the part played by the receptor in the reflex-arc is in the main what from other evidence it is inferred to be in the case of the receptors as *sense*-organs; namely, a mechanism more or less attuned to respond specially to a certain one or several of the agencies that act as stimuli to the body. We may suppose this

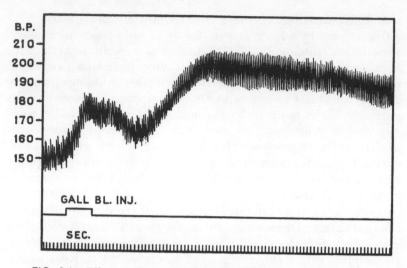

FIG. 2.1.   Effect of distension of common bile duct on arterial blood-pressure. Cat under CHCL₃ and curare; double vagotomy. Records from above downwards: Arterial blood-pressure: scale in mm. Hg. Signal line: rise of signal indicates rapid injection of 2.5 cc of saline solution into the common bile duct. Time in sec. Distension of the duct produces a rise of arterial pressure. (Sherrington, 1899.)

special attuning acts as does specialization in so many cases, namely by rendering more apt for a certain kind of stimulus and at the same time less apt for stimuli of other kinds. The main function of the receptor is therefore (Sherrington, 1900) *to lower the threshold of excitability of the arc for one kind of stimulus, and to heighten it for all others.* This is quite comparable with the low threshold for touch-sensation under mechanical stimulation applied to a hair (v. Frey, 1897) contrasted with the high threshold under electrical stimulation of the skin. Adaptation has evolved a mechanism for which one kind of stimulus is the appropriate, *that is, the adequate stimulus:* other stimuli than the adequate not being what the adaptation fitted the mechanism for, are at a disadvantage. Electrical stimuli are in most cases far the most convenient to use for experimental work, because of their easy control, especially in regard to intensity and time. But electrical stimuli not being of common occurrence in nature, there has been no chance for adaptation to evolve in the organism receptors appropriate for such stimuli. Therefore we may say that electricity never constitutes the adequate stimulus for any receptor, since it is always an artificial form of stimulus, and every adequate stimulus must obviously be a natural form of stimulation. It is therefore rather a matter for surprise that electrical stimuli applied to receptor organs are as efficient excitors of reflexes as they in fact prove to be. It is particularly in regard to a class of reflexes whose receptive cells seem attuned specially to react to nocuous agents, agents that threaten to do local damage, that electrical stimuli are found to be excellently effective. But the conditions of adaptation to stimuli appear here peculiar; and there will be better opportunity of considering them later.

We infer, therefore, that the main contribution made to the mechanism of the reflex-arc by that part of it which constitutes the receptor is *selective excitability*. It thus contributes to coordination, for it renders its arc prone to reply to certain stimuli, while other arcs not having that kind of receptor do not reply, and it renders its arc unlikely to reply to certain other stimuli to which other arcs are likely to respond. It will thus, while providing increase of responsiveness on the part of the organism to the environment, tend to prevent confusion of reactions (incoordination) by limiting to particular stimuli a particular reaction.

On the whole, we may regard the receptor as being concerned with the *mode of excitation* rather than with the features of conduction of the reflex-arc, and may now return to that conduction, which itself has important coordinative characters.

Nervous conduction has been studied chiefly in nerve-trunks. Conduction in reflexes is of course for its spatially greater part conduction along nerve-trunks, yet reflex conduction *in toto* differs widely from nerve-trunk conduction.

Salient among the characteristic differences between conduction in nerve-trunks and in reflex-arcs respectively are the following:

Conduction in reflex-arcs exhibits: (1) slower speed as measured by the latent period between application of stimulus and appearance of end-effect, this difference being greater for weak stimuli than for strong; (2) less close correspondence between the moment of cessation of stimulus and the moment of cessation of end-effect, that is, there is a marked 'after-discharge'; (3) less close correspondence between rhythm of stimulus and rhythm of end-effect; (4) less close correspondence between the grading of intensity of the stimulus and the grading of intensity of the end-effect; (5) considerable resistance to passage of a single nerve-impulse, but a resistance easily forced by a succession of impulses (temporal summation); (6) irreversibility of direction instead of reversibility as in nerve-trunks; (7) fatigability in contrast with the comparative unfatigability of nerve-trunks; (8) much greater variability of the threshold value of stimulus than in nerve-trunks; (9) refractory period, 'bahnung,' inhibition, and shock, in degrees unknown for nerve-trunks; (10) much greater dependence on blood-circulation, oxygen (Verworn, Winterstein, v. Baeyer, etc.); (11) much greater susceptibility to various drugs—anaesthetics.

These differences between conduction in reflex-arcs and nerve-trunks respectively appear referable to that part of the arc which lies in grey matter. The constituents of grey matter over and above those which exist also in nerve-trunks are the nerve-cell bodies (perikarya) (Foster & Sherrington, 1897) the fine nerve-cell branches (dendritic and axonic nerve-fibres), and neuroglia.

Neuroglia exists in white matter as well as in grey, and there is no good ground for attributing the above characteristics of conduction in reflex-arcs to that part of the arcs which consists of white matter. It is improbable, therefore, on that ground that the features of the conduction are due to neuroglia. Indeed, there is no good evidence that neuroglia is concerned directly in nervous conduction at all. As to perikarya (nerve-cell bodies) the experiment of Bethe (1897a) on the motor perikarya of the ganglion of the second antenna of *Carcinus*, and the experiments of Steinach (1899) on the perikarya of the spinal-root ganglion, also the observation by Langley (1901) that nicotine has little effect when applied to the spinal-root ganglion, though breaking conduction in sympathetic ganglia, all indicate more or less directly that it is not to the perikarya that the characteristic features of reflex-arc conduction are referable. Similarly, the experiments of Exner (1877) and of Moore and Reynolds (1898) detecting no delay in transmission through the spinal-root ganglion—though observations by Wundt (1876) and by Gad & Joseph (1889) had a different result—withdraw from the perikaryon the responsibility for another feature characteristic of reflex-arc conduction. Again, histological observations by Cajal, van Gehuchten and others, indicate that in various cases the line of conduction may run not through the perikaryon at all, but direct from dendrite stem to axone.

As to the nerve-cell branches (dendrites, axones, and axone-collaterals) which are so prominent as histological characters of grey matter, they are in many cases perfectly continuous with nerve-fibres outside, whose conductive features are known by the study of nerve-trunks; they are also themselves nerve-fibres, though smaller in calibre than those outside. It seems therefore scarcely justifiable to suppose that conduction along nerve-fibers assumes in the grey matter characters so widely different from those it possesses elsewhere as to account for the dissimilarity between reflex-arc conduction and nerve-trunk conduction respectively.

In this difficulty there rises forcibly to mind that not the least fruitful of the facts which the cell-theory rests upon and brings together is the existence at the confines of the cells composing the organism of 'surfaces of separation' between the adjacent cells. In certain syncytial cases such surfaces are not apparent, but with most of the cells in the organism their existence is undisputed, and they play an important role in a great number of physiological processes. Now in addition to the structural elements of grey matter specified above, there is one other which certainly in many cases exists. The grey matter is the field of nexus between neurone and neurone. Except in sympathetic (autonomic) ganglia, the place of nexus beweeen neurone and neurone lies nowhere else than in grey matter. We know of no reflex-arc composed of one single neurone only. In other words, every reflex-arc must contain a nexus between one neurone and another. The reflex-arc must, therefore, on the cell-theory, be expected to include not only *intracellular* conduction, but *intercellular* conduction. But on the current view of the structure of the nerve-fibres of nerve-trunks the conduction observed in nerve-trunks is entirely and only *intra*cellular conduction. Perhaps, therefore, the difference between reflex-arc conduction and nerve-trunk conduction is related to an additional element in the former, namely, *inter*cellular conduction. If there exist any surface or separation at the nexus between neurone and neurone, much of what is characteristic of the conduction exhibited by the reflex-arc might be more easily explicable. At the nexus between cells if there be not actual confluence, there must be a surface of separation. At the nexus between efferent neurone and the muscle-cell, electrical organ, etc., which it innervates, it is generally admitted that there is not actual confluence of the two cells together, but that a surface separates them; and a surface of separation is physically a membrane. As regards a number of the features enumerated above as distinguishing reflex-arc conduction from nerve-trunk conduction, there is evidence that *similar features, though not usually in such marked extent, characterize conduction from efferent nerve-fibre to efferent organ,* for example, in nerve-muscle preparation, in nerve-electric-organ preparation, etc. Here change in character of conduction is not due to perikarya (nerve-cell bodies), for such are not present. The change may well be referable to the surface of separation admittedly existent between efferent neurone and effector cell.

If the conductive element of the neurone be fluid, and if at the nexus between neurone and neurone there does not exist actual confluence of the conductive part of one cell with the conductive part of the other for example, if there is not actual continuity of physical phase between them, there must be a surface of separation. Even should a membrane visible to the microscope not appear, the mere fact of non-confluence of the one with the other implies the existence of a surface of separation. Such a surface might restrain diffusion, bank up osmotic pressure, restrict the movement of ions, accumulate electric changes, support a double electric layer, alter in shape and surface-tension with changes in difference of potential, alter in difference of potential with changes in surface-tension or in shape, or intervene as a membrane between dilute solutions of electrolytes of different concentration or colloidal suspensions with different sign of charge. It would be a mechanism where nervous conduction, especially if predominantly physical in nature, might have grafted upon it characters just such as those differentiating reflex-arc conduction from nerve-trunk conduction. For instance, change from reversibility of direction of conduction to irreversibility might be referable to the membrane possessing irreciprocal permeability. It would be natural to find in the arc, each time it passed through grey matter, the additive introduction of features of reaction such as characterize a neurone-threshold (Goldscheider, 1898). The conception of the nervous impulse as a physical process (du Bois Reymond) rather than a chemical, gains rather than loses plausibility from physical chemistry. The injury-current of nerve seems comparable in mode of production (J. MacDonald, 1902) with the current of a 'concentration cell,' a mode of energy akin to the expansion of a gas and physical, rather than chemical, 'volume-energy.' Against the likelihood of nervous conduction being pre-eminently a chemical rather than a physical process must be reckoned, as Macdonald well urges, its speed of propagation, its brevity of time-relations, its freedom from perceptible temperature change, its facile excitation by mechanical means, its facilitation by cold, etc. If it is a physical process the intercalation of a transverse surface of separation or membrane into the conductor must modify the conduction, and it would do so with results just such as we find differentiating reflex-arc conduction from nerve-trunk conduction.

As to the existence or the nonexistence of a surface of separation or membrane between neurone and neurone, that is a structural question on which histology might be competent to give valuable information. In certain cases, especially in Invertebrata, observation (Apathy, Bethe, etc.) indicates that many nerve-cells are actually continuous one with another. It is noteworthy that in several of these cases the irreversibility of direction of conduction which is characteristic of spinal reflex-arcs is not demonstrable; thus the nerve-net in some cases, for example, Medusa, exhibits reversible conduction (Romanes, Nagel, Bethe, and others). But in the neurone-chains of the grey-centred system of vertebrates, histology on the whole furnishes evidence that a surface of separation does exist between neurone and neurone. And the evidence of Wallerian secondary degeneration is clear in showing that that process observes strictly a boundary between neurone and neurone and does not transgress it. It seems therefore likely that the nexus between neurone and neurone in the reflex-arc, at least in the spinal arc of the vertebrate, involves a surface of separation between neurone and neurone; and this as a transverse membrane across the conductor must be an important element in intercellular conduction. The characters distinguishing reflex-arc conduction from nerve-trunk conduction may therefore be largely due to intercellular barriers, delicate transverse membranes, in the former.

In view, therefore, of the probable importance physiologically of this mode of nexus between neurone and neurone it is convenient to have a term for it. The term introduced has been *synapse* (Foster & Sherrington, 1897).

The differences between nerve-trunk conduction and reflex-arc conduction are so great as to require for their exhibition no very minute determination of the characters of either; but we may with advantage follow these differences somewhat further. In doing so we may take the reflexes of the hind-limb of the spinal dog as a field of exemplification.

SHERRINGTON'S EXPERIMENTS

Following the introductory overview Sherrington passed on to a lengthy presentation of experimental data. Sherrington's immense influence derives in appreciable measure from the way in which he illustrated his findings with experimental records showing reflex limb movements as a function of time since the onset of a stimulus or series of stimuli. I have extracted from the rest of the book experimental records that illustrate several of the 11 experimental findings enumerated by Sherrington (on p. 27).

Sherrington's method was the same in all of his experiments on reflexes. He began by cutting through the spinal cord just below the brain so as to remove the spinal mechanisms from the influence of the more complex processes mediated by the brain itself. In other words he began by radically simplifying the system, so that the operation of the basic mechanisms of the spinal cord could be observed without an overlay of higher activity. Having thus simplified his preparation, Sherrington attached the distal extremity of either the limb itself or an individual muscle to the lever of a kymograph. The lever held a pen (or other marking instrument) pressed against chart paper mounted on a revolving drum (see Fig. 2.2). Thus, time is represented along

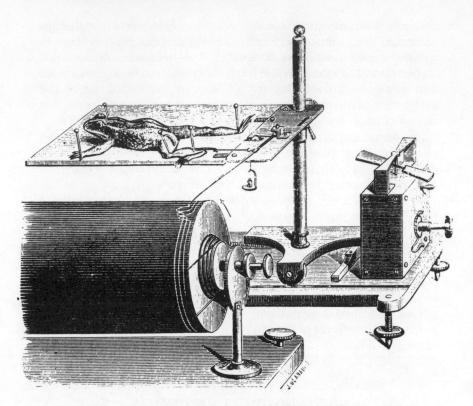

FIG. 2.2. Nineteenth century wood-cut, showing a kymograph set up to record reflex contractions in a leg-muscle of the frog. (From: Marey, E. J. *La Méthode Graphique dans les Sciences Experimentales.* Paris: Libraire de l'Académie de Médecine, 1885, Fig. 97)

the abscissa of the records and movements of the limb are represented by rises and falls in the line of the chart. The times at which Sherrington delivered the stimuli are indicated by appropriate markings on the chart (see caption to Fig. 2.3).

Figure 2.3 illustrates Sherrington's first point, namely, that conduction through a reflex arc is relatively slow. In the fastest case (Fig. 2.3a), one second elapses between the onset of the stimulus and the initial movement of the leg. The latency between stimulus onset and initial leg movement also depends quite a lot on stimulus strength (compare Fig. 2.3a to Fig. 2.3b). Sherrington took this finding to mean that somewhere in the pathway from the sensory neurons to the motor neurons there must be a "conduction process" whose dynamic properties (rates of rise and fall) were very different from the dynamic properties of the processes involved in conduction along nerve trunks. Extensive work by others had already shown that conduction along sensory and motor nerve trunks was much faster than the conduction rates implied by the data in Fig. 2.3. And the speed of nerve trunk conduction is little affected by stimulus intensity; whereas the comparison between panels (a) and (b) in Fig. 2.3 shows that stimulus intensity greatly affects the speed of conduction in a reflex arc. The latency of a reflex contraction gets shorter as stimulus intensity increases.

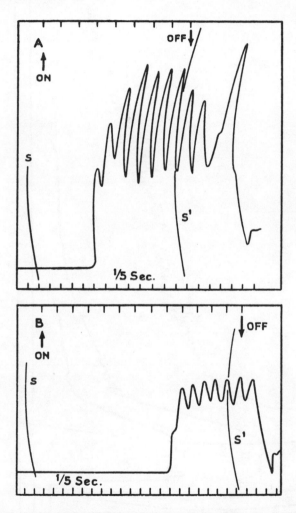

FIG. 2.3.   Records of the scratching movement elicited by a stimulus whose onset(s) and offset(s') is indicated on the graphs. The intensity of the stimulus in Panel *b* was less than in Panel *a*. Note that this weakening of stimulus intensity results in a much longer latency between stimulus onset and the onset of scratching. (From Sherrington, 1947, Fig. 2, p. 20)

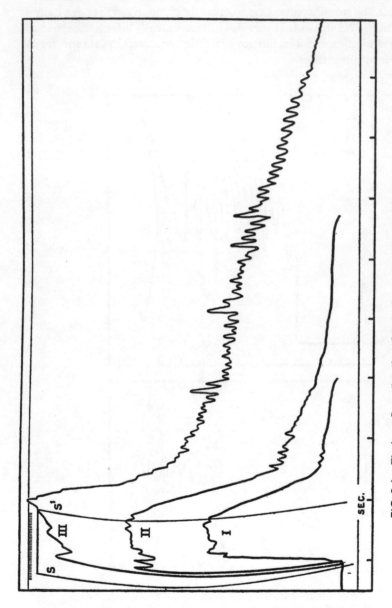

FIG. 2.4. Flexion reflexes (bending of the leg in response to a painful stimulus to the foot). The vertical arcs labeled S and S' show the onset and offset of the stimulus. Responses I–III were elicited by progressively stronger stimuli: Note that in the response to the strongest stimulus (response III), the reflex contraction outlasted the stimulus by more than 7 seconds. (From Sherrington, 1947, Fig. 5, p. 26)

In Fig. 2.4 is a record showing the lack of close correspondence between the cessation of a stimulus and the cessation of the reflex activity caused by that stimulus. The leg whose movement is recorded in Fig. 2.4 had not fully returned to its resting position several seconds after the stimulus ceased. One could not produce such a long after-effect by stimulating the motor nerve itself. Therefore the stimulus must have given rise (somewhere in the spinal cord) to a process that continued to excite the motor nerves long after the stimulus had ceased to act on the sensory nerves. Sherrington called this phenomenon "after-discharge" (see his point #2, p. 27).

Figure 2.5 illustrates Sherrington's third point, namely, that the temporal structure (rhythm) of the movements caused by the stimulus may be independent of the temporal structure of the stimulus. In a long series of

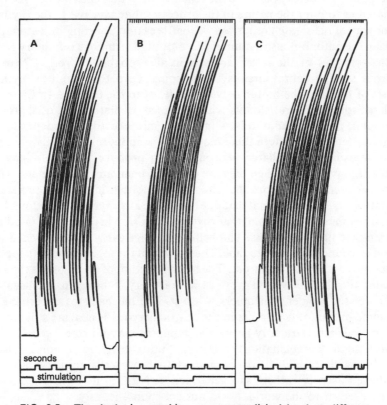

FIG. 2.5.   The rhythmic scratching movements elicited by three different stimuli: (*a*): The eliciting stimulus was light rubbing of the skin behind the shoulder. (*b*) & (*c*): The eliciting stimulus was a train of weak shocks (marked at top of panels). Note that the rhythm of the scratching movement was the same (about 4/sec) even through the temporal characteristics of the eliciting stimuli were very different. (From Sherrington, 1947, Fig. 14, p. 48)

experiments, Sherrington showed that the rhythm of the scratching movement of the dog's hind leg is about 4 scratches per second regardless of the rhythm of the stimulus that elicits the scratching. A continuous stimulus (rubbing the skin) elicits a four-per-secnd scratch and so does an intermittent stimulus consisting of a brief electric shocks delivered at rates from 10–100 shocks per second. When one stimulates the motor nerve itself, the temporal structure of the muscle response closely follows the temporal structure of the stimulus. Hence, Sherrington concluded that somewhere in the spinal part of the reflex arc there must be a process that can generate a rhythmic output with a frequency that is independent of the frequency of the stimulus.

The "refractory period" referred to in Sherrington's tenth point was not really an experimental finding, hence it cannot be illustrated. Sherrington's concept of a refractory period in the central part of the reflex arc derived from his attempt to infer the nature of the processes that gave rise to the rhythmic autonomy of the scratch reflex. As we shall see later, Sherrington's attempt to explain the autonomous rhythm of this output in terms of a refractory period in the synapses of the reflex arc was in all probability wrong. There are neurons and/or neural circuits in the spinal cord that produce rhythmic bursts of firing in the motor nerves that leads to the muscles. In Chapter 4 such neurons or neural circuits will be termed oscillators. An oscillator, by definition, produces an output whose rhythmic structure is independent of whatever temporal pattern there may be in the input to the oscillator. There are, for example, oscillator neurons, which produce bursts of signals at regular intervals even when they are divorced from any neural input. There are other oscillator neurons that fire rhythmic bursts in response to a steady neural input, an input signal that does not have any rhythmic structure. Even when the input has a rhythm, that rhythm is not seen in the output. Oscillator neurons are like bell-clocks. The bell-clock rings every hour provided only that it is wound from time to time. The rhythm of the input (winding) does not affect the rhythm of the output. The hourly rhythm of its ringing is the same whether the clock is wound every 24 hours, every 48 hours, or haphazardly, whenever the winder remembers to do it. The mechanisms underlying the rhythmic output of oscillators in the central nervous system are still not well understood, but refractory periods at synapses play no role.

Sherrington's explanation of the rhythmic structure of some reflexes reveals how thoroughly he was committed to the view that the nervous system conducted activity rather than generated activity on its own. The nervous system *reacted* to the world; it did not act spontaneously.

Figure 2.6 illustrates another rhythmic reflex—the "stepping" movements of the dog's hindleg. This rhythmic output is elicited by stimulating the paw of the contralateral leg with brief electric shocks at a high frequency (25–100 shocks/sec). The rhythm of this reflex is about 5 steps in 2 seconds (2.5Hz)— about half the frequency of the scratch reflex for the same limb in the same

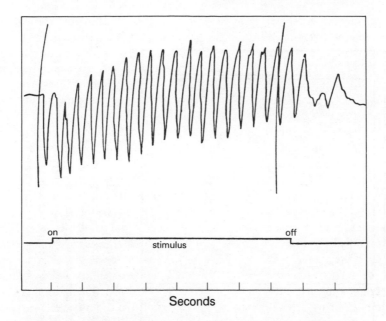

Seconds

FIG. 2.6. The stepping reflex. The leg steps about 5 times in 2 seconds, even though the stimulus eliciting the stepping is repeated 40 times/second. Note also that the frequency of the stepping movements is about one half the frequency of the scratching movements (cf. Fig. 2.3). (From Sherrington, 1947, Fig. 22, p. 66)

animal. Again, this rhythm is independent of stimulus strength and frequency. It is interesting to keep these two rhythmic "reflexes" in mind in reading von Holst's paper on the role of central oscillators in coordination (Chapter 4). Von Holst's emphasis on the role of central oscillators is frequently seen as standing in opposition to Sherrington's ideas. That Sherrington would not necessarily have insisted on this opposition may be surmised from the following passage. In the passage that follows Sherrington's reference to "refractory phase" refers to his conception of the mechanism underlying the autonomous rhythms he observed in some reflexes:

It is clear that an essential part of many reflexes is a more or less prolonged refractory phase succeeding nervous discharge.

Refractory phase appears . . . at the one end [in mantel movements of the very primitive *Medusa*] and at the other [end] of the animal scale as a factor of fundamental importance in the coordination of certain mobile actions. . . . in higher forms (dog) refractory phase occurs . . . not in the peripheral neuro-muscular organ, but in the centers of the nervous system itself [p. 69].

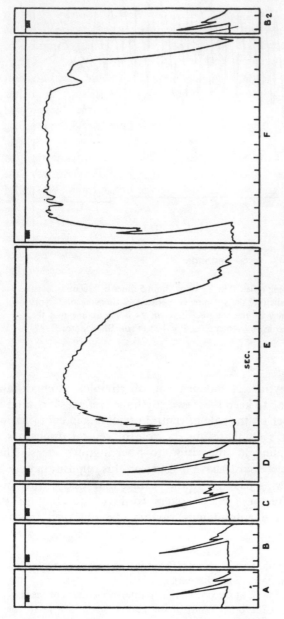

FIG. 2.7. The crossed-extension reflex (extension of the contralateral leg in response to a painful shock to the toe of a hindfoot) in response to stimuli of increasing strength (Panel *a*, weakest; Panel *f*, strongest). Note the tremendous increase in the amplitude and duration of the response from Panel *d* to Panel *e*. One characteristic of synaptic action in reflex arcs is this non-linear relation between the strength of the stimulus and the strength of the response: the first few increases in stimulus intensity produce only slight increases in the response (Panels *a–d*). The increase in the response at the fifth step (Panel *e*) is out of all proportion to what has gone before. (From Sherrington, 1947, Fig. 27, p. 76).

In other words, the spinal cord contains mechanisms that produce rhythmic outputs. Sherrington attributed these rhythmic outputs to refractory phases at synapses. In this he was in all probability mistaken. But he was very much in line with modern thinking when he recognized that oscillatory mechanisms in the central nervous system are a significant aspect of coordination in animals throughout the phylogenetic scale.

Figure 2.7 illustrates to some extent the highly variable amplification characteristics that Sherrington observed in reflex conduction. In other words, Fig. 2.7 illustrates Sherrington's fourth point—the "less close correspondence between grading of intensity of the stimulus and the grading of intensity of end-effect [p. 27]." The availability of processes whose amplification characteristics (relation between strength of input and strength of output) may vary is of great importance in the design of machinery that must organize the timing and relative strengths of its outputs. We make repeated use of this property in subsequent chapters.

Sherrington realized that the highly variable relation between stimulus strength and response strength was closely related to two other properties of the reflex arc. The first of these was the "considerable resistance of the passage of a single nerve impulse; but a resistance easily forced by a succession of impulses" (point 5 on p. 27). The second was the great variability in the threshold value for a stimulus (point 8, p. 27). What follows is his succinct discussion of the observations upon which these claims rest:

SUMMATION

SUMMATION of subliminal stimuli so that by repetition they become effective is practically unknown in nerve-trunk conduction. But it is a marked feature of reflex-arc conduction (Setschenow, 1863; Stirling, 1874). Nor is it attributable to the muscles whose contraction may serve as index of the reflex-response, since summation of this extent is not known for vertebrate skeletal muscle; though found by Richet (1882) in the claw-muscle of the crayfish.

We find striking instances of the summation of subliminal stimuli given by the scratch-reflex. The difficulty in exciting a reflex by a single-induction shock is well known. A scratch-reflex cannot in my experience be elicited by a single-induction shock, or even by two shocks, unless as physiological stimuli they are very intense and delivered less than 600 milliseconds (msecs) apart. Although the strongest single-induction shock is therefore by itself a subliminal stimulus for this reflex, the summating power of this reflex mechanism is great. Very feeble shocks, each succeeding the other within a certain time—summation time—sum as stimuli and provoke a reflex. Thus long series of subliminal stimuli ultimately provoke the reflex. I have records where the reflex appeared only after delivery of the fortieth successive double shock, the shocks having folllowed each other at a frequency of 11.3 per sec, and where the reflex appeared only after delivery of the forty-fourth successive make shock, the shocks having followed at 18 per sec. A momentary stimulus, for example, a break shock of fair physiological strength applied by a stigmatic pole (needle point) to a skin-spot in the receptive field of this reflex, produces in the nervous arc a change which though, as just said, unable of itself alone to produce the reflex movement, shows its facilitating influence (*bahnung*) on a subsequent stimulus applied even 1400 msec later. The duration of the excitatory change induced by a momentary stimulus is therefore in this mammalian arc (scratch-reflex) almost as long as that noted in the frog by Stirling, namely, 1500 msec.

With serial stimuli of the same frequency of repetition the latent time of the scratch-reflex is shorter the more intense the individual stimuli. Stirling (1874) conclusively traced length of latency to dependence on spinal summation of successive excitations. In accord with this in the 'scratch-reflex,' when the serial stimuli follow slowly, the reflex *ceteris paribus* is prolonged. A single brief mechanical stimulation of the skin (rub, prick, or pull upon a hair) usually succeeds in exciting a scratch-reflex, though the reflex thus evoked is short; but there is nothing to show that these stimuli, though brief, are really simple and not essentially multiple. A striking dissimilarity, therefore, between reflex-arc conduction and nerve-trunk conduction is that in reflex-arc conduction considerable resistance is offered to the passage of a single nerve-impulse, but the resistance is easily forced by a succession of impulses; in other words, subliminal stimuli are summed.

It follows almost as a corollary from this that the threshold excitability of a reflex mechanism appears much more variable than that of a nerve-trunk, if the threshold excitability be measured in terms of the intensity of the liminal stimulus. The value will be more variable in the case of the reflex mechanism, because there the duration of the stimulus is a factor in its efficiency far more than in the case of the nerve-trunk. In the scratch-reflex a single stimulus which is far below threshold intensity is found, on its fortieth repetition and nearly 4 sec after its first application, to become effective and provoke the reflex.

NONLINEAR SUMMATION

Sherrington's fourth and fifth points (variable amplification and response only to the cumulative effect of several stimuli) are both traceable to his eighth point (the variable threshold). Both phenomena are instances of *nonlinear* summation, a process of summation in which the effect of several stimuli acting together or in rapid succession is not equal to the sum of the effects of the individual stimuli acting in isolation. For example, a single electric shock elicits no scratch reflex. If the summation of stimuli in reflex conduction were linear, then repeating the shock a number of times would likewise fail to elicit a reflex, since $0 + 0 + \ldots + 0 = 0$. The fact that a number of stimuli delivered together will elicit a reflex even though no one of them elicits anything when acting alone indicates nonlinear addition of stimuli somewhere in the course of the reflex pathway (or, in Sherrington's terms, the summation of subliminal stimuli).

The phenomena that reflect nonlinear summation in reflex pathways were the focus of much interest in 19th century neurophysiology. The English termed such phenomena facilitation, because the first few stimuli in a train of stimuli were not themselves conducted to the effector organ, but seemed to make the passage easier for later stimuli. The German workers referred to this as Bahnung ("path-making"). Since most workers of the time tended to think of the nervous system as a structurally continuous passive conduction network, the ability of nerve signals to "change the resistance in a nervous pathway" seemed quite mysterious. This mystery inspired a good deal of complex and/or vague theorizing, despite the fact that Richet had offered a simple explanation as early as 1871.

Richet suggested that nonlinear summation phenomena (such as facilitation or Bahnung) implied the existence somewhere in the conduction pathway of excitation processes that were sluggish: These processes responded to a neural message with a relativley slow increase followed by a prolonged subsidence back to their original level. The effects of fairly widely spaced stimuli could partially summate through the agency of these slowly rising and subsiding excitation processes. Richet suggested that the sudden appearance of an observable response from the effector organ after some number of stimuli had been delivered implied that the summation excitation had to exceed some threshold before it could excite the next stage in the conduction pathway (see Fig. 2.8). The nonlinearity of the summation—the fact that the combined effect of several stimuli is not equal to the sum of their individual effects—is due to the presence of a high and/or variable threshold. Sherrington (1947, p. 156ff) offered a similar interpretation of at least one kind of nonlincar summation—irradiation (see Chapter 3).

Sherrington realized that the capacity for nonlinear or subliminal summation had far-reaching functional significance. In modern terms,

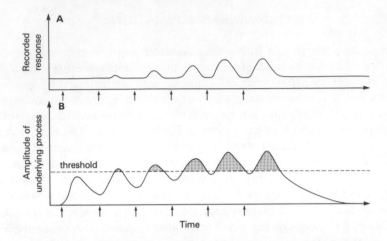

FIG. 2.8. (*a*) A kymographic record showing temporal facilitation. The regularly repeating shocks to the nerve are indicated by the vertical arrows. (*b*) A graphic presentation of a possible explanation. It is assumed that the processes set in motion by each shock to the nerve sum linearly. However, the sum must pass some threshold in order to produce the recorded effect. Hence, at the level of the recorded effect, the summation is nonlinear, even though at some level prior to the threshold the summation may be linear. (Modified from Richet, 1895, p. 150)

nonlinear summation permits "decision processes" that have the characteristics of logical AND gates. AND gates are devices that produce no output except in response to the *conjoint* occurrence of *at least* two inputs. They respond only to *x* and *y* in *combination*. They do not respond to either input alone. AND gates can be used in such a way that a complex spectrum of events must occur in order for a particular reaction to occur on the part of the organism. (For illustration, see Chapter 6, Fig. 6.9, and accompanying discussion).

As regards his sixth point—the irreversibility of conduction in a reflex arc—Sherrington again provides no illustrative experimental records, but he summarizes the evidence succinctly.

IRREVERSIBILITY OF DIRECTION
OF CONDUCTION

Another remarkable difference between reflex-arc conduction and nerve-trunk conduction is the irreversibility of direction of the former and the reversibility of the latter. Double conduction as it has been termed, is well established for nerve-trunks both afferent and efferent. It was shown by du Bois Reymond, for the spinal nerve roots, for peripheral nerves by Kuhne's gracilis experiment, for the great single electric fibre of *Malapterurus* by Babuchin (1876), for sympathetic nerve-cords by Langley & Anderson (1894), and by myself (1897) for certain fibres of the white tracks of the spinal cord. The nerve-fibres in all these cases, when excited anywhere in their course, conduct nerve-impulses in all directions from the point stimulated; that is, in their case both up and down, the only two directions open to them. Their substance may therefore be regarded as conductive in all directions along their extension.

From the Bell-Magendie law of the spinal nerve-roots we know that reflex-arcs conduct only in one direction. The stimulation of the central end of a motor-nerve remains without obvious effect. Bell (1811) and Magendie (1822) and their followers established that excitation of the spinal end of the severed motor root evokes no sign of reflex action or sensation. Evidently the central nexus between afferent channel and efferent is of a kind that though it allows conduction from afferent to efferent, does not allow it from efferent to afferent. The path is patent in one direction only. This is the special case which forms the first foundation of the law that conduction in the neural system proceeds in one direction only, the 'law of forward direction' (W. James, 1880). When the property of double conduction in nerve-fibres had been ascertained, the Bell-Magendie law of the spinal roots became more instructive. Gad (1884) argued that the dendrites of the motor root-cell are capable of conduction in one direction only, namely, toward and not away from the axone. It may, however, be that the irreciprocity of the conduction is referable to the synapse. The explanation of the valved condition of the reflex circuit may lie in a synaptic membrane more permeable in one direction than in the other. In other words, though intraneuronic conduction is reversible in direction, interneuronic may be irreversible.

Chain-cells of polarized conduction form the basis of the great majority of all the nervous reactions of the cerebrospinal system of higher animals. It appears, however, that not *all* pluricellular nervous circuits exhibit irreversible direction of conduction. The nerve-net of Medusa is a pluricellular conductor which exhibits reversibility of direction of conduction. In Medusa locomotion is effected by contraction of a sheet of muscle in the swimming-bell. When the swimming-bell, which resembles an inverted cup, contracts, its capacity is lessened, and some of the water embraced by it is expelled through the open end, the animal itself being propelled in the reverse direction by recoil. The mechanism is like that of the heart, but the heart propels its contents, the swimming-bell propels itself against its contents. The contractions of both recur rhythmically, though Medusa, unlike the heart, has periods of prolonged diastolic inactivity. At such a period an appropriate stimulus restarts the swimming-bell. The contractile beat begins from the point stimulated and spreads thence over the whole muscular sheet (Romanes, 1877). It spreads rapidly enough for the contraction not to have culminated at the initial point before it has set in at the most remote part. The beat is thus not only everywhere in progress at the same time, but is practically in the same phase of progress everywhere, and similarly synchronously passes off.

The arrangement of the nervous system of Medusa, *Rhizostoma*, is, according to Bethe (1897b), of the following kind (Fig. 2.9). The nerve-

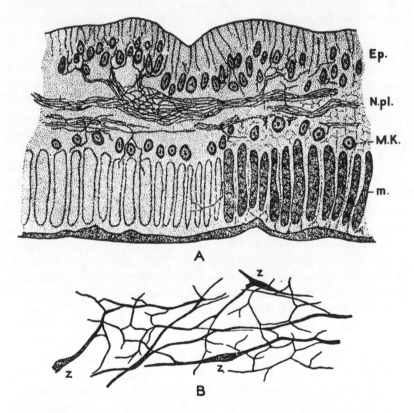

FIG. 2.9. (Bethe, 1897b). Nerve-net of *Rhizostoma* (*a*), radial section through a muscular field of the sub-umbrella; *Ep*, epithelium; *m*, muscle-fibres in cross-section; *M.K.*, their nuclei; *N.pl.*, nerve-plexus with fibres running into the epithelium and to the muscles. (*b*), nerve-plexus with scattered cells, from a horizontal section. Magnification 1200 in A, 200 in B.

cell has on one hand threadlike arms that extend to the surface of the sub-umbrella, and on the other hand others which stretch down to the sheet of contractile cells on the underside of the bell. Each nerve-cell has also long side threads which join similar side threads from other nerve-cells. By virtue of these lateral connexions the nerve-cells form a network of conductors spreading horizontally through the bell in a layer of tissue between a receptive sheet and a contractile sheet. From this nerve-net, throughout its extent, there pass nerve-threads to the adjacent muscle; it also receives at many points of its extent nerve-threads from specially receptive areas of surface.

The circularly arranged sheet of muscle does not form a continuous field toward the center of the disk; there are wide radial gaps in it. Across the gaps the 'conduction' passes: the microscope reveals no muscular tissue in these gaps, but the nerve-net can be seen to spread across them (Bethe, 1902). The presence of the nerve-net explains the conduction across them. It is therefore argued by Bethe that the spread of the contraction over the muscular sheet in *Rhizostoma* does not imply conduction of the contraction from one muscle-cell to another, but is the result of the spread of nervous action over the nerve-network. In its progress along the nerve-net, the nervous discharge, as it reaches each part of the nerve-net, spreads down the nerve-threads, descending thence to the underlying muscle-sheet. So long as the nerve-cell network is intact, *wherever* the point stimulated, the ensuing contraction is of the *whole* bell, that is, the nerve-impulses started at one point of the receptive surface, on entering the nerve-network, spread over it in all directions. When the bell-shaped disk is spirally cut into a long band, to whichever end of the band the stimulus be applied, the conduction spreads from that end to the other and over the whole strip (Romanes, 1877). The nerve-net therefore conducts nerve-impulses in both directions along its length. Therefore it is not a polarized conductor, conductive in one direction only. In the chains of nerve-cells of higher animals, such as Arthropods and Vertebrates, although the conduction is reversible in each nerve-cell—at least along that piece of it which forms a nerve-fibre—the pluricellular chain *in toto* constitutes a polarized conductor, conductive in one direction only. In such cell-chains the individual nerve-cells are characterized morphologically by possessing two kinds of cell-branches, which differ one from another in microscopic form, the one kind *dendrites*, the other *axones*. The difference in appearance between *dendrites* and *axones* is marked enough for recognition by microscopical inspection. Since in many well-known instances the dendrites conduct impulses away from their free ends, while the axone conducts towards its free end, it is possible on mere microscopic inspection of nerve-cells of this type to infer by analogy the normal direction of the conduction through the nerve-cell. But in the nerve-cells forming the nerve-network of Medusa there seems no such distinct differentiation of their branches into two types. Their cell-processes are not distinguishable into dendrites and axones.

Moreover, microscopic examination of the nerve-net of Medusa reveals another difference between it and the nerve-cell chains of higher animals. In these latter the neuro-fibrils of one nerve-cell are not found unbrokenly continuous with those of the next cell along the nerve-chain. Although the union may be close, there is not homogeneous continuity. The one nerve-cell joins another by synapsis. But in the nerve-net of Medusa the neurofibrils pass, according to Bethe, uninterruptedly across from one cell to another. Even if we admit the neuro-fibrils to be in a measure artifacts, the appearance of their continuity from one cell to another in one type, and of their discontinuity from one cell to another in the other type remains significant of a difference between the conduction-process from cell to cell in the two types. The nerve-net of Medusa appears an unbroken retiform continuum from end to end. Each nerve-cell in it joins its neighbors much as at a node in the myelinate nerve-fibre the axis-cylinder of each segment joins the next. Reversibility of conduction may be related to this apparent continuity of structure, and irreversibility to want of it. This points to the latter being referable to the synapse; if the *synaptic membrane* (Lecture I, p. 31) be permeable only in one direction to certain ions, that may explain the irreversibility of conduction. The polarized conduction of nerve-arcs would be related to the one-sided permeability of the intestinal wall, for example, to NaCl (Cohnheim).

The functional significance of the unidirectionality of conduction revealed by the study of reflexes is not readily appreciated unless one has some experience in the construction of organized signal systems, for example, relay or solid-state programming circuits. When a given control point ("common path" in Sherrington's terms) receives command signals from two different sources, one must always take measures to insure that the command signal from one source is not conducted back up the path from the other source. In electrical circuits one uses diodes, elements that allow current to flow in only one direction. In electronic circuits one uses elements called OR gates in order to prevent multiple inputs to the same point from generating "wrong 'way" signals in one another. Sherrington's emphasis on the unidirectionality of conduction is another instance of his deep insight into the properties of the central nervous system that are important from the standpoint of producing a functionally organized output.

INHIBITION

The last finding that has important organizational consequences is the inhibition mentioned in Sherrington's point #9. (Points 10 and 11 have important physiological and pharmacological consequences but are probably of little significance in the organization of outputs.) In vertebrates, when one stimulates motor nerves that are already being excited by some other means, the further stimulation simply accentuates whatever contraction is already in progress. Except under very specialized circumstances, stimulation of motor nerves never inhibits or cancels the excitatory effects of other stimuli. When one turns to the study of the muscular contractions that are elicited reflexly, that is, by the stimulation of sensory nerves, this is no longer true. Stimulation of one sensory area very often inhibits the muscular contractions that have been or are being elicited by stimulation of some other area.

Figures 2.10 and 2.11 illustrate the striking way in which one reflex stimulus can inhibit the effect of another reflex stimulus. In Fig. 2.10,

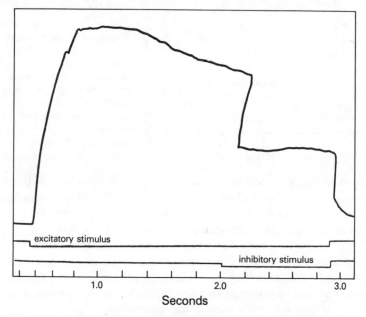

excitatory stimulus

inhibitory stimulus

1.0   2.0   3.0

Seconds

FIG. 2.10. Reflex inhibition. A painful stimulus to the foot (the excitatory stimulus) elicits a reflex contraction of a muscle that flexes the leg. A painful stimulus to the foot of the opposite leg (the inhibitory stimulus) elicits a reflex relaxation. In other words, the second stimulus partially counteracts the first. (Modified from Sherrington, 1947, Fig. 32, p. 99)

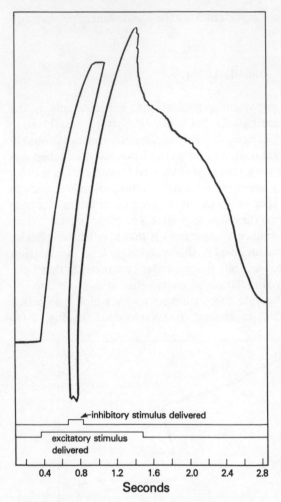

inhibitory stimulus delivered

excitatory stimulus
delivered

0.4   0.8   1.2   1.6   2.0   2.4   2.8
Seconds

FIG. 2.11. A negative twitch. Prolonged stimulation of the skin of the contralateral foot (the excitatory stimulus) elicits a sustained contraction of an extensor muscle. In the midst of this contraction, a brief shock to the skin of the homonymous foot (the inhibitory stimulus) elicits a momentary relaxation. (Modified from Sherrington, 1947, Fig. 33, p. 102)

stimulation of one foot elicits a sustained contraction of the hamstring muscle in the leg of that foot (the "homonymous" leg, or "leg of the same name"). Stimulation of the contralateral foot (the foot on the opposite side) then produces an abrupt, albeit incomplete relaxation of the hamstring muscle. This abrupt relaxation may be thought of as a "negative contraction," an effect opposite in sign to the effect of an excitatory stimulus. In Fig. 2.11 we see what might be called a "negative twitch," that is, a very brief *relaxation* of an extensor muscle in response to a brief stimulus to the homonymous foot delivered at a time when the muscle was contracting.

In summary, stimuli delivered to the motor nerves of vertebrates always have an excitatory effect. They cause the muscle to contract. Stimuli delivered to the sensory receptor areas may have effects of opposite signs; some cause the muscle to contract, others cause the muscle to relax. Sherrington saw that the relaxing effect of some reflex stimuli must mean that signals produced by these stimuli gave rise somewhere in the spinal part of the reflex pathway to processes that antagonize the excitatory process. Sherrington termed this antagonistic process inhibition. Thus, the spinal part of the reflex pathway can integrate both the signals that argue for the contraction of a given muscle and the signals that argue against the contraction of that muscle. The motor neuron signal, which drives the muscle, will increase or decrease as the arguments pro and con fluctuate in strength. All stimuli have excitatory effects on the afferent (sensory) pathways, but central processes can "invert" these effects, so that a stimulus may inhibit a motor process rather than excite it.

SUMMARY

These, then, are the kinds of central processes revealed by the study of what Sherrington termed *"the unit mechanism of the nervous system when that system is regarded in its integrative function* [p. 22]." In Sherrington's view, the reflex was the elementary unit of behavior, from which all coordinated action was constructed. Although it will emerge below that the reflex is only *one* of the functional units in the construction of coordinated sequences of action, this in no way detracts from the magnitude of Sherrington's achievement. He identified and experimentally characterized processes of far reaching functional significance.

In his analysis of the processes underlying reflex action, Sherrington was in every sense a modern psychologist. He was attempting to specify the general nature of the processes underlying integrated behavior. That he is known today primarily as a physiologist is owing in part to the fact that he was able to draw on recent anatomical advances to *infer the locus* of the processes whose general nature he had determined from behavioral study. Sherrington's inference was beautiful in its simplicity: He knew that the neural signals were relayed from the sensory nerve to the motor nerve over pathways that were fiber-like throughout most of their length except at a few points, namely, at the *junctions* between neural cells. At these junctions between neural cells there was no fiber-pathway to conduct the signals. So important was this fact in Sherrington's thinking that he opened his book with the sentence: "Nowhere in physiology does the cell-theory reveal its presence more frequently in the very framework of the argument than at the present time in the study of nervous reactions [p. 17]." The cell theory was embedded "in the very framework of the argument" because Sherrington attributed *all* of the differences between nerve-fiber conduction and reflex conduction to the only part of the reflex pathway that did not involve conduction along a fiber, namely, to the junction between cells. Here, the nervous signal had somehow to be transmitted *across* the barrier imposed by the walls of the two opposed neural cells. Since Sherrington attributed such far reaching significance to the transmission process at this locus, he coined a special word for the signal-transmitting junction between two cells—the *synapse*. It was, he inferred, the transmission process at the synapse that made the phenomena of reflex conduction so different from the phenomena of conduction in nerve trunks.

The last seventy years of neurophysiological work have richly supported most but not all[1] of Sherrington's inferences about the nature of the processes that occur at synapses. We now can explain the nature of synaptic transmission in terms of more molecular events such as the release of excitatory and inhibitory transmitter substances from the prejunctional membrane, the depolarizing and hyperpolarizing effects of these transmitter substances at the post-junctional membrane, the nonlinear conversion of the resulting depolarization into a conducted action potential, and so on. But this more molecular work need not concern us further. It has added little *of functional significance* to Sherrington's characterization of the process of synaptic transmission. Nearly all of the presently known aspects of synaptic transmission that play an important role in the construction of integrated sequences of muscular movement are clearly described in *The Integrative Action of the Nervous System*. These aspects are:

1. The capacity to integrate signals occurring over time intervals measured in seconds to minutes. This capacity derives from the wide range of rise times and decay times characteristic of excitation and inhibition at synapses.

2. The nonlinear summation of inputs so that several inputs acting together may produce an output even though any one input acting alone produces no output.

3. The control over the direction of signal flow so that signals arriving at a common point do not penetrate back up other input pathways.

4. The widely adjustable amplification characteristics that permit a strong signal to have no effect under some circumstances, while a weak signal may have a strong effect under other circumstances.

5. The ability to "invert" signals so that a signal from a given source can be used to excite one action and inhibit another.

For someone who is interested in the design of a system with complex adaptively organized ouputs the above list is an exceedingly useful set of properties to work with. The question now becomes what sort of combinatorial principles does the system use? That is, given a functional unit, the reflex, that manifests the above list of useful properties, how does the system combine these units to form complexes of units acting in coordination. Here too, Sherrington had many important insights.

---

[1]The most notable lack of support concerns Sherrington's inference of a long lasting synaptic refractory period.

3

Sherrington's Combinatorial Principles

THE PRINCIPLE OF THE COMMON PATH

For Sherrington, the reflex was *the* elementary unit of behavior. A complex behavior was a compound of allied reflexes, reflexes that operated simultaneously or in sequence and served a common purpose. The starting point for Sherrington's analysis of the problem of coordination was the principle of the final common path. This principle refers to a simple but important fact: Different reflexes involve the same muscles. A flexion reflex excites the motor neurons to the flexor muscles and inhibits the motor neurons to the extensor muscles. An extension reflex uses the same motor neurons, but to different effect. The motor neurons are a keyboard upon which different reflexes play. Any process in the nervous system that is to be expressed in action must use much the same set of motor neurons as any other. What distinguishes one reflex from another is the spatial and temporal pattern of motor neuron activity, just as one piece of music is distinguished from another by the spatial and temporal pattern in which the piano keys are struck.

The principle of the final common path means that we encounter the lattice-like pattern of hierarchical organization at the lowest level of the behavioral hierarchy. A motor neuron together with the muscle fibers it innervates constitute a motor unit. An impulse in the motor neuron causes a twitch in the muscle fibers. This twitch is the quantum of muscular contraction; no smaller contraction can occur and greater contractions are the sum of such twitches. When one diagrams the control of reflexes over motor units one creates a latticelike picture, as in Fig. 3.1a. Focus for a

A

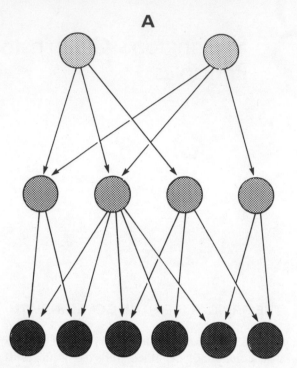

FIG. 3.1.   (*a*). Schematic illustration of a lattice hierarchy (*b*). Schematic illustration of a partition hierarchy.

moment on the lower two levels in Fig. 3.1a. Let the lowest level (darkest circles) represent motor units. Let the middle level (mid-gray circles) represent reflexes. The lines of control (arrows) from reflexes to motor units intersect to form a lattice. The competition among reflexes for control over motor units, which is represented schematically in Fig. 3.1a, is what Sherrington emphasized when he termed the motor neurons the final common paths of behavior.

The common path principle means that the pattern of hierarchical control underlying the actions of animals differs from the pattern of control found in many familiar hierarchically structured systems of control. The army, the church, and the governmental bureaucracy are all hierarchically structured systems of control that are not lattice hierarchies. Lower units in the systems—privates, parish priests, clerks—are subject to control by only one unit immediately above them in the hierarchy: The private is commanded by only one sergeant. Conversely, higher units do not compete for control over lower units: Sergeants do not compete for command over one and the same platoon of privates. Reflexes, on the other hand, do compete for control over motor units. In the army, the church, and the executive bureaucracy authority

B

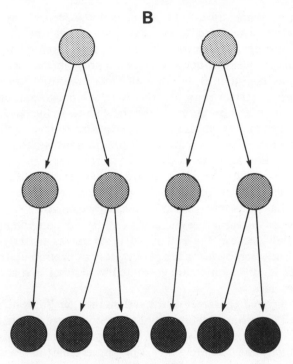

FIG. 3.1. *(contd.)*

over lower units is partitioned up. Lines of control do not cross. The organizational chart for these hierarchies is schematized in Fig. 3.1b. To distinguish this pattern of hierarchical control from the lattice pattern, I suggest the term partition hierarchy.

Although the partitioning of control is the pattern that comes most easily to mind, there are some well known systems of control that adhere to the lattice pattern. The control of doctors over nurses in a hospital is of this form. Indeed, in a hospital one may discern two levels of latticelike control. The orderlies, on the lowest level, are supervised by many different nurses. The nurses are supervised by many different doctors. Figure 3.1a schematizes such a three-level lattice hierarchy.

The structure of computer programs is an excellent example of a multilayered lattice hierarchy. A small computer may have about 20 elementary operations built into it. These operations are the elements of computer action, the lowest level of the hierarchy. The first level above this is the level of the "compiler language." The compiler language is a set of instructions, each of which activates a short and simple sequence of elementary operations. Different instructions from the compiler call on the same elementary operations, but in a different sequence, and, therefore, to different effect. The third level, that level above the compiler, is the programming language. Instructions in the programming language activate sequences of compiler instructions. Different program instructions call on the same compiler instructions, but in a different order and to different effect. These program instructions are the units of programming. All of the programs written by a programmer use these units. In the course of writing a complex program, the programmer creates fourth-level units called subroutines. A subroutine is a sequence of program instructions that performs some computation and that is called upon repeatedly in the course of the overall program. A complex program has many subroutines. Each subroutine makes use of almost the same instructions as any other subroutine, but in its own special sequence, with its own special result.

I have spelled out the lattice-hierarchy structure of computer programming in some detail because the pattern of organization underlying computer actions is closely analogous to the pattern of organization underlying animal action. Both kinds of action are generated by systems that are multilayered lattice hierarchies.

The multilayered character of the system that generates behavior did not impress itself upon Sherrington's thinking about coordination. For Sherrington, a motor scheme, that is to say, a complex action involving all of an animal's muscles and extending over some appreciable time, was a set of allied reflexes. This conception implies only a single level of functional organization—the reflex level. Sherrington's views recognized only chiefs and indians, reflexes and motor units. We will see in Chapters 8 and 9 that this is not the case. There are many intermediate units of organization between the elementary units of action and full-blown behavioral sequences, just as there are many intermediate units of instruction between the elementary operations of a computer and the computer program.

Although Sherrington did not make much use of the notion of multiple layers in the functional organization of behavior, he did recognize multiple layering at the anatomical level. Most motor neurons are contacted primarily by the so called interneurons (or internuncials in Sherrington's terms), that is, neurons that do not originate in sensory receptors, but rather are interposed between sensory neurons and motor neurons. Interneurons are by far the most numerous kind of neuron in any nervous system, and most interneurons contact only other interneurons. Thus, interneurons that drive a motor unit are themselves driven for the most part by other interneurons. In this way, a multilayered neuroanatomical hierarchy arises. Sherrington stressed that the common path principle (the lattice principle) extended to interneuron levels. He argued that the higher levels of the sensory nervous system gain control of a final common path not by any effect exerted directly onto that path, but rather indirectly, by means of excitatory and inhibitory effects exerted on intermediate levels (interneurons). Since the higher levels of the nervous system compete for control over these intermediate levels, these intermediate levels are themselves common paths (see Sherrington, 1947, p. 328).

PRINCIPLES GOVERNING COMBINATION

Because Sherrington recognized primarily the reflex level of organization, his analysis of coordination focused on the principles by which the system insured that reflex circuits active simultaneously or in rapid succession mediated allied or complementary movements, movements that served a common purpose. Thus, Sherrington's principles of coordination, to be elaborated momentarily, emphasized coordinative processes operating between units at the same level of function. We will see in later chapters that these within-level coordinative principles may be observed at every level of functional organization, including the highest, the motivational level.

Sherrington recognized three processes governing the compounding of reflex actions: facilitation between agonistic actions, inhibition between antagonistic actions, and chaining. He distinguished two kinds of facilitative interactions, induction and irradiation. But he also recognized that both of these manifestations of facilitation were traceable to nonlinear summation at synapses. All instances of facilitation may be thought of as an increase in the likelihood that a subsequent signal arriving at a synapse will exceed the threshold and produce a conducted signal in the postsynaptic neuron.

Induction

In reflex induction, two reflex arcs with complementary effects will facilitate each other. For example, if one elicits a weak flexion reflex in the hind limb of a dog by a mildly painful stimulus to a digit of the paw, a weak stimulus to the tail markedly strengthens the flexion. The stimulus to the tail, by itself, elicits tail deflection, not leg flexion. Another form of induction is when two subliminal stimuli, neither of which is effective by itself, together elicit a reflex. These induction phenomena reflect nonlinear summation in synaptic transmission. One input raises the excitation at synapses to the point where the addition of excitation from another input brings the sum above threshold, thereby producing an observable reflex action.

Irradiation

A closely related manifestation of the functional usefulness of nonlinear summation is the phenomenon of irradiation. Irradiation is the recruitment of more and more responses as the strength and/or duration of the exciting stimulus is increased. In the spinal dog a series of mild pricks delivered to the bottom of the hind paw elicits at first only a contraction of the hamstring muscle (flexing the knee joint). If the pricking is strengthened and/or prolonged, a contraction of the hip muscles flexes the hip as well. Further strengthening or prolonging the stimulus brings successively into play (1) a contraction of the extensor muscles in the leg on the opposite side, (2) extension of the elbow of ipsilateral ("same side") forelimb together with some retraction at the shoulder joint of this limb, (3) flexion of the elbow joint in the contralateral forelimb together with extension at the wrist joint and

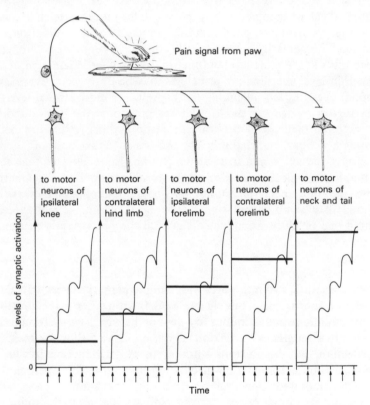

FIG. 3.2.   Schematic illustration of the way in which nonlinear summation at synapses can generate an "irradiating" sequence of movements. Each graph represents the excitation (depolarization) over time at the synapses subserving one movement. The arrows indicate the repeated pricks of the paw. The "staircases" indicate the build up of excitation through temporal summation of the excitation from each prick. The heavy horizontal lines indicate the threshold, that is, the level synaptic excitation must reach in order to fire the motor neurons and thereby produce muscle contraction. The knee bends first because those synapses have the lowest threshold. The neck and tail move last because those synapses have the highest threshold.

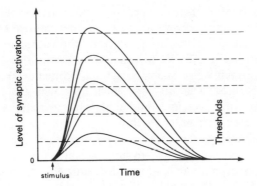

FIG. 3.3. The fact that stronger stimuli induce a more elaborate combination of movements is explained in the same way as irradiation. The horizontal dashed lines represent the same thresholds as the heavy bars in Fig. 3.2. The higher and higher curves represent synaptic excitation in response to stronger and stronger single stimuli. The response to the weakest stimulus only exceeds the lowest threshold, the threshold for bending the knee. The response to the strongest stimulus exceeds all the thresholds; hence it produces the complete spectrum of movements.

protraction at the shoulder of this limb, (4) turning of the head toward the side of the stimulation, some opening of the mouth, and diversion of the tail away from the side of the stimulation.

An irritating stimulus to the paw of an intact dog elicits a similar sequence of actions. Thus, we are dealing with an organized sequence of actions characteristic of the intact dog. Sherrington pointed out that nonlinear summation at synapses could explain this sequence. Figure 3.2 illustrates the sequential activation of more and more musculature by means of nonlinear summation. In Fig. 3.2 the irradiation occurs as the stimulus train is prolonged. Because the excitation produced by single stimuli decays slowly, the excitatory effects of the successive stimuli build upon each other (summate). Because the later responses in the irradiation sequence have higher thresholds, a larger and larger summated excitation is required for the appearance of each further response.

Instead of increasing the duration of the train of stimuli, one can increase the strength of a single stimulus. A similar irradiation sequence will be observed as the shock is strengthened (Fig. 3.3). The stronger the shock, the more components there are in the dog's response.

The use of nonlinear temporal summation to sequence responses is closely analogous to the use of the ramp-and-trigger principle in electronics. To control the order in which a series of units becomes active, the circuit designer arranges to feed a steadily increasing voltage (called a voltage ramp) to the "trigger inputs" of the units. The trigger on each unit is adjusted so that the unit acts when the input voltage reaches some particular level. The sequence or order in which the units become active is thus determined by their trigger thresholds. The voltage ramp corresponds to the increasing staircase of synaptic excitation in Fig. 3.2. We will encounter a modified version of this ramp-and-trigger principle in Chapter 5. In the modified version, the voltage ramp undergoes cyclical variation—up-down, up-down, etc. It triggers one action at one point in this cycle and another action at another point. Thus, the two actions alternate in a regular rhythm.

In summary, induction and irradiation are principles of reflex combination that depend on the synapse's capacity to sum together the excitatory effects of stimuli from different points in space or time and generate an output only when the sum exceeds a threshold.

Reciprocal Inhibition

A stimulus that excites a muscle on one side of a joint invariably inhibits excitation of the antagonistic muscle on the other side of the joint, and vice versa. Sherrington called this the principle of reciprocal inhibition. He applied this concept only to reflex effects on antagonistic muscles. In the case of antagonistic reflexes (e.g., the scratch reflex versus the flexion reflex in the hind limb of the dog), Sherrington (1947) referred to mutual or reciprocal interference. He pointed out, however, that this interference phenomenon was "tantamount to, if not the same thing as inhibition [p. 142]." There is now every reason to believe that Sherrington was correct: Part of the process by which one reflex wrests control of a final common path away from an antagonistic reflex involves inhibition of the interneurons in the antagonistic reflex pathway. Reflex arcs that compete for the use of a common path reciprocally inhibit each other.

In illustrating a reciprocally inhibitory network, I make a distinction that Sherrington did not make, namely, that between *precurrent* and *recurrent* reciprocal inhibition. Figure 3.4 shows a reciprocally inhibitory network of the precurrent type—the type that Sherrington has in mind in describing reciprocal inhibition of antagonistic muscles. Figure 3.6 shows a reciprocally inhibitory network of the recurrent type. As will be explained later, the recurrent configuration may be a more plausible representation of reciprocal inhibition between the interneurons of competing reflexes.

Precurrent Reciprocal Inhibition

In the precurrent network (Figure 3.4) a signal in path α_1 excites α_2, and inhibits β_2—and vice versa for a signal in β_1. If the stimulus that excites α_1, produces a contraction of, say, the flexor muscle of the knee (via α_2), it simultaneously produces a commensurate relaxation of the extensor muscle,

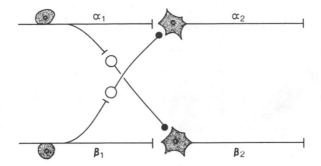

FIG. 3.4.   Reciprocal *precurrent* inhibition between two signal pathways. The T-like endings indicate an excitatory synapse; the solid-dot endings indicate an inhibitory synapse. It is generally found that a neuron (e.g., α_1) cannot have an excitatory ending on one neuron (e.g., α_2) and an inhibitory ending on another (e.g., β_2). Thus, an inhibitory interneuron (internuncial) is interposed whenever an inhibitory effect is called for. A signal in α_1 excites α_2 directly and inhibits β_2 via an inhibitory interneuron. A signal in β_1 does the opposite.

by way of its inhibitory effect on β_2. A stimulus to β_1 acts conversely; it excites the motor pathway to the extensor muscles and inhibits the motor pathway to the flexor muscles. This is the kind of reciprocal excitatory–inhibitory effect that Sherrington demonstrated to be at work on the atagonistic muscle pair that controls the flexion reflex in the hindlimb of the dog, (see Figures 2.10 and 2.11).

Precurrent reciprocal inhibition is analogous to the push-pull principle (or differential principle) in electronics. It makes downstream circuit elements (α_2 and β_2 in Figure 3.4) responsive to the difference between signals in upstream elements (α_1 and β_1) rather than to the absolute level of the input signals. The output does not respond to the signals that are common to both inputs. The network exhibits what is called common-mode rejection. It rejects whatever signal the two inputs have in common, transmitting only what they do not have in common, as illustrated in Fig. 3.5.

Common-mode rejection is a useful property in circuits whose elements are subject to spurious influences. These are factors (e.g., the temperature of the neural tissue) that affect the strength of the signal in a given pathway but must not affect the action controlled by the signal if the system is to function properly. In push-pull circuits irrelevant factors affect the signals on both sides to a similar extent, that is to say, the effects of the irrelevant factors are common to both sides of the circuit. The effects therefore cancel each other out; they do not influence the response of the downstream elements. Common mode rejection, then, immunizes a system against the effects of spurious factors.

Common-mode rejection may also compensate for a limited selectivity on the transducer (receptor) side of the system. As Sherrington was well aware,

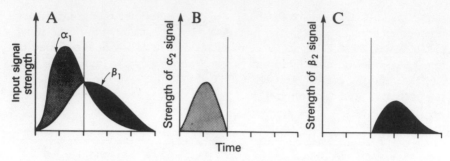

FIG. 3.5.   (a). The strengths of signals in the α and β pathways as a function of time. When $\alpha_1 > \beta_1$ (light stippling), only the α output (α_2) is active. When $\beta_1 > \alpha_1$ (dark stippling), only the β output (β_2) is active. (b). The lightly strippled area on A replotted to show what the signal in α_2 would look like. (c). The darkly stippled area on A replotted to show what the signal in β_2 would look like. Notice that at the moment (light vertical line) when the signals in α_1 and β_1 are equal, there is no signal in either output. This is common-mode rejection.

the receptors at the sensory end of the reflex arcs are by no means completely selective in the kind of stimulus energy or stimulus configuration to which they will respond. Touch receptors respond to noxious stimuli, such as strong shocks, as well as responding to small displacements of the skin (their "adequate" stimulus). The converse will no doubt prove true of pain receptors, if there eventually proves to be such a thing as pain receptors. Yet pain signals and touch signals lead to competing reflex responses (extension of the leg versus retraction of the leg). A precurrent reciprocal inhibition circuit may eliminate the overlap in these conflicting signals. Suppose a light touch is the adequate stimulus for α_1 in Fig. 3.4 and suppose further that a noxious stimulus is the adequate stimulus for β_1. The signal in α_1 will be stronger than the signal in β_1 when the stimulus is a touch and will block the β_2 response to the β_1 signal, leaving only α_2 (the touch pathway) active. In other words, reciprocal inhibition sharpens the stimulus distinctions that are only partially made by the "poorly tuned," stimulus transducers (receptors). The widespread use of reciprocal inhibition to sharpen afferent input may explain why electric shocks delivered directly to afferent nerve bundles are poor elicitors of reflexes: Electric shocks to the nerve produce signals of similar strength in all the sensory pathways; hence, no signal gets past the push-pull circuits, where the signals common to several pathways cancel each other out.

Recurrent Reciprocal Inhibition

The analysis of *recurrently* inhibitory networks (Figure 3.6) is more complex than it appears at first glance. Recurrent networks have a positive feedback loop in them that may be of considerable functional significance.

Paradoxically, the positive feedback loop exists because of the inhibitory interconnections. To grasp the positive feedback phenomenon, one must consider step by step the sequence of events that occur as the β pathway in Fig. 3.6 goes from less to more active than the α pathway. In Panel (b) of Fig. 3.6, the neurons of the recurrent inhibition circuit have been graphically rearranged to facilitate comprehension of the positive feedback loop created

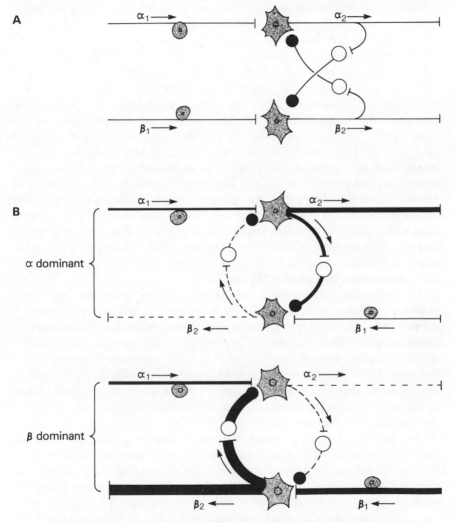

FIG. 3.6. (a). The *recurrent* reciprocal inhibition circuit, as it is ordinarily drawn. (b). The same circuit, redrawn to make clear how the recurrent inhibitory connections create a positive feedback loop that reinforces increases in either the α or the β pathway.

by the recurrent inhibitory pathways. When the α_1 signal is stronger than the β_1 signal, the α_2 neuron gives itself a further boost by way of its inhibitory effect on the β_2 neuron (top of Panel b). The β_2 neuron is inhibited by the strong signal in the inhibitory collateral form α_2. (This signal is indicated by the heavy line for this pathway.) Because β_2 is inhibited, there is little inhibition from β_2 back on to α_2. The weak or nonexistent signal in β_2 and its inhibitory collateral is indicated by the dashed lines for these pathways. Consider now what happens when the signal in β_1 becomes strong enough to overcome the inhibitory effect of α_2 on β_2 (bottom of Panel b). When the β_1 signal overcomes the inhibition from α_2, the β_2 pathway becomes active. The initial increase in the β_2 signal increases the inhibition that β_2 exerts on α_2. The increased inhibition of α_2 by β_2 weakens the α_2 signal. The weakening of the α_2 signal weakens the inhibition that α_2 exerts back on to β_2. The weakening of the inhibition of β_2 by α_2, which is a consequence of the initial increase in the β_2 signal, further increases the β_2 signal. And so on, around the loop again. Thus, an increase in the β_2 signal is self-reinforcing; it automatically promotes further increase. Decreases are, of course, also self-reinforcing. In a network with recurrent reciprocal inhibition changes in either direction are self-reinforcing. The parameters of the interaction can be chosen in such a way that the circuit has a flip-flop or teeter-totter characteristic: Either one output or the other is dominant. The in-between state where neither dominates is made inherently unstable, so that it cannot endure for any length of time. The outputs are like buttons on a car radio: Either the one is up and the other down, or the one is down and the other up; they cannot both be down at the same time.

The recurrent configuration seems more likely than the precurrent configuration as a representation of reciprocal inhibition ("interference") between the interneurons of reflex arcs that compete for control over a common path. The decisive "either-or" characteristics of the recurrent network explain Sherrington's observation that when a reflex supplants a competitor the transition is invariably abrupt. There is no period of compromise, during which the final common path manifests a mixed response consisting partly of commands from one reflex arc and partly of commands from the other.

One pair of competitive reflexes much studied by Sherrington was the scratch reflex of the dog's hind leg and the flexion reflex of this same hind leg. The stimulus for the scratch reflex is a mild irritation of the shoulder. The stimulus for the flexion reflex is a painful stimulus to the paw. These two reflexes have a markedly different temporal structure. The flexion reflex involves a unimodal excitatory command to the flexor motor neurons: The excitatory command rises to a single peak and then slowly decays. The scratch reflex, on the other hand, sends a rhythmically alternating series of excitatory and inhibitory commands to the flexor motor neurons. At some point there must be a neural network that decides which kind of command (unimodal or

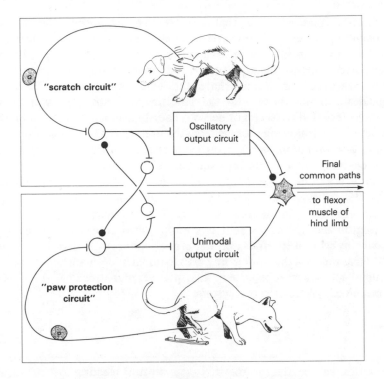

FIG. 3.7. A recurrent reciprocal inhibition circuit decides between two
opposed schemes of coordination that compete for control of the motor
neurons to the flexor muscles of the hind limb.

rhythmic) is to drive the final common path (the motor neurons). Figure 3.7
shows a recurrent reciprocal inhibition network mediating the competition
between the scratch and flexion reflexes. Placing the reciprocal inhibition just
before the stage where the two possible forms of command are generated
means that the final common path receives either an oscillatory command or
a unimodal command, but not both.

Recurrent reciprocal inhibition networks can promote decisiveness in the
competition between higher units for control over lower units. Such networks
may be used again and again, at every level of the motor hierarchy, wherever it
is necessary that *either* one *or* the other of two (or more) units have control
over shared lower units.

Chaining

The combinatorial principle that Sherrington relied on to account for lengthy
sequences of coordinated action was reflex chaining. This is the well known
notion that the action of one reflex gives rise to new stimuli that excite further

reflexes. Sherrington believed that the secret of neural coordination lay in the compounding of reflexes. Since reflex chaining ("sequential combination") was the only principle he enunciated that was capable of producing a coordinated sequence of more or less indefinite length, this combinatorial principle came to bear the lion's share of the explanatory burden. The chained reflex idea also took the brunt of the criticism from subsequent workers who did not believe that the secret of nervous coordination lay in the combination of reflexes. The following passage from the preface to the 1947 edition of *The integrative action of the nervous system* presents Sherrington's conception of reflex chaining. It also conveys something of Sherrington's ideas on the relation between mind and body. It is ironic that Sherrington was himself a dualist. He believed that when he cut the spinal cord, he isolated the neural mechanisms (body) in the spinal cord from the influence of the soul (mind). Sherrington thought of the soul as a nonphysical entity controlling higher behavior by way of its effects on the brain. The irony is that Sherrington's work did as much as the work of any man to undermine dualistic explanations of animal action and substitute in their place explanations based entirely on the machinery of the nervous system.

A 'reflex' can be diagrammatized as an animal reacting to a cosmical 'field' containing it. Animal and 'field' are of one cateogry, both being comprised within the physicist's term 'energy.' They are machines which interact—a point taken by Descartes. His wheel-work animals geared into the turning universe. Cat, dog, horse, etc. in his view had no thoughts, no ideas; they were trigger-puppets which events in the circumambient universe touched-off into doing what they do. It was a view less strange than might seem from this condensed epitome. But it lets us feel Descartes can never have kept an animal pet. Experiment to-day does, however, put within reach of the observer a puppet-animal which conforms largely with Descartes' assumptions. In the more organized animals of the vertebrate type the shape of the central nerve-organ allows a simple operation to reduce the animal to the Descartes condition. An overlying outgrowth of the central nerve-organ in the head can be removed under anaesthesia, and on the narcosis passing off the animal is found to be a Cartesian puppet: It can execute certain acts but is devoid of mind. That it is devoid of mind may seem a dogmatic statement. Exhaustive tests, however, bear the assertion out. Thoughts, feelings, memory, percepts, conations, etc; of these no evidence is forthcoming or to be elicited. Yet the animal remains a motor mechanism which can be touched into action in certain ways so as to exhibit pieces of its behavior.

An outline of the spatial arrangement of nerve illustrates how this comes about. From points within and on the surface of the animal, nerve-threads run to its muscles, but in their course thither are engaged by the central organ and are there relayed; the central organ becoming a sort of switchboard where muscles can be switched on or off. The starting-point of the nerve-thread is not equally responsive to all the various types of the field forces. Each starting-point is armed with a structure, the receptor, which reacts to one specific class of field agency, for example, one to light, not heat, another to heat, not light. The reaction of the nerve-thread itself is, in all nerve-threads, to generate a repetitive series of brief and minute electric currents which run away from the starting-point and, by relays through the central organ, reach this or that set of muscles determined by the topography of the starting-point concerned. As the play of the 'field' shifts over the animal, different sets of receptors come into and go out of action. The receptors thus analyse the successive situations occurring between animal and field in terms of the selective receptors, and ultimately in terms of the muscles of the limbs, etc. Change in the external situation brings corresponding change in the muscles brought into and released from contraction. A train of motor acts results therefore from a train of successive external situations.

The movements are not meaningless; they carry each of them an obvious meaning. The scope commonly agrees with some act which the normal animal under like circumstances would do. Thus, the cat set upright (Graham Brown), on the 'floor' moving backward under its feet walks, runs or gallops according to the speed given to the floorway. Again, in the dog a feeble electric current ('electric flea') applied by a minute entomological pin set lightly in the hair-bulb layer of the skin of the shoulder brings the hind paw of that side to the place, and with unsheathed claws the foot performs a rhythmic grooming of the hairy coat there. If the point lie forward at the ear, the foot is directed thither, if far back in the loin the foot goes thither, and similarly at any intermediate spot. The list of such purposive movements is impressive. If a foot tread on a thorn that foot is held up from the ground while the other legs limp away. Milk placed in the mouth is swallowed; acid solution is rejected. Let fall, inverted, the reflex cat alights on its feet. The dog shakes its coat dry after immersion in water. A fly settling on the ear is instantly flung off by the ear. Water entering the ear is thrown out by violent shaking of the head. An exhaustive list would be much larger than that given here.

The experiments of Graham Brown and of R. Magnus give excellent examples. But when all is said, if we compare such a list with the range of situations to which the normal cat or dog reacts appropriately, the list is extremely poverty stricken as a conspectus of behavior. It contains no social reactions. It evidences hunger by restlessness and brisker knee-jerks; but it fails to recognize food as food: it shows no memory, it cannot be trained or learn: it cannot be taught its name. The mindless body reacts with the fatality of a multiple penny-in-the-slot machine to certain stimuli, all of them, as in the case of the penny-in-the-slot machine, physical, and not psychical.

A point is that these mindless acts yet treat the animal's motor machinery as a united whole. Thus the mindless machine can walk, and run, and gallop; it can also spring. These acts include 'balance' and adjustments of poise as well as phasic movements duly coordinated. There is integration although purely motor integration. What is noteworthy is that such acts should be carried out in absence of mind, that is to say of mind in any ordinary acceptation of the term. Of course we do not forget that here what we observe is an artifact; but it is an analytic artifact. And that an artifact of such effectiveness should obtain in animals so highly mentalized as cat and dog, suggests that in creatures less mentalized than they a residuum of behavior still larger relatively to the total behavior will be 'reflex.' The behavior of the spider is reported to be entirely reflex; but reflex action, judging by what we can sample of it, would go little way toward meeting the life of external relation of a horse or cat or dog, still less of ourselves. As life develops it would seem that in the field of external relation 'conscious' behavior tends to replace reflex, and conscious acts to bulk larger and larger. Along with this change, and indeed as part of it, would seem an increased role for 'habit.' Habit arises always in conscious action; reflex behavior never arises in conscious action. Habit is always acquired behavior, reflex behavior is always inherent and innately given. Habit is not to be confounded with reflex action.

The examples of reflex action taken for study here have been for the most part isolated artificially by extracting them so to say from animal lives of relatively highly developed external relation, for example, cat and dog. Examples of reflex behavior could have been taken under much less artificial conditions by resort to animals of less complex external relations (of lower animal type), for example, the frog. But then the reactions, though more naturally obtainable, would have been more open to equivocal interpretation as to purpose and less rich in executive complexity.

OVERUSE OF THE CHAINING PRINCIPLE

For more than fifty years after Sherrington wrote, the physiologists' explanation of complex and prolonged sequences of muscular activity (as, for example, in walking) rested almost entirely on the chained reflex concept. Through the influence of Pavlov and Hull, the chained reflex concept also played a central role in psychological explanations of behavior. The Russian physiologist, Pavlov, who was a contemporary of Sherrington's, used the reflex concept to interpret his famous conditioning experiments. He argued that experience altered subsequent behavior by creating new reflexes. In Sherringtonian terms, this meant that at some level of the nervous system, reflex arcs—connections between sensory neurons and motor neurons by way of interneurons—were created by particular experiences rather than by the ordinary course of neuroanatomical development.

Clark Hull (1943; 1920) made the notion of experientially derived reflexes (or habits as he also called them) the cornerstone of his immensely influential theorizing about the proper scientific interpretation of such psychological concepts as knowledge, purpose, foresight, expectation and the like. Thus, behaviors that seemed to indicate knowledge (of the probable outcome), purpose (goal-directedness), and anticipation were all explained by appeals to the chained reflex principle. Although B. F. Skinner (1938) steered resolutely away from any attempt to anchor behavioral theories to physiologically defined concepts (like the reflex arc), he nonetheless made the concept of stimulus-response chaining a central part of his attempts to scientifically account for the behavior of organisms. Since Hull, Pavlov, and Skinner between them dominated Anglo/American and Russian work on behavior up until about a decade ago, it is fair to say that for most of this century the chained reflex notion was *the* central explanatory principle in psychology. Only within ethology, whose influence was largely confined to the German speaking world, did other conceptions have a chance to grow strong. Since so many of Sherrington's followers believed that the chaining concept explained virtually everything that was to be explained about coordinated action, the concept was understandably subject to harsh criticism by those who analyzed the many additional mechanisms and principles that are in fact necessary to explain lengthy sequences of coordinated behavior. We will encounter some samples of these criticisms in the work of von Holst and Weiss.

Doubts about the universal application of the chained reflex concept have been amply justified by subsequent research. Several seemingly transparent cases of chained reflexes, for example, the contractions of successive segments of the esophagous in swallowing, have proven on subsequent investigation to be mediated by central programs rather than by reflex chaining (Doty & Bosma, 1956). Although the chaining principle is less important than previously thought, it does play a role in many behavioral sequences. For example, when an object touches the cheek of a cat in a predatory mood, the head turns toward the side touched. The turn brings the object in contact with the lips. The lip contact elicits jaw opening. When the object touches the inside surface of the lips or the tongue, it elicits a snap like closure of the jaws. This three-reflex chain—turning, opening, closing—is an important component of the terminal portion of a predatory sequence of behavior (Berntson, Hughes, & Beattie, 1976; Flynn, 1972). We will see later that the elicitability of these reflexes is controlled by signals descending from regions of the brain that mediate motivation (Chapter 9). In Chapter 6 we will encounter the chaining principle in connection with non-reflex units of behavior, namely, the taxic orienting mechanisms of coastal snails. Thus chaining—whether of reflexes or of other units of action—is *one* of the principles underlying the construction of coordinated sequences of action. It is by no means the only one and probably not even the most important or frequently used.

SUMMARY

Many of the processes that Sherrington identified in his experimental analysis of spinal reflexes are used again and again in non-reflex mechanisms. Reciprocal facilitation and reciprocal inhibition are processes whose utility is by no means confined to the reflex context. Mutual facilitation between agonistic units and reciprocal inhibition between antagonistic units are general principles of coordination. More general still are the uses to which nonlinear (or subliminal) summation may be put. Firstly, the principle of summation beneath a threshold underlies the system's ability to make complex decisions. If the sum of the excitatory and inhibitory input falls short of the threshold, the decision is "no;" if the sum exceeds the threshold the decision is "yes." Secondly, the principle of summation beneath a threshold enables long lasting inputs (*tonic* inputs) to render a unit of action operative or inoperative. A tonic inhibitory input reduces the level of synaptic excitation so far below threshold that transitory (or *phasic*) excitatory inputs are ineffective—they do not generate sufficient excitation to exceed the threshold. In this way, tonic inhibitory input may render the neural circuit mediating some unit of action inoperative. Conversely, a tonic excitatory input may make a unit operative by bringing the sustained level of excitation close enough to threshold so that phasic inputs produce outputs. In Chapter 6, we see this use of nonlinear summation to switch on and switch off light-orienting taxes. In subsequent chapters this switching-on (potentiation) and switching-off (depotentiation) assumes a central role. It is the process by which higher units coordinate lower units. Ultimately, it is the key to understanding how motivation controls and directs behavior.

4 Von Holst's Coupled Oscillators

ENDOGENOUS RHYTHMICITY

In two of Sherrington's most studied reflexes—the scratch reflex and the stepping reflex—the rhythm of the response is independent of the rhythm of the stimulus. The spinal dog scratches at about 4 scratches per second (Fig. 2.5) and steps at 2½ steps per second (Figure 2.6) regardless of the frequency of the eliciting stimuli. The rhythms in these responses are autonomous—not dependent on the stimulus rhythm. Sherrington realized that movements with an autonomous rhythm were an important component of animal action. He explained the autonomy of the rhythms by postulating that some synapses in the reflex arcs had a refractory phase. The transmission of excitation rendered these synapses refractory, thought Sherrington. While refractory, the synapses would not transmit the excitation from the afferent neurons. At the end of the refractory phase, the synapse would again transmit excitation. The renewed transmission of excitation would render the synapse refractory again, and so on. Result: The synapses broke up afferent excitation into rhythmic bursts of excitation. The duration of the refractory phase determined the *period* of the rhythm, that is, the duration of a complete cycle.

Sherrington's (1947) explanation of rhythmic movement reflected his belief that the only function of nervous tissue is the conduction or transmission of signals: "From the point of view of its office as integrator of the animal mechanism, the whole function of the nervous system can be summed up in one word, *conduction* (p. 9)."

It was foreign to this conception to imagine a pacemaker that generated rhythmic signals all by itself. Sherrington knew that the heart muscle contained such a pacemaker. As many veterans of the introductory lab in biology know, the turtle's heart beats for hours after it has been removed from the turtle. The rhythm is endogenous, generated within the heart tissue itself. Despite this well-known example of endogenous rhythmicity, neurobiologists of the first half of this century were unwilling to entertain the idea that components of the nervous system were endogenously active. Neurons conducted signals; they did not originate them, or so it was thought.

Graham Brown (1914) showed that the rhythmic stepping and scratching movements of a spinal dog did not require a sensory input, as Sherrington's explanations assumed. Brown argued that the rhythmic bursts of motor signals were generated by oscillators in the spinal cord, little neural metronomes going tick-tock, tick-tock all by themselves. Each time an oscillator went tick, it sent a signal to one set of muscles. Each time it went tock it sent a signal to the alternate set of muscles. Brown argued that the rhythmic signals generated by these oscillators were one of the foundations of integrative activity. Brown's ideas were all but ignored by English-speaking psychologists and neurobiologists for fifty years.

In Germany, however, von Holst went over to Brown's way of thinking, after five years of research on rhythmic fin movements in fish. He did for central oscillators what Sherrington had done for the reflex: He discovered the special principles of coordination that apply to oscillators—*superimposition* and the *magnet effect* (or phase-dependent response)—the principles which this chapter explicates. Von Holst's work had little influence in the English-speaking world until the 1960s. In recent years, however, the evidence for oscillators in the central nervous systems of all sorts of animals has become overwhelming. Consequently, neurobiologists have abruptly and nearly universally embraced Graham Brown's suggestion that neural metronomes generate the alternating signals, the ticks and tocks, that underlie the rhythmic back and forth movements of the limbs in locomotion (Herman, Grillner, Stein, & Stuart, 1976). And, they have begun to demonstrate at the electrophysiological level the principles of oscillator coordination formulated by von Holst on the basis of his behavioral research.

It is now recognized by neurobiologists, if not yet by psychologists, that endogenously active oscillators constitute a second kind of elementary functional unit in behavior. It appears that this unit and the coordination principles peculiar to it may be the basis for the central programs or motor scores that underlie behaviors as diverse as eating (Kater & Rowell, 1973), drinking (Weisenfeld, Helpern, & Tapper, 1977), swimming (Stein, 1971), grooming (Fentress, 1973), molting (Carlson & Bentley, 1977) and the daily rhythm of life (Kavanau & Rischer, 1968; Richter, 1965; Wells, 1950).

One impediment to a wider appreciation of the role of oscillators in behavior is the unfamiliar terminology. Unless one is clear about the meaning of phase, period, periodicity, etc., the following reading by von Holst is hard to follow; and so is contemporary work on oscillators in behavior and neurobiology. What follows is an introduction to the terminology that describes simple and complex oscillation.

AMPLITUDE, PERIOD, AND PHASE

The curve in Figure 4.1a is a sine curve. For two reasons it is the prototype of all simple oscillations. It is prototypical firstly because many oscillations are sinusoidal—the angular position of a pendulum, the position of a point on a vibrating guitar string, the angular position of a fin in a swimming fish, the electrical potential in a pacemaker neuron in the cockroach's nervous system. When any of these quantities is recorded as a function of time the trace approximates a sine curve. The second reason for regarding the sinusoidal oscillation as prototypical is mathematical: The sine function is simply specified, and *any other oscillation no matter how complex can be obtained by adding together ("superimposing") a suitable series of sine curves.* This last mathematical property, known as Fourier's theorem in honor of the French mathematician who first used it, may have behavioral as well as mathematical significance, a point we will return to.

A sinusoidal oscillation is completely described by only three parameters: its *period* or frequency, its *amplitude,* and its reference *phase.* In Figure 4.1, the oscillation in Panel B differs from that in Panel A only in amplitude; the oscillation in Panel C differs only in its period or frequency; and the oscillation in Panel D differs only in its reference phase.

Amplitude and frequency are easily grasped; phase, on the other hand, causes confusion, because the term is employed in three more or less distinct senses or contexts: (1) to indicate a point in the cycle (*momentary phase*); (2) to position the oscillation in time (*reference phase*); (3) to indicate a segment of the cycle (*segmentary phase*). All of the uses of the term phase depend on the fact that simple oscillations repeat themselves at regular intervals called cycles. One cycle is a copy of any other, so the entire oscillation is described once a single cycle has been described. To describe a single cycle one divides the cycle into fractions of a cycle, most commonly into 360 fractions, called degrees. The choice of a fraction, such as a degree, enables one to specify where in a cycle one is, just as months (1st, 2nd, 3rd, etc.) specify where one is in the yearly cycle. The *momentary phase* of an oscillation is the number of degrees through the cycle at some moment (or instant) we are interested in.

The *reference phase,* on the other hand, is the point in the cycle at some arbitrarily chosen reference time, t_0. The reference time is usually of no particular interest. It is used only to position the oscillation in time, usually in order to specify the phase relationship between two or more oscillations. In Fig. 4.1, Panels a-c, the reference phase is 315° because each of these

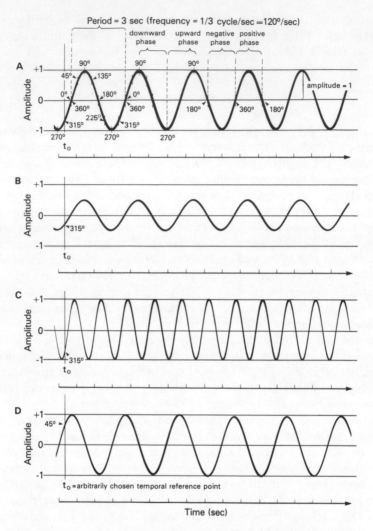

FIG. 4.1. (a) A sinusoid of amplitude = 1, period = 3 sec (frequency = 1/3 cycle/sec), and reference phase = 315.° The phase is referred to some arbitrarily chosen point in time, t_0. (b) A sinusoid identical to that shown in (a) except for amplitude. (c) A sinusoid identical to that in (a) except for period (or frequency). Note that were one to refer to some other t_0, the reference phase of this curve would not necessarily be the same as the reference phase of the curve in (a). Whether two curves of different frequency do or do not happen to have the same reference phase depends upon the choice of t_0. However, the two curves have the same phase *relationship* regardless of the choice of t_0. Which phase of one curve coincides with which phase of the other is not affected by the choice of t_0. (d) A sinusoid identical to that in (a) except for phase. Note that the phase *relationship* between curves (d) and (c) is not the same as the phase relationship between (a) and (c). This difference in phase relationship is independent of the choice of t_0.

oscillations is 315° through a cycle at the reference moment, t_0. In Panel d, on the other hand, the reference phase is 45°. This is the only way in which Panel d differs from Panel a: The amplitudes and periods are identical; only the reference phases are different. The reference phase positions an oscillation in time. *When we specify the phase at some one instant, we thereby determine what it must be at any other instant.* If Old Faithful erupts every hour and ten minutes (i.e., its period is 70 minutes) and I tell you that it was ¼ of the way through its eruption cycle (90° through) at 1:46 p.m. on April 3, 1741, you can calculate where in its cycle it was or will be at any other time in this or any other century. (I'm assuming Old Faithful to be more faithful than it actually is.) For this reason, one reference instant is as good as any other. However, when we compare several different oscillations we use the same t_0 for all of them. The importance of using a common reference will be obvious shortly, when we discuss superimposing two oscillations of different frequency.

The third meaning of phase, *segmentary phase,* is similar to momentary phase, but is refers to a segment of a cycle rather than a single point in a cycle (e.g., the segments marked downward phase, etc. in Fig. 4.1a).

SUPERIMPOSITION

Von Holst demonstrated that the principle of *combination* between the outputs of two oscillators running at different frequencies is *addition* or *superimposition.* Under a variety of circumstances, the movement of a fish's fin, a dog's leg, or a man's arm can be seen to be the sum of two sinusoidal oscillations with different frequencies. The tracing of the movement of the appendage can be obtained by superimposing two sinusoidal curves with appropriately chosen amplitudes, periods, and reference phases.

In superimposing two sinusoidal curves one adds the value of one curve at a given instant to the value of the other curve at the same instant; the sum of the two values is the value of the superimposition or compound curve at that instant. To obtain the complete compound curve (the complete superimposition), one repeats the process for every instant in time.

The value of a sinusoid at any instant is determined by its amplitude, its period, and its reference phase. The appearance of the compound, therefore, is determined by the amplitudes of the two elemental sinusoids, their periods, and their phase relationship. Most of the conceptual difficulty centers around the last of these factors, the phase relationship. Figure 4.2a shows the superimposition of two sinusoids of equal amplitude, but different periods. The two sinusoids are positioned in time so that the 0° point in the slower oscillation coincides with the 270° point in the faster oscillation (at t_0 on Figure 4.2a), the 90° with the 90° (at t_1), the 180° with the 270° (at t_2), etc. Figure 4.2b shows the superimposition of two sinusoids with a different phase relationship. In this phase relationship the 0° point in the slower component coincides with the 315° point in the faster component (at t_0), the 90° point with the 135° point, the 180° point with the 315° point, and so on. The change in phase relationship of the components, that is, the change in which points combine with which, alters the appearance of the compound. The bottom tracings in von Holst's Figures 4.7a & 4.7b (p. 88) are an empirical example of exactly such a change in appearance. These lower tracings are compound oscillations. The upper tracings in von Holst's figures portray the slower of two component oscillations. The faster components are not portrayed in von

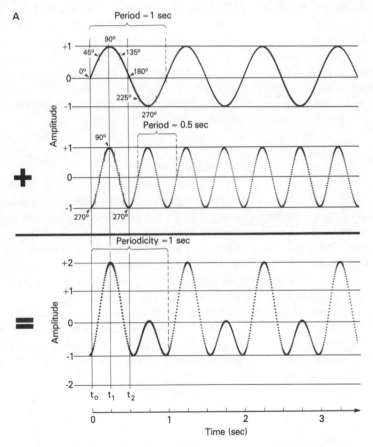

FIG. 4.2. (a) The bottom curve is the compound oscillation obtained by superimposing the top two curves. The periodicity of the compound is the period within which the compound goes through one complete cycle of variation. In this case, the periodicity of the compound is the same as the period of the slower component. However, this will not generally be so. (b) The bottom curve is again the superimposition of the top two curves. The top two curves are the same as in (a) except for their phase relationship. Note how the change in phase relationship alters the appearance of the compound.

Holst's figures because they were not directly observed: Their presence was inferred.

The nub of the confusion surrounding the concept of phase as it applies to oscillations of different frequencies is this: Although the difference in the momentary phases of the two oscillations changes from instant to instant, the phase relationship is fixed. In Fig. 4.2a, the difference in momentary phases at t_0 is 90° (360°–270°); at t_1 it is 0° (90°–90°); at t_2 it is 90°; etc. But, the overall phase relationship, that is, which points on the lower curve combine with which points on the upper curve, is fixed as soon as one specifies where the two oscillations happen to be at any single instant in time (e.g., at the arbitrarily chosen reference time, t_0). Thus, any two sinusoidal oscillations at different frequencies have a fixed phase relationship despite the fact that the difference in their momentary phases varies continuously. The momentary

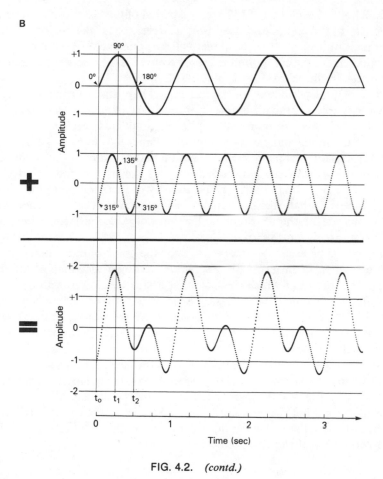

FIG. 4.2.   *(contd.)*

phases change from instant to instant and so does the difference between them, but *which* momentary phase in one oscillation coincides with *which* momentary phase in the other remains constant.

Periodicity

The periodicity of a compound curve is the time required for it to complete its pattern of variation. If one marks off the compound curve at intervals equal to its periodicity, the segments thus marked off are exactly congruent: The segment between any two marks may be placed on top of the segment between any two other marks and no discrepancy will be found.

The periodicity of a compound is the smallest number that is an integer multiple of the two component periods. In Fig. 4.2 the periodicity is equal to the period of the slower oscillation, because this period (1 sec) is an integer multiple both of itself and of 1/2 sec, the period of the faster oscillation. The periodicity of the compound need not, however, equal the period of either component. In Fig. 4.3, the components have periods of 2/3 sec and 1/2 sec; the periodicity of the compound is 2 sec, because 2 is the smallest number that is an integer multiple of both 2/3 and 1/2.

In Fig. 4.3, the periodicity of the compound happens to be the same as the interval required for the difference in momentary phases to go through one cycle. The difference in momentary phases completes a cycle whenever the graphs of the momentary phases intersect (Panel b in Figures 4.3 and 4.4). However, this interval from one intersection to the next need not be the same as the periodicity of the compound. In Fig. 4.4, the periods of the two sinusoids are .5 sec and .3 sec. The periodicity of their compound is 1.5 sec. Note, however, that the momentary phases intersect at t_0, when both oscillations are at the 0° point and again only .75 sec later, when both oscillations are at the 180° point.

The interval between two intersections on the graph of momentary phases may be thought of in terms of two racers circling a racetrack at different speeds. The instant at which the faster racer laps the slower is an instant of zero difference in momentary phase. The interval between such instants is the lap period, the time required for the faster to lap the slower. In Fig. 4.4, the faster oscillation laps the slower every .75 seconds. When we superimpose the two oscillations, however, the periodicity in the compound is not the lap period. It is the period from the instant when the faster laps the slower to the instant when the faster not only laps the slower again but laps it at exactly the same point. In Fig. 4.4, the faster oscillation laps the slower after .75 sec, but at the 180° point not the 0° point. Thus, .75 sec is not the periodicity. At 1.5 sec, the faster laps the slower again, and this time both are at the 0° point. This is the periodicity of the compound.

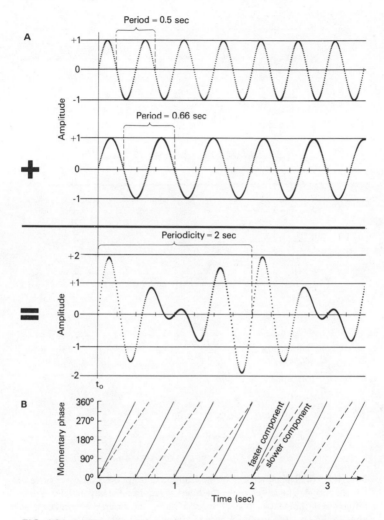

FIG. 4.3. (*a*) The periodicity of the compound is the smallest integer multiple of the periods of the components ($2 = 4 \times \frac{1}{2} = 3 \times 2/3$). (*b*) If the momentary phases of the components are plotted over time, then one notes that both graphs are at 0 phase at t = 0 and again at t = 2. The interval required for the two momentary phases to *simultaneously* arrive at their starting values is the periodicity.

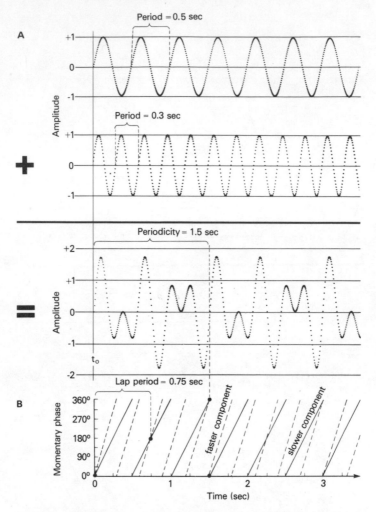

FIG. 4.4.   (*a*) The periodicity of the compound is not necessarily the same as
the lap period. The *lap period* is the interval required for any initially chosen
difference in momentary phases to recur. At t_0, the difference in momentary
phases is $0° – 0° = 0°$. This difference recurs at $t = .75$ (when $180° – 180° = 0°$).
(*b*) One may use the bottom graph to verify that the lap period is .75 sec
regardless of the choice t_0.

THE MAGNET EFFECT

Superimposing the outputs of two oscillators does not perturb the oscillators
themselves. *Superimposition is a principle for combining the outputs of
oscillators, not a principle for coordinating the oscillators themselves.* The

magnet effect, on the other hand, is the effect one oscillator exerts on another in order to maintain coordination between the two, in order, that is, to maintain a common tempo and a fixed phase difference.

The drill instructor for a marching unit exerts a magnet effect on the rhythmic stepping of each marcher. The instructor hollers out "hup" as his own right foot strikes the ground. The "hup" is a coordinating signal. The marcher's response depends on where he is in his own step cycle when he hears the hup. If the marcher's right foot has already struck the ground, if, that is, it has struck too early, the marcher *slows* his step cycle so that on the next step his foot strikes the ground at the moment of the coordinating command. If, on the other hand, the marcher is falling slightly behind so that his foot has yet to hit the ground when he hears the hup, then the marcher *speeds up* his step cycle. The coordinating hup from the drill instructor speeds up or slows down a marcher's stepping, depending upon what phase of his cycle the marcher is in when he hears the coordinating command. When the hup is heard in the phase just before the footfall, it speeds the cycle up; when heard in the phase just after the footfall, it slows the cycle down. The response to the command is *phase-dependent*.

Now suppose the marcher begins to day dream and begins to march to the beat of some distant drummer, drumming at a different tempo. The marcher's stepping no longer remains coordinated with the drill instructor's. Suppose, however, that the marcher retains a vestige of his former responsiveness to the instructor's hup, hup, hupping. He speeds up and slows down as before, but not enough to maintain the instructor's tempo. His marching is now in a state of what von Holst termed *relative coordination* with respect to the instructor. It is under the instructor's coordinative influence but not sufficiently to maintain absolute coordination.

Since, on the average, the marcher steps at a tempo different from that of the instructor, the difference in momentary phase between his stepping and the instructor's changes over time. For a while the day dreamer hears the hup just before a footfall. This makes him hasten his step a bit, but since he does not speed up enough, he falls gradually further behind. Eventually, he hears the hup after rather than before a footfall. This causes him to slow down rather than speed up. The drift in the momentary phase difference alternately speeds the marcher up, then slows him down, then speeds him up, and so on. The upshot is another kind of periodicity—a periodic alteration in frequency, first faster, then slower, then faster, etc., as is illustrated by the lower tracing in von Holst's Fig. 4.18 (p. 100). This periodicity is not the periodicity of a compound oscillation, but it is, in essence, a periodicity we are already familiar with, namely, the lap period.

The periodic fluctuation in frequency evident in most of von Holst's figures from 4.18 on depends entirely on the momentary difference in phase between *interacting* oscillators. It is determined by how long it takes the faster oscillator to lap the slower oscillator. If the oscillators had no effect on each other's frequency, then the lap period would be simply one over the difference in the two frequencies. If, for example, one oscillator is running at 5 cycles/sec, the other at 3 cycles/sec, then the faster is lapping the slower at: 5 cycles/sec — 3 cycles/sec = 2 cycles/sec. The lap period is thus ½ second, one over the difference between the two frequencies. However, because the oscillators are *interacting,* the frequencies do not remain constant. The frequencies fluctuate as a function of the fluctuating difference between the momentary phases of the two oscillations. Hence, the lap period is jointly determined by the difference in inherent frequencies and the strength of the *coupling,* that is, the strength of the coordinative interaction between the oscillators. If the coupling becomes strong enough, the two oscillations maintain a common tempo and a fixed difference in momentary phase. The lap period becomes infinite, because one oscillator no longer laps the other.

Von Holst perceived these two principles—the principle of superimposition and the principle of the magnet effect—in studying the movements of the fins in medulla fish. The medulla fish, like Sherrington's spinal dogs and spinal cats, has had its central nervous system simplified by a cut that separates the spinal cord (and lowest portion of the brain—the medulla) from the influence of higher brain processes. This cut allows one to study processes within the spinal cord itself. The spinal processes are no longer modulated by descending signals from the brain. These processes now show themselves in their true metronomic character. The fin waves back and forth, back and forth for hours in the absence of any stimulus.

The importance of the oscillator and of the principles von Holst discovered is only now being realized. We now know that animals carry within them oscillators whose periods may range from .001 sec (in weakly electric fish—Bullock, Orkand, & Grinnell, 1977, p. 332) to 24 hours (in nearly all animals). These neural oscillators enter into every sort of behavior. In fact, they may be the basis for most *central programs.*

Central programs generate complex sequences of muscle activity. From the Fourier theorem we know that any sequence, no matter how complex, can be generated by superimposing a properly chosen set of outputs from sinusoidal oscillators. In practice, a handful of oscillators can generate patterns of bewildering complexity. By varying the amplitudes and phase relationships, one can obtain many different patterns from the same handful of oscillators. In short, oscillators may be the alphabet with which central programs are written.

The paper that follows is the shorter of two reviews that von Holst wrote. The longer one, with many more experiments, and with examples of relative coordination in man and the higher mammals may be found in a collection of translated papers by von Holst, *The Behavioral Physiology of Animals and Man* (University of Miami Press).

On the Nature of Order in the Central Nervous System*

E. VON HOLST

In 1894, the physiologist Friedländer performed the following simple experiment: He bisected an earthworm and rejoined the two halves with a piece of thread. When the front half of the worm began to creep forward, the back half was carried along. Surprisingly, the peristaltic waves typical of the animal's movement passed in orderly fashion along the whole worm as if it had not been cut in half at all. The two halves of the worm moved *in coordinated fashion*. From this, Friedländer concluded that anatomical continuity of the ventral nerve-cord is not unconditionally necessary for conduction of nervous excitation. The *'reflex-chain,'* as J. Loeb has called this process, affects one worm segment after another in much the same way as toppling of the first bottle in a row will topple the other bottles, one after the other.

This concept of the reflex-chain rapidly achieved general acceptance since it seemed to facilitate understanding of numerous cases of nervous coordination. One was able to interpret the "wave"-movements of a swimming eel and a crawling caterpillar, the sequential leg-movements of a scurrying millipede, and even the running of a horse and dog, as a reflex-chain. It was only necessary to assume that each segment, or leg, elicits through a reflex the movement of the segment, or leg, next in the temporal sequence. Even the rhythmic repetition of the same movement, for example, the beating of a bird's wing and of a fish's fin, could be understood in a similar manner by assuming that each muscular contraction provides the reflex stimulus for the following contraction for the same muscle or an antagonist. To distinguish such a process from a reflex-chain it was referred to as a 'chain-reflex.' Such reflex performances

*This paper is a translation by R. D. Martin of: von Holst, E. Vom Wesen der Ordnung im Zentralnervensystem. *Naturwissenschaften*, 1937, 25, 625–631 and 641–647. The translation was published in *The behavioral physiology of animals and man: Selected papers of E. von Holst*, Vol. 1. Coral Gables: University of Miami Press, 1973. It is reprinted by permission of the University of Miami Press.

were and still are, frequently regarded as the basis for nervous coordination of movement.

In the meantime, however, there has been a rapid accumulation of research workers dissatisfied with this theory. People gradually began to recognize the less rigid, more autonomous variable activity of the nervous system. As a reaction against the chain-reflex theory, one began to talk of the 'holistic character,' the 'totality' and the 'plasticity' of the nervous system. In fact, at the present time there is apparently an ever-increasing number of adherents to the view that with the central nervous system (CNS) we are concerned with an organ which—either because of its great internal complexity, or because of the intervention of "supra-physical" factors—is fundamentally inaccessible to exact functional analysis. For example, one neurophysiologist writes of the 'physically and energetically indeterminable functions' of the CNS. He is of the opinion that this 'functional entity' contains 'its own intrinsic principles, which are inaccessible to purely analytically oriented research,' and that it 'appears to be impossible to investigate the intra-central processes with methods involving measurement.'

This paper is aimed at providing a brief survey of my own investigations in this domain, which have led me on to a new interpretation of the nature of nervous coordination.

We can begin with the earthworm as the generally recognized stock example of a reflex-chain. If conduction of nervous excitation along the worm's body is really a reflex-chain, then it must fulfill various conditions. The excitation must always affect one segment *after* the other, just as toppling of a row of bottles makes them fall one after the other. However, under certain conditions (e.g., after the effect of ether) this is not the case. Here, all of the segments extend and contract more or less simultaneously. In addition to this, nervous excitation should not be able to pass along a stretch of the ventral nerve cord on either side of which all of the nervous branches have been severed, since the reflex-chain has been interrupted. But, in reality, nervous excitation passes along such stretches of isolated nerve cord with an actual increase in velocity. Finally, in a section of the ventral nerve cord which has been dissected out of the worm and placed in a physiological solution, the rhythmic contraction impulses should no longer occur, since all possibility of a reflex stimulus has been excluded. In actual fact, the rhythm appears uninterruptedly in such an isolated piece of nerve cord. By recording of the electrical discharges of the ganglion cells, the continuance of the rhythm can be demonstrated over a period of hours (unpublished data). Thus, the central rhythm does not at all necessarily require peripheral stimuli; it is *automatic* and not reflex in nature.

If we consider another presumed reflex-chain, the rhythmic sinuous movements of a fish, we come to the same result. For example, if one takes an eel and severs all the peripheral nerves on both sides of a fair-sized middle portion of the dorsal nerve cord, so that the head and tail sections are only connected by nervous transmission along the dorsal nerve cord these two ends of the body still swim with the opposing order which they exhibited in the intact fish. This occurs even after exclusion of any possibility of mutual mechanical influence, just as if the middle muscular section were still functional. A reflex-chain would not be able to achieve this. And if one operates on a tench, severing all of the dorsal nerve roots on both sides whilst leaving the ventral roots intact (such that no further stimuli can be taken up from the trunk, since the centripetal pathways have been destroyed), the fish is still able to swim around— though its movements are considerably weaker. Thus, in this case too, the impulses which pass to the musculature through the ventral roots are automatically produced in the dorsal nerve cord; they do not require reflex elicitation. Over twenty years ago, Graham Brown performed the same experiment of severing the dorsal roots in mammals, with the same result. We shall later come to another, less crude, demonstration of the automatic nature of the locomotor rhythm. The nervous system is not, in fact, like a lazy donkey which must be struck (or, to make the comparison more exact, must bite itself in the tail) every time before it can take a step. Instead, it is rather like a temperamental horse which needs the reins just as much as the whip.

Objections have been made to the reflex-chain theory from a quite different direction, particularly by Bethe. Bethe saw that in many animals coordination of leg-movements is not rigidly, mechanically determined, but can alter considerably following certain interventions. For instance (taking an example from von Buddenbrock), a stick-insect—like the majority of insects—runs by moving the first and third pair of legs in the same sense, whilst the second pair is always in the appropriate, opposing phase. If the second pair of legs is amputated, the first and third pairs no longer move in the same sense as previously (i.e., in synchronous gait), but work in opposition (alternating gait) as in a lizard or a trotting horse. Guided by the hope that it would be more expedient to determine a certain regularity in such changes in animals with many legs, I studied various centipedes (Chilopoda) and discovered the following with *Lithobius:* The

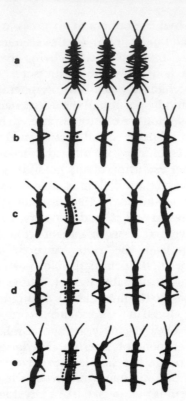

FIG. 4.5. Phases from the running movement of the centipede *Lithobuis* (from film records). *a*, normal animal. *b* and *c*, after amputation of all pairs of legs except two. *d* and *e*, after amputation of all except three pairs of legs. (The dots in the second diagram in each series indicate the numbers of segments between the legs.)

animal normally moves its legs in 'wave'-form. Each leg is separated from the next by a phase-lag of about one-seventh of a step, and each 'wave' thus covers about six to seven legs (Fig. 4.5a). If one amputates one pair of legs after the other, the phase-lag between the remaining legs consistently increases until the maximum of half a step is reached with three and two remaining pairs of legs (Fig. 4.5, b–e). Thus, a *Lithobius* with four legs runs with an alternating gait like a lizard or a trotting horse. What is remarkable about this is that, within certain limits, it is immaterial how great an anatomical gap is left between the remaining legs, whether it involves one, two, three, four or five segments. Therefore, one cannot speak of a fixed reflex locomotor relationship between the legs. A *Lithobius* with three pairs of legs consequently runs like an insect. If one repeats with this 'pseudoinsect' (Fig. 4.5d) the experiment described above for the stick-insect, the same result is obtained: After amputation of the middle pair of legs, the remaining legs are moved in alternating gait (Fig. 4.5c). Overall, one can derive the general rule that the smaller the number of legs present, the greater the phase difference between them. Other arthropods, admittedly with numerous exceptions, generally fit this rule. In more general terms, this rule means: *The processes in one ganglion are quantitatively dependent upon the processes in all other active ganglia.*

One can also reach an exactly corresponding concept of a quantitatively reciprocal relationship between the individual parts of the nervous system, by following another tack. It has already been known for about a hundred years that in arthropods extirpation of one half of the brain has the result that the operated animals subsequently run in circles enclosing the intact side. Taking a simple interpretation,[1] each half of the brain transmits to the ventral ganglia excitation which provokes inclination to the corresponding side. If both halves of the brain are active in equal strength, their effects are mutually eradicating; but if one is removed, the effect of the other becomes evident.

With centipedes, which regularly run in circles after unilateral brain-removal, one can perform the following experiment. One part (e.g., the last third of the ganglion chain) is put out of action by severing it or simply by cutting off the segments concerned. The result is that the front segments at once twist all the more sharply so that the circles traced in running are reduced in size by almost a half. It the ventral nerve cord is shortened even more from the hind end, the circles become still smaller. This can be exactly measured from tracks left on a powdered substrate. This signifies that in each ganglion of the ventral nerve cord *the strength of influence exerted by the brain increases with decrease in the number of ganglia exposed to this influence.* One might possibly imagine this process in terms of a given 'quantity' of 'brain excitation,' which in one case passes to several ganglia and in another only to a few. In the former case, each individual ganglion receives less of this excitation, and in the second case, more. Whether or not this interpretation is apt, there is once again an evident quantitative principle in the reciprocal functional relationships between components of the nervous system.

With the methods so far described—that is, observation of behavior following amputation of parts of the body and other major surgical interventions—one can, in my opinion, scarcely hope to uncover more than quite general guidelines of neural function, even if these experiments are greatly expanded. It was necessary to find a less disruptive process in order to permit insights into the more intimate processes of nervous coordination.

---

[1]In reality, the interpretation is somewhat more complicated, but this is not important in this context.

Before dealing with a process of this kind, we should consider the requirements which a method must fulfil in order to be useful . Difficulties of various kinds combine to bar the way to insight into central nervous processes. The first difficulty is the following: Central nervous function—in this case, the specific patterning of various movements in locomotion—always confront us as a ready-made, harmonic assembly. The pattern is at once present the instant the animal passes from rest to locomotion. It is therefore just as impossible to draw from this ready-made coordination pattern conclusions about the operative factors as it is for the developmental physiologist to draw conclusions from the finished organism about the driving impulses of its development. This difficulty forces us to search for subjects in which the fixed, absolute coordination between the individual locomotor organs is not the only possible relationship, but simply represents an extreme case. (The other extreme would be the lack of any mutual locomotor relationship.) Such subjects could possibly present us with all transitional stages, all degrees of reciprocal influence from the initiation of internal sounding to the strongest manifestation of reciprocal dependence.

The second difficulty lies in the multivariate complexity of the processes concerned. One can assume that several different forces, at least, are involved, and a useful method should enable us to extract (from this calculation with too many unknowns) individual quantities for examination.

The third difficulty is based on the well-known fact that in the intact animal no single movement is exactly like any other, so that exact measurements are never entirely successful. This phenomenon is interpreted by some as a sign of supra-physical direction, of free will, and by others as the consequence of continual variation in the external and internal influences upon nervous processes. This persistent irregularity would also have to be excluded in some way.

A process which meets the requirements listed above came to my knowledge at the Naples Zoological Station, to whose director— Professor Reinhard Dohrn—I owe a great debt of gratitude for extensive support and assistance. A fair number of different fish genera (*Labrus, Crenilabrus, Sargus, Serranus* and *Corvina*, among others) are distinguished by the fact that they do not swim along with the usual tail beats but maintain the main body axis immobile and glide smoothly along simply by performing even, rhythmic oscillations of the fins (pectoral, dorsal and anal). From straightforward observation and examination of film-strips, one can see that these individual fin rhythms are performed either in rigid harmony—in *absolute* coordination—or, in some cases only an instant later, completely independent of one another—that is, *without* any coordination. However, what occurs most frequently is that the individual rhythms are indeed exhibited with quite different, independent frequencies, but nevertheless exert an accompanying *quantitative* influence on one another. This behavior can be contrasted with absolute coordination as a new type of organization, as *relative coordination*.

There is a quite simple method for recording these movements: The fish is anaesthetized and the dorsal nerve cord is severed transversely at a specific point. With one sweep, this operation alters an unpredictable organism to give a *precision apparatus* whose movements are performed quite regularly as long as the external and internal conditions are maintained constant, but which responds to any influence with a quite specific change in activity. After the operation, respiratory movements are arrested;[1] the fish is placed in a water tank connected with a water inlet, its body is supported, and the individual fins are appropriately attached to light pen-operating levers. When fish of about the size of a human hand are used, it is sufficient if only two or three fin rays are left out of the entire fin. These are connected to the recording levers, and the other rays are cut away. Each individual fin ray has its own pair of small, antagonistic muscles, which move it to and fro and which are not noticeably hindered by the slight resistance of the recording lever, since they are adapted to overcome far greater water resistance. It should be mentioned that the individual fins, as can easily be observed, are not subject to any reciprocal, external mechanical influences. Between twenty minutes and two hours after the operation, one fin after the other begins to oscillate again, and this persists until the death of the fish (after three to five days with good preparations).

As has already been mentioned, the fins can move at different rhythms, and we must now find out what kind of influence is exerted by one rhythm upon another. Two different phenomena emerge, which will be dealt with one after the other.

Figure 4.6 shows a short segment of a curve indicating oscillation of one pectoral fin and the dorsal fin. The upper rhythm is completely regular and independent; the lower exhibits conspicuous periodicity affecting both amplitude and frequency. The external form of these periods varies in a quite specific manner with the frequency relationship between the two rhythms. For the unaided eye, this periodicity is most apparent in cases where the frequency

---

[1]The incision passes through the so-called respiratory center.

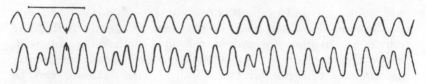

FIG. 4.6.   Recording of the movement of one pectoral fin (upper curve) and
the dorsal fin (lower curve) of *Labrus*. (The horizontal line indicates an
interval of two seconds.)

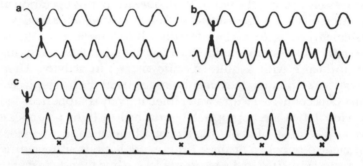

FIG. 4.7.   *Labrus,* recording as in Fig. 4.6. All three curve traces are taken
from the same fish. (Seconds indicated by the scale beneath *c.*)

relationship between the two rhythms is exactly 1:2, as illustrated in
Fig. 4.7 (a and b). Here, the same picture is continually repeated. (The
difference in appearance between Figs. a and b is based on a mutual
phase shift in the two participating rhythms, which can be
recognized from the coincidence markings.) We shall deal with Fig.
4.7c later on. All such curve segments are immediately reminiscent of
periodicity obtained by superimposition of two sinus curves. If such
a curve were recorded on a gramophone and played back, the result
would actually be the sounding of two notes, for example, two of an
octave in the case of Fig. 4.7. Thus, it would appear *as if* the
movement of one fin provides a motor picture of a process of
superimposition of two rhythmic excitation processes (of unknown
nature) in the spinal cord.

In order to evaluate these curves with greater accuracy, I did not in
fact make use of a procedure based on the principle of the Fourier
series, which is commonly adopted in technology. For the question
as to whether superimposition processes of some kind were involved
still had to be examined, and nothing of the sort could be
presupposed from the outset. Instead, I developed another procedure
which leaves the matter of the origin of the periodicity open to all the
various possibilities. This procedure provided more exact informa-

tion about the periodic change in frequency on the one hand, and in the speed of performance of each individual movement on the other, at the same time permitting analysis of the temporal relationships of these varaibles to one another and to the execution of the independent rhythm (Method of Time and Speed Tables). We shall have to do without a more detailed description here, as it is not altogether necessary for an understanding of what is to follow. It emerges that the periodic departures in the times (frequencies) and speeds, although they are quantitatively variable within wide limits, exhibit extensive qualitative agreement both in their relationships to one another and to the independent rhythm, and are virtually bound to one another. This qualitative agreement is of the kind one would expect in the case of central superimposition of automatisms. One point is particularly worthy of mention: Any increase in frequency of an individual movement is accompanied by a corresponding reduction in motor (contraction) speed, and vice versa. This fact excludes from the outset any attempt to explain the period-formation in one rhythm in terms of a periodically varying general 'excitatory' and 'inhibitory' influence exerted by the other rhythm. At the instant when the frequency is 'excited,' the contraction process itself evidently undergoes inhibition, and vice versa.

If the superimposition hypothesis is right, it should also fulfil a number of further requirements. As soon as one of the two superimposed rhythms is arrested, the other should at once continue evenly. This is always the case, as is illustrated by the trace in Fig. 4.8. One sees at first (Fig. 4.8a) the two independent pectoral fin rhythms

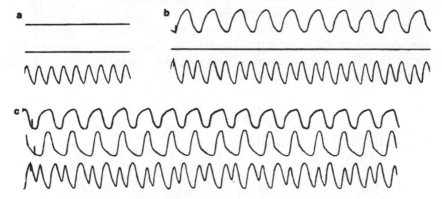

FIG. 4.8. *Labrus:* movement of one pectoral fin (upper trace), the second pectoral fin (middle trace) and the dorsal fin (lower trace). In *a*, the two pectoral fin rhythms are inhibited by pressure on the sides of the body; in *b*, only one pectoral rhythm is inhibited; in *c*, the two pectoral fins oscillate in alternation.

suppressed by means of a pressure stimulus on the sides of the body. Then one pectoral fin rhythm recommences (Fig. b), and finally both are operating (Fig. c). In this case, the pectoral fins beat in exact alternation and (as experience has shown) their operation always summates with the dependent dorsal fin rhythm. With oscillation of both pectoral fins, the effect is in this case roughly 90 per cent greater than with oscillation of just one pectoral fin.

This immediately leads on to another test. If the pectoral rhythms summate in their effects upon the dependent rhythm, as long as the pectoral fins oscillate in alternation, then they would logically have to *subtract* their effects with synchronous oscillation of the pectoral fins and thus cancel one another out by interference. It is, in fact, possible to influence the speed relationships between the individual rhythms in various ways. In the case to be considered (Fig. 4.9), alteration of the oxygen supply has the effect that one pectoral fin beats a little faster than the other, such that it overtakes the other by one beat in the trace shown. At the point where the two pectoral fins beat in synchrony (marked by '||'), the dependent rhythm does in fact temporarily become quite even. This is not because the pectoral rhythms no longer exert any influence but because their individual influences cancel one another.

In the example given in Fig. 4.8, the *independent* rhythm(s) were inhibited (Fig. a), and the dependent rhythm progressed evenly with its own, inherent frequency. Conversely, one can arrest the *dependent* automatism alone (e.g., by a pressure stimulus on the tail fin). The result is that the fin linked to the dependent automatisms does not remain still, but continues to oscillate with weak amplitude and in full *accord* with the *independent* rhythm. Inhibition of the independent rhythm, by contrast, also causes simultaneous arrest of the dependent rhythm. This experiment further supports the hypothesis of central superimposition and, in my opinion, cannot be explained in any other way.

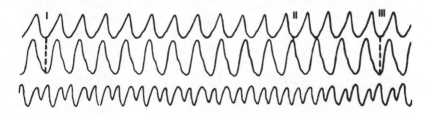

FIG. 4.9. Recording of the three rhythms as in Fig. 4.8. At I and III, the pectoral fins beat in alternation; at II they are temporarily synchronous.

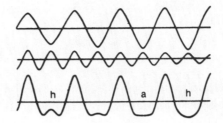

FIG. 4.10.   Two artificially produced sinus curve tracings, with increasing and decreasing amplitude respectively. Below: superimposition of the two curves (h = zero or rest position).

A further possibility for testing is the following: Fig. 4.10 shows two artificially traced sinus curves with a frequency relationship of 1:2. One trace increases in amplitude and the other decreases. Superimposition of the two traces initially still gives a large and a small oscillation, then the effect and couter-effect are exactly balanced such that the minor oscillation disappears (indicated by 'a'), and finally the superimposition tracing actually veers in the opposite direction at the point concerned. Thus, if the superimposition hypothesis is correct, under corresponding conditions with increasing strength of the superimposing rhythm there must come a time where one curve peak disappears, and later a point where, at the site where there was movement in one direction, there is actually a movement in the opposite direction. Again, this behavior could not be explained by 'excitation' and 'inhibition.' Whatever the strength of any inhibition, for example, it could never produce more than arrest and certainly would not produce a directional change in the movement. Let us look once again at the example already given in Fig. 4.7. In Fig. 4.7a, the superimposition is even weaker; large and small peaks alternate. In Fig. 4.7c, there is attainment of exactly the situation where the two automatisms balance one another. Only the characteristic curve form (flattened troughs and pointed peaks) and the minute bumps marked 'x' betray the fact that one automatism is running twice as fast as the other. In Fig. 4.11 one can see along a short stretch of the tracing the transition from almost no influence to the extreme case of directional reversal of the movement. The effect is obtained by gradually cutting off the water; the prepared fish was thus subjected to continuously changing physiological working conditions, which explains the inconstancy of the frequencies and amplitudes. Initially, at the left side of the trace, the central influence of the upper rhythm on the lower one is quite limited. It then gradually increases, and finally, at the points marked 'x' (analogous to the situation on the right of Fig. 4.10), there is an extensive downward excursion replacing the small upward bump. The

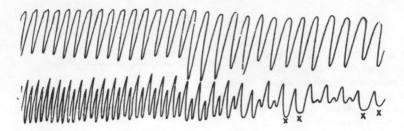

FIG. 4.11.   Recording of the pectoral fin rhythm (upper curve) and the dorsal fin rhythm (lower curve). The frequency relationship between the two automatisms is 1:2. Water supply to the prepared fish is gradually cut off. See text for further details.

hypothesis therefore proves to be watertight with respect to this experimental test as well.

In the examples so far considered there was always one independent rhythm and a second rhythm influenced by the former. However, it also occurs that the two rhythms have a reciprocal influence and one can also find a situation where two or three rhythms of different frequency exert an influence on a fourth. In all of these more complex cases, analysis has so far still consistently led to the theoretically expected result. The concept of central superimposition of the different rhythms can therefore be regarded at the present time as a well-supported theory. Thus we can talk, for *illustration,* in terms of *automatic neural 'two-,' 'three-' or 'four-tone' systems,* according to the number of rhythms involved; multitone systems which are reflected in the action of the peripheral musculature.

The fact that purely automatic processes are involved in this is indicated, for example, by the observation that one can sever all the nerves leading to a fin exhibiting rhythm-superimposition without abolishing the superimposition effect. The fin concerned is itself arrested, but the continuance of the automatic process underlying its movement remains visible through its superimposition on another automatism linked to a fin which projects *both* automatic rhythms into the external world.

Let us leave the fish for a moment and make a brief excursion, passing over all the other vertebrates to consider *man.* Any human being can without difficulty move both arms either synchronously or in alternation. It is considerably more difficult—for reasons which will be discussed later—to simultaneously beat out different rhythms with the two arms. However, it is usually quite easy to succeed at least in beating twice as fast with one arm as with the other. I therefore arranged for a number of people to perform this type of movement with their eyes closed, registering their activity with appropriate recording-levers. The experimental subjects were not told about the purpose of the experiment; they were simply requested to move both arms as evenly as possible. A perfectly typical example is shown in Fig. 4.12. One of the arms indicated in Fig. 4.12a exhibits periodicity of exactly the same kind as that which we have seen with fin rhythms (Fig. 4.7). In Fig. 4.12b, the slight bumps in the lower trace betray the fact that this rhythm was also influenced by the upper one. It is interesting to note that reciprocal influence between the two movements appears, as a rule, to occur subconsciously. The student who produced this particular tracing was afterwards very surprised at its appearance, since he had imagined that he had moved his arms with a continuous, steady amplitude. Of course, we cannot jump to conclusions from these and many other external signs of correspondence, assuming that superimposition is also involved here. This question is still under examination. Nevertheless, they do indicate that these things are not phenomena from some—possibly 'aberrant'—fish nervous system, but processes of general central significance. We shall now return to the dorsal nerve cord of the fish for the

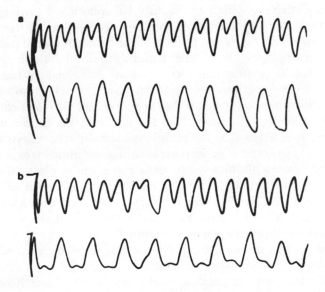

FIG. 4.12. Recording of voluntary up-and-down movement of the perpendicularly-held lower arms with a frequency relationship of 2:1. The experimental subject keeps the eyes closed and attempts to move each arm as evenly as possible (above: right arm; below: left arm. Both traces from the same subject).

simple reason that it is technically much more suitable for investigation.

The resultant concept of automatic, gradually increasing and decreasing excitation processes of some kind, as the cause of rhythmic muscle movements, presents difficulties as soon as one attempts to fit this with what we know of the activity of motor ganglion cells through measurements of action potentials from nerves and muscles. From such measurements, it is safely assumed that the active motor ganglion cell continuously transmits bursts of impulses in rapid succession along the nerve. These salvos of excitation exhibit varying frequencies, and each ganglion cell (as a general rule) possesses its own rhythm of discharge. It is consequently difficult to imagine how the activity of the motor neurons could be organized such that an evenly rising and falling excitation process results in the centre, and how—in any given case—several such processes can be summated. There is, admittedly, a way out of this dilemma, which would be to locate the automatic production of rhythms in *different* central elements and to regard the motor cells as intermediates between these elements and the peripheral musculature. We shall now have to examine this possibility in more detail.

Even in the course of analysis of relative coordination, phenomena repeatedly emerged which could only be understood through the assumption that the formation and superimposition of the automatic rhythms do not take a place in the motor cells which transmit the muscle impulses, but in other regions proximal to these cells. In essence, the following considerations are involved: When one automatism is superimposed upon another, the reflection of this process (the movement trace of the fin concerned) must indicate any increase or decrease in strength of the participating automatisms. However, it emerges that the peripheral activity (the extent of fin oscillation) can increase or decrease within wide limits in response to certain stimuli, without any apparent corresponding alteration of the relevant, underlying automatic excitatory process. An example will illustrate this. In Fig. 4.13, a mild jab with a needle has evoked performance of one double and one quadruple beat of the fin associated with the independent rhythm.

In this case, one would expect that the intensity relationship between the two automatisms should be considerably modified to favour the independent pectoral fin rhythm. In actual fact, however, the steady maintenance of the dependent rhythm indicates that this is not the case. This could be understood on the assumption that the stimulus magnifying the muscular action has not actually penetrated to the automatism, but has bypassed it to directly affect the motor

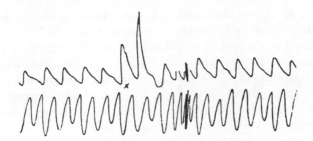

FIG. 4.13. *Sargus:* pectoral fin rhythm above, tail fin rhythm below. The frequency relationship is 2:3; the dependent rhythm continuously exhibits triplet periodicity. At *x*, a needle jab evokes two more powerful beats with the pectoral fin. Shortly after this, the recording surface was temporarily arrested (hence the apparent irregularities at that point).

ganglion cells, and thus the musculature. The converse effect—muffling of the automatic process—can also be evoked. In other words, the intensity of muscular activity apparently proves to be independent of the intensity of the automatism, within wide limits.

Whilst searching for a possibility to settle this dangling question in a more decisive manner, I uncovered the following phenomenon: The tail fin of the fish investigated does not oscilllate from side to side as an entire surface; the upper and lower halves of the fin move in opposite directions—when one moves to the right, the other moves to the left. This behavior can be exploited to provide an answer to our question, provided that one can successfully determine whether these oppositely oscillating fin-halves are underlain by two similarly opposing automatic processes in the spinal cord (case 1), or whether there is only one single tail-fin automatism (case 2), in response to which the musculatures of the two fin halves exhibit opposing (reciprocal) effects through the agency of some transmission mechanism. A decision is obtainable through the superimposition phenomenon explained with the schema in Fig. 4.14.

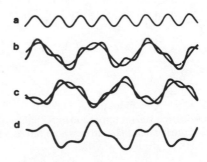

FIG. 4.14. Schema for explanation of Fig. 4.13. (See text for details.)

The finely developed sinus curves (b and c) would, in case 1, indicate
the opposing passage of the two tail-fin automatisms. The pectoral
fin automatism (a) would be superimposed upon them. From the
heavily outlined curves of (a) and (c), one can see that the fluctuations
evoked by rhythm (a) always occur in the same direction with both
rhythms, (b) and (c). Therefore, for case 1 one would expect
corresponding, accordant fluctuations in the oscillatory movements
of the two halves of the tail. In case 2, there is only one tail-fin
automatism (indicated by the faint trace in c) and, correspondingly,
only one superimposition process (heavy trace in c). One half of tail-
fin activity would have to correspond to this heavy curve (c), whilst the
other half of the tail would have to perform, at any given instant, an
opposing, mirror-image action—as indicated by trace (d). The
behavior actually observed is shown in Fig. 4.15: the traces are perfect
mirror images, even covering quite minor irregularities! Thus—
assuming that the superimposition theory is correct—it is proven
that one-and-the-same tail-fin automatism brings about operation of
the two halves of the tail fin. If this is the case, one can only
understand the opposing oscillation of the two halves by assuming
that between the automatic 'stimulus' on the one hand and the
musculature on the other there are further, intercalary neural
elements which fall into two groups, which exhibit contrasting
(reciprocal) response to the same automatic 'stimulus' and give rise to
the corresponding behavior of the two fin halves. Thus, the
'automatic' elements cannot be the ultimate motor elements from
which the muscle impulses emerge. In other words: *The automatism
is extraneous to the 'final common pathway'* along which all
excitation must be passed in order to reach the musculature.

This dualism of the automatic and motor functions of the CNS
represents *division of labor*. The automatic elements—we can briefly

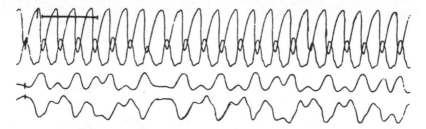

FIG. 4.15.   Recordings of the two pectoral fins, oscillating in alternation
(upper curve), and the upper and lower halves of the tail fin (lower curve). (A
central section of the tail-fin rays has been cut away.) Coincidence markings
are given on the left-hand side.

refer to them as automatic cells—determine the rhythm, the frequency of the muscular activity to be performed. The motor cells are the transmitters of the command, but they (more exactly, the number of impulses which they transmit) determine the intensity (amplitude) of the movement. The motor cells are not only dependent upon the automatic cells; they serve several masters. We have already seen that they can respond directly to peripheral stimuli, which do not even penetrate to the automatic cells (Fig. 4.13), and in the intact animal they are doubtless also accessible to impulses from the brain. Conversely, there are naturally additional effects which only influence the automatic cells, and which therefore only influence the tempo of the rhythmic movements. We shall consider such influences in more detail later on.

For the moment, we shall leave the description of rhythmic phenomena for a while, and turn to an experiment which initially appears to be far removed from the central theme, but whose interpretation leads back to the concept of superimposition.

It is a well-known fact that in all vertebrates normal postural orientation is guaranteed through the activity of the labyrinth system. All authors agree that this applies equally to fish. After destruction of the labyrinth, a fish is no longer able to maintain its equilibrium. However, I discovered that this statement is only conditionally valid. If a fish lacking its labyrinth is placed in a tank illuminated only from above by one light source, the previously disoriented fish once again swims around in normal fashion, as if it were intact. If the light is then projected into the tank *from one side*, such fish all immediately lie on their sides; and if the light source is placed *below* the glass tank, they all swim upside down, with their bellies pointing upwards. In other words: For a fish lacking a labyrinth, 'above' and 'below' is exclusively determined by the direction of incident light—the dorsal surface is always turned towards the light (von Buddenbrock's 'dorsal light reflex'). Thus, for a labyrinth-less fish, the eye provides a replacement static sense, and one would naturally like to know whether such optical equilibrating orientation is operative prior to the suppression of the labyrinth. This question can be answered quite easily. One only needs to illuminate a normal fish from one side. The result is that the fish does, in fact, incline to that side; but the inclination is not complete—it only occurs to a certain degree. The intensity of this lateral tendency can easily be determined. Measurements show that the inclined position exhibited with lateral illumination is maintained just as persistently as the upright position of a fish oriented exclusively by static means. The *degree* of inclination itself is quite

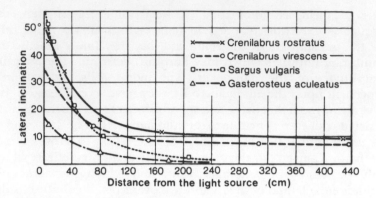

FIG. 4.16.   Graphical representation of the lateral inclination of free-swimming fish with lateral illumination from a 40-watt bulb. The degree of inclination is dependent upon the proximity of the light source and there are marked quantitative differences between the four fish species investigated.

exactly dependent upon the light intensity. The greater the intensity of the laterally incident light, the greater the degree of inclination of the fish. Fig. 4.16 shows, for four fish species, the inclination of the body (measured in degrees) in relation to the proximity of a lateral light source. As one can see, each fish species exhibits a characteristic inclination curve—a phenomenon which is extremely interesting from a comparative physiological and general biological point of view, though space does not permit fuller consideration here. The curves clearly show that the normal posture of the fish is a labile feature which is determined at any given time as a *central resultant* of the interaction of these two (apparently extremely different) forces—static and optical 'excitation'.

For an understanding of this central process, the following fact is important: If the fish is kept for a number of hours in darkness and is subsequently illuminated from one side, it at first swims exactly upright, with no apparent dependency upon the influence of light. It is a matter of minutes before the fish increasingly inclines towards the light, and the curve of this increase in inclination of the body exhibits a quite characteristic form. The optical equilibration component at first increases rapidly, and the fish inclines more and more to one side. Further increase in inclination then occurs at an ever-decreasing rate, and the ultimate condition of equilibrium between the two forces is only achieved after a number of hours—even days. On the other hand, with fish kept under illuminated conditions and then transferred to darkness, the changeover to exclusively static postural orientation is much more rapid and exhibits a different curve form. A period of 30-50 minutes in darkness suffices to prevent an immediate postural influence of light when the fish is re-exposed to illumination.

This whole phenomenon requires more detailed analysis in all possible directions. For example, it would be informative to study the influence of temperature upon this gradual conversion process and upon the behavioral resultant in general, or to investigate the effect of various substances which affect central activity, and so on. Whatever such experiments may show, it is reasonable to assume that there is, as with the previously described rhythmic processes, superimposition of two 'excitation processes' or 'substances' of an unknown nature. This provides the simplest explanation for the resultant character of the observed behavior. There is no fundamental distinction in the fact that we are concerned here with persistent conditions, whilst previously rhythmic processes were involved. The fin automatisms themselves are, in fact, not always uninterruptedly active in rhythmic fashion; situations can arise where there are pauses of several seconds between one beat of a fin and another, during which the superimposition phenomenon is approximately maintained. Superimposition in movement is then translated into superimposition in posture.

So far, we have only become acquainted with one of the two processes which play a part in the coordination of the objects of our investigation. Superimposition permits *quantitative* reciprocal adjustment of activities, regardless of whether these exhibit concordant or distinctive rhythms. What it cannot achieve is enforcement of the tempo of one rhythm upon another. Exactly as with a duet, each of the two automatisms remains quite uninfluenced by the other. However, the first striking property of coordinated movements is the accordance in tempo; somehow they are linked to one another. We shall now take a close look at the force behind this property.

When a father goes out for a walk with his six- to eight-year-old son, one can often observe the following: The boy would like to keep pace with his father, but this does not work for long. After a number of coincident steps, he gradually loses the tempo, and in order to fall into step once more he makes one or two rapid additional steps. By doing so, he once again falls in with his father's pace, and the game is all ready to start again. Exactly the same effect—translated into exact graphical form—is shown in Fig. 4.17a. One rhythm is even and independent, while the other exhibits a certain periodicity which is almost exclusively evident in the frequency and less obvious in amplitude. If we take the point marked 'x' as the starting-point, with

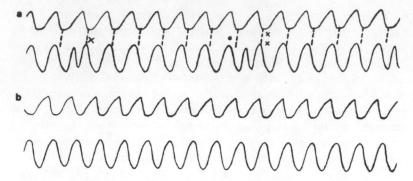

FIG. 4.17. *Labrus:* pectoral fin rhythm (upper curve) and dorsal fin rhythm (lower curve). (*a*), relative coordination; (*b*), absolute coordination (see text for details).

the aid of the reference lines we can follow how the dependent rhythm gradually becomes displaced with respect to the independent rhythm, until the phase relationship is reversed (●). There is then a much more rapid 'additional beat,' which achieves a return to the initial situation ($\overset{x}{x}$). Thereafter, the periodicity is repeated. A short while afterwards (Fig. 4.17b), the dependent rhythm has become completely aligned with the independent rhythm; the additional beats are lacking, and both rhythms exhibit the same tempo. *Relative* coordination has given way to *absolute* coordination. Figure 4.18 shows even more clearly that the influence concerned exclusively, or almost exclusively, affects the frequency. In this tracing, the frequency varies by a factor of two, whilst the amplitude of the movement remains almost constant. This alone demonstrates an externally obvious, fundamental difference between this phenomenon and that of superimposition, with which variation in amplitude is the first feature to strike the eye.

A further example in which the dependent rhythm is slower than the independent one is shown by Fig. 4.19. In this case, the dependent

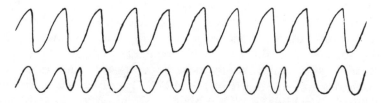

FIG. 4.18. A further trace from the same prepared fish as that providing Fig. 4.17.

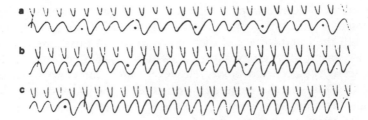

FIG. 4.19.   *Serranus:* pectoral fin rhythms (above; truncated to save space) and tail fin rhythm (below). The pectoral fin rhythm progresses smoothly; the tail fin rhythm accords with it periodically and exhibits occasional marked retardation (●). In (c), from the coincidence mark onwards, the tail fin rhythm is finally in full accord (absolute coordination).

rhythm does not exhibit occasional additional beats in order to keep pace with the other rhythm, but exhibits the opposite effect of periodic *ommission* of a beat. In 4.19c, accordance is finally achieved, and relative coordination gives way to absolute.

The fact that this phenomenon must involve something fundamentally different from the superimposition phenomenon is most clearly indicated by evaluation of such trace recordings using the method of 'time and speed tables' mentioned above. To mention just one important point, any increase in frequency in these cases is accompanied by corresponding increase in the speed of movement, and any decrease in frequency is associated with reduction in speed, whilst with superimposition exactly the opposite occurs. Detailed analysis of this coordination process has so far yielded roughly the following information: Both automatisms—dependent and independent—are involved in its production. The independent automatism operates by exerting a rhythmically rising and falling influence on the frequency of the dependent one; whilst the latter exhibits variations in accessibility to this influence, again with rhythmic fluctuation in degree. The influence itself varies according to the momentary phase relationship between the two rhythms. When close to a given reciprocal position the effect is one of attraction and attachment, whilst approach to the opposite position is accompanied by a repellent effect. Because of this polar opposition in functioning, I have proposed the term '*magnet effect*' for this peculiar process—though this, of course, implies no accompanying supposition about its physical nature, which is as yet indeterminate. Briefly stated, therefore, *the magnet effect is the 'endeavour' of one automatism to impose its tempo and a quite specific reciprocal phase relationship upon another.*

If we now enquire as to the reciprocal phase relationship which is imposed by one rhythm upon another, the question can be answered through the intermediary of the superimposition phenomenon. So far, we have only seen examples in which superimposition or the magnet effect occurred *alone*. However, such cases are far from typical. This behavior frequently occurs temporarily, or only under certain working conditions. As a rule, superimposition and the magnet effect operate together; but both phenomena can exhibit independent variations in intensity. When the two forces operate together, one can determine a quite specific, invariable relationship between them. The order into which the magnet effect seeks to align the two rhythms (as is finally achieved from 'x' onwards in the trace of Fig. 4.20) always exhibits the same phase relationship as that in which one rhythm augments the other in superimposition. Conversely, the phase relationship which results in *repellence* is the same as that in which superimposition produces weakening of the dependent rhythm (the places marked ● in Fig. 4.20). This, presumably, can only mean one thing. The magnet effect produces reciprocal stabilization with a phase relationship in which both central automatic processes are similarly oriented and *operate in the same sense*—since it is only then that *addition* of the effects can occur with superimposition. Thus, the magnet effect only provides the superimposition with a biological function when it continually stabilizes the two rhythms with a reciprocal relationship where one augments the action of the other.

One peculiarity of the magnet effect must be remarked upon. The manner in which 'attraction' or 'repellence' is exerted cannot be simply regarded as 'excitation' or 'inhibition.' For example, if the dependent rhythm is, at a given moment, temporally in advance of the phase relationship aimed at by the magnet effect, the latter has a slowing ('inhibitory') effect; whilst if it is falling behind, the effect is one of acceleration ('excitatory'). It is, so to speak, all the same to the magnet effect whether it operates in the form of excitation or inhibition; both influences are apparently unified and the nature of the magnet effect is not encompassed by such a distinction. The

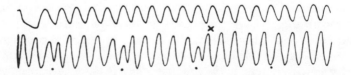

FIG. 4.20.   *Labrus:* pectoral and dorsal fin rhythms. Absolute coordination exists from 'x' onwards.

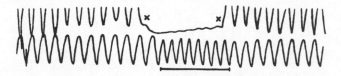

FIG. 4.21.   *Labrus:* pectoral and dorsal fin rhythms. Between *x* and *x*, the
pectoral fin rhythm is inhibited. (The corresponding segment of the dorsal
fin rhythm is marked with a horizontal bar.)

magnet effect represents the form in which one automatism fights for
control of another.

This struggle can remain undecided for some time, but with
augmentation of the magnet effect it must, after a given instant, lead
to defeat of the dependent rhythm, to surrender of its independence.
Such augmentation of the magnet effect can also be brought about by
certain peripheral stimuli. The question now arises as to whether,
following the definitive victory of the magnet effect (i.e., after
emergence of absolute coordination), the dependent rhythm gradually ceases to strive for independent activity with the passage of
time, or latently persists with the struggle. An answer is provided by
the experiment illustrated in Fig. 4.21. Absolute coordination exists
between the two rhythms; the lower, dependent rhythm had been
forced to fall in with the upper rhythm more than one hour
previously. Prior to that, the dependent rhythm possessed a
frequency which was one-third faster. In the trace (from x to x), the
independent pectoral fin rhythm has been stilled by pressure on the
anterior sides of the body, and one can see how, during this period,
the temporarily released dependent rhythm actually does continue
with its tempo increased by one-third. This apparently absurd
behavior, whereby the same stimulus inhibits one action and
simultaneously accelerates another, can easily be explained through
the disappearance of the magnet effect at this point. From this
experiment, which is at any time reproducible, we can only assume
that the struggle between the two automatisms persists even after
achievement of absolute coordination, though this is unsuccessful
for the dependent rhythm and therefore invisible to us. Perhaps for
the first time we can catch a glimpse of the tensions which are
continuously operating in the CNS without emerging visibly to the
exterior; tensions like those which many people must have
discovered, through introspection, in their own psychological
experience.

In this case, only two automatisms are in conflict with one another.
The situation immediately becomes more complex, however, when

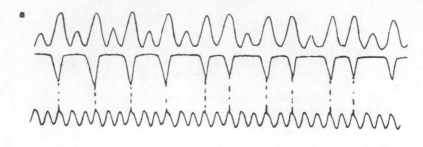

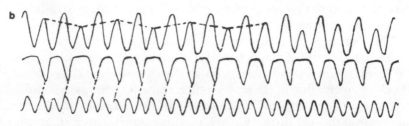

FIG. 4.22.   *Sargus:* periodicity produced through the combined operation
of the magnet effect and superimposition. (The dotted lines are included to
facilitate examination of the periodicity.) (*a*), transition from one order to
another; (*b*), a third combination. The traces represent selected examples
from a large number of different types of periodicity exhibited by the same
prepared fish.

three or more automatisms are involved and each attempts to
maintain its own tempo, particularly when the superimposition
phenomenon is added to this. This produces an unimaginable
wealth of possible combinations, and corresponding to these there
are just as many possibilities of variation in periodicity. The two
examples given in Fig. 4.22 are simply intended to demonstrate that
such periodicity always permits recognition of a rigid governing
principle, which enables us to determine the nature and intensity of
the various operative forces. There is, as it were, a parliament
continuously sitting in the spinal cord, where each power makes its
contribution of force: a parliament which continually reaches
compromises and which is only really distinct from its human
counterpart in that its decisions are never postponed! That ability is a
special gift of the brain.

I am inclined to believe that the magnet effect represents an
important instrument of central order. In fish, it emerges not only in
the interplay of locomotor rhythms but also in the relationship
between such rhythms and the respiratory rhythm. With terrestrial
vertebrates, this effect is almost certainly the basis for the fixed,
absolute locomotor order which characterizes these animals. When

we attempt to move our two arms with different rhythms, we are trying to overcome this magnet effect. In fact, some people can win the battle after some practice, at least as far as the arms are concerned. If we lie on our backs and attempt to do the same with our legs raised, we are not usually able to move them with different rhythms. Apparently, the magnet effect of the leg rhythm is stronger than that of the arm rhythms in human beings.

However, the magnet effect is not only the principle effecting order between the different individual automatisms. It seems to operate *within* each automatism as well, that is, between the individual automatic cells united into a group. This is most obvious when the harmony within an automatism is temporally removed, for example under the effect of anaesthetization or carbon dioxide administration. The entire fin then exhibits an irregular, fluttering movement. Yet if one records the movement of two adjacent, isolated fin rays, they are frequently seen to oscillate quite regularly; but each ray has its own, distinctive tempo. Thus, a group of otherwise cooperating automatic cells has in this case been dissolved to give smaller, independently operating units. Under suitable conditions, superimposition and the magnet effect can be demonstrated in the interaction between these lesser rhythms. Thus, within an automatism there is probably operation of the same process as that operating between various, more distinct rhythms. Since there is usually quite rigid coherence between the elements forming an automatism, the automatism as a whole generally follows the All-or-None Law, that is, it either discharges completely or not at all. This phenomenon, which was not to be expected in the CNS, is reminiscent of the same kind of regularity in vertebrate hearts; in fact, it leads on to a whole series of additional features which one had previously identified only in the heart and which provide a kind of bridge between the coordination types found in the heart (so far always treated as a separate category) and those found in the spinal cord. We shall not deal any further with this correspondence at this point, but finish off our excursion through the colourful and varied field of relative coordination with a brief forecast.

Relative coordination is a kind of neural cooperation which seems to be very important since it to some extent renders visible in peripheral muscle action the operative forces, which would necessarily remain invisible given absolute coordination. However, relative coordination is not only of interest in its own right; because of the great precision with which it works we can set questions using the prepared animal and obtain a clear-cut answer. Let us take just one example, concerning the problem of *gaits*.

It is a well-known fact that horses and dogs exhibit various gaits: walking, trotting and galloping. Such gaits also occur in fish. For example, the pectoral fins as a rule beat in alternation, but given certain central conditions they can abruptly 'switch' and beat synchronously. The converse also occurs. We can now ask: On what mechanism is this switch in the internal order, accompanying change from one gait to another, based? There are two possibilities; Either (1) the relationships between the two automatisms remain unchanged, and the response pattern of the motor cells alters such that they respond to the same automatic process in a manner different to that previously exhibited; or (2) the response of the motor cells remains unaltered, and the reciprocal phase relationship between the automatisms changes. This question must be answerable with the aid of relative coordination. If a third (dorsal fin or tail fin) rhythm is dependent upon the two pectoral fin rhythms, then the influence of the latter would necessarily remain unchanged following alteration of gait in the first case, whereas with the second case an abrupt transition would occur. Fig. 4.23 shows such a case of abrupt, spontaneous change from synchronous to alternating oscillation of the pectoral fins. The third rhythm appears to remain quite uninfluenced until the instant at which the 'switch' occurs. At the moment when the pectoral fins oscillate in alternation, however, the third rhythm is more or less dragged into the new tempo (note the bump in the tracing, marked 'x'), and subsequently it continues with increased intensity of actions. Thus, from the point 'x' onwards, the magnet effect and superimposition exert a powerful influence. Since this is *not* the case prior to 'x,' one must conclude that the pectoral fin rhythms were up to the point in opposition and had paralyzed one

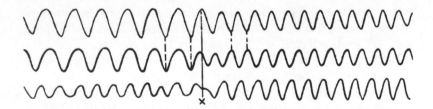

FIG. 4.23. *Sargus:* both pectoral fin rhythms (upper and middle traces) and the tail fin rhythm. Up to 'x,' the two pectoral fins beat synchronously (swinging backwards and forwards in unison). At 'x' there is a spontaneous 'switch' to alternating movement (one swings forwards, while the other is swinging backwards). Compare the dotted coincidence lines.

another in their effect upon the dependent rhythm. With this, our question is already answered. The change in gait is, in this case, based upon alteration in the reciprocal relationship between the automatisms themselves. In a similar manner, a number of other problems can be tackled with the aid of relative coordination; problems which we were previously unable to examine.

CONCLUSIONS

Although the foregoing account presents only a section of the results which have been obtained so far, we can nevertheless draw a number of more general conclusions. *Central coordination is not based upon chain-reflex mechanisms; it has a quite different nature. Its tools are processes which only occur within the CNS itself.* The 'reflex' is there in order to adapt this internal process at any given time to varying peripheral conditions, and to alter it in one direction or another. The reflex *is not the basic process itself,* as is so widely believed; it is either an *additional attribute of the central mechanism* or (probably in the majority of cases) a complex interplay of additional mechanisms with the active central forces described above. It is in accordance with the nature of these centrally operative forces that coordination is not fixed and machine-like, but variable, flowing and plastic. But this *plasticity,* contrary to the opinion of many supporters of the 'plasticity theory,' is not based on the fact that the CNS is comparable to a nerve net in which 'excitations' spread out, with decrements, on all sides. Instead, it is founded upon extremely refined (one might say *thoroughly engineered) internal organization.* Presumably, morphological structure—the arrangement of the cells and fibre connections—plays a large, but not exclusively decisive, role in the achievement of this order. If it were exclusive, the ordered behavior at any given moment could not be so very variable. What is important is the variable quantitative interaction of the internal forces (with some of which we have become acquainted). I suspect that these forces are attached to specific cell types or structures, though at the present time one cannot, of course, draw firm conclusions. Determination of the physiocochemical nature of these processes represents our next task. To accomplish it, the methods described here would have to be combined with chemical and bioelectrical approaches. It remains to be seen how far such a working association will be successful, and what will be discovered as a result.

RECENT WORK

In recent years, there has been much work on the mechanism of oscillation at the neuronal level and on the mechanism of the magnet effect (Ayers & Selverston, 1977; Hastings & Schweiger, 1976; Jacklet, 1977; Pinsker, 1977; Stein, 1974; Winfree, 1977). Many neural metronomes and neural clocks have been found. In some cases the oscillatory behavior is a consequence of interactions between neurons (Harcombe & Wyman, 1977); but more often it is, as von Holst conjectured, traceable to the inherently oscillatory behavior of certain neurons called neural pacemakers or neural clocks (cf. Russell & Hartline, 1978). Figure 4.24a portrays the output of the 24-hour neural clock in the eye of a marine slug (Aplysia). This clock is like the turtle heart, it runs for days after being removed from the animal. The output of this clock has an approximately 24-hour period under constant conditions. The day–night cycle plays the role of drill-master—accelerating or retarding the neural clock depending on whether the clock is fast or slow at daybreak or dusk. Figure 4.24b portrays electrical oscillations in the neural metronome (or pacemaker) that probably controls the stepping of the cockroach's leg (see Chapter 5).

Of more interest to psychologists is the impact von Holst's work has had on theoretical accounts of complex coordinations. In the next chapter Donald

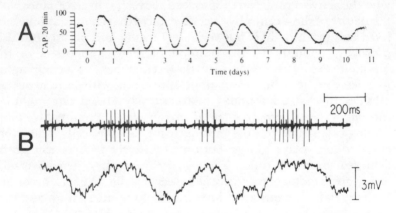

FIG. 4.24.   Two examples of neural oscillators. (a) The impulse frequency as a function of time in the output from the eye of *Aplysia*. The eye was dissected out and kept in a dish of seawater under constant conditions. The 24-hour rhythm of this neural clock derives from the endogenous activity of a population of neurons. [From Benson & Jacklet, 1977.] (b) The lower trace is a record of the sinusoidally oscillating electrical potential in a pacemaker neuron that (probably) establishes the stepping rhythm of the hind leg of a cockroach. The upper trace is a record of the impulses in a flexor motor nerve, the nerve that controls the muscles that swing the leg up and forward. The pacemaker neuron triggers a burst of impulses in the flexor nerve near the peak of each oscillation. [From Pearson and Fourtner, 1975].

Wilson addresses himself to the problem of accounting for leg coordination in the 6-legged animal whose intelligence was touted in Chapter 1. A system of coupled oscillators plays a central role in his account. And, Wilson's explanation of insect walking is representative of modern accounts of locomotion in all species that have been studied, including man (Herman, et al., 1976).

The emergence of coupled oscillators as an explanatory principle in the neural control of locomotion is only a foretaste of the role that von Holst's discoveries will eventually play in the explanation of coordinated action. It is now clear that many basic patterns of movement are generated by central programs even in primates (Taub, 1976). And these patterns frequently have a strongly rhythmic structure (see Carlson & Bentley, 1977; Fentress, 1973). This suggests that the central programs are arrays of oscillators coupled to each other in such a way as to maintain either constant phase relationships or constant lags (see Chap. 5).

SUPERIMPOSITION AND FOURIER SYNTHESIS

Any repetitive movement may be analyzed into the planar trajectories traced out by points on the limbs, torso, and head. And any such trajectory may be synthesized by superimposing a suitable selection of sinusoids. The Russian behavioral physiologist, Bernstein, spent years analyzing such trajectories in the skilled movements of craftsmen, industrial workers, and athletes. He recorded the trajectories by mounting tiny light bulbs at critical points all over the body and photographing the paths traced by the lights with a high speed movie camera. He found that in all cases he could synthesize the trajectory of a skilled repetitive movement, using no more than three suitably chosen fundamental sinusoids (one for each plane) and the first three harmonics of each fundamental. (The second harmonic has twice the frequency of the fundamental; the third harmonic, 3 times, etc.—see Bernstein, 1967, pp., 23–24.)

Bernstein's discovery suggests that the brain may represent learned movements by the sinusoids from which they may be synthesized. A relatively small selection of sinusoids (less than 100 as a conservative guess) would constitute an action-alphabet out of which any movement could be constructed.

The construction of a movement from its component oscillations would represent an application of von Holst's principle of superimposition. The three fundamental oscillators for a given movement would be set to oscillating and their outputs (and the harmonics thereof) would be superimposed to generate the actual movement. The maintenance of the requisite phase relationship between the three oscillators would be achieved by means of von Holst's other principle, the magnet effect or phase-dependent-response principle. This is, of course, highly speculative at the moment. However, Hinkle and Camhi (1972) have demonstrated diverse patterns of motor neuron discharge that are realized by varying the relative amplitudes of two oscillatory signals that drive the same pool of motor neurons in the locust. (For further discussion of the Fourier theory of movement coding, see Chapter 12.)

The next chapter points up the power and versatility of the central programs produced from the coupling of oscillators. It also shows how the pattern established by the central programs may be altered and adjusted by sensory inputs arising during the performance of the pattern. These last-minutes alterations and adjustments adapt the general pattern to momentary special circumstances. These reflex alterations of a general pattern specified by higher levels of the nervous system provide an important illustration of how interactions between levels of hierarchical command system give behavior an overall cohesiveness combined with flexible adaptations to momentary circumstances. Behavior begins to take on the intelligent qualities that Bruner and Bartlett emphasize.

5 The Role of Coupled Oscillators in Locomotion

COMPLEX UNITS OF BEHAVIOR

One of the more baffling aspects of the organization of behavior is that an action that we regard as unitary at one level of analysis dissolves into a bewildering variety of diverse descriptions when we shift to a lower level of analysis and description. When analyzed at the level of leg movements, "moving forward" is not a unitary phenomenon. The action of moving forward can refer to quite different sequences of leg movements. Take for example the sequence the cockroach uses when moving very slowly forward. First it lifts its rear leg (R_3) and advances it forward. Having planted the right rear leg, it lifts and advances the right middle leg (R_2) then the right front leg (R_1). The sequence of leg movements progresses along the body in the direction the body is moving, in this case the forward direction. Such sequences are termed metachronal. Having moved all three legs on its right side in this metachronal sequence, the roach now lifts and advances the left rear leg (L_3), then the left middle leg (L_2), and finally the left front leg (L_1). The description of this behavior when analyzed in terms of the sequence of leg movements is R_3, R_2, R_1, L_3, L_2, L_1, R_3, etc. On the other hand, we know from Chapter 1 that when the roach moves forward with maximum rapidity the sequence of leg movements is ($R_3L_2R_1$), ($L_3R_2L_1$), ($R_3L_2R_1$), etc., where the legs enclosed by parentheses are moved simultaneously.

At first glance, the rapid sequence has nothing in common with the slow sequence—other than the fact that both sequences move the roach forward. Is there any justification for lumping both sequences under a behavioral description that refers only to the net effect of the muscular activity? Perhaps this similarity of effect is accidental rather than essential. The neural machinery that generates rapid running may have nothing in common with the neural machinery that generates slow walking. In that case, lumping these two actions into a common category just because they happen to have a similar description at a grosser level of behavioral analysis leads only to confusion and paradox. On the other hand, an understanding of the process that generates the disparate sequences may reveal a common generative structure. If the two different sequences are instances of the output of a single underlying process, then regarding them as belonging to a single class of action is justified. Thus, the taxonomical problem of analyzing behavior into instances that should be regarded as belonging to a common class is intimately related to the problem of determining the structure of the processes that generate behavior.

One of the toughest problems in the analysis of learned behavior is to find appropriate units for the behavioral analysis. Does the organism learn to make a particular pattern of muscular contractions and relaxations, as conditioned reflex theories imply? Or does the learning experience operate at a higher level, a level that specifies, say, the direction a limb should move relative to some object, not the particular pattern of muscular activity to be used in accomplishing that movement? When should two movements that differ at some level of description be regarded as the same movement and when should they be regarded as different? This is the problem of response generalization in learning.

The problem is highlighted by Wickens' classic experiments on response generalization in the learning of a simple shock-avoidance movement by humans. In Wickens' experiments (1938, 1939), subjects had their forearm strapped to a board with the palm downward. The subject's middle finger rested on an electrode capable of delivering mildly painful shocks. Wickens conditioned an involuntary finger withdrawal response to a buzzer by giving several trials in which the buzzer preceded a shock to the finger. The response was involuntary in the sense that subjects could not inhibit the conditioned response when instructed to do so. In fact, one subject lost a small wager with the experimenter by failing to inhibit his conditioned withdrawal response after betting the experimenter that he could.

The question arises how we should describe the conditioned response? Should we describe it as a conditioned withdrawal response? Or should we focus down to the level of neuromuscular action? At the neuromuscular level of analysis, the response made by Wickens' subjects involved excitation of the motor nerves to the extensor muscles of the middle finger and a concomitant inhibition of the motor nerves to the flexor muscles (Sherrington's principle of reciprocal innervation of antagonistic muscles). The problem is that there is no one-to-one mapping between the description of the subjects' actions as a "withdrawal response" and the description of what happens at the level of neuromuscular activity. The two descriptions are by no means synonymous; nor does the one description reduce to the other.

That the description of the subjects' conditoned response as a withdrawal response does not reduce to a description in terms of extensor excitation and flexor inhibition is made clear by the next stage of Wickens' experiment. When the involuntary finger withdrawal response was thoroughly conditioned, Wickens unstrapped the subject's arm and then strapped it back onto the board again. Only now, the arm was turned over. The palm faced upward and the back of the middle finger rested on the electrode. Under these circumstances, the two descriptions of the subject's conditioned response—"withdrawal" versus "extensor-excitation and flexor-inhibition"—make opposite predictions about what will happen the next time the buzzer sounds.

In fact, most of Wickens' subjects made a rapid finger withdrawal response the next time the buzzer sounded. In other words, the buzzer triggered extensor inhibition and flexor excitation. From the standpoint of predicting the outcome of this learning experiment, we do better to describe the subject's action in terms of the direction of the finger's movement relative to the table rather than in terms of the neuromuscular activity that produces that movement in a particular instance. The nervous system somehow generates extensor excitation and flexor inhibition when that pattern of neuromuscular activity is required to withdraw the finger from the table and extensor inhibition together with flexor excitation when that pattern is required. This experiment illustrates a point that Weiss emphasizes: The hierarchial structure of behavior must be considered in any analysis of learning. One must always ask at what level in the structure the changes wrought by experience occur (see Chapter 8).

The problem from the standpoint of the organization of action is to describe the structure of the mechanism that translates a "finger-withdrawal" command into differing patterns of neuromuscular activity, depending upon the position of the finger relative to the table at the time the command is issued. Oddly enough, learning theorists have never addressed themselves very seriously to this problem. To be sure, they have given the problem a name—response generalization. But a name is not an explanation. Only an account of the response generating units at various levels of the motor system will enable us to predict all of the particular circumstances under which an effective finger withdrawing motion will occur when the buzzer sounds. Can the motor machinery generate any and all patterns of neuromuscular activity that circumstances require? Presumably not. But until we understand the principles underlying "response generalization" we will not be able to predict the spectrum of responses that the subject will give when he hears the buzzer. Response generalization is not an explanatory principle; it is merely a name for the fact that any learned action has a variety of manifestations at the level of neuromuscular activity. Until we understand the principles that organize the animal's neuromuscular activity we will never know what patterns of neuromuscular activity should be regarded as belonging to the class of actions that can be elicited by the buzzer after the conditioning experience. More generally, *until we understand the higher units that organize motor output we will not be able to predict the range of changed behavior that may result from a given learning experience.*

The relation between descriptions of action that derive from different levels of analysis is also central to modern linguistics. In linguistics this problem is known as the problem of paraphrase. If one witness to an assault testifies that *John hit Mary* and another witness testifies that *Mary was hit by John,* why are we justified in concluding that the two witnesses give the same testimony?

If we analyze the verbal actions of the two witnesses at the level of meaning, then *John hit Mary* and *Mary was hit by John* are two instances of the same meaning. Analyzed from the standpoint of word sequence, these two instances of the same thing appear to have little in common. The two utterances have many words in common—*Mary, John, hit*—but this is not decisive from the standpoint of meaning. Consider, *Mary hit John,* which uses the same words to achieve a different meaning, and *The male participant struck the female participant,* which uses different words to achieve roughly the same meaning. Is our feeling that the sequences from the two witnesses are two instances of the same thing a misguided inference based on the fact that the two sentences are likely to have similar effects on the jury's behavior? Or is there, at some deeper level, a generating process that is common to these two sequences and not common to other sequences employing the same words (e.g., *Mary hit John*)? If so, what is the nature of this process? This is the problem that Chomsky's (1965) transformational grammar attempts to solve.

Transformational grammars assume that all sentences derive from simple sentences or strings of simple sentences called deep structures. These deep structures may be remodeled by sequences of operations that combine sentences, alter word order, delete some words, add others (e.g., *by*), and so on. The rules governing these remodeling operations are termed transformations. Two different complex sentences have the same meaning if they derive from the same deep structure, if, that is, they are two different remodelings of the same set of simple sentences.

Just as Chomsky's transformational grammar specifies what, at an underlying level, is thought to be common to paraphrastic sentences, the following paper by Wilson specifies what, at a deeper level, is common to what might be called paraphrastic leg movement sequences. Chomsky's analysis applies to the different word sequences people use when they say the same thing. Wilson's analysis applies to the different leg movement sequences that cockroaches use when they do the same thing.

In other respects, however, the linguistic analysis and the motor coordination analysis are emphatically different. Chomsky's analysis makes use of a set of rewrite rules that transform the underlying deep structure into different surface sequences. Wilson's analysis makes use of a set of coupled oscillators, whose surface output varies as a function of a single parameter— the period of oscillation, the time required to complete a single stepping cycle. Chomsky's analysis and Wilson's analysis both, however, justify our intuitive scheme of behavioral categorization by showing that apparently disparate instances of intuitively coherent behavioral categories have a common generating structure. Our intuitive behavioral categories appear to be faithful to the underlying structures that generate behavior. Our intuitive behavioral categories justifiably disregard differences in the details of the movements that comprise behavior. We know intuitively that all those different leg movements are variations on the theme of walking. Wilson's analysis justifies our intuition by showing how a single mechanism generates all the variations.

Insect Walking*[1,2]

DONALD M. WILSON

The mechanics of various types of animal locomotion fall into two major categories; locomotion involving appendages and locomotion involving only two movements of the trunk. The latter includes either undulatory or peristaltic waves which move from anterior to posterior as the animal moves forward; the wave moves opposite to the direction of locomotion. Animals with appendages may move the appendages alone or also undulate the whole body, and the wave of activity ordinarily is metachronal in either case; it travels along the body in the direction of movement. This difference in direction of the wave of local mechanical activity in the cases of locomotion with and without lateral projections from the body surface seems to be rather general. In flagellated protozoans there are both simple flagella and

*Reprinted, with permission, from *Annual Review of Entomology*, Volume 11. Copyright © 1966 by Annual Reviews Inc. All rights reserved.

[1]The survey of the literature pertaining to this review was concluded in March 1965.

[2]Many of the uncredited observations are original and substantial parts of the older works have been repeated by the author. This work was supported by grants from the NSF (GB 2116) and NIH (NB 23927). I am indebted to Mrs. E. Reid for preparing the diagrams, and to Mr. R. J. Wyman for the critical discussion of the manuscript.

those with small projections, mastigonemes, fixed at right angles. In the latter type, the wave is in the same direction as locomotion, whereas in the simple type it is the opposite (Jahn & Bovee, 1964). Among the vertebrates, fishes, especially eel-like ones, use sinuous waves opposed to the direction of locomotion, whereas tetrapods use metachronal waves of limb movement, at least at low speeds.

Most arthropods move by means of metachronal waves of activity of the paired appendages (for reviews see Manton, 1953; von Holst, 1935a). Insescts are no exception, but the small number of legs tends to obscure this basic fact. Superficial examination of the gaits of insects reveals a bewildering assortment of different patterns. There are differences in single animals at different speeds, between species whether they use all six legs or fewer, and further differences when animals are deprived of their normal leg number by amputation. Several reviews of the diverse locomotory patterns and effects of experimental manipulation are available (Horridge, 1965; Hughes, 1957; Roeder, 1953; Ten Cate, 1936), and I will not survey the earlier literature again. Of especial interest in this literature is the introduction of the concept of *plastizität* by Bethe (Bethe, 1930; Bethe & Woitas, 1930). He used this term to indicate the lability of nervous function apparently needed to allow the animal to adopt immediately a new and adaptive gait after the removal of some legs. Although Bethe thought of plasticity as a central nervous process, later workers have usually used the plasticity phenomenon to argue that the legs are coordinated primarily by proprioceptive reflexes.

The first part of this review will be devoted to a hypothesis which describes all of the commonly observed gaits of insects, including those resulting from amputation, in a single framework. This hypothesis does not deal with physiological mechanisms. The hypothesis will first be presented in its simplest form, and then special cases which require its modification will be introduced. The second part will contain suggestions for mechanisms which could account for the descriptive scheme. The account will be largely limited to terrestrial locomotion.

A DESCRIPTIVE MODEL

I will begin with an eclectic description which amounts to an hypothesis regarding the relationships between the various locomotory gaits in insects. Most of the ideas contributing to the hypothesis are found in publications by Hughes (1952; 1965), or Wendler (1964a), and many are not original even there. Hughes summarized his finding in two rules:

1. A wave of protractions (forward movements of the legs relative to the body) runs from posterior to anterior (and no leg protracts until the one behind is placed in a supporting position).
2. Contralateral legs of the same segment alternate in phase.

In *Carausius morosus*, at least (1964a), the protaraction time is nearly constant. Since there are frequency variations, retraction time must vary and some intervals between steps of different legs must vary. Three more rules may be assumed in order to construct the simplest model.

3. Protraction time is constant.
4. Frequency varies (retraction time decreases as frequency increases).
5. The intervals between steps of the hindleg and middle leg and between the middle leg and foreleg are constant, while the interval between the foreleg and hindleg steps varies inversely with frequency.

With these five criteria one can construct the patterns of stepping shown in Figure 5.1, except for pattern *f* which appears to violate rule 1.

Using leg symbols as in Fig. 5.1, commas to denote minimal intervals, parentheses to enclose groups of legs moving approximately in synchrony, and dots to represent variable intervals, the patterns may be described as follows. There is a basic sequence, 3, 2, 1...3, 2, 1..., of stepping on each side. The sides alternate, so, at lowest frequency, the sequences are staggered

$$.. R_3, R_2, R_1 .... R_3, R_2, R_1 ....$$
$$........... L_3, L_2, L_1 .... L_3 \qquad \text{a.}$$

as in Fig. 5.1a. As speed increases the variable interval decreases and the sequences overlap,

$$... R_3, R_2, R_1 .... R_3 \ R_2, R_1 ...$$
$$L_2, L_1 .... L_3, L_2, L_1 .... L_3, L_2 \qquad \text{b.}$$

as in Fig.5. 1b. Front and hindlegs step in diagonal pairs and middle legs alternate between the pairs. With further overlap of sequences, due to increased frequency, two results are possible, depending upon whether contralateral legs alternate with exactly equal intervals

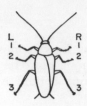

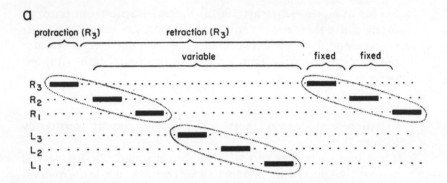

a

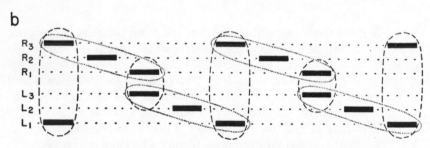

b

FIG. 5.1. Diagram illustrating an hypothesis relating the various six-legged gaits. The legs are numbered as in the drawing. The horizontal axis represents time. The solid bars indicate protraction (leg off ground and moving forward relative to the body and ground). For the purpose of making the simplest presentation, protraction time and interstep intervals between legs 3 to 2 and 2 to 1 are held constant and frequency changes are accomplished by varying only the interval between stepping in leg 1 and leg 3. Legs on opposite sides in the same segment are held in strict antiphase. Dotted enclosures indicate fixed basic sequences of steps of the legs of one side. In (a), the lowest frequency pattern is shown. Each leg steps by itself. In (b), the basic sequences overlap and some legs step in pairs (dashed enclosures). Removal of the middle legs, R_2 and L_2, would result in a diagonal stepping. In (c) and (d), the sequences overlap more. In order to have the sides alternate strictly, legs cannot step in exact pairs. Dashed enclosures indicate nearest temporal neighbor pairs. In (e), further overlap results in the tripod gait. Even the sequences on one side overlap so that legs 1 and 3 are synchronous. In (f), at the highest frequency the sequence beginning with leg 3 is started before the previous sequence has ended so that there is apparent reversal of the direction of the stepping sequence (dashed enclosures).

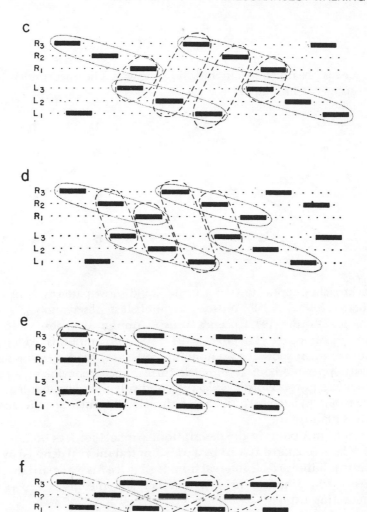

FIG. 5.1.   *(contd.)*

between steps as in Fig. 5. 1c and d, or whether the legs move in synchronous diagonal pairs as they often seem to do. In the latter case patterns result which are mirror images of an asymmetrical gait. Using the notation already described, the two patterns involving synchronous diagonal pairs are:

$$R_3, R_2, R_1, R_3 R_2, R_1, R_3.$$
$$L_1, L_3, L_2, L_1, L_3, L_2, L_1$$

c.

$$R_1, R_3, R_2, R_1 R_3, R_2, R_1$$
$$L_3, L_2, L_1, L_3, L_2, L_1, L_3 \qquad\qquad \text{d.}$$

These may be illustrated in the following way. The lines connect legs stepping synchronously.

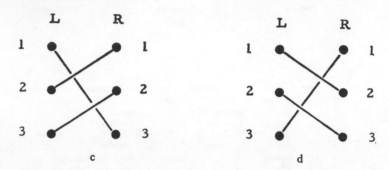

Cockroaches appear to stick to rule 2 and show patterns as in Fig. 5.1c,d (Hughes, 1952; Wilson, unpublished observations), while mantids (Roeder, 1937), beetles (Wilson, unpublished observations), and grasshoppers (La Greca, 1947; Wilson, unpublished observations) often show the asymmetric patterns. I have seen the same grasshopper use both asymmetric forms. Such behavior may have given rise to von Holst's (1935a) second rule that diagonal legs are synchronous, but most often, as Hughes (1952) points out, "the second rule is plainly false."

Up to this point in the description, symbols for legs on one side have been separated at least by a constant real interval denoted by the comma. If the variable interval from leg 1 to leg 3 is made still shorter, legs 1 and 3 appear to step together and the insect moves on alternating tripods.

$$(R_1 R_3), R_2 (R_1 R_3) R_2 (R_1 R_3)$$
$$L_2 (L_1 L_3), L_2 (L_1 L_3) L_2 \qquad\qquad \text{e.}$$

This is the well-known typical insect locomotory pattern shown in Fig.5.1e. Note that the basic sequence still operates on each side and the sides are 180° out of phase. For cockroaches no higher speed gait has ever been reported. Hughes (1952) in fact maintains that there is always a small delay between the protractions of leg 1 and leg 3. In the stick insect, however, this delay can reduce to zero or even become negative (Wendler, 1964a). A negative delay between legs 1 and 3 reverses the order of leg stepping from the metachronal one to

3 1, 2, 3 1, 2, 3 1, 2, 3 1

for each side, with the opposite side in antiphase. This new sequence can be seen to be the sum of overlapping basic metachronal sequences, however.

```
3  2   1
      3   2   1
          3   2   1
              3   2   1
      _____
3  2  31  2  31  2  31  2   1
```

The next extreme of overlap of the sequences would have all three legs of a side stepping at once, and we can probably expect not to find an example in nature.

All of the above illustrated sequential patterns have been observed in insects. To my knowledge, no other patterns, using six legs, have been reported for straight forward walking. A characteristic of the model is that the insect always stands on at least three legs which enclose the vertical axis through the center of gravity.

In order to make the easiest presentation of the model there has been some neglect of fact. I wish now to add a modifying condition which will accommodate much of the experimental evidence from different animals. However, this modification does not destroy the elementary simplicity of the model, which holds for most adult insect gaits. The most important and common deviation from the model behavior is that all the intervals between steps of adjacent legs vary with frequency and not just the interval from leg 1 to leg 3, even though the latter does account for most of the change in frequency. Hughes (1952) has constructed an alternative model in which no assumption is made about these intervals. He follows the two rules 1 and 2, holds frequency constant, and varies the ratio between protraction time and retraction time. In this way one can construct all of the above symmetrical patterns, but the model was not used to predict the highest speed ones, found later by Wendler (1964a). The Hughes model is equivalent to the present one normalized for frequency. However, its mode of construction is quite different and it does not form an appealing basis from which to begin a discussion of mechanisms.

In special cases the model is either inaccurate or does not hold at all. Some of the cases should be mentioned. Many insects normally walk with less than six legs. Mantids often hold the forelegs up and walk with only the other two pairs (Roeder, 1937). They use sequences which are the same as in the model, but with the first pair subtracted. Grasshoppers may hold the hind pair up and use normal patterns with the first two pairs (von Holst, 1943). According to La Greca (1947) the grasshopper *Tropidopola cylindrica* (Marsch.) at times walks with the hindlegs up and the legs of each segment stepping synchronously, with prothoracic and mesothoracic legs alternating. The abdomen forms the third point of support. This gait clearly breaks rule 2 as does jumping in grasshoppers and swimming in some other insects. Grasshopppers which normally walk using all six legs may use the hindlegs to some extent independently of the other four (von Holst, 1943). It is common in *Romalea microptera* (Beauvois) for the hindlegs to step only on every other cycle of the more anterior legs (Wilson, unpublished observations). Their stride is thus twice that of the others. They are correctly phased relative to the middle legs when they do step.

There is apparent escape from the condition, "no leg protracts until the one behind is placed in a supporting position," at the highest running frequencies. Even at lower speeds it is sometimes the case that more anterior legs step before the one behind is set down (Wilson, unpublished observations). This is relatively rare except under special circumstances such as turning, or after amputation of some legs. The same thing occurs commonly in many mammals, especially those with long legs, such as the giraffe, since otherwise the animal would kick its own foreleg.

Further differences from the above patterns are found in larval insects. Recently, Wendler (1964b) has studied the larva of *Cantharis fusca* and finds that the two sides may run at slightly different frequencies so that all phase relationships are shown between legs in the same segment, but with some preference for near synchrony. Adjacent legs of the same side alternated [fitting von Holst's old rule 1 (1935a)]. The adult of the same species walks with typical adult insect pattern.

CHANGES IN WALKING PATTERN
DUE TO AMPUTATION

Von Buddenbrock in 1921 described the results of experiments in which legs of stick insects were amputated and locomotory patterns observed. He showed that when one leg from each side of the animal is removed, regardless of what combination of four legs remained, the insect adopted the gait typical of a walking tetrapod; that is, the remaining legs formed combinations in diagonal pairs. Each pair stepped nearly together and in antiphase with the other pair. Bethe (1930) and von Holst (1935a) found similar results in some other arthropods which had all but four legs removed. Recent authors (Estartús & Ponz, 1951; Hughes, 1957; Wendler, 1964a) describe results which are in substantial agreement with the older work, although due to greater precision in their work they reveal differences in detail. Removal of only one leg has only relatively slight effect. In fact, the earlier reports indicated none. Hughes (1957) describes the results which do occur in cockroaches, but admits that they are not dramatic.

The best described and most interesting amputation experiment is that in which the two mesothoracic legs are removed. The result is surprising if one reasons from the old notion that insects generally walk with the tripod method. Removal of the two middle legs should result in an unstable walk with both remaining legs on one side alternating with the opposite two. However, when such amputations are made, the operated animal, without a learning period, changes to walking like a typical tetrapod. The alternating tripod pattern of walking,

$$(R_3L_2R_1), (L_3R_2L_1), (R_3\ldots\ldots\ldots\ldots$$

minus (should equal)

$$(R_3R_1), (L_3L_1), (R_3\ldots\ldots\ldots \qquad 1.$$

but

$$R_3, R_1, L_3, L_1, R_3\ldots\ldots\ldots \qquad 2.$$

or

$$(R_1L_3), (L_1R_3), (R_1\ldots\ldots\ldots \qquad 3.$$

results (according to most of the available literature).

The results are not so surprising when considered in the light of the whole known range of gaits of intact animal. Gait 2 is the natural result of subtraction of the mesothoracic legs from a slowly walking animal using gait a of Fig.5.1. Gait 3 is comparable to gait b in Fig. 5.1, minus the middle legs, and is used at a higher speed than gait 2. In fact, the whole set of recordable patterns from animals which have lost the middle legs can be predicted from the patterns used by whole animals. The most commonly observed results can be compared to the lower speed patterns for intact animal. However, it is true that in the amputee the lower speed gait of the intact animal continues to be used at relatively higher frequencies (Wilson, 1965; unpublished observations).

If it is true that the amputee gaits are just the speeded up, leg-deficient gaits of more slowly moving intact animals, then Bethe's plasticity phenomenon loses some of its intrigue. Although the plasticity is usually ascribed to adaptive reflex actions, it even seems possible that it is not altogether a reflex phenomenon. If it were not, then it might be possible to show that even nonadaptive amputee gaits occur under some circumstances. Amputee gaits 2 and 3 are part of the series of possible increasing frequency patterns which result after ablation of the mesotahoracic legs. Gait 1, with legs of one side in synchrony and sides alternating, is the next higher frequency pattern. Only recently, it has been shown that this pattern can be elicited in very excited animals (Wilson, 1965; unpublished observation). I have found this pattern in the grasshopper, *Romalea microptera*, the mole cricket or Jerusalem cricket, *Stenopelmatus*, and in the cockroach, *Blatta orientalis* Linnaeus (see Fig. 5.2). That it has not been seen in earlier studies on *Blatta* is probably the result of differences in equipment used for filming. Hughes' studies (1952; 1957) were made with a 32-frame per second camera which would be insufficient to allow resolution of leg movement patterns at the frequencies at which the novel gait occurs. On the other hand, the phenomenon can be observed in large grasshoppers without the aid of instrumentation, and it is surprising it has not been reported before. In the *Romalea*, mesothoracic amputee, the legs of one side move in synchrony when the frequency is only a few cycles per second (Wilson, unpublished observations). Under this condition the body falls from side to side as expected, the abdomen and even the thorax drag on the substrate, traction is very poor, and locomotion is quite inefficient. This pattern can only be elicited by sudden or extreme stimulation, the sort which ordinarily results in a rapid getaway. The behavior seems clearly a poor adaptation, not fitting the plasticity notion. Mole crickets show very similar behavior. In cockroaches the synchronous homolateral pair gait is used at very high frequencies and there does not appear to be any impairment of locomotion. The time available between leg steps does not allow for more than about one millimeter of fall of one side of the body of a two-centimeter long animal before that side is again supported by legs. In addition, at the speeds involved, some smoothing may occur due to aerofoil effects

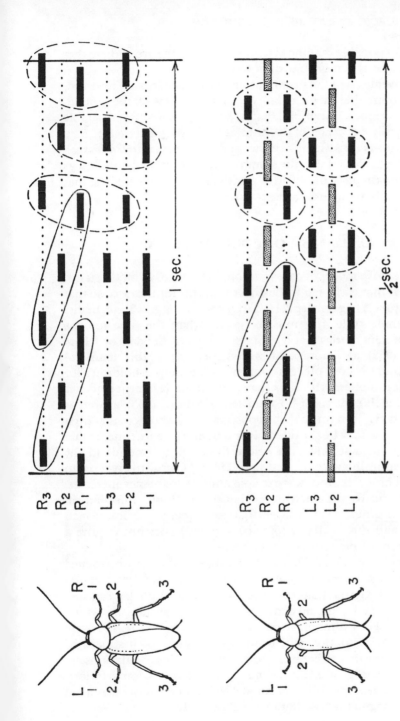

FIG. 5.2. A little known kind of result of amputation of the middle legs. The upper diagram records the movement pattern in a normal insect using the tripod gait. The lower diagram is from a rapidly running amputee. Stippled bars indicate protraction time for the stump of the amputated legs. The legs move in the tripod pattern, but only homolateral pairs are supporting weight much of the time. The amputee gait does not occur at the lower frequencies possible for tripod waking in intact animals. (from Wilson 1965.)

and it is also possible that the abdomen drags on the ground; neither of these has been demonstrated, however.

If the movements of the stumps of the amputated legs are recorded, it is often found that they oscillate without contact with the ground, and that their phase is normal, that is, halfway between comparable phase points in the cycles of the hindlegs and forelegs (see Fig. 5.2). This behavior is consistent with the model. However, in *Carausius*, Wendler (1964a) found that the stumps of the amputated middle legs moved approximately in synchrony with the forelegs, a finding that will apparently require a different explanation.

MECHANISM OF COORDINATION

In the most naive model of coordination, a chain reflex model, it can be supposed that each step is the direct stimulus for the next, so that stepping by leg 3 triggers leg 2, leg 2 triggers 1, 1 triggers 3, etc. In this case the whole cycle time must be greater than the time for one sequence of steps of the three legs of a side. The earlier data on *Blatta* (Hughes, 1952) are more or less consistent with this temporal requirement. However, other facts are not; for example, holding a leg still may not interfere with the others. Furthermore, recent evidence on *Carausius* (Wendler, 1964a) and *Blatta* (Wilson, 1965), as well as other insects (Wilson unpublished observations), shows that at high speed cycle time may be considerably less than sequence time, so that a hindleg steps a second time before the foreleg responds in the sequence beginning with the first step. This relationship gives rise to the reversal of locomotory wave propagation as frequency increases. Most emphatically it demonstrates that the oscillatory mechanism resides in a single segment, or that each segment contains an oscillator, and the oscillator (of each segment) does not require a resetting signal from another segment.

According to Bethe (1897c), and Matula (1911), legs on isolated insect thoracic segments can step alternately. Ten Cate (1928) reports that even after sagittal ganglionic hemisection a single leg can step rhythmically. Each segment contains oscillatory mechanisms which are capable of coordinating the muscles in the two legs. Likely mechanism of oscillation will be discussed later, but it should be pointed out here that either intraganglionic or reflex oscillations are possible. As a background for the more detailed discussion to follow, I will first suggest a coordinative model based on the idea of coupled endogenous segmental oscillators (Pringle, 1940).

Two other neuronally controlled behavior systems provide analogies. One is the control of the movements of the swimmerets of crayfish (Hughes & Wiersma, 1960; Ikeda & Wiersma, 1964; Wiersma & Ikeda, 1964). The swimmerets beat metachronally. If the abdominal nerve cord is isolated completely from input sources, a rhythm of motor discharge which is like that causing the normal beat persists. There is a delay between the ganglia of about 150 msec with activity always spreading from posterior to anterior. Repetition rate is about 1.5 c/s. The most posterior active ganglion (fifth) appears to drive the others. Removal of posterior ganglia does not stop the response, however. Both the fourth and third ganglia are capable of spontaneous action and can drive the ones ahead when they are disconnected posteriorly. The entire rythmic control mechanism, while inherent within the abdominal nerve cord and spontaneous, can be controlled by input including that from anterior centers via "command fibers" which need not have a rhythm related to that of the output.

A similar system is found in insects in the nervous control of ventilation. [For older reviews see Ten Cate (1931) and Fraenkel (1932), and for recent work Miller (1960) and Huber (1960)]. Each ganglion of the abdomen and thorax is capable of rhythmic respiratory control in the absence of peripheral feedback. The isolated ganglia have different rhythms, but when the ganglia are connected, the rhythms are coupled and the most rapid ganglion drives the others.

Several kinds of coupling of the segmental locomotory rhythms are possible. These may include both intracentral and reflex pathways. The segments may be connected either by means of excitatory or inhibitory influences and the influences may be either one-way or reciprocal. Several combinations of these possibilities could give rise to hypotheses which account for the described patterns of walking. A quite unproven but appealing one is the following. Assume that the three segments have different inherent frequencies under any given input situation, the metathoracic being the fastest. The ganglia have excitatory interconnections, but are self-limited so that mutual excitation does not lead to frequency runaway. An excitatory coupling will tend to draw the oscillators into synchronous activity, but if the coupling is weak the frequencies will remain different, and there will be only some statistical tendency for persistence of certain patterns of phase relationship between the oscillators ("relative coordination"). If the coupling is sufficiently strong, then all three will operate at the same frequency, but the inherently slower ones may lag in phase, producing the sequential timing of the legs. As the whole system increases in frequency, the phase lag may also increase, thus giving rise to the various frequency dependent patterns. A very similar model could be based upon inhibitory interrelationships between ganglia.

This model, depending upon loosely coupled oscillators, can also be applied usefully to some of the less common examples of insect locomotory patterns; those cases in which the phrase "relative coordination" is applicable (von Holst, 1939a; Wendler, 1964c). In these cases limbs may move at slightly different frequencies but still show preferential phase relationships. That is, two elements of the pattern will remain more or less constant in phase for many cycles but then begin to change in phase with each succeeding cycle until they come back to the original, relatively stable phase relationship. The coupling between segments is not sufficiently strong to produce phase locking or entrainment, and the phase drifts, but not uniformly. Wendler (1964b) has shown that the legs on the two sides of the larva of *Cantharis fusca* are not locked into regular alternation; instead they drift in phase but have a tendency toward synchrony. Adjacent legs on the same side alternate regularly. The adult *Cantharis* walks in typical insect style. During metamorphosis the organisms must both tighten, and reverse the sign of, the intrasegmental coupling. In the adult *Carausius* deprived of its middle legs and with its weight supported, Wendler (1964a) also showed "relatively coordination" between forelegs and hindlegs.

LEG REFLEXES AND EVIDENCE FOR PROPRIOCEPTIVE CONTROL OF LOCOMOTION

There is no question but the proprioceptive leg reflexes have a role in insect locomotion. Their presence is objectively demonstrated by the studies of Rijlant (1932a; 1932b), Pringle (1940), and Wilson (1965). Anatomical basis for the reflexes in *Periplaneta americana* (Linnaeus) is described in considerable detail (Dresden & Nijenhuis, 1958; Nijenhuis & Dresden, 1955), and electrophysiological studies of the sensory (Pringle, 1938a, b) and motor (Hoyle, 1964; 1965a) components are available. However, this knowledge of the existence and workings of the reflexes in isolation does not lead to an unambiguous understanding of their role in locomotion.

Tonic effect of proprioceptive input from the legs is evident in studies on posture Wendler (1961; 1964a) showed that specific sensory hair beds are involved in negative feedback control of body position in *Carausius*. Adding weight to the animal results in no change in the height of the body off the substrate until the weight on the legs is several times normal. Further increase results in abrupt collapse, apparently due to muscular insufficiency. When the hair beds are removed, regulation of height does not occur and body height and body weight are correlated. Hughes (1957) found that amputations led to alterations in the posture of the remaining legs of *Blatta*. The alteration is abrupt, but perhaps posture as well as walking coordination develop more precision of control as time goes on after the operation. Cockroaches can apparently learn a new leg coordination for cleaning the antennae after removal of the forelegs (Luco & Aranda, 1964). This learning most likely includes the perfection of a new posture which frees a mesothoracic leg from the function of body supporting. Studies on conditioned changes in leg position (Eisenstein & Cohen, 1964; Horridge, 1962) and motor neuron activity (Hoyle, 1965) may ultimately explain these long-term phenomena.

Phasic reflex effects are revealed when oscillatory inputs are used. The frequency and phase characteristics of reflex activity under oscillatory conditions have been largely ignored although such information is needed if the normal behavior is to be understood. From a very small number of examples one can select a wide range of variation of frequency capabilities in insect reflexes. In general, one expects at the upper end of the frequency spectrum of any reflex that the output will begin to lag in phase and finally the phasic component will attenuate to zero amplitude. To illustrate the range of possible frequency response capability, some diverse insect reflexes will be described.

Grasshoppers move the head in the following response when the visual environment is moved (the optomotor response). Thorson (1964) has shown that the response occurs with rotation velocities several times smaller than the relativel angular velocity of sun and earth. The animal responds to an oscillatory input of only 0.006 c/s, the response is maximal at 0.08 c/s, and the response fails at a few cycles per second. If leg reflexes were so slow, they could affect posture only.

Locusts have proprioceptive wing reflexes which are involved in flight control. In *Schistocerca gregaria* (Forskall) these influence a pattern of motor neuron activity which arises within the thoracic ganglia and which is not dependent upon the reflexes for its basic operation (Wilson, 1961). Stretch receptors at the base of each wing (Gettrup, 1962; 1963) are activated during the late part of each wing upstroke. The sensory feedback is thus capable of providing a timing signal for the CNS which could be used to keep central rhythm and wing movements in temporal register. However, experimental manipulation shows that the timing of the sensory return is irrelevant. Any pattern withthe same average frequency will produce the only known effect of this reflex; namely, the control of wingbeat frequency (Wilson & Gettrup, 1963; Wilson & Wyman, 1965). This reflex thus has a predominantly tonic effect analogous to that of postural regulation, even though the input contains information which could be used for cycle-to-cycle coordination. Other wing reflexes appear to be similar (Gettrup, 1964). Phase independence of the flight control system is not true for all inputs, however, as Waldron (unpublished data) finds synchronizing effects between wingbeat and a flashing light.

A faster reflex system is known in caterpillars of *Antherea pernyi*. Stretch receptors trigger motor responses at frequencies found in normal locomotion and these reflexes play a phasic role in peristaltic crawling (Weevers, 1965).

Proprioceptive reflexes in the legs of cockroaches have both a tonic and a phasic component. A sudden and maintained change of position imposed upon the leg results in greatly altered rate of firing of the motor neurons which then adapt to a new steady rate which is some function of the position (Pringle, 1940). The neuromotor changes resist the imposed movement of the leg. With oscillatory input, the response is also oscillatory at frequencies well above 20 c/s (Wilson, 1965). The maximum motor output occurs before the extreme position is reached and the phase of the output is constant over the whole frequency range found in walking (up to 20 c/s). During movement of one leg, the contralateral leg responds as well, but the response is opposite in phase (Pringle, 1940; Wilson, 1965). Again, the phase is constant over the frequency spectrum. Legs in other segments respond very weakly or not at all. When intersegmental proprioceptive reflexes can be demonstrated, they are always either exactly in phase or exactly out of phase with that of the moved leg. Their response is variable in sign, and it seems probable that this intersegmental reflex plays little role in walking coordination. They cannot account in a simple fashion for the phase relationships between the several legs, since the latter show a continuous variation over a wide range during walking.

REFLEX MODELS FOR WALKING COORDINATION

Proprioceptive reflexes of the type just described can be used to account for many of the observations on leg coordination (Horridge, 1965; Pringle, 1961). A simple idea which covers much of the observed behavior is that the separate legs are coordinated through their independent antigravity reflexes .Under this hypothesis intersegmental reflexes are not required. At rest, each leg supports a share of the body weight. If one or more legs are lifted, the remainder bear more weight and reflexly push harder. When the former legs reassume their load, others experience a lightening of theirs and tend reflexly to lift. An oscillation in one leg is thus the indirect cause of an antagonistic oscillation in legs which support the same body region. Within the segment the two legs oscillate reciprocally, partly because of direct proprioceptive reflexes. The rule that no leg lifts until the one behind is supporting can be due to this indirect coupling of separate reflexes via a purely mechanical linkage. While this kind of reflex effect undoubtedly occurs, it cannot explain intersegmental coupling in some situations. For example, in Wendler's experiments on *Carausius* (1964a), the animal was supported and the leg forces could not affect the weight borne by other legs (but the drag on one leg will be affected by other legs). Animals held upside down may move the legs in a coordinated way (von Holst, 1943). Cockroaches supported by the back may run in air for a few cycles (Hughes, 1957) or walk quite normally on a ball which they must hold up (Wilson, unpublished observations). In the latter case, the sign of all gravity reflexes would be reversed. Another argument against operation of a pure intrasegmental gravity reflex timing of the leg steps is that amputated legs continue to move their stumps, either in correct phase (Wilson, 1965) (Fig. 5.2), or in a new phase which is still dependent upon information about the phase of other legs (Wendler, 1964a).

Another kind of intrasegmental reflex is the step reflex described by Ten Cate (1936). If the whole cockroach or an isolated thoracic segment is dragged along a surface, the legs may step each time they are stretched a certain distance relative to the body. They lift, protract, and touch down, and are again stretched. This reflex is probably not of great importance in locomotion. It cannot time the stumps of legs not contacting the substrate, yet these stumps will often move normally. I have found that in grasshoppers which are walking with the hindlegs at a lower frequency than the others, the hindlegs have two different stride lengths with each protraction beginning at either of two widely separated points relative to the body. The protraction is triggered by a timing cue relative to the other legs, not a spatial cue related to its own posture. The stride length, however, may be determined by the degree of extension between steps.

It has been reported that coordinated walking can occur after an interruption of nervous connection between two thoracic segments

(Ten Cate, 1941). This is not easily confirmed (Hughes, 1957; Ponz & Estartús, 1951) and it is probably true that whatever intersegmental coordination remains is very poor. It is quite certain that normal walking utilizes nervous connections between the segments, since severing these connections always results in some deterioration of the ability to walk. These connections could be due to intersegmental proprioceptive reflexes also, although the elctrophysiological evidence for this is either negative (Pringle, 1940) or weak (Wilson, 1965). A kind of intersegmental reflex which might not be easily demonstrated with electrophysiological technique is one involving only inhibitory effects. It could be that one leg steps only when released from inhibition from a posterior one. However, holding one or two legs does not prevent the others from moving properly.

After amputation of some legs, the new gaits may or may not be consistent with models based upon intrasegmental antigravity reflexes or other intersegmental reflex coupling. Very often after amputation, protraction time for the remaining legs becomes smaller in proportion to stepping cycle time. Each leg must bear weight more of the time. The rule, "no leg can step until the next posterior is supporting weight," often holds (Hughes, 1957), but is clearly broken in the highest speed gain of mesothoracic amputees (Wilson, 1965; unpublished observations). Cockroaches suspended from a wire may use the diagonal rhythm without body weight sensation. According to Hughes, "This coordination persists for about 10 sec, after which the movements become more spasmodic and apparently discoordinated. These experiments indicate some measure of intersegmental coordination in the absence of drag or changes in the distribution of weight."

There is likely to be rather wide agreement now that, even though reflexes conspicuously affect insect walking, some degree of autonomous central nervous organization underlies the reflex superstructure (Bullock, 1965; Huber, 1962b; Hughes, 1965; Ponz & Estartús, 1951; Pringle, 1951; von Holst, 1948). Perhaps both central programming and reflex control are needed, or perhaps both exist and either is sufficient, as is true in earthworms (Friedländer, 1894). Interaction between central and peripheral rhythmic mechanisms is a subject of current interest (Bullock, 1961), and insect walking may provide a beautiful example. However, as yet there has been no clear demonstration of an inherent nervous rhythmicity related to walking behavior in any preparation. The most desirable test, deafferentation of the moving parts, seems only a remote possibility, though there is some separation of motor and sensory roots in the segmental nerves (Fielden, 1963).

Other autogenic nervous patterns have been demonstrated within central or ganglionic nervous structures in several phyla, however (Bullock, 1965). Within the Arthropoda several are known in addition to those mentioned in an earlier part [crayfish swimmerets (Hughes & Wiersma, 1960; Ikeda & Wiersma, 1964; Wiersma & Ikeda, 1964); insect ventilation (Fraenkel, 1932; Huber , 1960; Miller, 1960; Ten Cate, 1931); locust flight (Wilson, 1961)]. The classic demonstration was that of Adrian (1931) who showed a respiratory rhythm in the isolated nerve cord of *Dytiscus marginalis*. Similarly, the motor neuron discharge patterns controlling singing in cicadas (Hagiwara & Watanabe, 1956) and crickets (Huber 1962a; Huber, 1963), or heartbeat in crustaceans (Hagiwara, 1961; Maynard, 1955; 1960), or copulation in mantids and cockroaches (Roeder et al., 1960) do not require special temporal patterns of input.

Can any evidence be put forward which strongly favors a central rhythm hypothesis? There is the observation that an amputee, even at moderate speeds, may begin to walk with the rhythm appropriate to six legs, and then adjust to a new pattern (see Fig. 5.3). Another indication is that if a leg of a cockroach is injected with epinephrine it adopts a peculiar posture, flexed and not touching the substrate, due to gross hyperactivity of the campaniform sensillae, but if the animal is forced to run, the leg will be used in a normal fashion (Milburn, 1963). Another set of observations which seem consistent only with a hypothesis containing the central rhythm notion is the following. Electrical stimulation of the nerve cord of a beetle (*Edeodes* sp.) can elicit rhythmic leg movements in an animal held upside down (Wilson, unpublished observations). Stimulation of the thoracic ganglia themselves causes only spasmodic or tetanic contractions. If the stimulation is via the posterior nerves the hindlegs are usually tetanized, but in some cases all legs respond well. The segments may be independent or locked in some phase with respect to each other. The pattern is sometimes 3, 2, 1, 3, 2, 1, with opposite sides alternating. More often it is some pattern like 3, 2, 1, 2, 1, 3, 2, 1, 2, 1, or 3, 2, 1, 1, 2, 1, 1, 3, 2, 1, 1, 2, 1, 1. The more anterior segments are more easily activated and have the highest frequency. Holding or amputating a leg does not affect the pattern of the others. With the input at frequencies between 10 and 200 c/s, hundreds of stimuli are needed before a neat reaction pattern develops. The head is not necessary.

Pure nervous oscillators which could perform suitably are possible; at least electronic analog models based on networks of simulated neurons have been made (Harmon, 1964; Reiss, 1962). A good working hypothesis seems to be that each segment contains a

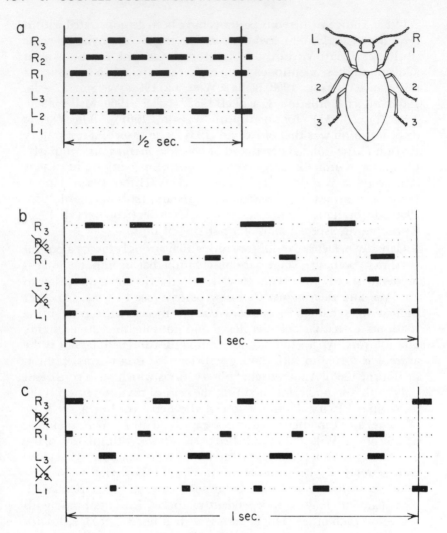

FIG. 5.3. Normal tripod walking in a beetle. Legs L₃ and L₁ were not recorded (*a*). After amputation of legs R₂ and L₂ the locomotion may begin with the tripod pattern minus the two legs and then become erratic (*b*) or gradually shift, without change in frequency, into a perfect diagonal rhythm (*c*).

reciprocal inhibition network which creates the timing signals for sets of antagonistic muscles and that the segmental oscillators are coupled intracentrally to provide the relative phasing. Reflexes are superimposed upon the central scheme, and in general reinforce it. When central rhythm and reflex feedback are not complementary, as after some amputation combinations, either may dominate. When central excitatory state is high, due, for example, to an extreme exteroceptive input, the central rhythm overrides the proprioceptive feedback. When central excitatory state is low, feedback reflexes dominate. At low walking speeds the latter situation prevails, but at the highest speeds the same central rhythm is manifest regardless of proprioceptive input conditions.

This idea is no more than an hypothesis, but it is in tune with current trends in neural theory. Bullock (1961) has said the pendulum is swinging from a dominant view in which reflexes were the main element of neurophysiological explanations, to a view which emphasizes the role of endogenous nervous rhythms. This changing view cannot be more dramtically illustrated than by the writings of one man. In 1935 von Holst wrote "Analysis of the separate factors concerned in coordination shows that the stimulation of proprioceptors in each leg during running is principally responsible both for the seriation of the leg in the order of leg movements and for the nature of this order itself," and in 1948, "An exact analysis of the coordination of movements in arthropods and vertebrates leads to the rejection of older explanations in terms of reflex physiology and to a dynamic conception of the process in the central nervous system, ... This conception carries with it the implication that locomotion is caused by automatic elements that work in the rhythm of locomotion and are prior to the motor elements."

THE WALKING SYSTEM: RECENT ANALYSIS

Thanks largely to the work of Keir Pearson and his collaborators, we now know something about the neural system that controls walking in the cockroach (see Pearson, 1976, for review). What we know is largely consistent with what Wilson assumed. In particular, we know that there are central pacemakers that generate the stepping rhythms of the legs–one pacemaker for each leg. Figure 4.24b portrays the electrical oscillations in one such pacemaker and the resulting rhythmic bursts of impulses in the flexor motor neurons. We also know that the six pacemakers send coupling signals to each other. One may actually record the "hups" passing back and forth between the pacemakers. These coupling signals are the neural basis for the magnet effects, the phase-dependent accelerations and decelerations of the pacemakers. The coupling signals coordinate the oscillators. The coordination between oscillators maintains the functionally coherent stepping patterns (gaits). Finally, we know that both the strength and the timing of the bursts of motor neuron activity triggered by the pacemakers is adjusted by reflex mechanisms.

This very recent advance in our understanding is worth spelling out in some detail. It has profound consequences for our understanding of behavior and for our understanding of the nervous mechanism of behavior. Because behavior exhibits sustained and coherent patterns of action, whose functional character is inescapable, we speak of purpose in behavior. Because the details of these patterns vary from moment to moment and from occasion to occasion in a manner that adapts the general pattern to particular circumstance, we speak of intelligence in behavior. The conceptual problem is to understand how these two properties of behavior can both be present simultaneously. How can one have the variety of action that leads us to speak of intelligence and yet adhere to the overall pattern or general tendency that leads us to speak of purpose and function? The functional coherence of most machine action is purchased at the price of extreme stereotypy. Variety of action matched to variety of circumstance is precisely what machines lack, a lack that makes machines seem stupid. If we conceive of animals as machines, we must ask how the actions of these machines can display so much variety while still adhering to a central purpose and promoting a given function. The modern analysis of locomotion illustrates one way in which this is possible. It thereby enriches our general understanding of behavior.

At the same time, the analysis casts new light on an old controversy about the neural mechanisms of behavior—the controversy between the connectionist school of thought and the holistic or nonconnectionist school of thought. The intelligence of behavior, the immense capacity to vary the details of action so as to cope with particular circumstances, is at the root of this controversy, too. The holistic school points to this variety and asks how such variety could be produced by a machine whose actions depend on the specific character of each part (each neuron) and the pattern of connections between parts (the pattern of synaptic connections). Would not such a machine have to have different parts or a different pattern of interconnections in order to produce each variation in the pattern of action? If so, a neural machine of this connectionist type cannot be the basis of animal behavior, because the variations in the patterns of even simple actions are infinitely numerous, or nearly so. The paper by Weiss in Chapter 8 develops this holistic criticism at some length. Lashley's famous paper on the problem of serial order in behavior makes a similar argument (1951).

The modern analysis of locomotion undermines the holistic argument by exhibiting a connectionist system that can generate an infinite or nearly infinite variety of outputs. Furthermore, the general pattern that one gets out of this system (the ballpark pattern, so to speak) is determined by a single control signal. Thus, the commanders of this system, the still higher units of behavior, may easily select one from among many possible forms of walking by setting the value of one signal. The walking circuit itself fills in all the details required by the specified form and then varies those details to adapt the chosen pattern to the fluctuating circumstances encountered during the walk.

The conceptual importance of this development justifies spelling out a model of the walking circuit that both goes beyond and simplifies the available neurophysiological facts. There is little doubt, however, that the outlines of the model are correct. Furthermore, the outlines apply with minor modifications to the explanation of locomotion in animals ranging from millipedes to mammals (Pearson, 1976; Stein, 1977).

The core of the walking system is the complex unit of action diagrammed in Fig. 5.4. This unit, which controls the stepping of a single leg, is dominated by an oscillator. The oscillator sets the pace by periodically triggering bursts of signals in the flexor motor neurons, as shown in Figure 4.24b. Accompanying the burst of impulses in the flexor motor neurons is an inhibition of activity in

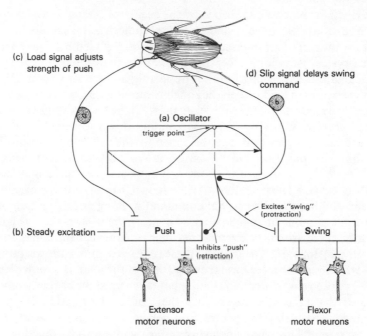

FIG. 5.4.   The circuit that controls the stepping of a single leg. Its components are: (a) An oscillator that gives the stepping rhythm. Near the peak of its cycle the oscillator triggers a swing command. The swing command excites the motor-neuron circuit that swings the leg forward and inhibits the push circuit, the circuit that presses the leg to the ground and draws it back, thereby pushing the animal forward. (b) A steady excitatory input that keeps the push circuit active whenever it is not inhibited by the swing command. (c) A sensory input from receptors in the leg joints that adjusts the strength of the push to match the load. (d) A sensory input that delays or prevents the swing command whenever a leg to the rear slips and fails to take up the load.

the extensor motor neurons. The excitation of the flexors protracts the leg—swings it forward through the air.

The duration of this protraction command is independent of the oscillator's period, which accounts for the third of Wilson's five rules, namely, "Protraction time is constant."

What varies when the pace of stepping varies is the retraction time, the interval during which activity in extensor muscles supports the roach and pushes it forward. The extensor motor neurons are active throughout the cycle except when interrupted by the protraction command, the duration of which does not vary. When the stepping period is long, when, that is, the stepping oscillator cycles slowly, the intervals of extensor activity are long. As the cycle period shortens, so does the interval of extensor activity. The variable duration of extensor activity accounts for Wilson's fourth rule, "Retraction time varies."

The rhythmic pattern established by the oscillator is modified by two other circuits, one a reflex circuit, and one a servomechanism circuit, or servo-circuit for short. The servo-circuit uses sensory signals fed back to the central nervous system from joint receptors and/or stretch receptors. The sensory feedback adjusts the strength of the supporting and pushing contractions to match variations in load. When the roach is running up a wall the load on the "pushing" muscles is great because they must lift the body's weight against the force of gravity. When the roach is running down a wall, no pushing is necessary because gravity draws the roach forward. These variations in the load that the pushing muscles must move necessitate compensatory variations in the strength of the contraction. A servo-circuit along the lines described by von Holst and Mittelstaedt in Chapter 7 takes care of this problem. Neither the circuits that command walking nor the oscillator that controls the stepping of a single leg need concern themselves about this detail.

Finally, there are reflex circuits that delay or prevent the command that swings the leg forward. The input to these reflexes comes from receptors that detect whether another leg has taken up some of the load. If another leg slips (or if it has been amputated), the load is not taken up at the ordinary time. The failure of the leg behind to take up the load in the fraction of a second preceding a to-be-triggered protraction delays or prevents the triggering of the protraction. This trigger-delaying reflex, whose normal function is now obvious, explains the intelligence of the post-operative roach, whose adaptation to experimentally contrived circumstances was celebrated in Chapter 1. The amputated middle leg fails to take up the load at the normal time. This failure delays the protraction of the front leg. When the rear leg hits the ground, it takes up some of the load, which releases the delayed protraction of the front leg. Result: The front and hind legs step 180° out of phase instead of in phase. The trigger-delaying reflex converts the tripodal gait to a diagonal gait. This intelligent adjustment of the pattern of movement is made automatically. It does not require the intervention of higher levels; nor does it involve learning. The intelligence is wired-in.

The complex unit of action that controls the stepping of a single leg combines all three of the currently understood elementary units of action—the oscillator, the servomechanism, and the reflex. This complex leg-stepping unit is in turn a component in the still more complex unit that controls walking. The six leg-stepping units in the walking unit—one for each leg—are coordinated by coupling signals that pass back and forth between the oscillators (Fig. 5.5). The oscillators that control legs directly across from one another maintain a constant phase relationship, a difference in phase of 180° (Fig. 5.5a). This accounts for Wilson's second rule, "Contralateral legs of the same segment alternate in phase."

On the other hand, the three oscillators ranged along either side of the animal do not maintain a constant phase-relationship. Rather, they maintain a fixed delay or temporal lag: The rearmost oscillator peaks first; then, at some fixed delay, the middle oscillator peaks; finally, after a further delay, the front oscillator peaks (Fig. 5.5b). The fixed lags between oscillators account for the first part of Wilson's fifth rule, "The intervals between steps of the hindleg and middle leg and between the middle leg and the front leg are constant..." The fact that the front oscillator lags the middle, which in turn

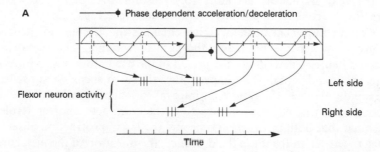

FIG. 5.5. Intrasegmental and intersegmental coupling of the stepping oscillators. (a) Intrasegmental coupling maintains a constant phase difference of 180°. In von Holst's terms, the coactive position of the two intrasegmental oscillators is 180° out of phase. Hence, bursts of electrical impulses in opposite flexor neurons alternate. (b) Intersegmental coupling maintains a constant temporal lag between adjacent oscillators. Each oscillator peaks at some fixed time after the oscillator behind it. Hence bursts of flexor activity proceed from back to front. The period of oscillation in this illustration would yield the diagonal gait portrayed in 5.1b. The form of intersegmental coupling assumed in this model derives from Stein's (1971) work on swimmeret coordination in the crayfish. Stein's findings are more congruent with Wilson's rules of insect walking than are the findings of Pearson and Iles (1973), possibly because the cockroach's walking does not conform strictly to the rules (Delcomyn, 1971 a, b).

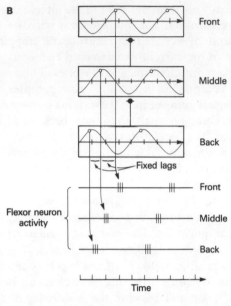

FIG. 5.5.   *(contd.)*

lags the rear oscillator, accounts for Wilson's first rule, "A wave of protraction . . . runs from posterior to anterior." (see Fig. 5.5b)

The final component of the walking circuit is the "command" neuron or neurons, by which the brain sets the pace of walking. The signal in the command neurons determines the period of the oscillators (Fig. 5.6). With a strong command signal—"Full speed ahead!" so to speak—the oscillators cycle rapidly. Hence, the retraction interval for each leg, which is the cycle period minus the constant protraction interval, gets shorter (Rule 4). Remember that both protraction time and the lag in protraction onset from one leg to the leg in front are fixed. Hence, the duration of the metachronal sequence of protractions is the same regardless of the period of oscillation. Hence, shortening the period (the cycle time for each leg) shortens the interval between a foreleg step, which marks the end of one wave, and a hindleg step, which marks the onset of the next (second part of Rule 5).

Increasing step frequency automatically changes the gait, as Wilson shows in Fig. 5.1. The changes in gait are simply changes in the phase relationship between the three oscillators on either side. As shown in Fig. 5.7, oscillators with a fixed-lag coupling *must* change their phase relationship when their period changes. Shortening the period increases the phase difference.

In summary, one signal from a higher level of the system, a signal that sets the speed of running, automatically determines a gait appropriate for that speed. By varying this one signal, many different gaits are obtained from a

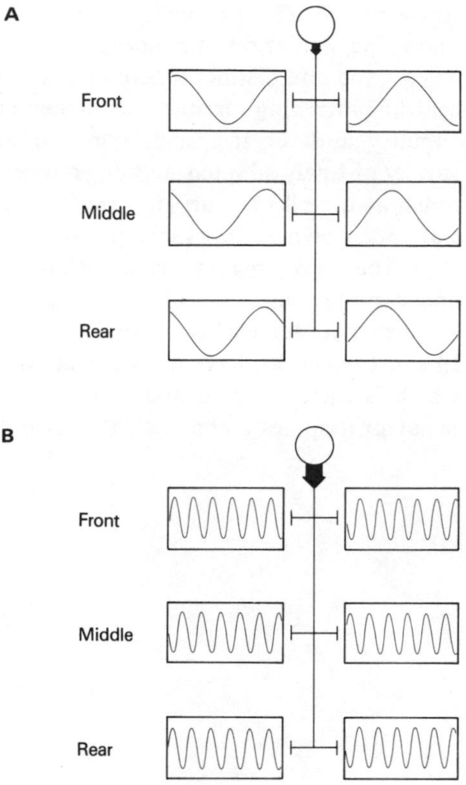

A

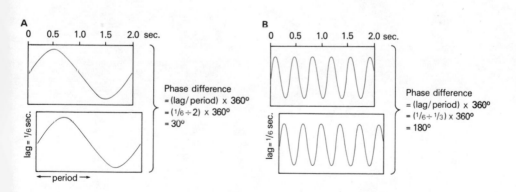

Front

Middle

Rear

FIG. 5.6. The gait is selected by means of a command signal from higher units. The schematic neuron passing down the middle of each panel, making excitatory synaptic connections with the oscillators, represents the carrier of the command signal. The stronger the command signal, the shorter the period of the oscillators. (a) A weak command signal (symbolized by thin arrow) yields a slow, one side at a time gait, such as shown in Wilson's figure 5.1a (b) A strong command signal (symbolized by thick arrow) yields a tripodal gait.

B

Front

Middle

Rear

A

0   0.5   1.0   1.5   2.0 sec.

lag = 1/6 sec.

←period→

Phase difference
= (lag/period) × 360°
= (1/6 ÷ 2) × 360°
= 30°

B

0   0.5   1.0   1.5   2.0 sec.

lag = 1/6 sec.

Phase difference
= (lag/period) × 360°
= (1/6 ÷ 1/3) × 360°
= 180°

FIG. 5.7. When the temporal lag between oscillators is fixed, the phase difference depends upon how rapidly the oscillators are cycling. (a) If they cycle once in 2 sec and the one lags the other by 1/6 sec, then the phase difference is 1/12 of a cycle or 30°. (b) If they cycle once in 1/3 of a second, then the phase difference is half a cycle, or 180°.

single system. This system is a connectionist system—a system that depends upon a particular set of connections between neural elements, each of which has a fixed and distinct function. The rich variety of gaits generated by this central patterning circuitry is further enriched by the load-compensating circuitry and the trigger-delaying circuitry. The result is the bewildering variety of finely adapted stepping movements that we actually observe in the roach as it walks at varying speeds through fluctuating circumstances—up walls and down walls, over rough and smooth surfaces frought with trips and slips. The steps it makes "have, within wide limits, a fluid order of occurrence and varying qualities." The walking is done "now in one way and now in another, but each way is . . . 'fitted to the occasion' (Bartlett, see Chapter 1)." In short, when we have a system of coupled oscillators set a basic pattern, which is then trimmed and modified by reflex circuits and servo-circuits, behavior assumes a character that is both purposive and intelligent.

6 Servomechanisms: The Control of Taxes in the Coastal Snail

SERVOMECHANISMS

The Sidewinder antiaircraft missile is one of the more spinechilling products of 20th-century engineering. It pursues its prey with a purposiveness and "intelligence" that would fascinate a Renaissance clockmaker. If the prey attempts to avoid the oncoming missile, the missile alters its course so as to nullify the evasive maneuvers of its prey. The basic principles underlying the design of this lethally purposive machine are the same principles that direct the movement of its biological namesake, the sidewinder rattlesnake, which preys upon small warmblooded animals in the deserts of the southwestern United States. The missile, like the snake, is steered by heat sensitive receptors. The missile has its infrared receptors in an array all around the nose; the snake has his in the pits beneath his eyes. Jet planes are excellent sources of infrared radiation; so are warm-blooded animals in the cold desert night (Bullock & Diecke, 1956; Dullemeijer, 1961; Noble & Schmidt, 1937; Shin-schi & Goris, 1974). The mechanism which keeps the missile oriented toward the hot rear-end of a jet plane is a servomechanism. The mechanism that keeps a snake oriented toward its intended prey is probably also a servomechanism, but we know more about the missile's machinery, so we will use the missile to explicate the concept of a servomechanism.

As shown in Fig. 6.1, the angle,α, of the missile's steering vanes is determined by the *relative* strengths of the infrared (radiant heat) stimuli impinging upon the heat sensitive "eyes" on opposite sides of the nose of the missile. In Fig. 6.1 the heat source is to the right of the missile's orientation, hence the right eye receives more heat than the left eye. The imbalance in the

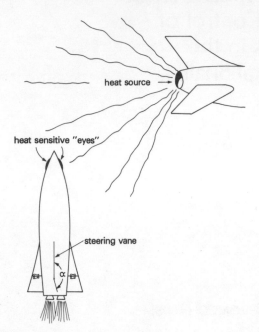

FIG. 6.1. A sidewinder missile turning in pursuit of the hot exhaust of a jet—an illustration of a servomechanistic orienting behavior of the kind called a taxis.

signals from the two opposed sensors causes the steering vane to bend to the right. The greater the imbalance between the two signals, the more the steering vane is bent. The bend in the steering vane causes the missile to turn toward the right. As the missile turns toward the right, the discrepancy between the heat received by the right eye and the heat received by the left eye grows less and less. In consequence, the bend in the steering vane grows smaller. When, the missile has turned so that it is oriented directly toward the source of heat, the two eyes receive equal amounts of heat and the steering vane is straight. Should the pilot veer his plane to the left, the missile's left eye will be more strongly stimulated than the right eye. This imbalance will be relayed to the steering motors, which will bend the steering vanes to the left. The resulting left-turning response on the part of the missile will continue until the missile again points directly at the heat source.

When the missile has approached close enough to the plane, a proximity detector triggers a reflex response in the missile—an explosion that destroys both the missile and the plane.

The orienting mechanism of the sidewinder missile is a servomechanism: There are two input signals, one from each heat-sensitive eye. These two signals are compared by simple electronic circuits, that is to say, the signal from one eye is subtracted from the signal from the other eye. The assignment of signs in the mathematical representation of this electronic subtraction is arbitrary, but, influenced no doubt by the traditionally negative attitude toward left-handedness, let us imagine that the signal from the left eye is subtracted from the signal from the right eye. Subtracting the left-hand signal from the right-hand signal yields an error signal. The sign and magnitude of the error signal is equal to the difference between the two inputs. In Fig. 6.1, where the source of heat is to the missile's right, the signal from the right eye is greater than the signal from the left, so the error signal is positive. If the heat source were to the left, the error signal would be negative. The error signal determines the action of the servomechanism. In the case of the missile, a positive error signal causes a turn to the right; a negative error signal, a turn to the left. The effect of the error signal on the response machinery (the steering vane) is such that the resulting turn tends to reduce the discrepancy between the two inputs, which reduces the error signal. This is termed negative feedback.

Distinction Between a Servomechanism and a Reflex

The central role of a negative feedback in determining the character of the movements produced by a servomechanism sets servomechanisms apart from reflex mechanisms. In a reflex mechanism, the feedback, if any, from the movement to the sensory input that triggered the movement is irrelevant. It has no effect on the ongoing movement. The ongoing movement is like an antiaircraft artillery shell, once launched its course is fixed. There are reflex orienting movements: The fast jump, called a saccade, which your eyes make when there is a flash in the periphery of the visual field, is a reflex orienting movement. But, the orienting actions of the sidewinder missile and of many animals under similar circumstances is a servomechanistic (or *cybernetic*) action. The feedback from response to input is crucial. If this feedback is altered, the character of the movement changes.

Suppose, for example, a source of heat is attached to one side of the misile, so that when the missile turns the source turns with it, as illustrated in Fig. 6.2.

heat source

FIG. 6.2.   An homunculus (little man) alters the output–input relation in a sidewinder missle. Normally, turning the steering vane (output) reduces the inequality in the heat received by the eyes (the input). Here the right eye continues to receive most of the heat from the torch, no matter how strongly the missile steers to the right. Hence, it steers ever more strongly to the right and flies in tightening circles. A unilaterally blinded moth does the same thing, because no matter how much it turns, the unblinded eye transmits a stronger signal than the blinded eye.

This arrangement alters the feedback from response to input. Turning toward the hotter side no longer reduces the discrepancy between the heat received by the two eyes. As a result, the missile turns ever more tightly toward the side on which the source of heat is fixed. An analogous experiment may be conducted with a moth. Moths orient toward light with a servomechanistic response closely analogous to the heat orienting response of the missile; that is, they turn toward the more brightly illuminated eye until both eyes are equally illuminated. If one eye is blinded, a moth flies in ever tightening circles, because no matter how much it turns, the signal from the unblinded eye remains stronger than the signal from the blinded eye (Fraenkel & Gunn, 1961).

Taxes

When a servomechanism maintains an animal's orientation with respect to some stimulus while the animal walks, crawls, flys, etc., the resulting oriented progression is called a *taxis*. Taxes are distinguished firstly by the stimulus to which the animal orients. If it orients to light, the mechanism is called a phototaxis; if to gravity, a geotaxis; and so on. Taxes are distinguished secondly by the direction maintained with regard to the stimulus. If, for example, a snail orients away from the pull of gravity, the mechanism is a negative geotaxis; if it orients toward light, the mechanism is a positive phototaxis.

From the description of the missile's (and moth's) orienting mechanism, one might think that it did not have a positive or negative sense. After all, the eyes are equally illuminated, and there is therefore no turning tendency, whenever the animal (or missile) points either directly toward or directly away from the source of stimulation. Both of these orientations are *equilibrium* orientations, orientations at which the two inputs cancel and there is no error signal. However, as shown in Fig. 6.3, only one orientation is a *stable equilibrium*, an orientation to which the animal will return whenever it deviates.

The two input signals whose comparison generates the error signal in a servomechanism need not both originate from sensory receptors. One input may be derived from sensory receptors while the other input, called a command or set point signal, derives from complex processes at higher levels of the motor system. One example of this use of a servomechanism is described by von Holst and Mittelstaedt in the paper reprinted in the next chapter: Many organisms sense the direction of gravitational pull by means of organs called *statocysts*. Figure 6.4 is a highly schematized representation of a statocyst. The statocyst is a sac lined with sensory hairs upon which a little stone sits. As the animal tilts this way and that the weight of the stone bends the hairs more or less in one direction or another. By this simple means the

A
Unstable equilibrium

B
Stable equilibrium

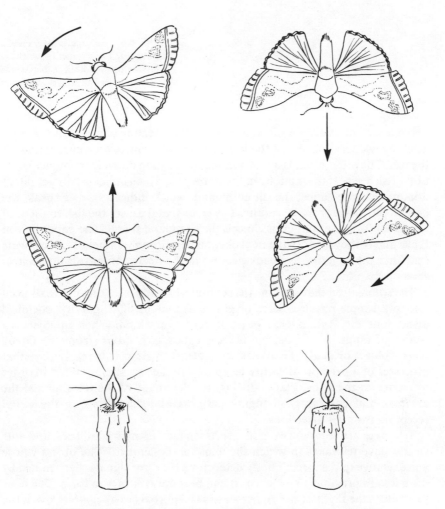

FIG. 6.3. (*a*) The light tropotaxic steering mechanism in a moth flying directly away from the source of light is in unstable equilibrium. So long as the moth maintains its course perfectly (lower picture), the steering mechanism will steer straight ahead because both eyes are equally illuminated (the equilbrium condition). However, any deviation from the equilibrium condition (upper picture) results in a steering movement that increases the deviation, turning the moth toward the light, away from the unstable equililbrium. The turn continues until the moth faces the light. (*h*) When the moth is flying directly toward the light (upper picture) its steering mechanism is in stable equilibrium; any deviation (lower picture) results in a steering movement that decreases the deviation. Thus, the moth always returns to this orientation.

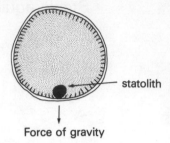

statolith

Force of gravity

FIG. 6.4.   Schematic diagram of a statocyst. The manner in which the little stone (statolith) bends the sensory hairs indicates the direction of gravitational pull.

nervous system receives a signal indicating the direction of gravitational pull. Such signals serve as one of the inputs to the tilt control servomechanism in the fish. The other input is a "tilt command" coming down from higher levels of the fish brain. If the input from the statocysts, which indicates the actual tilt does not exactly cancel the tilt command, which indicates, so to speak, the desired tilt, an error signal results. The error signal causes the fish to tilt until the signal from the statocysts cancels the command signal. The paper by von Holst and Mittelstaedt in the next chapter describes a number of experiments that alter the negative feedback process in the operation of this tilt-control servomechanism.

The stimulation that governs the servomechanistic orienting in a taxis need not be a simple physical force or gradient, such as light, gravity, chemical dispersions, etc. Rather it can be an object of some kind. When an object is a source of input to a taxis, the taxis is called a *telotaxis* (from the Greek telos = object or goal). Telotaxes, in contrast to simpler taxes, require that processes of a perceptual nature be applied to the raw sensory input in order to recognize the telos, that is distinguish the image of the telos amidst the complex and constantly changing patterns of light falling on the visual receptors from all directions.

Telotaxes are common even in insects. In fact, many wasps, bees, and ants clearly have telotaxes in which the telos can be learned! The object whose angle relative to the insect's body determines the error signal is determined by the animal's previous experience. It can be quite arbitrary in form. The telos that guides the flight of the digger wasp as it approaches its egg-burrow, is the pattern of sticks, stones, pine cones, etc. that surround the location of the hole (Tinbergen & Kruyt, 1938). Improbable as it may seem to psychologists, there is compelling evidence that the wasp commits this pattern to memory during a spiral reconnaissance flight that it makes before leaving the vicinity of the hole! (See Chapter 11.) Clearly, such a taxis involves perceptual mechanisms of a high order, and a memory as well.

It is lack of insight into the nature of pattern-recognizing processes that has until recently defeated man's attempts to built telotaxic missiles. Indeed, an early proposal for a telotaxic missile suggested the use of a biological pattern-recognizer (Skinner, 1960). Pigeons were to be trained to peck at the images of battleships on a radar screen. The pigeons were then to be installed in radar-equipped missiles. Objects within the radar field would be projected onto a radar screen inside the missile, before which stood the animate pattern recognizer. If the radar image of a battleship appeared on the screen, the pattern recognizer would go into action, that is, the pigeon would begin pecking at the image. The error signal was to be derived from the locus of the pigeon's pecks. The farther from the center of the screen the pigeon pecked, the greater the error signal. I mention this proposal here to emphasize the fact that the difficulties in constructing telotaxic machines center around the problem of pattern recognition and not around the problem of generating appropriate motor commands once pattern recognition has been achieved. In recent years computer engineers have solved the pattern recognition problem sufficiently to permit the construction of terrain recognizing guided missiles. These missiles physically embody the telotaxic principle.

Taxes, like reflexes and oscillators, may be combined to produce integrated behavior sequences. In the following paper Fraenkel shows that combinations of three simple taxes—a negative geotaxes, a negative phototaxis, and a positive phototaxis—may underlie an appreciable part of the entire behavioral repertoire of one organism: the coastal snail.

On Geotaxis and Phototaxis in *Littorina*

The coastal snails (genus) *Littorina* have been a frequent object of study in sensory physiology. Mitsukuri (1901) initiated the investigation of the phototaxis in *Littorina*. He gave a good description of the negative phototaxis, but did not recognize the negative geotaxis. Instead, he spoke of a negative hydrotaxis, which was his name for the snail's tendency to crawl up out of the water. Bohn (1905) published an extensive analysis of the sensory

*Translated from: Fraenkel, G. Beiträge zur Geotaxis and Phototaxis von Littorina. *Zeitschrift für vergleichende Physiologie (Abt. C der Zeitschrift für wissenschaftliche Biologie)*, 1927, 5, 585–597. Used by permission of Springer Verlag and G. S. Fraenkel. Translated by C. R. Gallistel, who is grateful to Gottfried S. Fraenkel for reviewing the translation.

physiology of *Littorina*. From the responses of *Littorina* he evolved a theory of tropisms. Several important observations from his experiments have so far been ignored, while other observations, for example, the response to two black screens have led to strong controversy. Later, his ideas on the periodic movements of the snail in synchrony with the tides were further investigated by Morse (1910) and Haseman (1911).

That the different authors worked with different species should perhaps not be overlooked. Mitsukuri worked with *Littorina exigua* in Japan, Bohn experimented on Littorina rudis on the coast of Normandy, the Americans worked with *Littorina littorea* in Woods Hole, while here in Naples the little *Littorina neritoides* has been available for my studies. Perhaps some of the controversy can be traced to differences in the experimental animals. By and large, however, it has been established that despite certain species-specific characteristics the behaviors are markedly similar.

In view of these numerous previous investigations, my intent has been only to expand our knowledge of certain aspects of these interesting snails. Namely, it seemed to me of interest to attempt to construct a picture of the life of *Littorina neritoides* out of results from experiments on its sensory physiology together with field observations.

THE GEOTAXIS

The geotaxis was extensively investigated by Kanda (1916) at Woods Hole. His method was as follows: He let a number of snails crawl upon an inclined plane and determined the percentage of snails who crawled upward as a function of the inclination of the plane. The result was unequivocal: The greater the inclination the greater the percentage of snails that crawled upwards. Only under two conditions could downward crawling be observed: (1) When direct sunlight came from above, snails crawled downward. This response can be traced to a negative phototaxis rather than a positive geotaxis. (2) On a dry surface the snails oriented themselves with the head down and crawled downwards. This was taken as a true case of a positive geotaxis. I could not find this behavior with my Littorina. On a dry surface the snails would not crawl, once the accompanying water had evaporated. Rather they remained stationary, glued themselves to the substrate, and closed their shell.

Kanda posed the question whether the negative geotaxis might not be a purely mechanical effect of the distribution of mass to the shell. The snail might orient upwards because the heavy shell pulled the rear end down. This notion is controverted by Kanda's observation of a positive geotaxic response when the snail is on a dry substrate. If the negatively geotaxic orientation is to be explained by a purely mechanical effect, then at least the positive geotaxis will have to be explained on some other basis.

The assumption that the snail is forced to crawl upwards by the downward pull of its shell can be refuted in a simple fashion. I stuck a piece of wax to the snail's shell. The wax had a lighter specific gravity than water and the piece was chosen sufficiently large so that the shell was pulled (floated) upwards. If the shell determined the orientation, the snails should have crawled downwards. That was in no way the case. The animals gave a completely unaltered negative geotaxis when placed on a vertical wall, although the shell was clearly pulling upwards. *This proves that the pull of the shell does not determine the orientation.*

Finally, Kanda noted that a small percentage consistently responded differently from the rest. If orientation arises from the distribution of mass, then every normally constructed snail must respond with a negative geotaxis. The fact that exceptions occur indicates that the orientation arises from internal factors and not external conditions. This conclusion is not completely compelling. The occurrence of exceptions could mean that some snails are differently directed. The direction by purely mechanical orientation from the pull of the shell could influence the response as well as an orientation through statocyst stimulation.

Littorina possesses a highly developed statocyst with a refined statolith and it is likely that the geotaxic orientation is a function of the statocyst. A direct proof is difficult, because extirpation [of the statocyst] is almost out of the question in such a small snail.[*]

The geotaxis of *Littorina* can be beautifully demonstrated on a turntable. The centrifugal force is in principle the same as the force of gravity. Both forces impart an acceleration to a body. If the snail finds itself on a turntable it is to be expected that the animal will crawl toward the axis of rotation against the pull of the centrifugal force. This is in fact the case.

A large number of *Littorina* were placed near the rim of a round glass dish 28 cm in diameter. When the snails had firmly attached themselves to the dish, the water was poured out, so that it would not spill during centrifuging. The turntable turned at approximately 160 rotations per minute. The result can be seen in the photographs (Fig. 6.5a–d). Picture (a) was taken before the beginning of rotation. The animals are all near the rim. Picture (b) shows the distribution after 5

---

*Editor's note: This has since been done—Geuze, 1968; Lever & Geuze, 1965; Wolff, 1975, 1970.

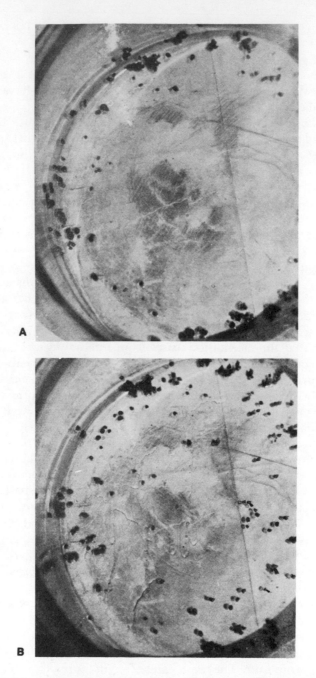

FIG. 6.5. The centripetal movement of *Littorina* on the turntable at four moments: Picture (*a*) before the onset of rotation; picture (*b*) after 5 minutes; picture (*c*) after 10 minutes; picture (*d*) after 15 minutes. The turntable was placed perpendicular to the incident sunlight (November midday sun). Because of shadows, the camera could not be placed directly over the turntable.

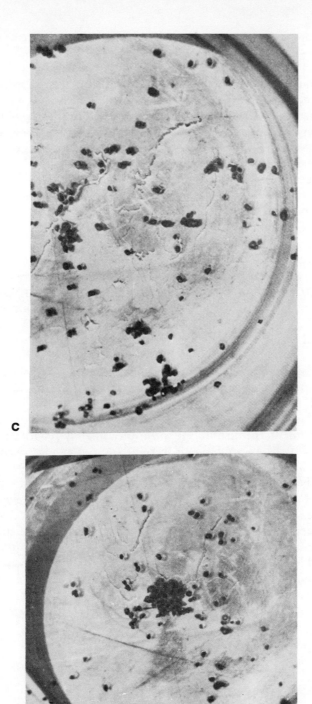

FIG. 6.5. *(contd.)*

minutes, Picture (c) after 10 minutes, and Picture (d) after 15 minutes of rotation. Clearly the animals wander away from the rim toward the axis of rotation. They assemble in a clump at the center. It is also easy to see that nearly all of the snails are oriented with their head toward the center and the tip of the shell toward the outside. That not all snails are so oriented is because between the stopping of the rotation and the taking of the photograph some moments elapsed and some snails reoriented themselves toward light and gravity.

The centrifugal acceleration at 160 rotations per minute is very great. It is given by the formula

$$\text{Centrifugal acceleration} = 4r\pi^2 n^2$$

where r is the distance from the axis and n the number of rotation per second. At the beginning of the experiment r was about 12 cm. The rotation per sec was 2.7. Thus, the centrifugal acceleration was

$$4 \cdot 12 \cdot 3.14^2 \cdot 2.7^2 \simeq \approx 3000 \text{ cm/sec}^2$$

which is approximately three times the acceleration imposed by the earth. The acceleration decreases in proportion to the snail's approach to the center, until it is equal to zero.

If one uses lower rates of rotation one obtains the same result. In one experiment, the turntable made approximately 100 rotations per minute. Out of 42 animals 10 were at the center after 5 minutes rotation, and all 42 after 30 minutes rotation.

Initially I was particularly interested to see if the crawling speed depended on the strength of the centrifugal force. However these experiments did not produce results. This was to be expected because even under normal circumstances the crawling speeds of different individuals are so different that no comparisons can be drawn. It appeared to me that at 160 rotations per minute the snails assembled more rapidly in the center than at 100 rotations per minute. However, it must be kept in mind that at 100 rpm the centrifugal force is already less than the force of gravity when the snail is within 8 cm of the center.

GEOTAXIS AND PHOTOTAXIS

We turn now to an investigation of the way in which geotaxis and phototaxis in *Littorina* work together and/or against one another.

A number of *Littorina* crawled on a vertical plate. The plate stood alternately either perpendicular to or parallel to the direction of incident light. Thus, the animals were illuminated alternately from directly overhead or from one side. The incident light was approximately parallel to the horizon. Thus, the negative phototaxis causes the animal to crawl in a horizontal direction. If the plate is vertical and parallel to the incident light, then the negative geotaxis and negative phototaxis will be simultaneously active. If we imagine the effects of the light and gravity as incident forces, then theoretically the animal should move along the resultant of the two acting forces.

This is in fact the case, as Fig. 6.6 shows. The animals crawled on the rough side of a plate of milkglass. It is easy to trace-off with a pencil behind the animal the course of crawling. During the segments of the trail marked *a*, *c*, and *e* the plate was perpendicular to the incident light. Under these circumstances, only gravity is effective, because the snails are illuminated from overhead. The courses run more or less vertically. During the segments *b* and *d* the

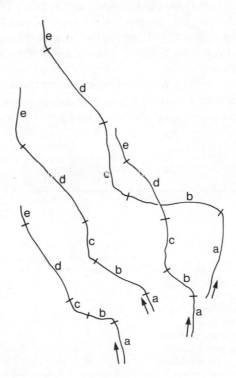

FIG. 6.6. Crawling traces from 4 *Littorina* on a vertical plane of milkglass. During the segments marked *a*, *c*, and *e*, the incident light was perpendicular to the milkglass, during segments *b* and *d* the incident light was parallel to the milkglass, coming horizontally from the right.

plate was parallel to the incident light. The courses run along a resultant of the two impinging forces. The angle the animals pursue with respect to vertical is not quite the same for different animals. This indicates that the relation between the physiological effects of the light and gravity stimuli varies from snail to snail.

With strong illumination the negative phototaxis can be so strong that no negative geotaxis is evident. One hundred snails were placed in a 12 cm high beaker filled with water to a depth of 4 cm. The beaker was illuminated alternately from above or below by a 50 candle power light at a distance of 50 cm from the bottom of the beaker. At the beginning of each experiment the snails were on the beaker bottom. After, in each case, a 10 minute period of illumination, the snails were distributed as shown in Table 6.1.

This experiment shows that the geotaxis is weakened by the phototaxis (when the phototaxis acts in opposition, as in Experiments 2 and 3). In addition it emerges that the effect of the light is stronger outside the water than in the water. With illumination from above the snails do not crawl out of the water (though many crawl up to the waterline).

In no case could I detect any appreciable number of snails crawling downward. Even when strongly illuminated from above, they never turned around and crawled downward, rather they either glued themselves firmly to the glass or they released their hold and fell down.

The just described experiments show that phototaxis and geotaxis can be simultaneously and independently operative. This produces an orientation along the resultant of the light and gravity stimuli: In

TABLE 6.1

	had crawled up to the waterline	had crawled up out of the water	of which x number had reached the top of the beaker	had remained on the bottom of the beaker
Experiment 1: Light from below-------	5	80	40	15
Experiment 2: Light from above-------	50	10	—	40
Experiment 3: Strong midday (August) light from above--	20	3	—	77

contrast, experiments are now described which lead to the conclusion that the phototaxis can depend qualitatively on the geotaxis [or, more accurately, on the direction of the gravitational force relative to the snail].

A number of snails were placed in a glass beaker filled to the rim with water. A cover was carefully slipped over the beaker so as to leave no airspace. The animals first crawled in the direction of (i.e., away from) the (horizontally) incident light, then climbed up the wall whose (inside) face was toward the light. Upon reaching the cover, they crawled over onto the underside of the cover and now, surprisingly, they crawled upside down along the cover toward the incident light. When they arrived at the vertical wall toward the light, they stopped. Evidently they could go no farther. They did not crawl downwards, nor would they crawl away from the light along the underside of the cover. In a short time, all the snails were assembled at this point.

This experiment is particularly clear under the following arrangement. Two cuvettes 12 × 13 × 3 cm are placed one atop the other in a water filled beaker. Figure 6.7 shows a cross-section of the experimental arrangement. The open end of the cuvettes face the light. A number of *Littorina* are placed on the lowest surface. They soon begin to crawl. They crawl along the ground away from the light, climb the vertical wall, crawl in photopositive fashion along

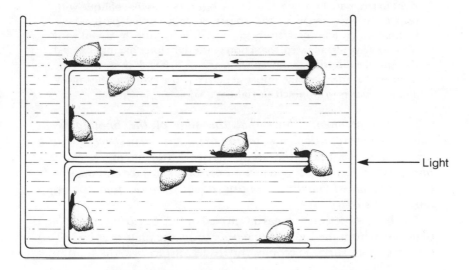

Light

FIG. 6.7.   Crawling path of *Littorina* placed on the lower inside surface of two glass cuvettes one atop the other. Shown in cross section.

obliquely
incident light

FIG. 6.8.   Path crawled by *Littorina* on the inside of a cylinder illuminated by light oblique to the axis of the cylinder.

the underside of the horizontal surface. Upon arriving at the end, they crawl upwards into the second cuvette. Here the course continues in the same fashion. The course ends atop the uppermost surface at the wall away from the light. Here the snails can go no further; they remain stationary.

In looking through the literature I found that this behavior had already been recognized by Bohn. He illustrated this change in the sign of the phototaxis by an elegant experiment (see Fig. 6.8). In describing this experiment I want to use Bohn's words (Bohn, 1905):[1]

Repetition on the interior of a horizontal glass cylinder. Glass tube placed approximately along the axis of the light field. The littorina follow at first the course of the inferior genetrix of the cylinder, from right to left; but, if the direction of the light is somewhat oblique with respect to this genetrix, the snails enter a curved path whose inclination grows progressively greater; little by little, in accord with what we have already seen, the action of the light force having changed its sign, the direction of movement becomes inverted; thus, when the littorina have reached the upper genetrix of the cylinder, they move along it, but now from left to right [p. 33].

These experiments show that the sign of the phototaxis in Littorina *depends upon the situation of the animal in space, that is to say, it depends upon the static sense.* Littorina *are negatively phototaxic when crawling upon a horizontal surface and positively phototaxic when crawling hanging down from the underside of a horizontal surface.*

The basic experiment is easily carried out: A *Littorina* crawls on a plate away from the light. If one now turns the plate over by 180° so that the upper surface becomes the under surface and the snail now

---

[1]Translator's note: In Fraenkel's text the quotation is given in the original French.

hangs down while crawling, then the snail turns round and crawls straight toward the light. *However, the change in the sign of the phototaxis only occurs under water. In air,* Littorina *respond photonegatively even when upside down.*

One might think that the sign of the phototaxis is determined by the pressure or the pull of the shell. This is, however, clearly not the case. If one fastens a piece of wax to the shell, then during right side up crawling the shell pulls upward and during upside down crawling the shell is pushed against the animal.

THE RESISTANCE OF *LITTORINA*

It has long been known that *Littorina* remain alive for many days out of water. They close their shell, and, when returned to water, become active again. Bohn (1905) reported that *Littorina rudis* could endure dryness for at most 6 days. Issel (1918) kept *Littorina neritoides* 3-4 weeks in dry air and found them all alive afterwards. Since June, 1926, I have kept a number of *Littorina neritoides* in a can open to the dry air. After 7 months all were still alive and awoke in water after 10-20 minutes.

If one brings Littorina into fresh water, they instantly pull back into their shell and keep the shell tightly closed. If one tosses a *Littorina* with a closed shell into fresh water, then under a binocle one can readily see that the cover is opened a small crack and then immediately reclosed. One sees this happen some number of times and then the shell remains firmly closed. After 8 days in fresh water, 7 animals were dead, the other 3 became immediately active when returned to seawater.

THE LIFE OF *LITTORINA NERITOIDES* IN NATURE

From the results of the sensory physiology investigations in conjunction with field observations,[2] I wish now to attempt a reconstruction of the life led by *Littorina neritoides* under natural conditions.

Littorina neritoides lives in the Mediterranean on rocky coasts. The animals sit 3-8 meters above the waterline in cracks and crevices. Normally the snails are in dry surroundings. They have their shells

---

[2]Carried out for the most part at the marina piccola in Capri.

closed and are firmly glued to the rock. When the rocks are wetted by waves the animals crawl about. Their nourishment consists of algae on the rock walls.

Assume that a *Littorina neritoides* finds itself on the bottom in shallow water near the shore. *Littorina* crawl toward dark objects. The rocks on the shore must appear dark relative to the open water. Therefore the snail turns toward the shore (negative phototaxis). Having reached the rocks, it crawls upward (negative geotaxis). On the way up, it encounters a crack that cuts horizontally across the rock wall. The snail crawls without hesitation into the depths of the crevice (negative phototaxis). Arriving at the depth of the crevice, it crawls back upside down along the roof of the crevice out into the open. The obstacle is overcome. Were the phototaxis incapable of changing its sign, the snail would remain hanging at the innermost part of the crack and never reach the surface of the water. The change in the phototaxis has, in other words, an important biological significance.

The snail reaches the surface of the water. The crossing of the surface offers no difficulty (the opinion of Haseman to the contrary has been refuted by Kanda). The snail stops, however, at the waterline if the sun shines brightly down upon the rocks. Once out of the water the snail crawls upward so long as the substrate is moist. If, on its way, it encounters a hole or crack, it crawls in (negative phototaxis). It does not, however, ordinarily crawl out, because the reversal of the phototaxis only occurs in water. Thus it stays in the innermost angles of the cracks and holes. Those are the places where Littorina are to be found in nature. The biological significance is clear. In the cracks the animals are shielded from direct sunlight. Here also moisture can long be retained.

If the water in the crack dries up, the animal pulls back into its shell and closes the cover. If the crack is filled with water by high seas, then the animals come to life again. Now they can crawl out along the ceiling of the crack. Finally they reach the zone that is only reached by the waves of a strong sea. Here the periods of dry sleep become longer and more frequent. That the snail is in danger of drying out is improbable. According to my observations the snails withstand the danger of drying out for at least half a year and probably much longer. The intervals between big stormtides are appreciably shorter. According to field observations *Littorina* never reaches the zone that is sprayed only by strong storm tides; rather they remain appreciably lower, so that the highest snails must endure at most a few weeks of dryness even in summer. One must consider that the animals live on steep shores where waves can lick extraordinarily high up.

SUMMARY

1. *Littorina* crawl on a turntable away from the centrifugal force straight toward the axis of rotation.
2. The geotaxic orientation does not occur for purely mechanical reasons through the pull of the heavy shell, rather it is probably a function of the statocysts.
3. When gravity and light act simultaneously, *Littorina* crawl along the resultant of the two forces.
4. *Littorina* when right side up on a horizontal substrate crawl negatively phototaxically, when hanging upside down from a horizontal substrate they crawl positively phototaxically. The sign of the phototaxis is dependent on the situation in space.
5. On the basis of the results of the sensory physiology investigation and field observations it is possible to construct a picture of the life of *Littorina* in nature.

POTENTIATION AND DEPOTENTIATION

In addition to showing that taxes may be combined to generate a behavioral sequence, Fraenkel's paper introduces a principle of coordination that will play a fundamental role in our analysis of action when we consider the hierarchical structure of action systems. The principle, which one sees in the reversal of the snail's phototaxes, is the principle of potentiation and depotentiation. Sensory signals indicating that the animal is upside down and under water reduce or abolish the potential for activity in the neural circuit that mediates the snail's negative phototaxis. Reducing the potential for activity in a neural circuit is what I shall call depotentiating that circuit. At the same time, the potential for activity in the neural circuit mediating the snail's positive phototaxis is increased. If the snail is exposed to a light gradient (a necessary activating condition), this circuit will now control the snail's orientation vis-a-vis that gradient. This effect—increasing the potential for activity in a neural circuit so that it readily comes into play given the relevant external input—is what I shall term potentiation. The appropriate external inputs I will call the activating conditions.

The potentiating and depotentiating effects of being upside-down and underwater constitute a new role for sensory input to play in the shaping of behavior. In the reflex, the function of the sensory input is to elicit or trigger the action of the unit. In the oscillator, sensory pathways play a variety of modulatory roles. They modulate the frequency of the oscillator; they modulate the trigger points, that is, the point in the oscillator's cycle at which a particular output is triggered; and they modulate the duration and intensity of an output once it has been triggered. In the taxis, the sensory input guides the action of the animal's steering mechanisms. The sign (plus–minus, left–right, up–down) and the intensity of the motor signal to the steering musculature is determined by the discrepancy between two different sensory signals or the discrepancy between a sensory signal and some internally generated reference signal. Thus, each type of functional unit has introduced a new role for sensory input to play.

The "upside-down" and "underwater" sensory signals, however, play none of these roles: They do not elicit a motor action, since in the absence of an appropriate guiding input the snail does nothing. They do not modulate frequency, trigger points, or the strength and duration of motor signals; nor do they guide the motor action by giving rise to error signals through a comparison process. Rather, they enable (potentiate) or disable (depotentiate) a functional unit. That is, they place one functional unit in a state of readiness to be active. As we will see in the chapters on hierarchical control, descending potentiating and depotentiating signals regulate all of the functional units. Indeed, they regulate whole systems of functional units by potentiating and depotentiating circuits at higher levels of the nervous hierarchy that coordinate the activity of ensembles of functional units.

Neurophysiological Mechanism

The capacity for summation beneath a threshold (i.e., nonlinear summation), which Sherrington recognized as a salient feature of the synaptic transmission process, provides a physiological mechanism for mediating potentiating and depotentiating effects in behavior. A potentiating input can raise the level of excitation at a synapse (or remove an inhibitory influence) without producing enough excitation to exceed the threshold for an output. This potentiates the synapse: Other inputs may now sum with the effects of this potentiating input and thereby exceed the threshold for output. The potential for transmitting excitation is increased. Depotentiating inputs act in just the opposite fashion: They reduce the likelihood that other inputs will be able to produce an output, that is, they reduce the potential for transmitting signals across the synapse.

Figure 6.9 portrays this hypothesized neurophysiological basis for potentiation and depotentiation. The neuron labeled b represents interneurons in the servo-circuit that mediates the positive phototaxis. These interneurons relay signals originating in the eye ("light signals") to the turning machinery. However, the threshold for excitation of neuron b by these light signals is so high that these signals are ordinarily ineffective. The interneurons

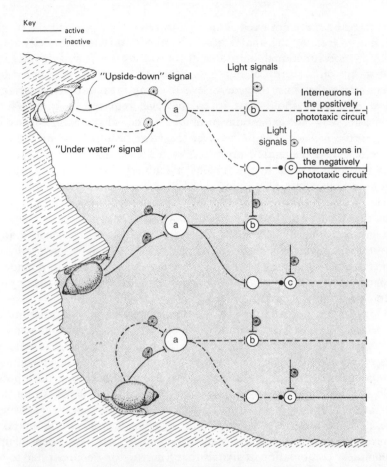

FIG. 6.9. A highly conjectural neural circuit, showing that the principles of synaptic function elucidated by Sherrington can explain how the snail's positive light taxis becomes operative only when the snail is upside down and under water, while his negative light taxis is operative at all other times. The operation of the same circuit is shown at three different stages in the snail's progress from the ocean bottom to a niche above the water, where it stops. The neurons that are active (i.e., transmitting signals) at a given stage in its progress are drawn in solid lines. Those that are not transmitting are drawn in dashed lines. At the top and bottom of the figure neuron *a* is inactive, hence neuron *b*, which would be potentiated by *a*, is also inactive. Since the inactive *b* is a crucial component of the circuit mediating the positive phototaxis, the snail has no functional positive phototaxis. In the middle of the figure neuron *a* is active, because both its inputs are active. Hence, *c* is depotentiated (inhibited) and *b* is potentiated. Now the positive phototaxis is functional and the negative is not. The illustrated mechanism is one among many possible. One plausible alternative would be to have the circuits mediating the opposing phototaxes depotentiated and potentiated by the imposition or removal of presynaptic inhibition (a mechanism explained in any text on neurobiology, e.g., Kuffler & Nichols, 1976).

163

represented by b are not excited enough to relay the signals to the turning machinery. Hence, the snail's positive phototaxis is ordinarily depotentiated—non-functional, incapable of controlling the flow of signals to the muscles (bottom and top of Fig. 6.9). When the neurons represented by a become active, they raise the general level of synaptic excitation in b, bringing it close to the threshold, that is, to the level required to initiate signal conduction. Now, the excitations produced by the light signals easily exceed the threshold for activating b because these excitations build on the near-threshold level of excitation produced by the tonic input from a. Hence b relays the light signals to the turning machinery and the snail's positive phototaxis comes into play (middle of Fig. 6.9).

Activity in a also depotentiates synaptic transmission at interneurons in the circuit that mediates the negative phototaxis. In Fig. 6.9, these interneurons are represented by c. The short inhibitory interneurons between a and c convert the signals in a into an inhibitory effect, that is, an excitation-suppressing action at c. The tonic suppression of excitation in c renders c incapable of relaying light signals to the turning machinery; so the negative phototaxis drops out of play.

In Fig. 6.9, the potentiating and depotentiating effects of a are assumed to be mediated by the effects of a upon b and c. There are other well-known ways of accomplishing the same result. For example, activity in a might control the effectiveness of the light signals in the two circuits by means of a mechanism known as presynaptic inhibition, in which case a would act upon the inputs to b and c. Only very recently has it become possible to demonstrate these potentiating and depotentiating effects electrophysiologically (Krasne & Wine, 1975; Wine & Krasne, 1972), so the exact mechanism is still unknown. However, the principle is clear: Potentiation and depotentiation depend upon the nonlinear combination of signals that Sherrington demonstrated to be a special feature of synaptic transmission. The combination of signals is nonlinear because the combined effect is greater than the sum of the individual effects. Neither the light signals acting alone nor the potentiating signal acting alone can produce activity in neuron c. Acting in combination, however, they do produce conducted activity.

The nonlinear combination of synaptic inputs must also underlie the biconditional decision-making function of neuron a. A biconditional decision is a decision that depends on two conditions being met. The decision to potentiate the positively phototaxic circuit and depotentiate the negatively phototaxic circuit occurs only when the snail is *both* upside down *and* under water. In Fig. 6.9 it is assumed that this decision hinges on whether the neuron a is or is not active. Neuron a becomes active only when both inputs to it are active, the input that indicates the snail is upside down and the input that indicates the snail is under water. Neither input alone activates a; but in combination they do. In this case, the nonlinear combination of synaptic inputs mediates a biconditional decision. The same principle may be used to implement multiconditional decisions. In fact, the electronic equivalent of this nonlinear combination of inputs—the so-called AND gate—is the basis for all of the decisions that a computer makes.

The principle of selective potentiation and depotentiation, operating within the latticelike hierarchy of the neural circuits that control behavior, will be examined at length in subsequent chapters. In the next chapter, however, we consider a final set of principles that play an important role in coordinating the interactions between units whenever several units are "on stage" at the same time. These principles come under the head of reafference and efference copy. The next chapter defines and explicates these concepts, and, in the process, extends our sense of the important role that servomechanisms play in behavior.

7

Reafference and Efference Copy

The servomechanisms featured in the preceding chapter were taxes. Another kind of servomechanism, the so-called optokinetic reaction, provides a point of departure for considering reafference and efference copy. In visual taxes, the error signal derives in one way or another from visual angle, that is the angle between the stimulus source and the longitudinal axis of the animal's body. The more this angle departs from some equilibrium, the more the animal attempts to turn back toward the equilibrium orientation. In the optokinetic reaction, the turning tendency depends upon angular velocity rather than upon angle per se. That is, the strength of the turning reaction depends upon the rate at which a patterned field of light sweeps across the photoreceptive surface of the eye.

The optokinetic reaction can readily be demonstrated by placing almost any visual animal inside a large vertical drum with black and white vertical stripes painted on its inside wall. In these introductory remarks I use the common housefly as the subject, but a human being reacts similarly. If the drum begins to revolve around the animal, alternating dark and light bands sweep across the visual receptors. The number of degrees of visual angle that the pattern moves across the animal's eyes in one second is termed $d\alpha/dt$ in Fig. 7.1. This symbolization of the rate of motion of the pattern is the standard way of indicating the change in angle ($d\alpha$) per change in time (dt) in the calculus. The movement of the pattern across the animal's photoreceptors

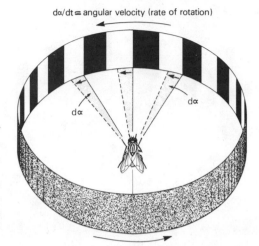

dα/dt = angular velocity (rate of rotation)

dα

dα

FIG. 7.1.   The angular velocity of the pattern of light on the eye is the ratio between the change in visual angle ($d\alpha$) and the change in time (dt). In this illustration, the fly is assumed to be standing still, so the rate at which the pattern sweeps across the eye is equal to the rate at which the drum rotates.

causes the animal to rotate in the same direction as the pattern is moving. The more rapidly the animal turns, the more slowly the light pattern sweeps across its photoreceptors. If the animal rotates at exactly the same rate as the visual field itself, then the light pattern on the eye is stationary; $d\alpha/dt$ = 0. In other words, the optokinetic reaction slows or arrests the sweep of patterned light across the eye.

The rate at which the pattern sweeps across the eye is the difference between the rate at which the drum turns and the rate at which the animal turns. If we let the turning rate of the visual field (the drum) be represented by dF/dt and the turning rate of the animal be represented by dA/dt, then the equation

$$d\alpha/dt = dF/dt - dA/dt$$

expresses the physical facts. To belabor this point still further, I represent the same set of facts diagrammatically in Fig. 7.2a. The point needs belaboring because it is easy to forget that the sensory signal (m) that indicates visual field motion does not depend simply upon the objective motion of the visual field, that is, it does not depend simply on dF/dt, the rate at which the drum is turning. Rather, the sensory signal, upon which the rest of the animal's brain must depend for information about what the world is doing, depends upon $d\alpha/dt$, the rate at which patterned light sweeps across the photoreceptors. And, what is happening at the eye is not necessarily the same as what is happening out there in the real world. What is happening at the eye is $d\alpha/dt$, which is the difference between what the world is doing and what the fly is doing. The fact that the motion signal from the eye to the brain must depend on the difference between dF/dt and dA/dt is represented diagrammatically in Fig. 7.2b.

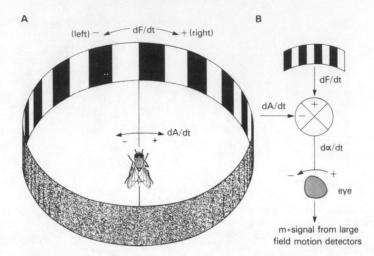

FIG. 7.2.   (*a*) The rate at which the pattern sweeps across the fly's eye is the difference between the rate at which the field rotates (*dF/dt*) and the rate at which the fly rotates (*dA/dt*). (*b*) The neural signal, *m,* indicating motion of the visual field across the eye depends on *dα/dt*, which is the difference between *dF/dt* and *dA/dt*. Keeping track of the flow of cause and effect in an action controlled by a servomechanism can be difficult. Block diagrams, of which this is an example, are useful in keeping things sorted out. However, one must be careful to keep the signs straight. Note that if *dF/dt* = –2 (i.e., the field is rotating *left*ward at 2°/sec) and *dA/dt* = +2 (i.e., the animal is rotating *right*ward at 2°/sec), then *dα/dt* = (–2) – (+2) = –4; hence, the motion signal would be proportional to 4 and have a *negative* sign (i.e., the signal would indicate that the visual input was sweeping toward the *left* edge of the eye).

EXAFFERENCE AND REAFFERENCE

Because the motion signal depends on the difference between *dF/dt* and *dA/dt*, the same signal arises from two completely different states of affairs: Either the world may be moving or the animal may be moving. When the drum turns to the right and the animal stands still, the motion detecting circuits in the eye give a signal indicating motion to the right (Fig. 7.3a). In this case, the signal represents what the world is doing. When the world stands still and the fly in Fig. 7.3b turns to its left, the motion detecting circuits give the same signal as before. Now, however, the signal no longer represents what the world is doing; rather it reflects what the fly is doing. The problem for the fly's brain is how to distinguish one case from the other. In one case, the sensory signal (called an *afference* in neurobiology) is called *exafference* (ex meaning "from outside"). In the other case, the exact same afference is a *result* of the animal's own action; hence it is called *reafference*. The problem for the animal's nervous system is to distinguish reafference from exafference.

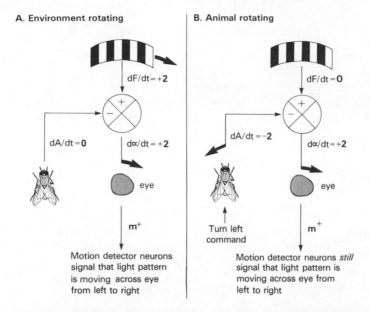

A. Environment rotating

B. Animal rotating

$dF/dt = +2$

$dF/dt = 0$

$dA/dt = 0$ $d\alpha/dt = +2$

$dA/dt = -2$ $d\alpha/dt = +2$

eye

eye

m^+

Turn left command

m^+

Motion detector neurons signal that light pattern is moving across eye from left to right

Motion detector neurons *still* signal that light pattern is moving across eye from left to right

FIG. 7.3.   The problem of distinguishing exafference from reafference arises from the fact that two very different events can make the visual input sweep across the eye. (*a*) The animal stands still and the field rotates to the right; hence the visual input sweeps across the eye toward the eye's right edge, producing a positive (=rightward) signal from the motion detecting neurons in the eye. The signal (*m*) is called an *ex*afferent signal because it was generated by *ex*ternal movement, movement of the environment. (*b*) the environment stands still and the animal rotates to the left; hence the visual input again sweeps across the eye toward its right edge. Since this is the same input as received by the eye under the conditions portrayed in (*a*), the signal (*m*) is also the same. Only now the signal is called a *re*afferent signal because it is a *re*sult of the fly's own movement.

The experimenter—a *deus ex machina*—is perfectly well able to distinguish exafference from reafference. He observes from outside the situation and can tell whether the motion signal represents motion of the visual field, motion of the animal, or both. The motion detectors in the eye can not make this distinction. They respond when a pattern moves across them—whether because the world is moving, because the animal is moving, or because both the animal and the world are moving. If the organism judged motion solely on the basis of what the eye told it, it would have no way of distinguishing signals caused by environmental motion from signals caused by the animal's own motion: *It would have no way of distinguishing exafference from reafference!*

One consequence of this ambiguity is that animals ought to be paralyzed by their optokinetic reaction. Suppose some other functional unit sends out motor commands that produce a rotation of the animal to the left (at say a

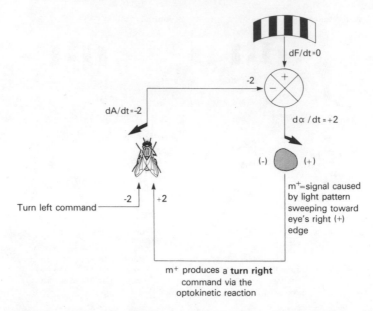

FIG. 7.4.   The diagram of the optokinetic reaction that we began constructing in (*b*) of Fig. 7.1 is now complete. It allows us to see that any turn-producing motor command from some other functional unit (the turn-left command) should generate an opposing command from the optokinetic unit.

rate of 2°/sec). This rotation to the left results in the pattern of light from the world sweeping across the fly's eyes *toward the right* (Fig. 7.4). Such a stimulus should give rise to a *reafferent* "right motion" signal from motion detecting circuits in the eye. The optokinetic unit feeds these motion signals to the motor system in such a way as to cause a correctional turning, that is, a rightward turning (Fig. 7.4). The correctional turning from the optokinetic system opposes the turn that gave rise to the reafferent signal in the first place. The question arises: What keeps the animal from being paralyzed by the opposing actions of the initial turn command and the subsequent optokinetic reaction?

EFFERENCE COPY AND COROLLARY DISCHARGE

Von Holst and Mittelstaedt's influential answer to this question was the concept of *efference copy*. Before putting forward the efference copy explanation, they rejected the first explanation that springs to mind. Once it is realized that the optokinetic reaction would counteract turn commands from other functional units, it seems reasonable to assume that any such commands from other units are accompanied by a strong inhibition of the optokinetic reaction. This inhibition would prevent the optokinetic unit from counteracting the commands.

There have been two versions of this theory. Some theorists have followed the Sherringtonian idea that interactions between functional units must be mediated by way of a sensory stimulus to one unit produced by the motor action of another unit. They have suggested that the inhibition of the optokinetic reaction came from sensory receptors in the muscles and joints that would be excited by the animal's moving. Other theorists have suggested that the signal inhibiting the optokinetic interneurons was centrally generated at the same time as the command to rotate. Thus, the inhibitory signal to the optokinetic reaction would be a corollary of the turn left signal. Centrally generated corollaries of motor commands have been termed *corollary discharge.* Von Holst and Mittelstaedt begin their paper on "The Reafference Principle" with an experiment demonstrating that both versions of the optokinetic inhibition theory are wrong for the simple reason that the optokinetic reaction is *not* inhibited during spontaneous turning.

The experiment involves twisting a fly's head 180° around the axis of the neck. A fly with its head thus twisted has the right and left edges of its eye reversed. When the fly spontaneously turns to its left, the reafferent motion signal from the motion detectors in its eye has a sign opposite to the sign it would ordinarily have. Ordinarily a light pattern that moves toward the eye's right edge also moves toward the fly's right side. When the head is rotated 180° about the the neck, the reverse is true. A light pattern that moves toward the fly's right moves toward his eye's left! The result (Fig. 7.5) is that the optokinetic reaction— *if it is not inhibited during "spontaneous" turning*— should reinforce and prolong any spontaneously arising turn command. Since this reinforcement and perpetuation of spontaneously initiated turning is what von Holst and Mittelstaedt observed in their experiments, they concluded that the optokinetic reaction is *not* inhibited when a turn is commanded by other functional units.

So, if the optokinetic reaction is not inhibited during turns commanded by other functional units, why does it not counteract the commands from other sources? And, more generally, how does the nervous system distinguish exafference from reafference? Von Holst and Mittelstaedt postulate that the animal makes use of a copy of the initial turn-commanding signal. Any motor signal is called an efferent signal, or simply an *efference,* by neurobiologists. A copy of such a signal is an *efference copy.* Von Holst and Mittelstaedt realized that a copy of the initial command was just what one needed to offset the reafferent signal generated by the commanded action. Suppose some event in the environment, for example, the movement of an object in the periphery of the animal's visual field triggers a reflex turn to the left. Assume that the strength of the motor signal to the turning apparatus is *minus* 2, where the minus signifies left and 2 indicates how fast a turn is ordered. When the turn is

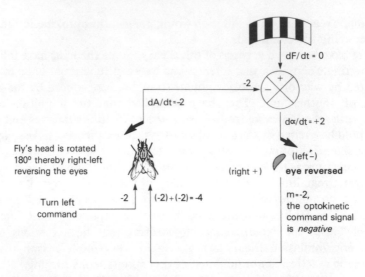

FIG. 7.5. Normally the optokinetic reaction would oppose the turn commands from other functional units, as shown in Fig. 7.4. But if the eye is rotated 180°, as in this figure, the sign of the reafferent signal is thereby reversed. When the animal turns to the left, the signal (*m*) produced in the motion detecting neurons by that movement is negative rather than positive. Hence, the turn command generated by the reafferent signal has the same sign as the command that initiated the turn. The optokinetic reaction now reinforces the turn commands from other units rather than opposing them, and the animal turns continually.

executed, the visual field sweeps toward the eye's right side at a rate proportionate to the speed of the turn. Hence, the commanded turn produces a reafferent visual signal whose value we may set at *plus* 2, because plus signifies "to the right." This positive reafferent signal will be cancelled out if we add to it a copy of the negative (leftward) efferent signal that caused the turn. A –2 efference produces a +2 reafference. Conversely, a +2 efference produces a –2 reafference. The efferent signal and the reafferent signal are equal and opposite. Therefore, adding a copy of the efference to the reafference will cancel it out.

The efference copy theory explains why the optokinetic reaction does not normally interfere with turning. Whenever another functional unit sends a turn signal to the muscles, it sends a copy of that signal to the optokinetic unit, as shown in Fig. 7.6. The optokinetic unit treats this signal as though it were a command originating within the optokinetic unit itself! That is, the optokinetic unit *could* pass this efference copy onto the muscles, as though it were a command from the optokinetic unit. However, the reafference opposes this, as shown in Fig. 7.6. The efference copy signal and the reafferent

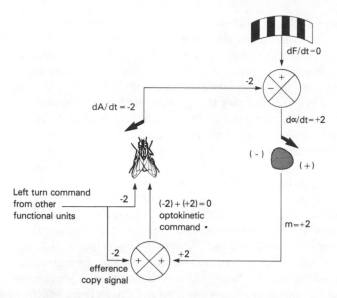

FIG. 7.6.   When another functional unit generates a command to turn, it also generates a copy of this command (the efference copy signal). Note that a command to turn left has a negative sign; but, the reafference generated by such a turn (the signal in *m*) will have a positive sign, because turning left sweeps the visual input toward the eye's right. Since the efference-copy signal and the reafferent signal are equal and opposite, they sum to zero when added algebraically. Thus, adding a copy of the command signal to the motion detector's signal cancels out the reafferent component in the motion-detector's signal. The commanded turn is therefore carried out accurately, without interference from the optokinetic reaction.

signal cancel each other. The optokinetic unit does not oppose the initial turn command, and the turn goes ahead undisturbed.

The efference copy theory and the corollary discharge theory are closely related. Indeed, efference copy and corollary discharge are two names for the same signal, a signal that is sent off to other units at the time a command is issued. The two theories differ with regard to how the copy of the motor command is employed: In corollary discharge theory, the copy of the command is used to inhibit any units whose response to the reafference would interfere with the commanded action. In efference copy theory, the copy of the motor command is actually fed into the sensory pathway of other units in such a way as to algebraically offset the reafferent signals in those pathways. The result is the same; the units to which the efference copy is sent do not respond to the reafference.

The difference between the two theories becomes noticeable only when for some reason the reafference is abnormal, so that it and the efference copy no longer cancel. The head-twisting experiment of von Holst and Mittelstaedt creates exactly this sort of abnormality. It reverses the sign of the reafferent signal. The efference copy and the reafference no longer cancel, they reinforce. Now, as shown in Fig. 7.7, the efference copy actually becomes a component of the optokinetic reaction. It reinforces the original turn command. We see now that the fly with his head on backwards is in even worse shape than portrayed in Fig. 7.5. Not only does the reafferent signal reinforce the original turn command, the efference copy signal does also. The original command is doubly incremented, once by the reafferent signal and once by the efference copy. This reinforcement effect distinguishes the efference copy theory from the corollary discharge theory. If the copy of the original command simply inhibited the optokinetic reaction, then it would not matter what the sign of the reafferent signal was. There would be no way that the copy of the original command (the corollary discharge) could become itself a motor command, which is what happens in Fig. 7.7.

It seems that the nervous system employs the simpler approach—inhibiting other units that would be activated by the reafference—only when the action of those units could never *complement* the action from which the corollary discharge originates. An instance of this use of corollary discharge has been documented by an electrophysiological analysis of the crayfish escape

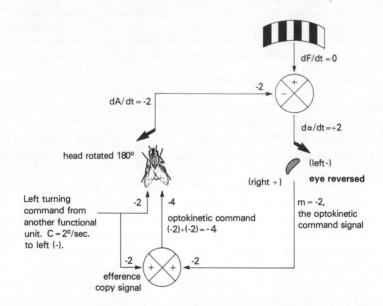

FIG. 7.7.   Rotating the head reverses the sign of the reafferent signal produced by a turn. The efference copy signal and the reafferent signal no longer have opposite signs. When added they reinforce rather than cancel: The original command is thereby doubly reinforced, once by the reafferent signal and once by the efference copy signal.

response (Wine, Krasne, & Chen, 1975). The response—a vigorous flip of the tail—is triggered by a disturbance of sensory hairs on the tail. The response itself massively disturbs the very same hairs, but a corollary discharge from the motorneurons prevents the reafferent signal from triggering a second flip before the first is finished. The use of the more sophisticated approach— offsetting the reafference—is probably reserved for situations in which the action of the unit receiving the efference copy may complement the action of the unit sending it. The optokinetic reaction will complement the action of the object-orienting reflex whenever the fly is standing on a perch that moves relative to the rest of the world. Under these circumstances, an optokinetically controlled turn may coincide with an object orienting turn. The combined effect will be better than if the optokinetic reaction were shut out, because the actual turn the fly makes will correct for the movement of its perch. In turning toward the object, the fly's machinery automatically takes into account the movement of the fly's perch with respect to the rest of the world. The optokinetic reaction, which is what takes the movement of the perch into account, is driven only by the exafferent component of the visual field motion, the component due to the movement of the perch. The reafferent component of visual field motion, the component due to the object-orienting turn is canceled out by a copy of the command that causes this turn.

The use of efference copies to offset reafferences is an unconscious, low level process within the motor mechanism. However, when the efference copy and the reafference that it anticipates are for some reason no longer equal and opposite, the resulting failure to cancel may show up in conscious perception. The most striking examples occur when the eye muscles are paralyzed with a drug, such as the Indian arrow poison curare, which blocks the transmission of excitation from nerve to muscle. Paralyzed or otherwise pathological muscles result in abnormal reafference because the commanded action does not occur or occurs at less than the commanded rate. Hence, the reafference fails to cancel the efference copy. Just as uncanceled efference copy is passed on to the fly's turning machinery, so too uncanceled efference copy is passed on to the human conscious perception. When a man with paralyzed eye muscles tries to glance to the right the world appears to jump to the right even though the pattern of light falling on the paralyzed eye has not moved. Uncanceled efference copy has created an hallucination of movement, a sensory experience for which there is no sensory basis. The image of the world on the retina does not move, but one "sees" the world move.

EXPECTATION

The concept of canceling reafference by efference copy is of particular psychological and even philosophical interest because it constitutes perhaps the simplest and most physiologically explicable instance of an expectation.

By expectation I understand an anticipation of some kind, a model of forthcoming sensory experience that arises before the fact. If the experience that does materialize matches the anticipatory model, an expectation is confirmed; if it does not, an expectation is disconfirmed. If the expectation is strong and the disconfirmation unequivocal, we are surprised. It is very surprising indeed to order your eyes to glance to the right and perceive instead that the world jumps to the right. In this case, of course, the expectation—the efference copy—was unconscious. Our conscious expectation is that the perceptual world will stay put as we glance here and there. This conscious expectation exists only because unconscious expectations (efference copies) anticipate the immediate and equally unconscious sensory consequences of our eye movements and cancel out these reafferences. Thus, the following paper is interesting both for what it teaches us about the role of servomechanisms in behavior and for what it suggests about the physiological basis for one kind of expectation.

The Reafference Principle
*(Interaction between the central nervous system and the periphery)**

E. VON HOLST
WITH HORST MITTELSTAEDT

INTRODUCTION

Ever since the physiology of the central nervous system (CNS) came into existence, one question has remained the focus: What regular relationship exists between the impulses which arrive in the CNS, following evocation by stimuli, and those which are then transmitted (directly or indirectly) to the periphery, that is, between *afference* and

*This paper is a translation by R. D. Martin of: Holst, E. von, & Mittelstaedt, H. Das Reafferenzprinzip. Wechselwirkung zwischen Zentralnervensystem und Peripherie. *Naturwissenschaften*, 1950, *37*, 464-476. The translation was published in *The behavioral physiology of animals and man: Selected papers of E. von Holst*. Vol. 1. Coral Gables: University of Miami Press, 1973. It is reprinted by permission of the University of Miami Press.

efference. The CNS is portrayed as the image of an automat which produces, in a 'reflex' manner, a given travel voucher in exchange for a specific coin. With simple protective reflexes—such as sneezing and retraction following a pain stimulus—this interpretation is an appropriate one, and it has similarly been used to explain more complex responses, for example equilibrating and orienting movements. Rhythmic locomotion can also be understood on this basis, if it is assumed that every individual movement reflexly sets in motion its antagonistic partner and that every extremity provokes movement in its temporal successor (reflex-chain theory). Finally, the higher, experimentially modified behaviour patterns are fitted into the picture as 'conditioned' reflexes.

This *classical reflex theory* by and large dominates the field although many facts have been recognized which do not concord with it. We know that the respiratory centre continues to operate even without rhythmic stimulus impulses, that the central locomotor rhythms of some invertebrates (von Holst, 1932, 1933, 1938) persist without afference, and that in fish (Lissmann, 1946; von Holst, 1935b) and amphibians (Gray, 1950; Gray & Lissmann, 1946; Weiss, 1941) an almost negligible residue of afferent nerves suffices for continued movement of *all* parts in a coordinated fashion. In addition, analysis of *relative coordination* (von Holst, 1935-43) in arthropods, fish, mammals and men has demonstrated the existence of central organizational forces—coupling and superimposition phenomena—whose interaction leads to rules which are formally quite similar to those discovered for the subconscious organization of sensory perception in Gestalt psychology (von Holst, 1939a, 1948).

These new results resist any description using reflex terminology, and it is therefore comprehensible that, whilst they have had a certain influence upon comparative behavioral research (Lorenz, Tinbergen and others) and upon human psychology (Metzger), they have not been assimilated in studies of the actual physiology of the CNS. Even quite recent textbooks are still entirely constructed on the classical reflex concept.[1] The fact that the intact CNS is an actively operative structure in which organized processes are continuously taking place without stimulus impulses, and that even resting and sleeping represent no more than special forms of central nervous activity,

---

[1]This applies, for example, to the comprehensive work of Fulton (1943), *Physiology of the Nervous System,* which leads the reader from the simple spinal reflexes up to the operation of the entire nervous system (the conditioned reflex) without attributing any part to spontaneous endogenous activity or to autonomous organizational forces in the CNS.

strikes many physiologists as being an unscientific concept. It is believed that the only possible 'cause' of any central process must be 'the stimulus.'[2]

This attitude is, after all, understandable, for nobody will readily give up a simple theory—particularly when it is regarded as a 'fact' because of its long history—before a better one is available. The new theory must incorporate both the old *and* the new results and permit predictions above and beyond the area which one has so far been able to understand. New experiments have led us to an interpretation which we think lives up to this expectation, within demonstrable limits. This interpretation will be explained with examples, and its applicability to well-known, but previously unexplained, phenomena will be examined. The characteristic feature of this new conceptual framework is a rotation of the point of attack through 180°. Rather than asking about the relationship between a given afference and the evoked efference (i.e., about the reflex), we set out *in the opposite direction* from the efference, asking: What happens in the CNS with the afference (referred to as the 'reafference') which is evoked through the effectors and receptors by the efference?

AN INTRODUCTORY EXAMPLE

Let us begin with an example. If a cylinder with vertical black and white stripes is rotated around an immobile insect (e.g., the fly *Eristalis*) the animal rotates itself in the same direction—it 'attempts to stabilize its visual field' (Fig. 7.8a). This well-known 'optomotor reflex' can be immediately elicited at any time. However, as soon as the animal sets itself in motion, one can see that it performs arbitrary turning movements both in the (immobilized) striped cylinder and in an optically unstructured environment. The question then arises as to why the 'optomotor reflex' does not return the animal to its former position whenever a turning movement is initiated, since the displacement of the image of the retina is, after all, the same as with the rotating cylinder. The reflex theory answers as follows: Because the optomotor reflexes are 'inhibited' during 'spontaneous' locomotion. But this answer is erroneous!

---

[2]This misunderstanding probably has psychological motives as well. It is much more satisfying in view of the naïve requirement for causal explanation to be able to relate a visible motor activity of the body to a visible alteration in the environment, than to invoke invisible energy turnover within the CNS. The latter is apparently felt to be semi-psychological.

FIG. 7.8.   Behavior of an insect
(*Eristalis*) with a striped surface
(SW) which is rotated around to the
right: *a*, normal aminal; *b*,
following rotation of the head
through 180° around the axis A—
A. R, right eye; L, left eye. (The
ommatidia are numbered.) The
arrow drawn on the animal
indicates its direction of active
rotation.

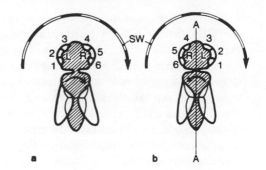

The animal has a thin, mobile neck, and the head can be rotated through 180° around the longitudinal axis and then glued to the thorax so that the two eyes are spatially interchanged (Fig. 7.8b; see also Mittelstaedt, 1949). In this way, a situation is produced where rotation of the striped cylinder in a clockwise direction produces the same migration of the image across the retina as with anti-clockwise rotation of the cylinder around the normal animal. Accordingly, the resting animal promptly responds to rotation of the cylinder to the right with a movement of its own to the left. If the animal begins to run around in the immobilized cylinder, locomotion should occur unaffected as in the intact animal, assuming that the 'optomotor reflexes' are now inhibited. *No normal running* occurs in the striped cylinder: *Eristallis* continuously turns in small circles to the left or the right, or there are brief, pronounced right—left turning movements until the animal becomes immobile 'as if frozen' in an atypical posture. When the head is rotated back to its former position, the behavior also returns to normal.

This result contradicts the 'reflex-inhibition' hypothesis, since it shows that, in 'spontaneous' running as well as in the rotating cylinder situation, retinal displacement exerts an effect upon locomotion. For the time being, this can be formulated as follows. The running animal 'expects' a quite specific retinal image displacement, which is neutralized when it occurs. If, on the other hand, retinal image displacement occurs in a direction *opposite* to that expected following interchange of the two eyes, this immediately elicits optomotor body-turning. But this turning movement itself magnifies the unexpected retinal image displacement, and the process is therefore self-reinforcing. As soon as any turning movement is initiated, the animal is optically propelled around in the same direction of rotation. If it attempts a movement in the opposite sense, the same dilemma appears. The result is evidently a central catastrophe!

If this provisional interpretation is valid, we must ask: How does the CNS 'know' which particular image displacement it should expect when the animal is moving? Such knowledge could have two sources. Either the CNS preserves for a period of time certain data (regarding the efference transmitted to the legs) which are computed against the retinal image migration; or, if it does not possess this simpler capacity, it relies upon the reafference from the receptors in the moving legs to 'calculate' the direction and speed of running, in order to compute the result against the retinal reafference. These two possibilities are not mutually exclusive. We shall leave these alternatives open here and turn instead to another example which allows clearer appreciation of the situation.

MORE DETAILED FORMULATION
OF THE PROBLEM

In the labyrinth system of the vertebrates, there is on either side of the head a flat stone—the utriculus statolith—which is situated horizontally on a sensory surface in the normal head position. This organ responds to gravity. Experiments on fish (reported in von Holst, 1950a, 1950b) show that a force parallel to the resting surface represents the adequate stimulus. When the head is inclined away from the normal position, the gravitational force increases sinusoidally and produces in the postural center a similarly sinusoidal increasing disequilibrium in activity (a 'central turning tendency') which evokes motor responses which return the animal to the normal posture. This apparatus operates with great precision without habituating. In the terminology of the reflex theory, the organism is maintained exactly in its normal position through its 'postural reflexes.' However, one can often observe with all animals and in human beings that they can adopt a posture *different* from the normal position for varying periods of time. For example, fish can position themselves with an almost vertical upward or downward inclination, turn on their sides and so on when searching for food, hunting prey, fighting or taking part in courtship.

In view of the continuously evokable 'postural reflexes,' how are these deviant postures possible? As before, the reflex theory would state, 'through complete or partial inhibition of the "equilibrium reflexes".' Yet it can easily be shown that this interpretation is *not* valid. These 'requisite postures,' which deviate from the norm, are actually restored through the *same* correcting movements, when disturbed by some external impulse, as those which are seen in restoration of the normal posture!

One might therefore think that the reflexes are not extinguished but simply diverted into other pathways by a higher-level switching mechanism, that is, that the higher center merely sets the points which determine the pathway from afference to efference (the 'steered reflexes' of W. R. Hess). This interpretation also involves an experimentally testable corollary: someone who is changing points performs the same work whatever the number of trains passing over the line. In other words, the effect of such reflex steering should not be affected by the magnitude of the afference. Once again, this is *not* the case.

One can increase the mechanical force which the statolith exerts upon the sensory surface by applying a constant centrifugal field. If the weight of the statolith is doubled in this way, there is a constant doubling of the shear stimulus produced by any departure from the normal posture. If one in fact records the frequent, spontaneous postural deviations (snout pointing upwards or downwards) in a free-swimming fish, it emerges that they become increasingly restricted with increase in weight of the statolith. The *'voluntary movement'* proves to be *dependent upon the afferent return stream* which it evokes!

To take another example. Fish orient their longitudinal axis in the direction of a water current by optically 'attaching' themselves to the immobile environment. This is also largely true when the current comes from obliquely above (or below). The greater the success in pointing the snout towards the current, the less is the energy required to prevent displacement downstream (von Holst, 1950a). If one goes on to investigate the behavior of a fish swimming freely against a constant current within a cage, it emerges that the fish has decreasing success in maintaining its longitudinal axis parallel to the current, as one approaches a 'vertical' current direction, with increasing weight of the statoliths (Fig. 7.9). The fish does, in fact, then attempt to oppose the current *dorsally;* but this is far less successful, as it tires rapidly. This difference disappears following removal of the statoliths; whatever the strength of the mechanical field, the snout is oriented directly into the current.

Thus, one can see that the higher central factor which determines the *requisite posture* deviating from the norm is not a point-setting or steering mechanism, since the reafference indirectly produced by its command has a quantitative influence upon the posture which actually appears as a result. Despite this dismissal of the concept of

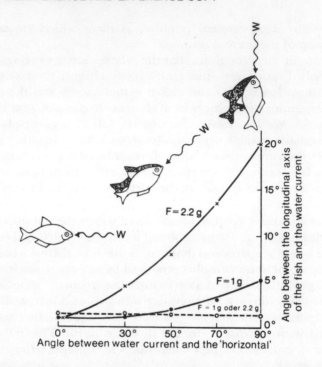

FIG. 7.9.   Orientation of a fish swimming freely within a cage against a constant water current. the current direction is altered from horizontal to vertical and the strength of the mechanical field (F) is increased from 1 g to 2.2 g (through a centrifugal field). (The 'vertical' is a resultant of the grativational and centrifugal forces.) ● and x represent the intact fish; o represents the fish after an operation to remove the statoliths. The white fish outlines illustrate the behavior of the intact fish at F = 1g, whilst the black outlines indicate the behavior at F = 2.2 g. W is the water current. (The current velocity is approximately one fish length per sec.) The hydrostatic pressure is maintained constant, and the values are taken from five experimental series involving three fish (*Gymmocorymbus* and *Hypessobrycon*).

the 'steered reflex,' the following pronunciations on the approach to the problem and the conceptual framework involved are quite closely related to the works of W. R. Hess (although the methodology is quite different). The 'steering device' must perform *more work*, the *greater the number of trains* which pass along the line! How can this be interpreted?

We can obtain a quite simple picture if two reliably demonstrated physiological facts are taken as a basis:

1. The sensory cells of the labyrinth, like many (perhaps most) other receptors, exhibit a continuous endogenous rhythm—the *continuous trace* prior to any stimulation. The shear stimulus of the statoliths merely increases or decreases the resting frequency, according to the direction of shear. This *automaticity* of the receptors has been verified through our own experiments on fish and also by direct electrical recording either from the afferent fibers (e.g., O. Lowenstein, 1950) or from the vestibular nucleus (Adrian, 1943).

2. A *continuous stream of impulses* links the higher and lower centers even when there is external motor inactivity. This fact has also been demonstrated for various central areas through electrophysiological investigations, and is indirectly evident from the 'shock'-like reduction in activity which occurs on transection of certain ascending inter-central pathways. The 'spinal shock' of lower motor centers following destruction of (for example) the *tractua vestibulospinalis* corresponds to the 'shock' suffered by the left vestibular nucleus following destruction of the left labyrinth. In both cases, a continuous activating stream of arriving impulses is disrupted.

These two preconditions are necessary for the interpretation explained in Fig. 7.10. The 'postural center' (a complex of ganglion cells whose spatial distribution is irrelevant at this point) consists of two halves, each of which receives a stream of impulses from the statolith epithelium and from higher central areas. If both halves are charged at the same level (i.e., at the same level of activity), they both send impulse streams of equivalent intensity to the lower motor centers of the spinal cord, which in this case too have no more than a charging function (Fig. 7.10a): the well-known 'tonus'-effect of the labyrinth (Ewald; see von Holst, 1950a). If the fish is passively inclined to the right (Fig. 7.10b), the shear of the right statolith produces—as has been verified in experiments (von Holst, 1950a)—an increase in the continuous afference, whilst that of the left is reduced. The resulting difference in level between the right and the left halves of the postural center produces an imbalanced impulse stream to the spinal cord, which brings into operation local motor apparatus which, as a whole, leads to a turning movement to the left. This process is referred to in classical terminology as the *postural reflex*.

However, a corresponding difference in level within the postural center can also arise as a result of imbalanced impulses arriving from

FIG. 7.10.   Schema explaining the interaction of higher centers (Z_n) with the lower postural center (Z_1) and the static apparatus (St) in the postural orientation of a fish (along the longitudinal axis). The thickness of each arrow denotes the intensity of the stream of impulses (number of discharges per unit time) flowing from one component to another, and the shading of the half-centers of Z_1 indicates the momentary level of discharge (activity). St = statolith; the arrows above it in *b* and *d* indicate the direction of shear, and the large arrow in the center of *b* and *c* indicates the direction of the rotational tendency. *a;* normal situation; *b;* rotational tendency towards the normal position following passive inclination of the animal; *c;* active (spontaneous) rotational tendency towards the left; *d;* resulting inclined 'requisite posture.'

the higher center (Fig. 7.10c and d). The result is *the same* motor action as before.[3] This process is known in physiology as a *'voluntary movement.'* It is instructive that the *inclined* 'requisite posture' is *protected* against passive disturbances through the afference from the statolith apparatus in exactly the same way as the previously maintained normal posture. Any passive alteration in posture will lead to a difference level within the postural center and thus produce a 'postural reflex' without any involvement of higher centers.

---

[3]The concept that higher centers have the function of distorting the excitatory equilibrium in lower antagonistic centers was first developed in the analysis of relative coordination in rhythmic locomotor movements (von Holst, 1936, etc.). Recently it has been further validated by investigations of 'action currents' (Bernhard & Therman, 1947).

We can now consider verifiable corollaries of this model interpretation:

1. Destruction of the left statolith apparatus, as a result of simultaneous lowering of the level within the postural center, must produce a persistent turning tendency towards the left. This tendency must exhibit a maximum when the fish is on its right side (maximal charging afference from the right) and a minimum when it is on its left side. This applies to all vertebrates and has been quantitatively validated in fish (von Holst, 1950a). The same also applies, as is well known, to the injury or destruction of the postural center itself (vestibular nucleus; Spiegel and Sato, 1927).
2. When the left half of the postural center has recovered from the removal of the statolith on the same side and has been re-charged to the normal level,[4] any turning tendencies occurring with a change in posture should only exhibit half of their former value, since the left level remains constant, whilst only the right level is dependent upon posture. This has been quantitatively demonstrated in fish (von Holst, 1950a).
3. Amplification of the intensity of the mechanical field, and thus of the afference, must also amplify in a regular fashion the part played by the statolith apparatus relative to that of other equilibrating organs (e.g., the eye in fish) in postural orientation. For example, doubling of the intensity of the mechanical field exactly compensates the lack of one statolith (point 1).
4. Following exclusion of the higher centers, no further active departures from the normal posture should occur. This has also been demonstrated (Magnus, 1924, etc.).
5. Spontaneous changes in the requisite position, or those produced by other afferences passing through higher centers, should produce a *decreasing* alteration in posture with *increase* in the intensity of the mechanical field, and thus of the *shear stimulus* of the statoliths. In this point too, as we have seen, the expectation is fulfilled: the balancing of the two halves of the postural center is achieved with approximately *the same shear*, that is, with a corresponding *smaller angle of inclination* of the animal when the statoliths are heavier.

---

[4] Our co-worker L. Schoen (1949) has quantitatively examined this central compensation process, but no further discussion of this can be conducted here.

6. Conversely, following bilateral exclusion of the afference, imbalance in the stream of impulses arriving from higher centers should lead to *exaggerated* movements, since in the absence of reafference—mechanically speaking—there is loss of the 'stop' which arrests the initiated movement at the right moment. This phenomenon can also be observed at any time with free-swimming fish and amphibians, and it has frequently been reported. Animals lacking the labyrinth on both sides exhibit postural alterations which are so pronounced that general tumbling often results[5]. In terrestrial vertebrates, this behavior is less obvious because of the loss of tonus following removal of the labyrinths and because of the pronounced part played by muscle receptors in the movement (see pp. 197–202). Nevertheless, the phenomenon can be observed following loss of just one part of the balance receptors. For example, following destruction of both horizontal semi-circular canals, a slight, unstable rocking movement of the head in the horizontal plane occurs in intention movements (particularly in birds).

Thus, one can derive a number of valid corollaries from this conceptual model—corollaries which cannot be explained by the reflex theory.

MORE GENERAL FORMULATION
OF THE REAFFERENCE PRINCIPLE

The key feature in the example explained above is the role played by the reafference produced by active movement. This extinguishes the alteration in conditions produced in a lower center by a motor command from a higher one, so that the former equilibrium is restored. If this afference is removed under experimental conditions, if it is too large or too small, or if its sign is altered (as in the rotated head of *Eristalis*), predictable alterations in the locomotor process can occur.

---

[5]Schöne (1950) has reported entirely analogous observations on insect larvae. The larva of *Dytiscus*, which normally presents its back to the light, will (for example) perform somersaults when swimming upwards head-first following blindings of the forward- and backward-directed eyes. This is apparently because there is absence of the reafferent 'stop' (stronger illumination of the forward-directed eyes and lesser illumination of the backward-directed ones) which normally arrests the correcting movement. (Schöne's own interpretation runs in a similar manner.)

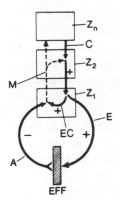

FIG. 7.11. General schema for the explanation of the reafference principle. For explanation see text.

It is now necessary to provide a more general formulation of this principle and then demonstrate its validity with examples from different neuromotor mechanisms.

Let us consider (Fig. 7.11) a given center Z_1 which has sensory and motor connections with an effector EFF. This effector can be a muscle, a limb or the entire body. One or more further centers (Z_2 to Z_n) are superior to the center Z_1. Any *command* from Z_n—that is, a specific *change* in the stream of impulses descending to Z_1, produces an efferent series of impulses (E) from Z_1, which produces a closely correlated alteration in activity—the *efference copy*, EC—which spreads through the neighboring ganglionic mass with a specific temporal delay. The efferent stream E flowing out to the periphery evokes the corresponding reafference A from the effector, and this reafference interacts with the efference copy. The efference and its copy can be arbitrarily marked with a plus (+), whilst the reafference is marked with a minus (-). The efference copy and the reafference exactly cancel one another out in Z_1, whilst the command descending from Z_n flows outwards without interruption. As soon as the entire afference is too large or too small, as a result of some *external influence* acting upon the *effector*, either a + or a - remains as a residue in Z_1. As we shall see, *this residue is transmitted* upwards, sometimes to the highest centers; it can be referred to as a *message*, M. The ascending message can branch in Z_2 on its way (although it *does not necessarily* do so), where once again it summates with the descending command. In this case, the system from Z_2 downwards will maintain itself in equilibrium, thus producing a *feedback system* of the kind recognized in technology.[6] Let us assume, for

---

[6]We owe our acquaintanceship with technological cybernetics to Dr. Böhm (see also Böhm, 1950).

example, that an influence affecting the effector EFF produces an *increase* in the – afference in Z_1, in which case the ascending message to Z_2 *reduces* the + command until an equilibrium is reached once again. Conversely, an externally produced *decrease in* the –afference in Z_1 will bring about a + residue which will *amplify* the + command through Z_2. Thus, in both cases, *the efference is modified until no further message is sent out by Z_1.*[7] We have already encountered a feedback system of this kind in the example of postural orientation.

In addition, we can refer to the alteration of the afference which is *not* a direct consequence of an efference but arises through *external* influences (through proprioceptors or exteroceptors) as an *exafference.* The *exafference* in our schema is thus the + or – residue in Z_1 which proceeds upwards as the message.

The schema outlined incorporates two physiological assumptions:

1. Different impulse sequences can mutually amplify or cancel one another (addition). There are various indications that this occurs. One example in the area of motor activity is the superimposition of locomotor rhythms of different frequency in relative coordination (von Holst, 1935b), where two rhythms can summate or cancel one another according to their phase relationship. An example from the field of coordination of sensory data is the exact linear superimposition of statically and optically produced central activity differences and the similarly purely additive positive or negative interaction of surgically-induced activity differences in the postural center of fish (von Holst, 1950a).

2. The efference from the lower center leaves behind it a certain alteration in conditions as a 'copy.' This assumption is plausible *a prior* for higher centers and can nowadays be regarded as true even for the lowest centers. Recent investigations of action currents in the spinal cord, using antidromic (backward flowing) impulses in motor fibres, have shown that it is quite probable that normal discharge of a motor ganglion cell, apart from passing through the efferent fibres, also spreads through the small dendrites ramifying in the vicinity and hence produces an alteration in conditions

---

[7]It should be emphasized that this 'negative feedback' is not a necessary component of the reafference principle and that it should not be confused with the latter! The decisive point in the principle is the mechanism distinguishing reafference and exafference. This distinction plays no part in cybernetic technology.

within the neighboring intermediate neurons. Tönnies (1949) refers to this process as 'central feedback' and ascribes to it great importance in the control of excitation in the spinal cord. For our purposes, it is sufficient that one can conclude that our assumption is physiologically plausible.

APPLICATION OF THE REAFFERENCE PRINCIPLE TO DIFFERENT NEUROMOTOR SYSTEMS

Eye Movements

We can now test the reafference principle to see which phenomena not explained by the reflex theory can be correctly predicted. In order to make use of perception as a source of information, let us begin with the human being, taking the optical system. We can assume that simple relationships exist in this instance, since the eye—which is a protected sphere located in the head—will not be adapted for mechanical disruption of its movement.

Reafference from the actively moved eyes could have two sources: (1) the retinal image displacement and (2) impulses from the receptors in the eye muscles. Only the first source is accessible to conscious perception; the participation of the second can only be deduced. Let us set out from an assumption which is critical, since it is improbable *a priori*. When the eye is immobilized and the muscle receptors are excluded (Fig. 7.12a), following the command 'visual sweep (eyeball rotation) to the right!' (taking all directional indications relative to the experimental subject), the efference copy must return upwards from the lowest center in full force as a 'message,' owing to the lack of any reafference from the retina or the muscles. Further, this 'message' must be the same as that which normally produces an environmental shift of the same size and in the same direction with the resting eye (Fig. 7.12b).[8] The entire environment has made a leap (of the same size as the intended eye movement) to the right.' This prediction is actually borne out! It has long been known from people with paralyzed eye muscles that any intended movement produces perception of an evidently quantitative environmental shift in the

---

[8]This must be fulfilled, since with this environmental shift a retinal image displacement occurs opposite to that which would emerge with a completed visual sweep to the right. In our schema, the direction inversion signifies a change in sign of the afference from - to +, so that a + message equivalent to the + efference copy must pass upwards.

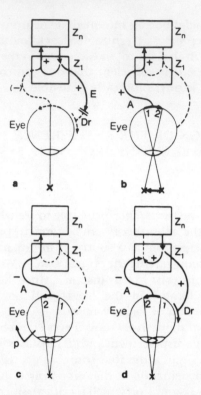

FIG. 7.12. Explanation of perception of movement by the eye under normal and experimental conditions, using the reafference principle. The eye is in primary position; viewed from above, Z_1 = lower optical center; Z_n = higher optical center. The efference (E) passing to the eye musculature and the corresponding afference (A) produced by displacement of the image on the retina are indicated as in Fig. 7.11. In *a*, the immobilized eye receives the command impulse to glance to the right (turning impulse, Dr, for rotation to the right). In *b*, the viewed object (x) objectively migrates to the right, moving from 1 to 2 on the retina. In *c*, the eye is passively (mechanically) turned to the right, as indicated by the arrow p, and the immobile x moves from 1 to 2 on the retina. In *d*, the eye performs an active (commanded) gaze movement to the right (turning impulse = Dr, as in *a*, and the immobile x moves from 1 to 2 on the retina. (Further details in text.)

same direction, and Kornmüller (1932) has provided more detailed verification of this by carrying out experiments on himself, following anaesthesia of his eye muscles. This 'apparent movement' cannot be distinguished from 'objective' perception of movement, as is to be expected, since according to the reafference hypothesis the *same* message arrives in both cases. Thus, in this experiment there is, so to speak, *directed visual recognition of the efference copy*.

Following Hering (cf. Trendelenburg, 1943, p. 240 et seq.), this phenomenon is interpreted as 'displacement of attention' in gaze movements. So far, a plausible physiological explanation has been lacking. We shall see shortly that 'attention' has nothing to do with this, since the same phenomenon is found with non-conscious eye movements. Perception is, for us, simply a comfortable indicator for an otherwise relatively inaccessible physiological process.

The same perception of movement as that described above— though in the opposite direction, to the left—is obtained when the eyeball is passively rotated to the right with a pair of forceps (Fig. 7.12c). In this case, the movement command is lacking and the retinal exafference passes upwards unhindered as the message, once again producing 'pseudoperception': 'the landscape jumps to the left.'

If we now combine the first case with the second, that is, by passively turning a paralyzed eye to the right in synchrony with the movement command (or by making a gaze displacement to the right with the *intact* eye, which is of course simpler), then two mutually complementary streams of impulses are actually produced (Fig. 7.12d): an efference copy which indicates movement of the environment to the *right*, and an exafference indicating movement to the *left*. Since these two streams cancel one another out at a low level (Z_1), there is *no* ascending message and neither stream of impulses is perceived. As we all know, the environment remains immobile, which in *this* case is also 'objectively' true. The 'correct' perception proves to be the sum of two opposing 'false' perceptual processes.

As with all technical constructions, this central apparatus has noticeable limits of accuracy. It only functions reliably in an intermediate visual range and with moderate speeds of movement. For example, if the gaze is turned markedly to the right and then rapidly passed up and down a vertical junction in a room, the latter undergoes pronounced 'apparent rotation' (Hoffmann, 1924). This is based (according to our interpretation) on the fact that the efference copy in this movement (following Listing's Rule) of a rotating eye only partially cancels out its afference, such that a message is passed upwards. The landscape also appears to leap markedly in the opposite direction when the gaze is rapidly moved back and forth from right to left. In this case, the efference copy is apparently produced too slowly, such that a restricted message is passed upwards in the first instant.

The fact that one can produce pronounced apparent movements of the environment, either through passive movements of an otherwise intact eye or through intended gaze movement with a mechanically fixed eyeball (a fact which was already known to Helmholtz), shows that the afference of the muscle receptors can only be of restricted significance (if at all) for our approach. If these receptors were always capable of indicating the position of the eyeball, as is the case with receptors in the limbs (see pp. 202–207), then apparent movements could only appear following their exclusion (Kornmüller's experiment). The role of these muscle receptors has apparently been so greatly overestimated—as we shall see in other instances as well— because the reflex theory does not provide for any concepts involving an intra-central feedback process.

The reafference principle is valid not only for so-called 'voluntary' movements, but also for those of an involuntary kind in which the eye 'scans' the visual field by sequentially fixating one point after another. This 'scanning' occurs both in active movement of the eyes (e.g., in reading a book, where every line requires four to five steps) and in turning of the head and body (labyrinth nystagmus) or presentation with a traveling landscape (optomotor nystagmus). In all of these cases, we do not usually perceive anything of the stepwise displacement of the image across the retina. Instead, we perceive the environment as traveling smoothly in one direction or (in the case of reading) as remaining stationary.

An interpretation of this phenomenon in terms of reflex physiology runs as follows. If the landscape passes by our eye (e.g., when looking out of the window of a train), the eye is initially carried along 'reflexly.' The consequent movement of the eye muscles indicates—through muscle receptors—the speed and direction of the environmental movement, since retinal displacement (which could also possibly act as an indicator) is lacking or negligible. When the muscular tension has reached a maximum, there is a further 'reflex' motor impulse in the opposite direction (the rapid nystagmus phase). The afference of the resulting, opposing displacement of the image across the retina is 'inhibited' or fails to reach the conscious level because of its rapidity.

Among other things, this interpretation contradicts the fact that one can produce an after-image on the retina by fixation of a bright cross and that this after-image, which persists in the dark, can be seen to wander alternately first in one direction (slowly) and then in the opposite direction (rapidly) with labyrinth nystagmus (which can be produced at will after practice). Thus, the image is *not* extinguished in the rapid phase (Fischer, 1926). As will be demonstrated shortly, this behavior would be predicted by the reafference principle.

The much-discussed nystagmus apparatus can best be understood when the term 'optical scanning apparatus' is taken quite literally. Consider, for comparison, the locomotor apparatus of an arthropod

FIG. 7.13.   A small fragment of an arthropod (*Geophilus*) which is drawn across the substrate with a hook attached to the anterior end. The legs raised from the ground are actively swung forward (→) in such a manner that each leg is placed exactly in the track of its predecessor and the resulting, overall pattern resembles the track of a bipedal animal.

(*Geophilus;* von Holst, 1933) following separation of the higher centers (Fig. 7.13). Through continuous (e.g., electrical) excitation of the ventral nerve cord, the locomotor system can be activated such that the legs perform coordinated walking movements, just as a uniform stream of impulses from higher centers sets nystagmus in operation. In addition—as with nystagmus—it can also be activated by unidirectional movement of the 'fixed landscape,' by pulling the remaining fragment of the animal across the substrate at varying speeds. The legs *actively* accompany this latter movement: Even those legs which are in the act of swinging forward will exactly follow every alteration in speed imposed upon the legs resting upon the substrate. The propulsive phase corresponds to the slow nystagmus phase: Steered by the exafference, the legs and the eyes fixate the substrate. The swinging phase corresponds to the rapid nystagmus phase: The legs and eyes suspend the fixation and perform a pace in the opposite direction. In neither case do the higher centers need to receive information from the individual paces. Just like the continuous stream of impulses from above, there is a reverse stream passing upwards, indicating the relative speed between the subject and the environment. The pacing apparatus fails when the moving substrate is unstructured (e.g., *Geophilus* on the mercury surface, or the eye passing over a homogeneous visual field), or when the relative movement becomes too rapid, in which case the legs and the eyes remain 'blocked' in an extreme backward position.

Let us now try to give a more exact interpretation of this scanning apparatus. The landscape begins to move past the eye and there is a resultant retinal displacement which immediately passes to the higher areas as a + message, bifurcating to Z_2 and the pacing center Sz (Fig. 7.14a). This + message, in turn, at once descends from Z_2 as a + command and evokes a movement of the eye. The image is consequently returned to its previous position on the retina, producing a – afference which cancels out the + efference copy in Z_1, so that the eye movement would be arrested (Fig. 7.14b) if the process

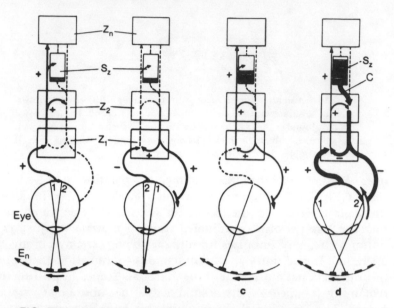

FIG. 7.14. Explanation of the scanning movement of the eye in the example of optomotor 'nystagmic' movement accompanying movement of the environment (En). The schema follows those in Fig. 7.11 and 7.12. Z_1 and Z_2 are lower motor centers; S_z is the scanning center responsible for the rhythm; and Z_n is a higher optical center. In a, the eye is at rest, the environment is slightly displaced, and an (arbitrarily selected) element of the visual image wanders across the retina from 1 to 2. In b, active accompanying movement has started, and the given element of the image has wandered back to its former position on the retina. In c, the eye moves with the same angular velocity as the environment and the image remains immobile on the retina. In d, the scanning center S_z discharges and produces a powerful, opposing motor command in C. During the time elapsed with the rapid movement phase, the environment continues to move, and an arbitrary element of the image thus passes from 1 to 2 across the retina. The thickness of the arrows indicates the intensity of the streams of impulses. (Further explanation in text.)

in Fig. 7.14a did not immediately reappear. The movement thus oscillates in an equilibrium condition (Fig. 7.14c). The eye moves so rapidly that there is no further retinal displacement (or almost none), and the entire feedback system maintains itself.

The scanning center, S_z, is thus charged up until it abruptly discharges (acting as a 'ratchet system[9]') and returns the eye to its

---

[9]A. Bethe (1940), in particular, has performed important experiments on physical ratchet oscillations as a model for physiological rhythms.

starting position (Fig. 7.14d). This is the rapid phase, during which the efference copy and the afference cancel one another out, apart from the small *ex*afferent residue which is brought about by the movement of the landscape and which continues on its upward path as a message independent of the phase-change. The same set of events is then repeated.

One can see that the entire apparatus is *not* a 'reflex mechanism' since, with sufficient auto-excitation or stimulation from above, it must pass over to autorhythmicity following *removal of all afference* (cf. Fig. 7.14c!). This is actually observed under experimental and pathological conditions.

Accommodation

We shall now turn from eye movements to another process: that of *accommodation*. At rest, the eye is set for long-distance vision, since the elastic lens is flattened by suspensory fibres. Proximal accommodation is ensured by a circular muscle which operates antagonistically to this tension and allows the lens to swell. As is well known, this apparatus—along with other criteria—operates in association with the retina to permit perception of the approximate distance and size of a viewed object. The retinal image, when uniformly focussed, is perceived as large and distant or small and nearby, according to the accommodation setting. Or, to use the usual formulation, the 'subject size scale' depends upon the 'imagined distance.'

The reflex theory can only explain this fact through the assumption that receptors in the accommodation apparatus, according to its setting, 'reflexly' exert a reducing or magnifying influence upon the image which is transmitted upwards. However, this possibility is discounted by the well-known fact that when the accommodation mechanism is paralyzed with atropine, the—unsuccessful—attempt to fixate nearby objects makes everything appear to shrink in size (micropsia), although the incapacitated peripheral mechanism is naturally unable to elicit any 'reflexes.' Conversely, everything appears to become large (macropsia) when one attempts to fixate objects some distance away following tetanic contraction induced with eserine. The reafference principle explains this outcome.

Let us set out from a simple case (a), producing a sharp afterimage of a nearby cross on the retina and then gazing at a wall some way off. The command for adaptation to distance produces in the lowest center the corresponding efference to the musculature, together with its accompanying efference copy. Since the image of the cross on the retina remains sharp and unaltered, no reafference appears; the efference copy proceeds upward as the message and indicates a *positive perceptual process*, which (as is well known) reads as follows: 'The cross is (now) much larger.' We now proceed to (b), directly regarding first a large cross and then a small one at the same distance from the eye. In this case, an accommodation command is lacking; the exafference—as a result of absence of any efference copy—proceeds unimpeded upwards as the message and indicates a positive perceptual process: 'The (second) cross is smaller.' Following this (c), we take the larger cross, look at it close by and then move it just far enough away so that its image on the retina is exactly as large as the previous image of the small cross (in b). It now emerges that there is *firstly* the already described message from (a) stating 'the cross is larger' and *secondly* the message from (b) stating 'the cross is smaller.' Both the efference copy and the exafference cancel one another out in a lower center, and *no* message passes upwards. Consequently, the perceptual mechanism must conclude: 'The cross has remained the same size'; which is exactly what it does do! Once again, the 'correct' perceptual process originates from two compensatory 'false' perceptual processes.

With this interpretation we can also easily understand the above-mentioned effects of micropsia and macropsia. When the peripheral musculature is unable to follow the efference, the retinal reafference must be absent, and the efference copy which passes upward as the message must indicate to the perceptual mechanism a size alteration in the predicted direction.

Once again, it is interesting that the reafference and the efference copy only cancel one another exactly within certain limits. Where accommodation no longer takes an active part—far away or very close by—one sees objects become smaller or larger, as is to be expected. The apparatus is also unable to follow rapid alterations in distance, such that an object which approaches rapidly appears to increase in size.

The principle set out here for the distance adaptation of the individual eye can be applied in just the same way to active binocular distance measuring devices—the convergence of the eyes, which increases with the closeness of the fixated object. This will not be discussed in detail here since we cannot yet reliably state whether (and to what extent) reafference from the eye muscles is involved in the process.

Limb Movements

Let us now consider another apparatus: the moving limb. Here, more complex relationships are to be expected, since—in contrast to the protected eye—passive (mechanical) alteration of posture is possible in many respects, and the CNS must receive information about the latter in order to operate in an appropriate manner. Perception involves distinction of at least four different qualities of mechanical influence: touch, pressure, tension ('force'), posture. The first two are well known to everybody, and they overlap with one another. The fact that tension and limb posture are sharply distinguished can be clearly experienced when the intensity of the mechanical field is increased in a centrifugal field. If one's weight is more than doubled in this way, raising of the arm (for example) requires an astounding quantity of perceived force, although no external pressure is imposed upon it. Nevertheless, one is correctly informed about the momentary arm position or movement, and no surprise is encountered when the arm is examined following movement to a required posture.[10] This indication of posture is primarily given by receptors in the connective tissue external to the muscles; for measurement of tension there are further receptors both in the muscle fibres themselves and in the tendons. Together, they provide the so-called 'kinaesthetic sense.'

One can at once begin with a concrete question. How would a muscle respond to external loading if its centers incorporated interconnection of the efference and afference of the tension-measuring elements in the tendons, following the same pattern as that found in the postural mechanism of fish? A mildly stretched muscle is extended so that the tension increases (Fig. 7.15a). The increased afference (exafference) passes upward to Z_2 and indicates the size of the preceding efference; the muscle actively relaxes. When the muscle is unloaded, the converse will occur; the + efference copy passing from Z_1 to Z_2 increases the overall efference: the muscle activity contracts (Fig. 7.15b).

The limb, however strong the muscle tonus may be, will 'spastically' follow the movement imposed from the outside. Mechanisms of this kind are widely distributed and they occasionally occur in quite pure form in pathological cases. An example in this direction is again provided by an operated *Geophilus* (see Fig. 7.13) which is actively following an imposed speed of movement. Exactly

---

[10]Based on observations on myself, conducted in an encapsulated experimental chamber rotated by a kind of centrifuge.

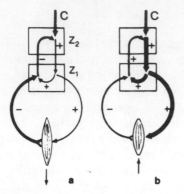

FIG. 7.15. Explanation of the behavior of a loaded muscle whose central apparatus is so constructed that—in analogy with Fig. 7.11—it will actively adapt to supplementary passive stretching *a*, and shortening *b*, while the tonus determined by a higher command (C) remains the same.

the same thing can be seen in vertebrates (dog; toad) in which the spinal cord has been transected at the thoracic level; when the substrate is pulled away backwards, the back legs begin to move.[11]

With an actively innervated muscle of an intact warm-blooded animal, the response to loading is, of course, usually opposite in nature: There is contraction to an extent which will balance the load. This much-investigated *endogenous reflex* (P. Hoffmann *et al.*) passes from the sensory neurone directly to the motor neurone and therefore operates without participation of an efference copy and without 'computation' in a higher center. Its receptors are the muscle spindles, fine contractile fibres (representing about 1 per cent of the transverse area occupied by the remaining fibres with exclusively motor connections) which have both motor and sensory connections. If we imagine the afference from the muscle spindles as passing directly to the motor neurone leading to the remaining mass of the muscle we can understand the operation of the endogenous reflex (Fig. 7.16).

If the *unloaded* entire muscle contracts or relaxes, the spindles remain silent, as long as they and the other muscle fibres alter their lengths to the same extent. If the resting or contracting muscle is loaded, the spindles are stretched as well, and they 'fire off' until they are discharged by contraction of the remaining muscle fibres.[12] Thus, the CNS determines the required position or movement, and the endogenous reflexes maintain this against external resistance. The

---

[11]Nevertheless, supplementary locomotor activity is necessary for the forward movement (swinging phase of the legs).

[12]We owe thanks to Dr. Lissmann, Cambridge, for valuable data on proprioceptor function (verbal communication) taken from sources inaccessible to us, and to Prof. P. Hoffmann, Freiburg, for providing important literature.

FIG. 7.16. Behavior of a muscle (M) mildly stretched through a higher command (C), whose central apparatus is so organized that it actively opposes any additional external loading (↓). CE = efference produced by the higher command, passing to the muscle and the muscle spindle fibre; EE = supplementary muscle efference which is directly produced by the afference of the stretched spindle; MSp = muscle spindle; TSp = tension receptor in the tendon ('tendon spindle') with a high stimulus threshold, which leads to the central apparatus illustrated in Fig. 7.15.

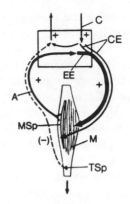

tension receptors in the tendons, which have a higher stimulus threshold, may be ascribed with the function of switching off this reflex mechanism when there is inordinate loading and switching on the above-described adapting mechanism, so that the muscle does not tear apart.

With this refined trick, Nature has ensured that the organism maintains its equilibrium simply through muscular auto-regulation. If an impact from the left causes an animal standing at rest to sway to the right, the extensors of the right legs will stiffen as a result of increased loading, before the labyrinth has time to come into operation. An undisturbed animal standing or walking with mild resilience receives a solid support just at the moment of disturbance and only in the affected place. One can imagine the enormous saving in higher command impulses and muscular energy which this entails.

Thus we can see that the reafference principle is apparently replaced by a differently operating *peripheral* mechanism in the endogenous reflexes, but that it is otherwise also operative in limb movements. Let us now make use of perception in order to follow this question somewhat further, as we did with the eye.

At first sight, the well-known fact that disruption of the afferent pathways (dorsal roots) does not lead to perceptual illusions when the arm (for example) is moved, despite the lack of reafference, seems to disprove the reafference principle. However, the argument does not hold up. Any possible perception of apparent movement of any object is dependent upon a perceived object, so it will in this case be bound to touch and pressure afferences, which are similarly lacking. Similarly, in a quite analogous fashion, the feedback message from the efference copy of an eye actively moved *in the dark* of course does *not* lead to optical 'apparent movements of nonperceived objects.' A human being with an amputated arm does indeed continue for some time to dispose of the appropriate central representation; he can open and close the missing 'phantom hand,' and he can say in which direction it is moving.[13] However, as many statements indicate, all this takes place in an 'imaginary sphere' which literally penetrates the 'real' (i.e. afference-induced) sphere.

Let us therefore test our question instead on the basis of concrete predictions which the reafference principle can make for perception.

If the 'kinaesthetic sense' of a limb is reduced, then (apart from the extinction of the endogenous reflexes and the associated emergence of muscular weakness) active movement on a solid substrate must produce a *positive* perceptual process. As a result of inadequate reafference from the tension receptor, the efference copy must proceed upwards as a message in association with any movement which loads the limb: 'The contacted object is moving away.' This prediction is accurate! For example, when the kinaesthetic sense of the extensor muscles of the legs is markedly reduced, as with polyneuritis, one has the impression (for instance, when stepping down from a stool onto the floor) that the substrate moves downwards elastically.[14] Presumably, the same interpretation can be applied to similar reports concerning *tabes dorsalis,* indicating that the floor is 'like rubber.'

As the motor counterpart to this effect, one should expect *overextensive* limb displacement in active movement. As has already been explained for postural orientation, reduced reafference is accompanied by lack of what we have referred to as a 'peripheral stop,' using technical terminology. In the lowest center, the normal equilibrium state is not achieved, the efference continues and the limb movement becomes too extensive. The exaggerated, excessive movements of an atactic *tabes*-sufferer actually demonstrate this quite clearly.

To take another example: according to the reafference principle, it should make a great difference in perception whether pressure differences on the sole of the feet are produced by active movement or by a surface passively pressed against the sole. In the first case, one should notice no pressure differences, whilst such differences should be perceived in the second. D. Katz (1948) has found that when one stands up and actively loads the sole of the foot to differing extents by displacement of the body weight, by supporting the arms, by

---

[13]Unfortunately, there has apparently been no investigation to settle the important question as to whether motor impulses also pass into the stump of the arm.

[14]Personal observation reported by L. Lorenz (verbal communication) and others.

performing knee-bends, and so on, the perceived *difference threshold is twenty times higher* than when one lies on one's back and a corresponding pressure is exerted upon the sole.[15]

Thus, perception once again demonstrates the validity of the reafference principle. The mechanism in this latter case is doubtless to be found in a fairly high central area, since the behavior of the four limbs is taken into account in one framework.

Reafference and Locomotion

We can consequently measure the extent of reafference incorporated *as an integrating component* in a neuromotor apparatus according to the degree of exaggeration and inexactitude of the movement following destruction of the sensory pathways. In this respect, some interesting differences are observed: In lower swimming and crawling forms (fish; amphibians), locomotion is still completely normal following deafferentiation; in walking mammals, it is extremely atactic, and the complex motor sequences of the human hand can only be performed as individual, greatly exaggerated and disorganized fragments (Foerster, 1936). From this, it follows that with the simple, monotonous movement patterns the CNS, in principle, performs everything independently and thus has an 'automatic' character (von Holst; P. Weiss), whilst higher motor patterns *do not need 'reflex stimuli,'* but *do apparently need reafference!* The series from swimming through crawling, running, climbing and grasping to touching (hand; tongue) passes from movements which are adapted for no afference, through those which require reafference and exafference to movements which are primarily adapted for exafference.[16]

The old controversial question: 'Is movement of the limbs a reflex or an automatic process?' can, in this light, be set aside. The alternative was false! To give a pictorial illustration: The locomotion of a swimming fish takes place blindly into the dark, whilst the moving hand needs an illuminated environment. A deafferentiated hand is like a blind man, who cannot go on his way since he does not know where he is. This does *not* mean that the central motor drive for the hand is weaker than that of a swimming fish. And exactly as the sense of touch guides the blind man, the eye

---

[15]The author himself attempts to explain this fact in terms of a 'Gestalt interpretation of the entire range of bodily experience.'

[16]Like the expressive musculature of the face, the tongue does not possess proprioceptors; in the fingers, the proprioceptors are the most important providers of exafference.

aids a sensorially paralyzed hand: Both move around much better with such auxiliary afferences.

The Interaction of Several Afferences

The situation in the CNS becomes somewhat more complex where afferences from different parts of the body which can be moved in opposition to one another are involved in the posture and movement of the entire animal. A simple example: In arthropods, the direction of running is determined by ganglia in the head. If the right oesophageal commissure is transected, thus eliminating operation of the right sensory center (supraoesophageal ganglion), there is a resultant turning tendency—analogous to that found with postural orientation following unilateral suppression of the vestibular nucleus—which in this case produces movement to the left. The animal flexes towards the left when moving forwards and to the right when moving backwards, thus producing circles to the left in both cases (von Holst, 1934b).

If we make the justifiable assumption that the command displacing the tonus in the segments originates from a subordinate center (suboesophageal ganglion), it is to be expected in accordance with the reafference principle that reduction in the number of segments will increase the curvature exhibited by the remaining segments. This is because the loss of reafference, which produces a further imbalance in level in the higher command center, can only be countered by a corresponding increase in the range of movement, producing additional reafference. This expectation is borne out in practice: if a many-limbed arthropod (e.g., *Lithobius*) is shortened by removal of the posterior segments, the curvature increases with increasing reduction in length (Figs. 7.17 and 7.18), such that half of the animal will describe circles which are scarcely half as big as those produced by the entire animal (von Holst, 1934). This is a curious fact in the light of the reflex theory!

It is also to be expected that in an intact animal which is moving in a straight line, *passive* deflection of the posterior end (for example)

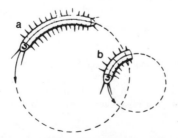

FIG. 7.17. Arthropod (*Litho-bius*) following transection of the oesophageal commissure on the right side. It describes circles with a specific mean diameter: *a:* otherwise intact animal; *b:* animal shortened posteriorly.

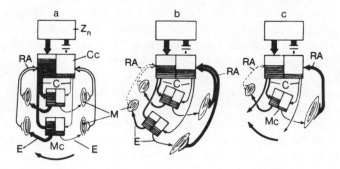

FIG. 7.18. Schema to explain Fig. 7.17. Zn = higher sensory center (supraoesophageal ganglion); Cc = command center (suboesophageal ganglion); C = command to the lower motor segment centers (Mc), of which only two are represented; E = efference to the muscle, M; A = afference; R = reafference from postural indicators in the joints of the body. The thickness of the arrows indicates the intensities of the streams of impulses. The right stream from Z_n to Cc has been disrupted. In *a*, the asymmetrically charged command center produces an equivalent asymmetry in the motor centers, and the efference of the latter produces body curvature (tonus displacement) to the left (lower arrow). In *b*, the reafference of this curvature charges the command center in a balanced manner and produces an equilibrium between the required asymmetry of innervation and the asymmetry in reafference. In *c*, after removal of the second motor center the reafference is once again inadequate, and there is further disequilibrium which necessarily leads to an increase in tonus displacement (lower arrow).

will lead to an *active* counter-deflection of the anterior end—as long as other disruptive effects are absent—since the exafference from the posterior end must be compensated by an opposing afference from another area in order to produce, *in toto*, the correct overall afference on the way up to the higher center. This behavior is also well known for many arthropods under the name of the 'homostrophic reflex' (Fig. 7.19).

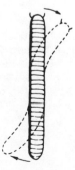

FIG. 7.19. Arthropod (*Iulus*) in which the posterior end is passively deflected to the left and the anterior end is subsequently actively turned to the right ('homostrophic reflex').

We can now turn to a more complex case, that of postural orientation in higher vertebrates and man. In the fish, postural orientation can be easily surveyed, since the static sensory organ is rigidly incorporated in the body. In addition, the motor system has no additional task to perform, whatever the required posture, since the mechanical equilibrium is of no importance. By contrast, *our* upright posture is labile and every requisite posture necessitates special innervation relationships. Furthermore, the head, body and limbs can be moved relative to one another. In active or passive inclination of the head, the labyrinth *must not* elicit any 'limb reflexes,' since the latter would only jeopardize bodily equilibrium! Let us look at the behavior which actually occurs (Fig. 7.20a–d).

The head and body of a resting animal are passively inclined to the right: a realigning compensatory movement is made with the limbs (Fig. 7.20b). If the head is immobilized in its spatial location and only the body is inclined, the same movement appears (Fig. 7.20c). If the head alone is inclined, the attempt is made to restore it to an upright position, but the body remains immobile (Fig. 7.20d). These observations can most easily be understood if it is assumed that the postural receptors are located in the body, as has often been suggested (Trendelenburg, 1906, 1907; Fischer, 1926). However, the behavior of the eyes does not fit in with this at all. In (b), the eyes are rotated slightly to the left (relative to the head), in (c) they are rotated slightly to the right, and in (d) pronounced rotation to the left occurs, so that they once again exhibit roughly the same position to the body. This is entirely analogous to the orientation of the head and the posterior extremity with the 'homostrophic reflex.'

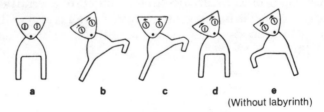

a   b   c   d   e
                                    (Without labyrinth)

FIG. 7.20. Sketch explaining the correcting movements of the limbs and eyes of a warm-blooded animal (mammals; birds) accompanying passive changes in posture (direction of inclination indicated with respect to the animal). *a:* normal posture; *b:* head and body inclined to the right; *c:* only the body inclined to the right; *d:* only the head inclined to the right; *e,* there is the same situation as in *d,* but after removal of the labyrinths (cf. Fig. 7.21c).

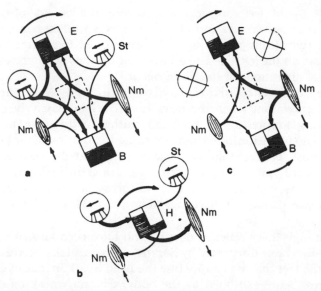

FIG. 7.21.   Schemata (analogous to Fig. 7.10) explaining the behavior of a warm-blooded animal with an intact statolith apparatus (*a, b*) and following removal of the latter (*c*), when the head is (passively) inclined to the side (cf. Fig. 7.20d, e). *a* and *b* equally apply to active inclination of the head. Postural centers: B = for the body; E = for the eyes; H = for the head; Nm = neck muscles. In *a* and *c*, the head postural center has been omitted in the interests of clarity; it is represented in *b*. The extent of afference from the statolith apparatus and from the postural receptors of the neck muscles is indicated by the thickness of the arrows. Unequal charging of the eye postural center (E in *a* and *c*), the head center (H in *b*) and the body center (B in *c*) in each case provokes a turning tendency indicated by the curved arrow. (For further details, see text.)

The simplest explanation of the overall behavior runs as follows: *two* afferences (at least) are involved in the posturing of the body, head and eyes; one originates from the statoliths in the head and the other comes from postural receptors in the neck muscles. These two streams of impulses are mutually subtracted in respect to the posture of the body and added in respect to the direction of the eyes (Fig. 7.21a). If this interpretation is correct, one should—according to the reafference principle—expect a quite specific functional disruption as soon as the afference from the two sides of the neck is artificially brought into imbalance. the CNS would evaluate this intervention as 'inclined body relative to an erect head' and produce an appropriately compensatory movement of the limbs. This actually proves to be the case. If a cold, wet compress is applied to the left side of the neck below the mastoid area and a hot compress is applied symmetrically on the right (thus producing a slower impulse frequency from the receptors on the left side and a faster one on the right), the expected postural alterations of the limbs occur.[17]

The reafference principle also requires exactly the same misinterpretation when the head is actively or passively inclined following suppression of both labyrinths. In this case, too, since there is no further information regarding inclination of the head, the CNS must 'believe' that the head is erect and the body inclined, consequently proceeding to correct the apparent inclination of the latter. This has also been known for some time as an actual occurrence (Dusser de Barenne; Magnus, 1924; cf. Figs 7.20e and 7.21c).

Although 'neck reflexes' of this kind have been known for some time—they were discovered by Barany—it has usually been assumed, from the fact that we can incline the head in all directions *without* 'reflexes' being exhibited by the body, that such neck reflexes are typically lacking in man. This widespread accepted opinion is once again a probable outcome of the reflex theory, which dictates that a 'stimulus' must always be followed by a movement—a movement which is in this case lacking.

The described extinction of the labyrinth and neck afferences only applies to the stream of impulses descending to the limbs on the trunk; it does not affect the eye where the two components are additive. Inclination of the head to the left produces rotation of the eye to the right (as can be easily observed with a mirror), which is exactly the same as that produced by inclination of the entire body without movement of the neck and by bending of the neck whilst the head is maintained erect (i.e., turning of the body to the right).[18] This effect was already known to Magnus and his co-workers. This summation ensures that, when the head is moved, the eyes retain their position relative to the vertical plane and thus maintain their visual field to some extent.

As far as the head itself is concerned, the observed behavior is easily understood. The center for head posture receives its afference

---

[17]The phenomenon was first described by Griesmann (1922) and confirmed by Fischer and Wodak (1922). Goldstein and Riese (1925) used it as an argument for a general theory of plasticity. As far as we are aware, no physiological interpretation has been presented.

[18]The relative contributions of the two afferences, in this case represented as equivalent (Fig. 7.20), can also be unequal for control of the eyes.

exclusively from the labyrinth and transmits its efference to the neck muscles. The head together with its neck muscles is comparable to the entire musculature of the fish (Fig. 7.21b). When passively inclined, it returns to the erect position, and it can also be actively inclined (command from higher centers). In both cases, the reafference flowing to the centers for body and eye position from the labyrinth and the postural receptors in the neck muscles is the same. Thus, we can understand that active or passive movement of the head makes no difference for the body and the eyes. One can give equally plausible explanations for the fact that the body and the limbs can similarly be moved to various requisite positions, whilst the head independently maintains its spatial location.

Through this interaction between the neuromotor mechanisms one can understand why the organism behaves *as if* the 'postural sense' were normally located in the body and as though it were able to wander up into the neck following removal of the labyrinths, such that inclination of the neck would abruptly produce 'postural reflexes.' This really does pose a problem for the reflex theory!

CONCLUSIONS

This account represents a preliminary, rough outline. Nevertheless, it may clearly show why we believe that the reafference principle possesses an advantage over other interpretations. The reflex theory describes everything which is evoked by stimuli with the same term. This, in itself, is inoffensive—after all, we need collective concepts— but this term is underlain by the seductive reflex-arc concept, which almost always presents us with false explanations. The counterpart of the reflex theory—the *plasticity* theory (Bethe)—according to which everything is connected up with everything else and excitation can spread in all directions in the CNS as in a nerve reticulum, is doubtless justified in its negation of the reflex interpretation; but neither these two theories nor any other given theory of the CNS can predict in a concrete case what will actually happen—*and what happens is never arbitrary.*[19] The reafference principle provides.

---

[19]Bethe himself is presumably in agreement with this interpretation. This is demonstrated by his various attempts to give a more detailed explanation of actual events, using physical models. In our opinion, his derived principle of mechanical 'transitional coupling' (Bethe & Fischer, 1931) represents a good model; the discussion on pp. 180–207 of the present paper is simply a detailed representation of transitional coupling.

concrete predictions which can be tested to show the validity of the principle and its limits. It represents *one* mechanism *among others* and does not prejudice the possible occurrence of automaticity, coordination and spontaneity. It would therefore seem appropriate to link the opposing interpretations one to another. Since the reafference principle explains in a uniform manner particular phenomena throughout the CNS from the lowest processes (passive and active positioning of the limbs, relationship between the different parts of the body) to those at a very high level (spatial orientation, perceptual processes, sensory illusions), it provides a bridge between the lower levels of neurophysiology and higher behavioral theory.

It has often been asked whether insects can distinguish their own movements from movement in their surroundings. Mathilde Hertz (1934) instinctively answered this question positively, but was unable to give a plausible explanation of the manner in which it occurs. Other investigators have followed von Buddenbrock (1937) in giving a negative answer on the grounds that the relative movement between the animal and the external environment is, of course, the same in both cases. We can now recognize the following fact: The *eye* is indeed unable to distinguish between its own movement and that of the environment, but the *animal*—which, after all, does possess a CNS consisting of more than connecting leads between the receptors and the muscles—is *well able* to distinguish the two. With the aid of the reafference principle, it achieves recognition of the *constancy of its own objective environment*.

Such *constancy phenomena* in fact play a major part in human psychology. Well-known examples are the perception of an immobile environment when the eyes are moving (spatial constancy) and the perception of an object as retaining a particular size independent of distance (size constancy). As we have seen, the reafference principle explains both of these phenomena. The fact that it does not explain other constancy phenomena into the bargain (e.g., 'color constancy' of optically perceived objects) is not a drawback but an advantage of the principle, which—because of its concrete formulations—does not permit pseudo-explanations of heterogeneous factual matter.

Finally, the reafference principle also provides a quite specific contribution to the question of the *objectivity of perception*. We have repeatedly seen that the 'correct' information is simply the resultant of two 'false' bits of information, each of which possesses in its own right the character of 'correctness.' For a lower center which receives only *one* afference, all information is 'correct' in the same way. The question whether a perceptual process can also be *'objectively'* correct, or whether it is only 'apparent,' can only arise where several different afferences are combined. 'Objectively correct' then means no more than coincidence of different bits of information, and information is evaluated as 'apparent' when it does not fit in with other information. In this respect, the lowest center is unconditionally stupid—but we must also consider the fact that even the highest center can never be more intelligent than its afferences permit, and that every individual afference is 'fallible.'

It is hoped that this article will contribute to the gradual disappearance of attempts to describe the functions of the highest developed organ of the body with a few primitive expressions. The sooner we recognize the fact that the *complex higher functional Gestalts* which leave the reflex physiologist dumbfounded in fact send roots *down to the simplest basal functions of the CNS*, the sooner we shall see that the previously terminologically insurmountable barrier between the lower levels of neurophysiology and higher behavioral theory simply dissolves away.

8

The Hierarchical Stucturing of Action

COHERENT COMBINATIONS

The preceding chapters have introduced three distinct kinds of functional units—reflexes, oscillators, and servomechanisms. These are some of the building blocks of coordinated action. The higher levels of the nervous system construct complex action sequences (e.g., the building of a nest or a search for food) by allowing appropriate combinations of functional units to operate either simultaneously or in suitable sequence. Reflexes, oscillators, and servomechanisms do not exhaust the major categories of functional units. There remain, no doubt, basic units of action whose essential features have not yet been given a clear experimental characterization. But the three categories that have been experimentally documented provide a foundation for considering principles of hierarchical organization.

We have seen that each category of functional unit has interaction principles associated with it. Reflexes interact by facilitation of agonists and inhibition of antagonists (Chapter 3). Oscillators interact by means of phase shifting effects on each other ("magnet effects" in von Holst's terms, Chapters 4 and 5). Interactions with servomechanisms frequently involve the efference copy principle (Chapter 7). Both reflexes and taxes may interact through the chaining principle (Chapters 3 and 6); and so on. These diverse modes of interaction do not, however, by themselves insure the coherence of coordinated action. The coherence and purposefulness of sustained action depends upon a hierarchical structuring of the units. By means of this hierarchical structure, the highest levels of neural integration impose an overall direction on behavior.

The isolated action of a lower unit of behavior will not usually serve any purpose for the animal. Suppose, for example, that the unit controlling the stepping of a single leg were active all by itself. What good would that do the cockroach? A single leg, stepping all by itself cannot propel the roach anywhere. It can only waste energy. Other units must be active at the same time in order that the action of a leg-stepping unit may make a useful contribution to behavior. Nor can these be just any collection of other units. Insects use their front legs for grooming as well as walking. They rhythmically stroke their front "feet" (tarsi) over their head and down their antennae. There is also a distinctive pattern of leg movement when the roach is on its back and trying to right itself. It obviously will not do to have some legs stepping, some grooming, and some making righting motions all at the same time. In order that diverse lower units may act in concert to generate a coherent behavior of the whole animal, there must be higher levels of organization, levels that permit only those actions that fit together.

An elementary functional unit, *when it is permitted to act,* directly controls the motor neurons to the muscles, the final common paths for the expression of all behaviors. But, any given elementary unit is only permitted to act some of the time. The elementary unit that underlies the positive light orientation of the coastal snails, when it is allowed to act, directly controls the motor neurons that determine direction of turning. However, it is only allowed to act—it is only *potentiated*—when the snail is upside down and underwater. When the snail is right side up and/or out of water, the positively phototaxic mechanism is depotentiated—not allowed to act. Control over the motor neurons passes to the negatively phototaxic mechanism.

The example of the positive and negative phototaxes in the coastal snail displays a three-level hierarchy. At the lowest level are the motor neurons. They directly activate and deactivate the muscle fibers that comprise a muscle. At the second level are the positive and negative phototaxes. These neural circuits do not control muscle fibers directly; rather, they control the pattern of firing in the motor neurons to the muscles. At the third level we have a "decision" circuit. Its control over muscle fibers is twice removed; it determines whether the positively phototaxic or the negatively phototaxic circuit is potentiated. The potentiated taxis controls the firing in a subset of motor neurons, and the motor neurons in turn control the contraction and relaxation of muscle fibers. The decision circuit controls behavior by way of the control it exerts over lower level units (the orienting units), much as a general controls the footsoldiers by way of the control he exerts over their commanders. This layering of control processes is what one means by hierarchical organization in action. And, the pattern of neural connections which determines that the decision circuit controls the phototaxes but not the geotaxis is what one means by the *structure* of the hierarchical control system. The structure of the system determines what controls what.

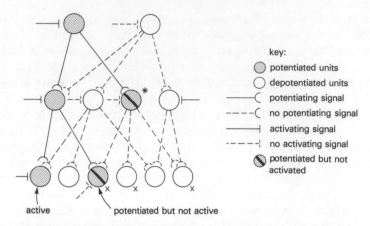

key:
- ⊙ potentiated units
- ○ depotentiated units
- ⎯C potentiating signal
- ----C no potentiating signal
- ⎯⊣ activating signal
- ----⊣ no activating signal
- ⊘ potentiated but not activated

active   potentiated but not active

FIG. 8.1.   A schematic rendering of the manner in which potentiating signals descend from higher to lower levels of a lattice hierarchy. Potentiated units have a high potential for becoming active and depotentiated units a low potential. Activating conditions are the conditions that cause a potentiated unit to actually become active. In the case of elementary units (lowest level), the outputs from the active units go directly to the muscles. In the case of higher units, the outputs from the active units descend from them to potentiate and depotentiate lower units. For example, if the activating conditions for the potentiated unit marked with an asterisk were to arise, the lower units it controls (marked with an X) would become potentiated. Note that one of these lower units already is potentiated by way of a different intermediate unit.

At any given moment in the life of the organism only some of the organism's repertoire of functional units are potentiated (Fig. 8.1). Only potentiated units are free to interact with each other to determine the pattern of commands to the musculature. The other units, units whose actions would be at cross-purposes to the prevailing direction of the animal's behavior, are depotentiated. Their access to the final common paths is blocked by inhibition of their interneurons and they play no role in the ongoing behavior. The direction of ongoing behavior is determined by the pattern of potentiation and depotentiation. By potentiating a coherent selection of lower units the higher levels impose a general tendency upon behavior. The animal reacts to the world in many different ways as activating conditions vary (Fig. 8.1). But, the different reactions initiated by different activating conditons have a common tendency. Reactions that do not have this tendency are depotentiated and cannot occur. The selective potentiation of actions that have a common or complementary tendency is the source of the coherence and direction that are such salient features of behavior, the source in other words, of purposiveness.

The patterns of behavior that are possible for a given animal are determined by the patterns of potentiation and depotentiation that the higher levels of the animal's nervous system can impose upon the lower level units of action. The richer and more varied the possible patterns of potentiation and depotentiation, the richer and more varied the animal's behavioral repertoire. The variety and intricacy of the selective potentiations and depotentiations available to an organism is determined by the structural intricacy of the hierarchical control system in which the basic building blocks of action are embedded. The basic building blocks of actions are embedded in a hierarchical system and the structure of the hierarchy limits the sequences of muscular activity the animal may produce. The limitation that the structure of an animal's coordinative hierarchy imposes upon its behavioral options is superbly illustrated by the work of Paul Weiss (1941) on the coordination of forward and backward walking in salamanders.

WEISS'S APPROACH

Sherrington stressed the hierarchical arrangement of neural activity, but his evidence for it was largely anatomical. His followers in clinical neurology, most notably Denny-Brown, made the hierarchical conception the foundation of their analysis of neurological disorder. The effects of accidental or pathological brain lesions in humans and experimental brain transections or lesions in higher animals give abundant evidence that the brain exerts its determining effect on behavior primarily by modulating the interplay of spinal mechanisms. Damage to higher levels of the brain seems to unbalance the flow of potentiating and depotentiating signals to the functional units in the spinal cord. Some categories of functional units become chronically potentiated and others chronically depotentiated. It is difficult, however, to extract from such data a clear conception of the functional components in the motor hierarchy and how these components are tied together into a pattern of subordination and superordination. The insults to the nervous system that produce these neurological data do not ordinarily split the system along functional lines. It is rather like trying to analyze the executive structure of a large corporation by bombing one wing of the headquarters building. The experimental intervention takes out a mixed bag of division managers, vice presidents, secretaries and office boys. It would be much more instructive if one could send all the vice presidents on vacation for six months. From the resulting dysfunction, if any, one might perceive what it is vice presidents contribute to the integrated functioning of the company.

Weiss's approach to analyzing the hierarchical integration of forward and backward progression in the salamander left the CNS intact. To demonstrate centrally patterned activation of lower level units, Weiss made these patterns more salient by divorcing them from their ordinary functional effects. He reversed a salamander's front limbs, so they pointed backward rather than forward. Whenever the muscles controlling these limbs showed the pattern of contraction and relaxation that would ordinarily propel the salamander forward the effect was instead to propel the salamander backward. In this way, Weiss developed a clear and experimentally documented conception of the intermediate functional units in the hierarchically structured neural machinery. He showed that the coordination of front limb stepping with hind limb stepping depended on the organizing effect of a central programming unit that specified a particular, centrally mediated pattern of interaction between the lower units controlling the individual legs. The coordination between legs was *not* achieved by way of the kind of peripherally mediated process postulated by chained-reflex theories of coordination. The stepping of the front legs was not triggered by sensory signals resulting from the mechanical effects of the stepping movements of the hindlimbs (and vice versa). Rather, the units controlling the hind limbs and the units controlling the front limbs were constrained by some central program to interact in such a way as to produce one or another pattern of stepping across all four limbs. The great merit of Weiss's experiments was to show that these higher order constraints operated whether or not the resulting four-limb stepping patterns were functional. The centrally coordinated interaction between the units that control the individual limbs was in some ways as rigid and blind as the computer programs that relentlessly call up the prescribed series of subroutines even when the input to the computer is such that the computations carried out by the subroutines no longer make sense.

At the time Weiss wrote, we had little grasp of what the units controlling individual legs might be and even less grasp of how a higher unit could constrain these lower units to interact in a particular way. Now, however, it seems likely that the lower units are the oscillator-dominated units discussed in Chapter 5. The higher unit—the unit that coordinates walking—constrains the interaction between these oscillators by controlling the flow of coupling signals from one oscillator to the other. This idea will be spelled out in more detail at the end of this chapter.

The lengthy paper by Weiss that follows is remarkable for the incisive introduction to the general nature of the problems posed by the phenomena of motor coordination. As he points out early on, the subject is frequently discussed in a maddeningly vague way. His introduction is also remarkable for its concise and critcial review of the major schools of thought—the preformistic structural (innate connections), the heuristic (learned associations), and the systemic (Gestalt) schools.

IN DEFENSE OF CONNECTIONISM

Weiss goes to some lengths to point out the deficiencies in the preformistic structural school of thought, the school which holds that coordinated action is determined by genetically specified patterns of connections between neurons. The most common objection to this school of thought concerns the ontogenetic aspect—the assertion that the basic determinants of coordination are genetically specified. This is emphatically not Weiss's objection; a central argument in the complete version of Weiss's paper is that the basic determinants of coordination are indeed inherited (or, better, self-differentiated).[1] I have edited out a great deal of this argument, because the original paper is very long and because I want to focus on the mechanisms of coordination, *not* on their ontogeny (i.e., not on the processes and variables that bring the mechanisms into being). Despite my editing, it will nonetheless be obvious that Weiss's objections to the preformistic structural school do not center around the school's claim that the determinants of coordination are preformed. Rather they center around the school's claim that what determines coordination is the pattern of connections between neurons, the microanatomy of the nervous system.

Weiss advances two very different lines of argument against the notion that the microanatomy of the nervous system (which neurons connect to which) is a major determinant of the patterns of muscular activation in coordinated action. The first and today most interesting line of argument is that the bewildering variety of patterns generated within one and the same set of muscles would seem to require an equally bewildering variety of different neural circuits. Even if one were willing to grant the existence of as many distinct neural circuits as there are distinct temporal sequences of muscle activation, one would still not have explained how the system determined which neural circuit was to be allowed to control the muscles at any given moment. Weiss develops this line of argument in his Introduction (see pp. 225–229) and returns to it from time to time later on.

This line of argument loses most of its force as soon as one abandons the idea that the reflex is *the* functional unit of organization in action, and that all neural circuits are therefore reflex circuits. In Chapter 5 we saw that all of the different temporal sequences of leg movements observed in insect locomotion can be generated by one and the same coupled-oscillator circuit. Indeed, the vast, as yet unrealized importance of coupled-oscillator circuits lies precisely in this: By varying the strength of one or two signals (frequency setting signals) and/or by varying the direction and strength of a few inter-oscillator coupling signals, one can generate a rich variety of output patterns from a single basic circuit. Servo-circuits, such as the neural circuits mediating the taxes and the optokinetic reaction also have the property that a system of such

---

[1]Weiss is too subtle a developmental biologist to use the vague and confusing term "inherited." He prefers the subtler, but more precise and defensible term "self-differentiated," that is, "differentiated in their essential characteristics independently of the actual intervention of function" (p. 223).

circuits may display a variety of actions, depending on the constantly changing values of the error signals.

Both servo-circuits and coupled-oscillator circuits, despite their versatility, are determined by the nature of the neuronal elements composing them and by the pattern of interconnection between these elements. They are, in other words, determined by the microanatomy of the nervous system. Thus, as soon as one recognizes that many neural circuits are not organized in accord with the reflex concept, but rather in accord with other more versatile conceptions, then one is no longer forced to posit as many distinct neural circuits as there are distinct patterns of behavior.

Weiss's second line of attack on the notion that patterns of neural interconnection determine patterns of action rested on experimental conclusions that have subsequently been disproven. Many of Weiss's experiments involved the regeneration of motor neurons into the muscles of limbs that had been grafted on to unusual locations (as when a front limb from one salamander was grafted on to the upper back of another salamander). Weiss believed that the motor neurons that found their way into, say, the biceps muscle of the grafted limb were not motor neurons that would ordinarily innervate a biceps muscle. Despite the muscles of the grafted limb being innervated seemingly at random by motor neurons, the muscles contracted when they should. The biceps muscle of the grafted limb contracted and relaxed in synchrony with the biceps muscle of the normal limb, and so on. Since a given muscle responded at "its" time in the overall pattern regardless (so Weiss thought) of the motor neurons that happened to innervate it, the appropriately timed activation of that muscle could not depend on any specific set of neuronal interconnections. However, Sperry (1945) subsequently showed that the muscles of the grafted limb were not reinnervated randomly: Only motor neurons that ordinarily innervate a biceps muscle functionally reinnervate a transplanted biceps. Sperry's findings removed the foundation for Weiss's second line of attack on the specific-connections school of thought.

That Weiss's attack on the connectionistic school has not been sustained by more recent work on nerve regeneration in no way invalidates his penetrating analysis of the problem of coordination. Nor does it have any bearing on his demonstration tht the *basic* patterns of muscle activation are generated by central scores (central programs). In fact, this contention has been confirmed by virtually all modern neurobiological work on the mechanisms of coordination (Bizzi, et al., 1971; Carlson & Bentley, 1977; Deliagina, et al., 1975; Elsner, 1972; Evarts, et al., 1971; Fentress, 1973; Grillner, 1975; Herman, et al., 1976; Kennedy & Davis, 1977; Murphy & Phillips, 1967; Peretz, 1969; Truman, et al., 1976; Weisenfeld, et al., 1977; Wyman, 1977).

The extent to which this work has so far failed to influence the thinking of psychologists may be estimated from a recent paper by Adams in the

Psychological Review (1977), entitled "Feedback theory of how joint receptors regulate the timing and positioning of a limb." Adams puts forward a Sherringtonian analysis of the control of limb movements, claims that there is no "organ of time" (i.e., pacemaker) in the nervous system, and vigorously attacks the central program viewpoint. The paper is remarkable for the selectivity with which it treats the recent neurophysiological literature on motor mechanisms. The lengthy list of references given above will convince anyone who troubles to consult them that Adams' views are not tenable. The list of references demonstrating unequivocal instances of centrally derived patterning in one behavior after another in species from every branch of the phylogenetic tree can be lengthened indefinitely.

In summary, the paper that follows gives a penetrating analysis of the problem of coordination and a concise characterization of the major schools of thought. It also provides compelling evidence that many behaviors are produced by hierarchically structured programming circuits in the central nervous system.

Self-Differentiation of the Basic Patterns of Coordination*

PAUL WEISS

THE PROBLEM OF COORDINATION

Introduction

Motor behavior is effected through the coordinated operation of the musculature. The problem of the ontogenetic origin of behavior, therefore, resolves itself essentially into the problem of the ontogeny of coordination.

Whether "coordination" is a *constitutional* (i.e., prefunctional) faculty of the central nervous system or an *acquired* property, gained by experience, has long been a matter of dispute. The main objective

---

*Reprinted, in edited form, with the permission of Paul Weiss and the publisher, Johns Hopkins Press, from *Comparative Psychology Monographs*, 1941, Vol. 17, No. 4. Copyright ® 1941 by Johns Hopkins Press. All rights reserved.

of this paper is to present direct experimental proof that *the basic patterns of coordination arise by self-differentiation within the nerve centers, prior to, and irrespective of actual experience in their use.* In addition, experimental data will be reported indicating what coordination consists of, and how it is laid down in the centers. So specific and articulate has this experimental information been that we would forego the full benefit of its instructiveness if we were to report it in the general inarticulate language in which the problems of coordination are conventionally treated. Since the experiments have produced answers much more differentiated and detailed than any of the questions commonly being asked, we must prepare the ground for their presentation by reformulating the questions with greater precision. One cannot discuss "coordination" profitably so long as the term is kept on the abstract level; ill-defined, and noncommittal in regard to concrete implications. We, therefore, shall try to dissect the general concept of "coordination." By breaking it down into more tangible issues, we make it tractable and give experimental analysis a chance to substitute knowledge for conjecture.

Thus, with a view to discontinuing the practice of speculating about "coordination" without a clear mental picture of just what it implies, we shall first review the facts and reformulate the problems, and only then proceed to present the experiments and, in their light, scrutinize the existing theories of coordination. The notable confusion about terms and facts in this field would justify a much more thorough reconsideration of the whole subject than can here be afforded. However, such an ambitious attempt had better be postponed until more concrete building stones for a good and sound theory of coordination have been gathered than are now avilable. It is only a few of these building stones that the present paper aims to contribute.

There is a striking disproportion between our knowledge of the physiological properties of nervous *elements* and out understanding of the operation of the nervous *system* as the coordinator of those elemental activities in the service of the organism. While the combined efforts of electrophysiological, histological, biochemical and mathematical studies have produced a great wealth of data concerning the *elemental* activity of the neurone, our conception of the *systematic* activity of their organized totality has essentially remained pegged to the level to which it had been raised by *Sherrington's* classic work on the "Integrative Action of the Nervous System." We do not mean to imply that some progress has not been made here and there. Brain physiologists and neurologically-minded psychologists, in their efforts to interpret behavior in terms of the function of the nervous system, naturally had to focus on the system as such. From their studies, they were led to conclusions which partly supplemented, partly discredited, the synthetic conception of the nervous sytem to which preoccupation with the nervous elements had led. Yet, although they succeeded in pointing the direction toward a more adequate theory of central functions, the actual progress made thus far appears small when contrasted with the spectacular growth of our information about the nervous units during the same period. A mere comparison between the volume of attention currently paid to the issue of synaptic transmission— whether chemically or electrically mediated—on the one hand, and the almost complete neglect of the problem of how central transmission has come to be so discriminatory and selective as to lead to coordinated responses, rather than to unorganized convulsions, on the other, puts the situation into sharp relief. A restoration of sounder proportions should be attempted, of course, not by detracting from the current vigorous trend toward the isolated elements, but by reviving interest and revitalizing research in matters which concern the integrative aspects of the nervous system. If such course is to be followed with profit, it will pay, at the outset, to examine the possible reasons of its lag in the past.

A few explanations suggest themselves quite readily. The most obvious one is the infinitely greater difficulty and complexity of the task facing the student of the nervous system. This may be a challenge to inquisitive minds, but it certainly does not predispose the subject for mass attack by routine methods. So long as one clings to the study of elements, one is dealing with well-circumscribed units, a well-defined subject, presenting clearcut problems, and one can call on familiar and approved methods of analysis. As soon as one raises the eye from the unit to the whole system, the subject becomes fuzzy, the problems ill-descript, and the prospect of fruitful attack discouraging in its indefiniteness. This may explain why a considerable number of able experimental workers prefer to circle around the focal problems at a respectful distance rather than heading straight at them. It also explains why discussions of central nervous function operate so much more liberally with words than with facts; for it is remarkable how general the tendency is in this field to cover up factual ignorance by verbalisms. The average attitude is somewhat like this: the "whole" gets a large share of one's thought and talk, but the elements get all the benefit of one's actual work; here the problems seem to be so infinitely more tangible. Adrian (1932) has expressed this very plainly at the conclusion of his lectures on "the mechanism of nervous action." He says:

> The nervous system is built up of specialized cells whose reactions do not differ fundamentally from one another or from the reactions of the other kinds of excitable cell. They have a fairly simple mechanism when we treat them as individuals. Their behavior *in the mass* may be quite another story, but this is for future work to decide. (p. 93, italics added).

The search for that "other story" deserves encouragement.

However, a second point which has detracted from a vigorous pursuit of this search is not to be overlooked. This is the reiterated expression by highly competent students of the nervous system of their conviction that a thorough understanding of what is going on in the isolated peripheral nervous units, will eventually explain the operation of the centers, too. Gasser (1937), for instance, in his Harvey lecture on "the control of excitation in the nervous system," states this belief quite explicitly:

> Admittedly the nervous system can be understood only as it is operating as a whole, but it is equally true that an insight into its working can be gained *only* by a detailed analysis of its parts. If the isolation of a part results in the sacrifice of some of its qualities, the loss is compensated for by the acquisition of a degree of simplicity making the part more amenable to investigation. The organization of the nervous system is such that an understanding of the mode of activity of any part of the ganglionic apparatus would mean a long step forward, for all parts of the nervous system are fundamentally alike. We can, therefore, proceed, confident in the belief that when the parts are understood, they *can be added together into larger units,* and that, as the addition takes place, the lost qualities will again emerge and be recognized. Bit by bit it should be possible in the end to build back to the elaborate patterns of activity which are characteristic of the intact organism. (p. 171, italics added).

This stand seems justified if one accepts the premise proposed by Keith Lucas and quoted and amplified by Gasser, "that the phenomena taking place in the central nervous system could be explained without the assumption of any properties which could not be experimentally identified in peripheral nerve." "If the reactions in the central nervous system are to be explained on the basis of occurrences in peripheral nerves,... it is evident that the starting point of all discussions must be a thoroughgoing understanding of the physiology of nerve fibers" (p. 173).

At the same time, the opinion is growing that this precept of Lucas has not worked, and cannot work, in bringing us real understanding of the centers, in spite of numerous ingenious hypotheses designed to make it work. Forbes, for one, once an outstanding exponent of Lucas' scheme, expresses this change of opinion poignantly, when he declares (1936):

> In developing these schemata no attempt was made to offer a final theory of the workings of the central nervous system, but merely to see whether research had yet brought to light any facts which were utterly incapable of explanation in terms of the phenomena of peripheral conduction. As newer information has come to light, the subsidiary hypotheses needed to explain the facts in terms of the nerve impulses alone have made it increasingly improbable that these working hypotheses would be adequate, until now they have become of little more than historical interest (p. 164).

Without arguing the issue any further, we merely present it as a symptom of the discouragement not uncommonly held out to those who might have wanted to give the central nervous system an independent examination as a system in its own right.

Consequently, a large group of workers who did concern themselves primarily with the nervous system accepted the thesis of the "elementarians," that inasmuch as central activity can be conceived of as merely a proper linking together—"association"—of individual neurone activities, understanding of central activity can be pieced together from bits of knowledge about the elements. Thus the theory that "associations" form the basis of behavior, which is the psychological version of the theory of the "reflex" as the basis of central nervous action, played into the hands of the elementarians and greatly increased their prestige. Now, we still are not saying that they may not in the end turn out to have been right; but we do want to point out that the question as to whether there is more in the centers than there is to be found in the peripheral elements is a purely empirical question which cannot be solved on *a priori* grounds and which should not be prejudicated by recommendations for procedure which by their very nature preclude any but the anticipated answer. Nobody is likely to do prospecting in an area where he is constantly assured by experts that nothing worthwhile can be found; nor is he going to be encouraged by the repeated warning that whatever he is looking for has already been found—or, at least, will most certainly be found—by his neighbor. In this sense, the denial that the central nervous system presents problems *sui generis,* has undoubtedly been a potent deterrent from a vigorous attack on those problems.

It is not to be questioned that the attempt to identify in the central nervous system properties familiar from peripheral nerve elements has met with spectacular success. In fact, faith in the fundamental identity of both has been rewarded by discovery in the peripheral elements of properties which had formerly been known only to occur within the centers (see Gasser). However, by confining attention to those phenomena which the peripheral and central systems have in common, we plainly relegate the specifically central phenomena to continued obscurity; by "specifically central" we mean the ones that are not recoverable from peripheral investigations. *Coordination* is a case in point, and this brings us to our immediate subject.

Even though we can interpret other central phenomena, such as reaction time, summation, rhythmicity, inhibition, irradiation, fatigue, etc., in terms of known properties of neurones, the specific *order* in which the units are brought into play so as to produce effects serviceable to the organism, is nowhere accounted for in this scheme. It is this order that is commonly referred to as "coordination," with implications that are not always clearly realized. Coordination means the *selective* activation of definite groups of units in such combinations that their united action will result in an organized peripheral effect that makes sense. But what principle is there in operation in the centers to make the appropriate selection? And in what terms is the choice being made? Here is a question aimed at a "specifically central" phenomenon, evidently of fundamental importance, and yet one that is hardly ever asked explicitly, and still more rarely answered in anything but the most general of terms. Really only a very few have taken the trouble of penetrating beneath the surface of the problem, and although, as we shall show below, none of their efforts have as yet yielded wholly acceptable results, they have at least emerged with some definite suggestions that can be put to test and serve as points of departure for further clarification. In addition to the few who have given the matter mature thought, practically every biologist and psychologist carries in his mind some sort of notion, specific or hazy, of the mechanism of coordination, which he has usually acquired unconsciously and by accident.

Disregarding their various shades, we can class these notions, both rational and instinctive ones, into three different groups: the *preformistic,* the *heuristic,* and the *systemic* theories. All three start from the fact of the transmissibility of excitation from one nerve element to another, and go on to explain why transmission in the normal nervous system does not occur indiscriminately, ending up in mass contraction of all muscles, but remains confined within certain channels, yielding an orderly and differentiated response. For the time being, we may ignore the fact that by stamping the problem as purely one of controlled transmission we subject our search to an unwarranted limitation from the very start. Inasmuch as most speculations on coordination have tacitly accepted this limitation, they do not essentially differ on that point. From here on, however, they diverge.

THE THEORIES OF COORDINATION

The Preformistic-Structural Concept

The first and most popular interpretation of coordination is the reference to stereotyped inherited anatomical neurone connections in the centers. It is based on the study of reflexes, the observation that in many simple reflexes there is a fairly definite and constant relation between the point of stimulation and the nature of the response ("reflex-arc"), and the assumption that the chain of events leading from stimulus to response is anatomically preformed in a chain of neurones leading from the sense organ through the centers to the effector. The biological adequacy of the response, according to this concept, is a result of the correct construction of the anatomical apparatus, that is, among other things, of the suitable distribution of the peripheral and intracentral neurones, suitable arrangement of the central switches among neurones, suitable arrangement of the muscles on the skeleton and suitable form of the joints; "suitable" in the sense of making the whole response come out as of service to the organism. In other words, the body has its coordination built in.

In designating this concept as "preformistic," we do not use the term "preformation" in the sense in which it is used in embryology. There it refers to the existence of organized patterns in the egg prior to the onset of *development*, while in the present connection it merely implies the presence of definitely organized innervation patterns in the centers prior to the onset of their actual *operation*. Developmentally speaking, these patterns have, of course, been differentiated according to the same principle of progressive (epigenetic) determination which dominates embryonic development in general (P. Weiss, 1939). Only in functional regards may we call them "self-differentiated," that is, differentiated in their essential characteristics independently of the actual intervention of function.

Movements with only one degree of freedom give an excellent illustration of this kind of anatomically preformed coordination. All a clam can do with its shell, is to open and close it, the contraction of the adductor muscle effecting the closure, and the elastic ligament over the hinge effecting the opening when the muscle relaxes. The whole performance is rigidly determined by the construction of valves and hinge. The situation would not be fundamentally different, if the opening of the hinge were effected by another muscle, instead of an elastic ligament, as is the case in bivalve brachiopods. In this case, the "suitability" of the situation implies, in addition to the hinging of the joint, the insertion of the two muscles on opposite sides of the joint (mechanically antagonistic action) and the ability of the nervous system to contract one muscle while the other relaxes (reciprocal innervation). If one admits the possibility that, for instance, tactile receptors are connected with the shutting muscle, and chemoreceptors with the opening muscle, the differential response of the animal—closing after mechanical disturbance and opening in the presence of food—would be accounted for on purely anatomical grounds.

Cases have been reported in which the anatomical predisposition to produce a given peripheral effect is even visibly expressed by the nervous elements so predisposed. The giant nerve fibers of the earthworm are the mediators of certain fast responses only while other fiber systems serve slower reactions of different pattern (see Prosser, 1934). Making use of the fact that thicker fibers conduct faster (Erlanger & Gasser, 1937), the anatomy of these animals has provided for a system of central superhighways for undelayed through traffic. Still more spectacular is the case of the innervation of the mantle of the squid. The giant nerve fibers to the mantle muscles, which radiate from an anterior ganglion, increase both in length and thickness in anteroposterior order (J. Z. Young, 1938). In view of the proportionality between thickness and conduction speed, this provision enables a simultaneous discharge from the ganglion to arrive at all muscles at approximately the same time, producing a powerful synchronized over-all contraction in spite of the graded lengths of the supplying nerves (Pumphrey & Young, 1938). But for this anatomical provision, the result could be achieved only by having the impulses go off staggered in definite regular intervals, beginning with the longest fibers. Here, too, coordination is efficiently preformed in the anatomical structure of the nervous system. Similarly, the fast and slow reactions of the claws of crustaceans are mediated by different sets of nerve fibers, either set being predisposed for its function by appropriate constitutional properties (Wiersma & van Harreveld, 1938).

There can be no doubt, therefore, about the existence of built-in coordination. The only question is whether these observations can be generalized and made the basis for a theory of *all* coordination. In point of fact, they have been generalized without much opposition. For instance, the flexing and bending of a knee joint has been viewed much in the same light as the opening and closing of the valves in a brachiopod. However, we must reiterate that the brachiopod exemplifies a system with only a single degree of freedom of motion. The only two movements compatible with the rigid mechanical limitations occur both in the same plane, and the muscles merely determine whether the joint will move one way or the other. It is after this sort of model that the anatomical theory of reflex action has been fashioned, and one recognizes immediately the close resemblance with the conventional description of the stepping movements of a vertebrate limb. The main action of the joints is represented as occurring in one plane, with two groups of antagonistic muscles producing excursions of opposite sign, which, depending on whether they reduce or increase the angle of the joint, are designated as "flexion" and "extension." To represent a limb movement in this manner involves a deliberate abstraction, in that we confine our attention to those joints which, in crude approximation at least, can be considered to conform to the model, that is, to true hinge joints (Fig. 8.2a). Under these conditions, simplified to the extreme, peripheral coordination would appear simply as the alternating contraction of two antagonistic muscle groups, and the central basis of that coordination might pass for merely an oscillation between the excitation of a "flexor" and that of an "extensor" center, each attended by inhibition of the other ("reciprocal" innervation).[1] An underlying anatomical neurone setup is conceivable, and several such schemes have been promoted in the past. They have become so firmly ingrained in our thinking that most textbooks deal with them as realities.

This is no place to evaluate the merits of the various anatomical switchboard concepts which have been advanced in explanation of simple type reflexes, and, in further consequence, of coordinated behavior in general. But it will be well to keep in mind what Herrick,

---

[1] It is irrelevant in the present context whether this oscillation is regarded as due to alternating stretch-reflexes (Sherrington) or to autonomous rhythms of the centers (Graham Brown, 1914).

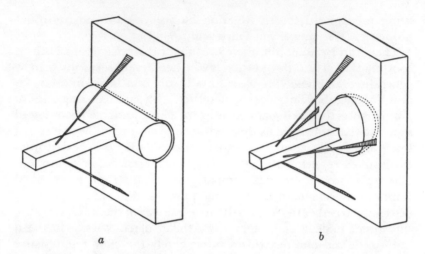

a   *b*

FIG. 8.2.   Models of Joints. (*a*) hinge joint with single degree of freedom; moved by a pair of antagonistic mucles; (*b*) ball joint with free rotational motion, operated by four muscles.

that most judicious student of the anatomy of the central nervous system, had to say in this connection (1930):

> No complication of separate and insulated reflex arcs, each of which is conceived as giving a one-to-one relation between stimulus and response, and no interconnection of such arcs by elaborate switchboard devices can conceivably yield the type of behavior which we actually find in higher vertebrates.... These facts are regarded as incompatible with the traditional dogmas of reflex physiology, with its precisely localized and well-insulated reflex arcs and centers of reflex adjustment....The mechanisms of traditional reflexology seem hopelessly inadequate (p. 645).

However, even if the concept of a rigid anatomical neurone linkage were adequate to explain the single pendulum-like action of a hinge joint, it must utterly fail as a basis of coordination in any more general sense. For most joints are constructed so as to allow of more than one degree of freedom and, therefore, require more than two sets of muscles, inserting and acting in different planes.

A ball joint, such as the shoulder joint, can be moved in any plane laid through its center (Fig. 8.2b). The direction in which it actually moves at any given moment, is determined by the resultant of muscular tensions acting from all sides. Depending on the combination of active muscles and the relative strength of their contraction, an infinite variety of positions can be assumed. Variety of movement is thus made possible by varying the combination of muscles called into action. While it is easy to separate the muscles of a hinge joint sharply into agonists and antagonists, such classification is no longer applicable to a ball joint. Any two muscles may facultatively operate as agonists or antagonists. The following example, which refers to a specific case dealt with later in this paper, will help to make this clear.

Let us consider the shoulder joint of a tetrapod. Ignoring the finer details of the distribution of its muscles, we recognize four main groups converging upon the humerus from four different directions, schematically along the four edges of an imaginary pyramid (Fig. 8.2b and 8.3). Acting individually, these muscles—listed in counterclockwise order—would pull the humerus upward, forward, downward, and backward, respectively, and they may be designated accordingly as elevator (El), abductor (Ab), depressor (De), and adductor (Ad). Through their graded contraction in proper combinations the humerus can be made to describe a full circle, eight representative stages of which are reproduced in Fig. 8.3. To bring

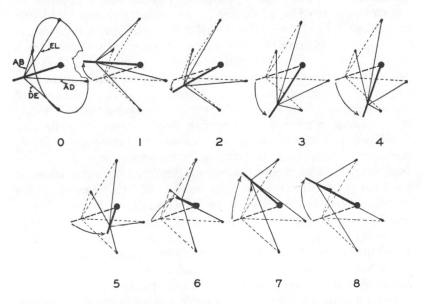

FIG. 8.3. Eight positions of the ball joint of Figure 8.2b, assumed through the contraction of its muscles in the combinations listed in Table 8.1. The posture in which all muscles are evenly contracted is pictured in phase 0; it is indicated throughout the following phases by dotted lines, the arrows showing the direction of the excursions.

TABLE 8.1

Phase	Muscles in Action	Resulting Movement
1	El, Ab, De	Craniad
2	Ab, De	Cranio-ventrad
3	Ab, De, Ad	Ventrad
4	De, Ad	Ventro-caudad
5	El, De, Ad	Caudad
6	El, Ad	Caudo-dorsad
7	El, Ab, Ad	Dorsad
8	El, Ab	Dorso-craniad

the humerus into any of these eight positions, the following muscle combinations must enter into action (Table 8.1).

According to the table, any one muscle may be engaged either in phase or out of phase with any other muscle. The diagram (Fig. 8.4) expresses for each pair of muscles and phases when they act synergically (convergent arrows) and antagonistically (divergent arrows). Thus, in contrast to the hinge joint with its single direction of motion, the ball joint presents the centers with a problem of multiple choice: The grouping of the muscles changes with the movement to be effected. The problem of coordination, therefore, is no longer simply one of alternative innervation of one out of two muscle groups ("flexors" and "extensors"), but it involves the selection of a definite combination of muscles out of a large number of possible combinations. If we add that a change in the intensity of the contraction of any one muscle necessarily changes the direction of the resulting movement, we realize that none of the schemata developed for hinge joints are applicable to this more general case, and, particularly, that this type of coordination must defeat any interpretation in terms of monotonous central connections. Here the problem of coordination presents itself in its full meaning: *What determines the choice of muscles to be engaged in a given movement, and how is this selective activation being put into effect?* Viewing the problem in the light of the ball joint, sets it into the right perspective, while the overemphasis of the flexor-extensor pendulum essentially misses the problem and thus helps to sidetrack rather than to solve it. We shall return to this subject later in the paper.

From a correct appreciation of the implications of the problem, several theories have arisen, striving to replace, or, at least, supplement, the thesis of pure structural preformation of coordination. We may call them the *heuristic* and the *systemic* theories.

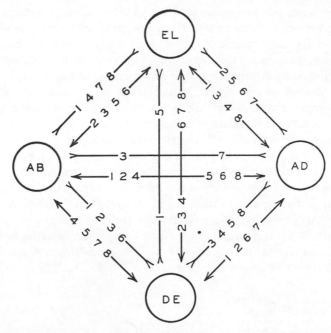

FIG. 8.4. Diagram illustrating the changing agonistic ()–() or antagonistic(↔) relations between any two muscles in executing the eight movements of Figure 8.3.

The Heuristic Concept

Any theory which submits that the common appropriateness for the body of motor effects has been developed ontogenetically under the molding action of practice and experience, may be called *heuristic*. The animal is thought to be capable of activating each one of its numerous motor effectors independently. Through repeated trials with constantly changing combinations it is supposed to produce a kaleidoscopic variety of peripheral effects, of which some are successful from the standpoint of the body and its needs, some are failures, and some are indifferent. Combinations leading to useful effects are somehow preserved in the central organization and fixed and improved by repetition, while those leading to useless or adverse effects are eliminated. According to this view, patterns of coordination arise through the accumulation of nervous "associations" which have proved their usefulness for the body. The essential point is that the *effectiveness* of a response is thought to confer selective value, and hence stability, upon the originally wholly tentative grouping of the muscles through which it is brought about. Whether the trials in this "trial-and-error" procedure are entirely random, or whether they show some method and direction; whether the drive to move is produced within the organism or furnished by external stimulation; whether the "associations" are to be viewed as nerve fiber connections, or whether—following behavioristic maxim—one had better refrain from such attempts at visualization; all these are relatively minor matters compared with the basic tenet in which all heuristic theories agree: that the central nervous system is a plastic mold upon which experience gained in actual performance gradually inscribes the patterns of coordinated behavior, with the adequacy of the effect for the organism as a whole serving as the standard of rating. This concept has been advanced for the lowest (Jennings, 1931) as well as for the highest forms of animals (Pavlov, 1927), and it has been variously applied to the development of nervous coordination from the highest cortical acts down to the most elementary motor functions.

The Systemic Concept

The systemic theories of coordination have in common with the heuristic theories the assumption of practically unlimited *plasticity* of the nervous system. However, instead of letting coordination become built up bit by bit through trial and error methods, they concede to the nervous system a *primordial dynamic ability* to respond to any change in the external stimulus situation by a total response of maximum adequacy for the organism as a whole. According to this view, entirely novel stimulus situations, neither provided for in the organization of the animal nor previously experienced, can be met by a primary response of great suitability. This view, shared by many Gestalt psychologists, has been particularly elaborated by Bethe (1931) and Goldstein (1939). The contrast between the heuristic and systemic concept can perhaps be expressed as follows: according to the former, partial reactions (elementary sensomotor responses) of no definite directiveness are variously recombined until they finally compose a chain the resultant direction of which has affirmed its value for the organism; whereas, according to the latter, resourceful dynamics of the central nervous system lay down the general direction of the total response as a sort of frame through which the partial reactions necessary for its execution are forced in channels consonant with the general "intention." In this view, the drive toward a certain real or visualized goal would directly produce the proper muscular innervation necessary to attain that goal.

SUMMARY

Reduced to the terms of the preformistic-anatomical (1), heuristic (2), and systemic (3) theory, respectively, the coordinated advance of the organism toward a desirable goal, and its coordinated retreat from a harmful situation, could be expressed as follows:

1. Beneficial and nocuous stimuli enter through different adequate receptors, activate each a system of separate pre-arranged lines which, in turn, engage a pre-arranged selection of muscles in a pre-arranged time order, the combined action of which then becomes manifest as a motion of advance or withdrawal. The appropriateness of the response is based on the appropriateness of the inherited pre-arrangements; the individual itself deserves no credit for it.

2. Either kind of stimulus evokes ubiquitous random reactions, including excursions of limbs and trunk of continuously varying patterns, which are tried and discarded and repeated and altered, until eventually the correct composition and sequence is discovered; the animal is to be given credit for its resourcefulness in producing ever changing assortments of undirected responses, as well as for its faculty to choose and retain those that prove to lie in the right direction.

3. Any stimulus produces a general response the character of which is directly determined by the constellation of the external field of stimuli and the internal state of the centers, resulting in a primarily directed movement; the centers get credit for their ingenuity.

To reduce the various theories of coordination to such simple formulae, admittedly involves a great deal of abstraction and oversimplification. Moreover, many authors, in discussing these matters, have failed to take an explicit stand, which puts it up to the interpreter to extrapolate their basic beliefs from casual remarks; which is a doubtful task. Again, some have taken compromise attitudes, contaminating one theory with admixtures from another, which makes a strict classification of their views impossible. Hence, no more than practical significance should be attached to the attempt of the preceding pages to group all existing theories of coordination into the three outlined categories. The justification for that attempt lies merely in that it serves to crystallize the issues. It puts into specific form the premises and implications of the various current theories and thus prepares them for the experimental tests to which they must be subjected for verification.

THE EXPERIMENTAL STUDY OF COORDINATION

The Central Hierarchy

To decide between the performistic and the heuristic concept of coordination, is an empirical problem. Here is the alternative which the experimental investigator faces: If coordination is preformed in self-differentiated central impulse patterns, which yield adequate peripheral effects only by virtue of what may be called evolutionary precedent and in the individual case amounts to predesign, they should prove stable and conservative even if experimentally prevented from producing appropriate functional effects. If, on the other hand, functional effectiveness is all that counts in shaping the patterns of coordination, one should expect any experimental reduction of that effectiveness to be followed by corrective modifications of the impulse patterns—evidence of plasticity and of lack of intrinsic organization.

It is evident that the decision cannot be reached by even the most intimate study of the *normal* organism, with its inherited stereotypism of central structures, peripheral structures and nerve connections. For this stereotypism means that the same standard central patterns and the same standard effects appear always in conjunction. A crucial experiment, therefore, must aim at disrupting the monotony of central-peripheral correspondence. It must upset either the discharge pattern of the centers or the play of muscles or the distribution of nerve connections in such a manner as to make the established central impulse patterns yield incongruous effects for the body. If, thereafter, the body recovers more efficient use of the affected part—either instantaneously by systemic reaction, or gradually by heuristic procedure—, the systemic or heuristic theories would score. If, on the other hand, corrective changes fail to occur and the nervous system continues to operate the part according to the old standard scheme of innervation now rendered inadequate, this would be incontestable proof of the *preformation* of coordination in form of definite central impulse patterns which do or do not produce appropriate effects, depending on whether the effector system for whose operation they are predesigned is intact or disarranged.

All this seems so plain that one might expect the issue to have long been settled one way or the other. In fact, the indicated experimental course has been followed by some authors in the past. If, nevertheless, there is, even at this date, a basic lack of agreement, this suggests that either the experimental results or their interpretations have remained inconclusive. The reasons for this failure will become increasingly clear in the course of this paper. Two of them may be specifically mentioned here: preoccupation with higher mammals, particularly man; and injudicious generalization of concepts of "learning" or "conditioning."

The substitution of a healthy muscle for a paralyzed one is standard practice among orthopedic surgeons. The replacing muscle is sutured to the tendon stump of the incapacitated muscle and thus the mechanical part played by the lost muscle is taken over by the substitute. To be physiologically effective, the transposed muscle must, of course, be operated according to a new time schedule. Its former functional associations must be dissolved and replaced by new ones in accordance with its new function. To be sure, tendon transposition as such, even without retiming of muscle actions, produces some degree of improvement, simply owing to the restoration of a more normal balance of tensions around the joint. For the shift of a muscle from the vigorous to the frail side not only reduces the bulk of muscle left on the intact side, but also cancels part of the remaining muscle power of that side by the opposing action of the shifted portion contracting simultaneously. Further post-operative adjustments are brought about by compensatory changes in the strength with which other, unimpaired, muscle groups are being engaged, still according to the original time pattern.

However, there is incontrovertible evidence to show that the gradual restoration of relatively efficient limb coordination in patients with translocated tendon insertions is not merely due to changes of the kind just mentioned, but involves an actual modification of the original time pattern of innervation, the transposed muscle assuming functionally—that is, with regard to its phase of innervation relative to other muscles—the place formerly held by the muscle which it has replaced mechanically. While there seem to be limitations to this adaptive change of coordination (Scherb, 1938), there is consensus of opinion that some "re-education" of the play of muscles can be attained by proper training in all human beings.

By sheer extrapolation it was then conjectured that what is true of man, would likewise hold for other animals. A broad experimental foundation of this assumption seems to have been neither sought nor offered. Some pertinent experiments were made on the coordination of eye movements after muscle translocation in mammals (Marina, 1912), but the results have remained controversial (Dusser de Barenne & de Kleyn, 1929; Olmsted, Margutti & Yanagisana, 1936). An isolated report of reorganization of limb coordination in the frog (Manigk, 1934) was shown to have arisen from a faulty interpretation of the underlying experiments (Taylor, 1936). But in spite of this lack of convincing experimental proof, the view seems to prevail that the locomotor apparatus of an animal can undergo essentially the same kind of adjustive "re-education" which has been demonstrated in man.

Critical experiments on amphibians, however, have contradicted this view decisively. As will be reported below in greater detail, these animals show no trace of readjustment of muscle coordination under comparable circumstances. To avoid misunderstandings, it may be added that while the basic coordination mechanisms through which all locomotor acts must be executed are in themselves quite unmodifiable in amphibians, the total behavior of these animals can be somewhat modified by training. They can learn to advance or retreat on different occasions, but they cannot learn to change their manner of walking or retreating. Similarly, recent experiments on the rat have definitely shown that the time pattern of coordination of the hind limb muscles of these animals, too, is rigidly fixed and remains incorrigible even after the crossing of antagonistic muscles resulting in permanent reversal of movements (Sperry, 1940). There may be a trace of re-adjustment after transposition of muscles in the *fore* limb of the rat (Sperry, see below), and as we extend the examination to higher and higher mammals, we may expect to find a growing faculty for such corrective measures of the nervous system. The essential point, however, remains that this faculty is a very late evolutionary acquisition of the central nervous system, practically still absent in as high an animal as the rat, and consequently entirely unfit as a model of the principle of coordination in general. (See p. 264–268.)

We must once and for all renounce the idea that the type of muscular control with which we are most familiar, namely, our own, or at least that part of it of which we are consciously aware, represents the fundamental type of vertebrate coordination. Man can learn to engage individual muscles independently, but most animals cannot. This is why the anthropocentric approach to the general problem of coordination is misleading and has failed to produce results of general applicability whenever attempted.

The issue has often been further obscured by ill-defined and unverified generalizations of the concept of "learning." "Learning," that is, an adaptive modification of behavior in response to recurrent stimulus situations, has been demonstrated to occur, at least in traces, in most branches of the animal kingdom, from the lowest forms up. However, the strict constitutional limitations of this learning ability do not seem to be generally realized, or if so, have certainly not received due emphasis. There is agreement that the total motor performance of an animal can be modified by experience, but since the total performance is an integrated act, involving shifting combinations of partial performances of more elementary character, it remains to be demonstrated whether the modification concerns those elementary acts—the building blocks of behavior, as it were—as such, or merely their combination into more complex actions on a higher level. The mere assertion that the response mechanisms of the animal as a whole are not absolutely rigid but provide for some degree of adaptation, does not reveal whether this plasticity extends to all parts of the behavioral mechanism alike or is a privilege of certain components only, and if so, of which. Adaptive behavior presupposes functional reorganization somewhere; but where? Is the whole nervous system one vast pool of equivalent elements whose functional relations can be infinitely varied by experience, or is adaptability confined to some of its divisions or some of its functions only, while the rest are immutable?

The question is no longer whether learning is a common faculty or not. The answer to this has become a matter of course. What we need, is to know precisely what functions are amenable to change and what others are not; further, what functional elements, or groupings of elements, remain constant and unmodifiable even as the behavior pattern of which they form integral parts changes. Behavior results from the activities of a hierarchy of functional levels, each of which may or may not be adaptable. Plasticity on any one level neither implies nor precludes plasticity on any other level; the only means to test their capacities is by way of experiments.

Let us briefly illustrate the various levels.[2] Confining ourselves to metazoans possessing a differentiated nervous system, we may dismiss subcellular entities and start right at the cellular level. There we find as the lowest recognizable elements to which a measure of functional stability may be conceded, the individual *motor units*, the

---

[2]This list is more pertinent than one published on an earlier occasion (P. Weiss, 1925).

term signifying, according to Sherrington, a motor neurone with its attached muscle fibers (level 1).

The orderly contraction of a whole *muscle* is the result of collective action of its constituent motor units, and the characteristics as well as the grading of the resultant contractile effect depend largely on the proportion of active to inactive units, on their rate of alternation, on the time relations of their activation (synchronization or temporal dispersion), on the frequencies of their discharges, and several other factors. In other words, in order that a muscle may function properly, its motor units must be definitely under common control. What happens when motor units act without control and at random, is impressively demonstrated by the functional inefficiency of a muscle in the state of pathological fibrillation. The level of integration of the motor units of a given muscle may be designated as level 2.

Next, we must remember that every *joint* or other movable part (e.g., eyeball) is operated not by one, but by several muscles. The relative strength and timing of their contractions determine the direction and speed of the movement and the duration and stability of the resulting position. Thus the simple muscular actions of level 2 are integrated into orderly functions of muscular complexes relating to a single joint (level 3).

Again, in order to obtain an efficient movement or to maintain a definite posture of a segmented structure, such as a limb or the spine, containing *several joints,* the activities of the various muscle groups of level 3 must be finely correlated among one another, a task which gains in complexity in those cases in which a single muscle spans two joints, moving either one or the other or both, depending on the degree to which it is opposed at the time by other muscles. Thus, limb movement requires a higher level of integration (level 4) than does single joint action.

On the next higher level (level 5), we find movements of the various locomotor organs (limbs, trunk segments, tail) combined in orderly fashion so as to yield a definite act of the entire *locomotor system,* such as ambulatory progression and regression, jumping, swimming, or the like. The integration of widely separated muscle groups in the act of breathing (laryngeal, intercostal, abdominal, diaphragmal muscles) is obviously of the same order.

Finally, on the highest level common to all animals (level 6), the various motor acts are put into the service of the *animal as a whole* under the control of the sensory apparatus, whose reports are evaluated by the centers in accordance with the external stimulus situation, the internal state of the animal, the inherited response mechanisms of the centers, and such modifications of the latter as past experience may have brought about. It is in their bearing on this level that all motor acts of the lower levels gain *biological significance*. Viewed from this level, "progression" becomes an instrument of "preying," regression" of "escaping," "eye movements" of "orientation in space," and so forth.

For abbreviated reference to the various levels, we shall use the following symbols:

Level 1, i.e., level of the Neurone.......................................N
Level 2, i.e., level of the Muscle ....M
Level 3, i.e., level of the muscle Group ....G
Level 4, i.e., level of the Organ...O
Level 5, i.e., level of the organ System ....S
Level 6, i.e., level of the organism as a Whole ....W

Now, after this survey, let us repeat the question: On which one of these levels does "learning" occur? Possibly on all of them? Or on the highest (W) only? Or the lowest (N) only?

To those who are either unaware of the hierarchical principle of nervous function or may think to have grounds for denying it, these questions must seem utterly senseless. For them there exists no central organization on a level higher than that of the neurone, and as they would describe all behavior merely in terms of connections among indiviudal neurones, so they would naturally be disinclined to conceive of "learning" otherwise than as of a free rearrangement of individual neurone connections. In the terms of our question this amounts to asserting that "learning" occurs on the level N, and exclusively there. There is no room in this concept for stability and unmodifiability of functions of lower order in an organism whose behavior has been demonstrated to be adaptable. It is either plasticity all the way, or rigidity all the way. "Learning," according to this view, proceeds by tentatively engaging, disengaging, and re-engaging independent efferent neurones in varying constellations, letting the biological value of the results for the organism decide which ones of the tried combinations are to be preserved, and which to be discarded. If this were true, the problem for an animal would be the same, whether it faces the necessity to substitute one established pattern of locomotion for another established pattern (e.g., hopping for running; see Bethe and Fischer, 1931), or to make modifications *within* a standard pattern (e.g., longer strides in trotting; swimming in circles instead of straight), or to use its healthy legs for unusual tricks, or finally to return limbs with arbitrarily disarranged muscles to their usefulness as instruments of locomotion. There would seem to be no reason why an animal which can change the rhythm of its several limbs in the acts of locomotion should not be equally adept at changing the rhythm of the several muscles within the limb, if in last analysis it all comes down simply to rearranging neurone linkages.

However, this view is strictly contradicted by the facts. We have already quoted evidence to show that in amphibians, and even the rat, the time order according to which muscles execute a limb movement is unalterably fixed, while at the same time the total behavior of these animals is amenable to reconditioning by training and other regulatory adjustments. In the light of these facts, the distinction between rigid and plastic functional levels assumes great significance, as indeed the neglect of the hierarchical principle would lead, and has led, to serious confusion. In brief, the fact that an animal can learn (on levels S and W) to use its limbs differently in moving the body, does not necessarily imply that it can likewise learn (on levels O and G) to use its muscles differently in moving a limb. Adaptive functional reorganization is a prerogative of certain functional levels only. Therefore, in raising the question of learning separately for each level, we merely give expression to realities.

The preceding pages may suffice to bear out our contention, that progress in the study of coordination has been held up both by lack of restraint in extrapolating from higher mammals to animals in general, and by lack of precision in the application of the principle of learning. In this state of affairs it is not surprising to find the changes observed after tendon transposition, muscle transplantation, nerve crossing, sectioning of central tracts, destruction of brain portions, and similar interferences, lumped together indiscriminately under the common headings of re-education, regulation, functional restoration, reconstitution, reparation, reorganization, readjustment, and the like. If in the future more discretion will be exercised in the use of these terms and if the mere statement, that a behavioral change has occurred, will be amplified by precise information as to what this change has consisted of and where it has taken place, the gain for our understanding of nervous function will be enormous. Then, all the mentioned interferences, instead of merely serving to tell whether or not "functional recovery" can occur, become discriminative assay methods, revealing the degree in which the various functional levels participate in the noted "adjustment." It is in this assaying capacity that the transplantation experiments to be discussed below have been used, and since this method invites much wider application, a few comments on general methodology seem appropriate.

Experimental Methodology

As all biological experiments, those dealing with the nervous system fall essentially into three classes: *defect* experiments, *isolation* experiments, and *recombination* experiments (compare P. Weiss, 1939, p. 147 f.). Given a system Y, consisting of parts A, B, C, D, and so forth, the experiment aims at establishing the relations between the system and its parts, as well as among the constitutent parts, by severing the existing relations. Singling out, for instance, part A, the *isolation* experiment determines the properties and capacities of A, when completely released from the rest of the system, while the *defect* experiment, complementary to the former, ascertains the properties and capacities of the remainder of the system (Y minus A). In both cases the relations between the system and the part are permanently interrupted. It is left to the *recombination* experiment to supply the positive part of the story by restoring connection and relations between the severed components, however, with such added variations from the orginal condition that it will be possible to discern whether and in what respect the relation between the system and part A differs from its relation to parts B, C, and so on. Part B is supplanted for part A, and vice versa, and the subsequent conduct of the altered system is studied. If the system behaves as before, we conclude that A and B are equivalent; if it behaves differently, the change is ascribed to the differential between A and B.

In the past the defect experiment has been by far the predominant method in the study of nervous function. The value of the isolation experiment is increasingly appreciated; witness the work on isolated nerve fibers and isolated brain parts. The recombination experiment, however, has been largely neglected. Yet, its instructiveness greatly exceeds that of the defect experiment. In what respect, can be easily shown.

Let us quote an example. We cut a tendon and note subsequently that limb movements are changed. Now, the operation has altered a number of conditions in one stroke: It has caused trauma, produced a gap in the elastic continuity of the tissues, interrupted the transmission of pull from muscle to skeleton, abolished stretch reflexes from the affected muscle, and, as a result, changed the mechanical and innervatory balance of other muscles. What each one of these factors contributes to the common defect, cannot be immediately discerned. Their effects can be separated, however, by resuturing the tendon stumps in various modifications—under slack or shortening; to the old muscle or to an antagonist; with or without concomitant denervation of the muscle;—in other words, by restoring certain, but not all, of the severed relations.

Similarly, peripheral nerve section leads to a complex functional disturbance the net effect of which—impairment of motility—does not reveal its composite nature. The locomotor apparatus suffers changes which are partly due to the trophic and mechanical by-products of muscle denervation in general, partly to the fact that a particular nerve (not just innervation in general) has been lost, partly to compensatory reactions of other muscle centers not directly affected by the operation, with every one of these effects telling on all levels, from the simple movement of a joint up to the aimed behavior of the animal as a whole. We know that all these factors enter into the result, but only systematic recombination experiments, consisting in this case of the replacement of old peripheral nerve connections by new ones, with or without rearrangement of tendons, can help us to disentangle them. Only then can we learn what difference it makes whether a muscle is merely supplied with nerves or actually receives impulses: whether it is just innervated or innervated by one particular nerve rather than another; whether it merely contracts or actually moves the skeleton; whether it operates the skeleton to good use or in a mechanically inefficient manner; whether it contributes to an act of biological significance or one that runs counter to the interests of the organism as a whole.[3]

The rest of this article is essentially a detailed account of how problems of this kind, refractory to other methods, could be solved by recombination experiments. It is hoped that the advantages of the method will become sufficiently evident to encourage its extension to problems not yet hitherto tackled, but entirely within its reach. In view of the fact that endocrinology owes much of its rapid progress to the introduction of routine transplantation methods, it is surprising that neurology has not yet adopted analogous methods to any appreciable extent.

---

[3]The lack of distinction in these matters is clearly reflected in the anatomical nomenclature of muscles. Some muscles received their names from some constitutional characteristics, such as shape, (e.g., m. trapezius; m. piriformis), some from their topographic relations (e.g., m. intercostalis; m. subscapularis), some from their skeletal connections (e.g., m. ileo-fibularis; m. coraco-brachialis), some from their kinetic effects (e.g., m. levator scapulae; m. extensor carpi; m. corrugator supercilii), some from their biological function (e.g., m. masseter [from $\mu\alpha\sigma\sigma\alpha$ $\epsilon\sigma\vartheta\alpha\iota$, to chew]; m. risorius, the "laughing" muscle; m. vocalis, the "vocalizing" muscle).

AN ANALYSIS OF COORDINATION IN AMPHIBIA

The Principle of Myotypic Response ("Resonance")

Transplantation experiments carried out after the scheme just outlined have led to an astonishing discovery concerning the manner in which the central nervous system controls the musculature. They have revealed a series of phenomena, commonly referred to, somewhat vaguely, as *resonance* phenomena, which have provided us with an assay method of nervous function of much greater discriminatory power than any other method available. Since the results obtained with this method have been amply reported and reviewed on previous occasions, only those points will be recapitulated here which have an immediate bearing on the problem of this paper. (For the latest comprehensive review, see P. Weiss, 1936.)

Reduced to the simplest formula, the results have shown that muscular control is based on a principle of selective correspondence between nerve centers and indiviudal muscles, which enables the centers to identify and engage any given muscle by its *name*, irrespecitve of its mechanical effects, or the biological effects which the latter have for the body as a whole. Each individual muscle owns some distinctive constitutional characteristic through which it is differentially distinguished from all other normal muscles. By virtue of this distinctiveness, in a manner not directly discernible from the experiment, the central nervous system can discriminate muscle from muscle, regardless of where they are attached and how they act. Each muscle is centrally represented by units of corresponding specificity, and these, in turn, are activated by the centers selectively. The basic elements of motor function are specific central "calls," one for each muscle, and each so organized that it will affect just those motor units belonging to the appropriate muscle, and no others. The totality of "calls" at the disposal of the centers represent the code or vocabulary, as it were, of which all central messages are necessarily composed.

All of these statements contain no hypothetical implications, but represent merely the net result of a large series of experimentally established facts. Presented in a nut shell, the underlying facts are the following.

In amphibians[4] it is possible to graft an extra muscle, or group of muscles, or even a whole limb, to the body wall and provide motor

---

[4] All statements in this chapter relate only to young amphibians, for which direct experimental proof is at hand, while the possibility of extending the results to other groups will be discussed later.

innervation for these transplants by diverting to them some motor nerve branch from one of the normal host limbs. The amount of deviated nerve fibers can be held to such insignificant proportions that no perceptible change in the function of the host limb results. This small nerve source is fully adequate to assure complete re-innervation of the transplant, inasmuch as nerve fibers in the course of regeneration undergo profuse branching. The experiments were so devised as to insure that the muscles of the transplants would be re-innervated for the most part or wholly by nerves with which they formerly had no relations. After transmissive connections between the regenerated nerve fibers and the grafted muscles had been restored, the supernumerary muscles began to exhibit regular and strong contractions whenever the host limb, from which their nerve supply was derived, moved.

The stress, however, lies not so much on the fact that the transplanted muscles had become re-engaged in functional activity, but on the peculiar time order in which they were found to operate. Extensive studies, under a great variety of conditions, of the precise times when a transplanted muscle starts to contract and ceases to contract, as well as of the degree of its contractions during that active period, has revealed a principle of such definiteness and constancy that it amounts to a law. *The phases of activity of an extra muscle correspond precisely to the phases in which the muscle of the same name,* or *synonymous* muscle, *is found to be active in the host limb innervated from the same plexus of the spinal cord.* Whether the transplant consists of a single muscle, or a group of muscles, or a whole limb, each individual muscle as such duplicates the action of the synonymous muscle in the normal limb nearby. This phenomenon has been described, and ever since been referred to, as *"homologous response"* of synonymous muscles. The term signifies that if a body district is provided, instead of with a single muscle of a given kind, with two, three, or even four homologous muscles of the same kind and name, all of them will act in unison, the contractions beginning at the same moment, developing the same proportional tension and subsiding at the same time; the only prerequisites being, that all of them receive their nerve supply from the same side and the same general level of the spinal cord (e.g., limb level in the case of limb muscles), and that the transplantation be done in young, preferably premetamorphic, animals.

Now, what does this phenomenon of "homologous response" actually mean? In spite of the ample attention given to it in the past, it does not seem that the majority of authors have succeeded in seeing it in the correct light. Many authors, while reporting the phenomenon correctly, yet have missed the point which it so clearly proves, namely, the existence of correspondences of a specific kind between nerve centers and individual muscles. Thus, the phenomenon was variously described as demonstrating almost unlimited "plasticity of coordination," "learning capacity" even at the lowest level, "adjustments" of the nervous system to the introduction of a new organ, integrative action of the spinal cord, and so forth. Some of these interpretations are strictly incorrect, others merely besides the point. It would be idle to try to fix the blame of these misinterpretations. Part of it can probably be ascribed to lack of clarity in the earlier descriptions of the phenomenon, as well as to misleading terminology, part to the fact that the problem of coordination, to which the phenomenon offered a clue, was not usually presented in the correct light. It thus becomes necessary once more to explain the intrinsic meaning of this phenomenon of "homologous response" of synonymous muscles.

To begin with, to emphasize the fact that the transplanted muscle and the synonymous muscle act in unison, is already putting the wrong slant on the phenomenon, because in stressing the association of the two peripheral parts, we give prominence to a rather irrelevant aspect. We make it appear as if the transplanted muscles, or rather their centers, have in some way learned to imitate the synonymous normal muscles, even though it would be difficult to find any plausible reasons why they should have done so. To avoid this misconception, it must be stressed that in all these experiments the normal muscles simply serve as *indicators* of the hidden activities of the central nervous system, and that their actual presence is in no way required for the appearance of the phenomenon. Even if all muscles of the normal limb are removed, the transplanted muscle keeps on functioning at precisely the phases when the removed synonymous muscle would have functioned if it were still present. But so long as a normal limb is available, we use it as a detector to tell us which combination of muscles the central nervous system tends to activate in any given phase of a locomotor act.

Let us now forget for a while that effective limb movements are of service to the animal, and let us consider them simply in their service to the observer as convenient instruments for the visible registration of the content of the varying central commands. To be used for this purpose, movements must be resolved into muscle actions. This can be done directly or indirectly—directly, by connecting the muscles with mechanical or electrical recording devices, as is commonly done in the study of simple reflexes with fairly constant stimulus-response relations; indirectly, by taking cinematographic records of the movements and reconstructing the muscular activity from the measureable changes in the angles of the various joints. The former method, besides being limited to animals above a certain size, has the disadvantage of interfering with the free execution of the movements, while the latter falls short in two respects: First, it fails to register isometric contractions, which produce tensions to overcome resistance without producing excursion of the joints, and second, the individual muscular contributions to the movement, instead of self-registering, are only indirectly recoverable from the record. In the work on homologous response both kymographic registration and slow-motion picture analysis have been employed. However, experience has shown that the former method is by far less suitable in the study of coordination, because the technical measures necessary for direct muscle registration (anaesthesia, strapping, fixing of joints, tendon dissection, etc.) interfere with the execution of most of the regular locomotor repertoire of the animal to such a degree that little insight into the normal, unrestrained, performance can be gained.

By slow-motion picture analysis, a complex movement can be resolved into the constituent muscular actions: The sequence in which different muscles become dominant and the duration of their phases of activity can be determined. We thereby obtain a time record—a chronological *"score,"* as it were,—of the central activities through which the various muscles are engaged. Thus, when the forearm is bent against the upper arm, we take this to signify that the central nervous system has set into action chiefly that group of neurones which innervates the biceps muscle. As the flexion slows down and finally reverts into extension, we interpret this as central activation of the triceps neurones. Doing this for all muscles involved in a given movement, we compose a master chart of the central timing mechanism effecting the movement. Such a master record of coordination may be compared to the score of a piece of orchestral music in which onset, intensity, and duration of each instrumental part are recorded separately, except that in the case of our muscular orchestra no instrument can produce more than a single tone: contraction of the particular muscle. It is herewith proposed to call this master time record of all muscles particpating in a given movement, the *myochronogram.*[5]

---

[5]Although we have used myochronograms as the simplest method to represent movements for years, none were published until 1937 (P. Weiss, 1937b). Coincidentally, it was then found that a Swiss surgeon, Scherb (1938), had been using the same method to symbolize movements under the name of "myokinesiogram." If we give preference to the term "myochronogram," it is only because *"kinesiogram"* means record of motion, whereas *"chronogram"* simply means "time record," thus providing for the inclusion of non-motile, isometric, muscle contractions.

As a concrete example on which to carry on our further discussion, we reproduce here the myochronograms of the fore limbs of a salamander in the act of walking on solid ground (Fig. 8.5). For the sake of simplicity, only the shoulder and elbow joints are included, while the wrist has been ignored. Furthermore, only six major muscles have been selected as representatives. These muscles are shown in a dorsal view of the left fore limb in the inset (upper left of the figure). The shoulder muscles chosen are the same as those of Fig. 8.3, namely, an elevator ($\triangle$), an abductor ($\bigcirc$), a depressor (X), and an adductor ($\bullet$). The upper arm muscles are represented by a flexor ($\square$) and an extensor ($\blacksquare$) of the elbow. The two central strips of the picture reproduce in diagrammatic ouline six phases of one complete walking cycle, both in dorsal and rear views. Double rings indicate the fixed points on the ground in which the animal sets down its wrist and around which as pivotal points it swings the body forward. The muscles in action are marked by their respective symbols.

In phase 1, the right hand takes hold on the ground ($\circledcirc$), and presently (phases 2 and 3) depression (X), adduction ($\bullet$), and extension ($\blacksquare$) of the right arm swing the animal forward, while at the same time the left arm is lifted ($\triangle$) and brought forward ($\bigcirc$, $\square$). At point 4, the left hand is then set down and serves as pivot around which the body is swung forward through phases 5 and 6, while the right arm in turn is lifted from the ground and brought forward. The top and bottom records represent the myochronograms of the left and right fore limbs, respectively, as each goes through the illustrated phrases. In order to be truly representative of the resulting movements, these records should include an account of the varying intensities of the muscular contractions. Since these cannot be directly observed, we confine ourselves to the score of time relations.[6]

With sufficient practice it might be possible in reading a myochronogram to visualize the resulting movement just as an orchestra conductor reads a muscial score. To determine how much variation in detail there is in the play of muscles in moving a limb, would require much more intimate studies. However, all observations thus far concur in demonstrating that the essential chronology expressed in the above myochronograms is typical. Walking is always effected by the same general sequence of muscular activities in all animals of the same species. In other words, the muscular integration of the level O of our hierarchical scale (p. 236) follows a stable chronological pattern.

---

[6]The overlap between antagonistic muscles in these diagrams has not been directly observed, but put into the records in accordance with the work of Wachholder (1923), showing that the contraction of antagonistic muscles actually sets in some time before the reversal of the movement becomes visible.

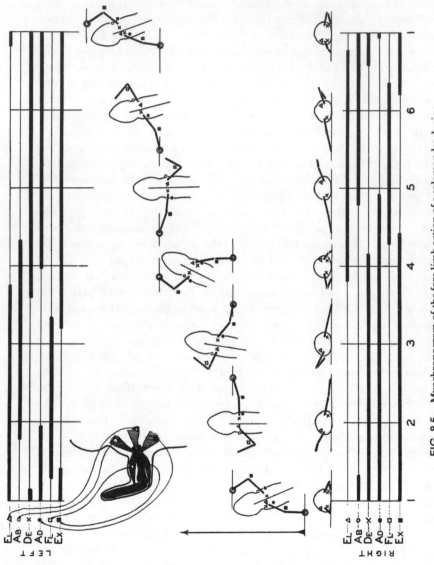

FIG. 8.5. Myochronogram of the fore limb action of a salamander during ambulatory progression over solid ground.

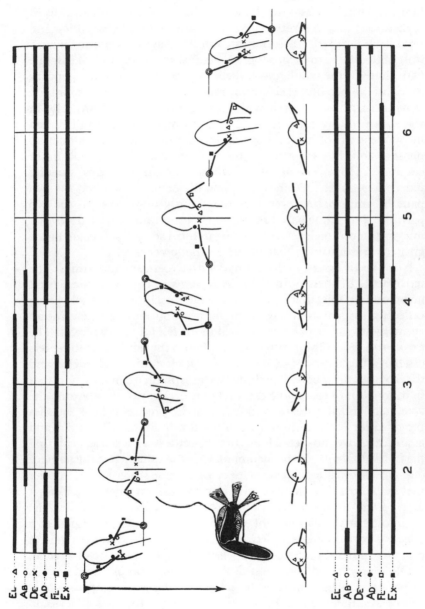

FIG. 8.6. Myochronogram of the fore limb action of a salamander with interchanged, that is, reversed fore limbs during ambulation.

Compared with this firmly set pattern for a given limb, the association between left and right fore limb, or that between fore limbs and hind limbs is much looser. That is to say, while usually in undisturbed and vigorous walking the alternation between left and right limb is as strict as is indicated in the diagram, amounting to a shift of the lower myochronogram against the upper one of just one half phase of the whole cycle, there is also frequently independent action of the two limbs, either one moving without the other, or both moving in phase, or even both entirely out of turn. Similarly, in vigorous walking there is usually an intimate correlation between the movements of hind limbs and fore limbs in that the adduction phases, and likewise the abduction phases, of diagonal limbs coincide. However, at other times, the hind limbs operate independently of the fore limbs, and dissociation between the two pairs of limbs occurs even more commonly than between the two partners of the same pair. Simple observation thus demonstrates that integration on the level S of the hierarchical scale is subject to much greater variation than that found on the lower level O.

Now, let us return to the animals with supernumerary limbs. The movements of their normal limbs serve us to construct the central myochronograms, that is, to reveal what muscles are centrally being called up for action at any given moment. Suppose we examine an animal with an extra limb attached to the left fore limb plexus. The myochronogram informs us that in phase 3 the left fore limb centers discharge impulses destined to engage the elevator, the abductor, and the flexor of the elbow. Watching the transplanted limb, we note that in it, too, out of the whole extra set of muscles, just the elevator, the abductor, and the flexor respond, that is, precisely those muscles provided for in the central score. Since this holds for all muscles and at all times, we must conclude that the centers, in a sense, "call up" the individual muscles by their names; further, that when the name of one muscle is called, all muscles of that name react, which implies that each muscle is endowed with some peculiar property enabling it to respond to the calls of its own kind selectively. Thus, the "homologous" response of supernumerary muscles signifies a selective correspondence between central impulses and peripheral effectors rather than a tie-up between synonymous muscles as such.

Obviously, the designation of the phenomenon as "homologous response" has been misleading in that it places the emphasis on a technical rather than on an essential feature. For this reason, it would seem more to the point to speak of a principle of *"myotypic response,"* which means "muscle-specific response." This change of terminology is herewith proposed.

The factual content of the phenomenon of myotypic response can be reduced in essence to two points: (1) The protoplasm of each individual muscle has a specific and distinctive constitution, distinguishing it from all other muscles. (2) This constitutional specificity is instrumental in establishing a selective relation between the centers and any muscle of that particular kind of specificity.

This formulation merely expresses logical conclusions to be drawn from the observed facts. It contains no reference whatever as to just how those specific relations between muscles and centers are effected. If we are to consider this latter question, we find ourselves no longer on the same solid ground as before. Here the experiments fail us. While they have set up a definite frame within which any explanation of central-peripheral correspondence must hold itself, they carry no further positive suggestions. The tentative explanation currently favored and presented in the following pages should, therefore, be considered as entirely hypothetical. Whether or not it will ultimately prove to be correct, does not affect the validity of the principle itself. The reality of the myotypic principle remains a fact, its mechanism a matter of further research.

At this point, I have omitted a several page discussion of the possible models for how the motor nerves to reinnervated muscles come to carry the motor command signals that are appropriate for "their" muscle. Current evidence indicates that collaterals from the functionally relevant motor neurons are guided to the appropriate muscles by some as yet poorly understood mechanism. If all of the functionally appropriate neurons are unable to enter the to-be-innervated limb, then functionally inappropriate motor neurons may innervate the muscles of the limb. Contrary to what Weiss thought at the time he wrote this paper, normal limb motion does not reappear when muscles are reinnervated with functionaly inappropriate motor neurons (Gaze, 1970; Szekely, 1976). The principle of myotypic response depends on the fact that the muscle a given motor neuron should innervate is specified by something inside the motorneuron. This "something" tells the motor neuron that it should innervate, for example, the biceps muscle. This internal specification of the muscle to be innervated induces the regenerating motor neuron to seek out the biceps muscle wherever it may be (within limits). Thus, a biceps muscle, wherever the experimenter may place it and whatever its experimentally contrived function, will contract at those moments when a normal biceps muscle would contract, for the simple reason that it is always innervated by the motorneurons that normally innervate the biceps muscle. If the experimental procedure is so drastic that the correct motor neurons are unable to find their way to the displaced muscle, then the muscle never again becomes functionally active. Other motor neurons will not command the biceps muscle, only "biceps" motor neurons will.

As Weiss himself emphasized, however, the manner in which myotypic responses are achieved has no bearing on the implications of the myotypic response principle for our understanding of the general nature of coordination. The fact remains that coordinated action depends ultimately on elementary functional units that contract and relax specific muscles in certain patterns, regardless of the functional effect those patterns may or may not have. The patterns realizable through the elementary functional units are the raw materials that the higher levels must work with. The higher levels may select one or another elementary pattern of muscular activity, but the higher levels cannot (in lower animals) produce just any pattern that circumstances may require. Even in higher animals, where there is some capacity for reprogramming even very elementary patterns of muscular activation, there is reason to believe that at any given time the higher levels must synthesize complex actions out of a limited set of elementary units that command particular patterns of muscular activation. The primate, like the salamander, may readily change the occasions on which it advances or retreats, but it cannot readily change its manner of advancing or retreating. The elementary units and intermediate units controlling the pattern of muscular activity in locomotion delimit the primate's options with respect to the manner in which it walks.

MYOTYPIC RESPONSE AS ASSAY METHOD

Having established the general validity within known limits of the principle of myotypic response, we may pass on and use it to assay central coordination. How, will become clear from the following example.

Let us consider what is conventionally described as a *flexion reflex*. A stimulus applied to the toes results in the withdrawal of the foot and leg. This reaction occurs essentially on the level O of the hierarchical scale, implying operations on the subordinate levels G, M, and N. In terms of the top level (W) it can be rated as part of an escape reaction from a harmful stimulus. In terms of the organ level (O) it means approximation between base and tip of the limb. In terms of the muscle group level (G) it amounts to reducing the angles of the ankle and knee joints, commonly designated as "flexion"; and on the level of the individual muscle (M), it simply means contraction of these muscles which happen to be inserted on the flexor sides of the joints (e.g., hamstring at the knee; tibialis at the ankle). Our problem is to decide in terms of which of these levels the coordination of the withdrawal reflex is laid down.*

It is here that the assay function of a transplanted muscle can prove its value. For we can transplant a flexor muscle in such a fashion that it will have the mechanical effect of extending the joint instead of flexing it, as it did before. Thereby we alter the relation between the M level and all higher levels. When a "flexion" reflex is now elicited, will the response still be "flexion," or will it be a contraction of what used to be the "flexor" muscle now producing extension? Or we can change the insertion and orientation of a whole limb with regard to the body in such a manner that, while the muscles will continue to produce the normal kinetic effects within the limb, the net result of the limb action for the body as a whole will become quite different from what it was before. Thereby we upset the relation between level O and the higher levels S and W. Will coordination patterns within the limb thereafter remain as they were before, perpetually in discord wtih the needs of the body, or will they be remodeled and re-integrated with the levels S and W so as to restore harmonious operation of the whole?

Applying these experimental tests, it was found that a stimulus which normally yields a "flexion" reflex will invariably lead to a contraction of the hamstring muscles and the tibialis group, no matter whether the resulting movement comes actually out as flexion, or, owing to transposition of the muscles, as extension, rotation, or any other joint excursion, irrespective also of whether or not the resulting flexion or extension, as the case may be, leads to an effect which can be considered adequate from the standpoint of the body.

Now, let us go one step farther. Let us change the nerve supply of a "flexor" muscle, either one that still flexes, or one that has been transposed to the extensor side, by substituting an "extensor" nerve for the original "flexor" nerve. As we have outlined before, the result will vary with the age of the animal at the time of operation. Late operations will lead to neurotypic response; that is, the muscle will contract during "extensor" phases only and, hence, not take part in the "flexion" reflex (cf. Sperry, 1941). Early operations, however, will result in continued myotypic response, that is, a "flexion" reflex will

---

*Editor's footnote: The reader will note that this is the same question that arose in connection with the Wicken's conditioned finger "withdrawal" experiment.

bring in the "flexor" muscle even though it is now innervated from an "extensor" nerve and may have been switched over to the extensor side so as actually to produce extension. Whatever we do to it, the muscle with the "flexor" constitution will be the one to respond in the so-called "flexion" reflex (see Table 8.2).

Such being the situation, it would seem much more to the point to speak of a "tibialis-semitendinosus-semimembranosus" reflex, rather than of a "flexion" reflex, and to describe the "flexion" reflex about as follows: A stimulation of sensory fibers from the skin of a toe sets off a central discharge pattern, which selectively engages all motor neurones, however much scattered over the central district, which bear the specific "tibialis," "semitendinosus," and "semimembranosus" tags previously acquired from their respective muscles, with no regard to the actual kinetic and biological effects of the resulting contractions. The fact that the contraction of the hamstrings produces flexion, which has given the reflex its name, is, physiologically speaking, pure coincidence; fortunate from the standpoint of the animal and, of course, fixed by virtue of that very fact during the phylogenetic evolution of the species, but entirely dependent on the skeletal attachments of the muscles being and remaining what they are. If we disrupt this anatomical wisdom, we note no tendency of the centers to maintain the integrity of the response in terms of its effect ("flexion," "withdrawal"), but a blind continuance of the inherited central impulse scheme, delivered in terms of muscle-specific calls, in spite of the adversity or, at best, indifference to the individual of the resulting effects.

We have chosen a reflex as our first example because reflexes are usually conceded to be sufficiently rigid to fit into this picture. Therefore, the statements of these last pages do not exact much revision of current thinking, except in so far as they show that the response called for in a given reflex is not due to firmly set central connections, but that the nerves are conditioned for their response by their muscles. All the other conclusions could have been reached without knowing about the myotypic principle. It is only on the level of the more complex motor activities that uncertainties arise which it might not have been possible to clear up without the aid of the myotypic test.

A transplanted supernumerary limb can be of no use to the body unless possibly in the very special case where it has been inserted exactly in the same orientation as the near-by normal limb so that the pair can execute parallel action. In all other cases the actions of the transplant are sheer waste from the standpoint of the body. Conditions can even be created in which the action of the transplant

TABLE 8.2

Effect of a "Flexion" Reflex on a "Flexor" and "Extensor" Muscle Before and After Tendon Crossing or Nerve Crossing or Both

		Insertion		Innervation		Reflex Effect	
Operation	*Operated Muscle*	*Left on*	*Transferred to*	*Original*	*Transposed*	*Contracting Muscle*	*Kinetic Effect*
Control	Flexor	Flexor side		Flexor nerve		Flexor	Flexion
	Extensor	Extensor side		Extensor nerve			
Tendon crossing	Flexor		Extensor side	Flexor nerve		Flexor	Extension
	Extensor		Flexor side	Extensor nerve			
Nerve crossing[a]	Flexor	Flexor side			Extensor nerve	Flexor	Flexion
	Extensor	Extensor side			Flexor nerve		
Tendon and nerve crossing[a]	Flexor		Extensor side		Extensor nerve	Flexor	Extension
	Extensor		Flexor side		Flexor nerve		

[a]Nerve crossing prior to loss of ability of re-modulation.

is distinctly harmful in that it counteracts the normal limb (P. Weiss, 1937a). No adjustment or elimination of the wasteful action has ever been observed. It was suggested by Bethe and Fisher (1931, p. 1119) that the disturbance caused to the animal by the extra limb might not have been sufficiently vital for the centers to do something about it. It was argued that so long as the host limbs could continue in their normal function, the incentive to change the functional pattern might not have been strong enough. This criticism, however, has been invalidated by later experiments in which the nuisance value of the transplant was so aggravated that it created a serious predicament for the animal. Since these experiments illuminate the problem of coordination most clearly, we shall recount them here briefly, adding a number of comments that were not contained in the original publication (P. Weiss, 1937b).

UNMODIFIABILITY OF LOCOMOTOR SCORES

In larval salamanders possessing developed and functional limbs, the two fore limbs were mutually exchanged under preservation of their original dorsoventral orientation. Since the two limbs are mirror images of each other, this operation amounts to replacing one limb by another limb which has the same assortment of muscles but in exactly the reverse arrangement. A comparison between the insets of Fig. 8.5 and 8.6 explains the situation. Of the six muscles which represent the limb in our myochronograms only the elevator ($\triangle$) and the depressor ($\times$) have retained their normal positions relative to the body, while the adductor and abductor of the shoulder, and likewise the extensor and flexor of the elbow, have traded places. Adductor ($\bullet$) and extensor ($\blacksquare$) now lie at the anterior instead of the posterior border of the limb and abductor ($\circ$) and flexor ($\square$) lie on the posterior instead of the anterior side.

After being re-innervated by regenerating nerves, these limbs resume function. The characteristics of this function are outlined in Fig. 8.6, in which six phases of a full walking cycle have been reproduced diagrammatically. Strips of the moving pictures from which these diagrams were reconstructed have been reproduced previously, and the reader may be referred to the earlier publication (P. Weiss, 1937b) for further details. The functional effect of the anteroposterior reversal of the whole muscle apparatus was so obvious that it seems hardly necessary to add much to the story, as it unfolds itself in a comparison between Fig. 8.5 and 8.6 (pp. 246–247).

All movements of the trunk, hind legs, and other parts which have been left untouched by the operation, are identical with those of a normal animal in the act of progression. Hence, we can use these normal parts to identify the successive phases of locomotion and to line them up with the corresponding phases of the normal animal in the diagram. This being done, we realize immediately that the position of the transposed fore limb (Fig. 8.6) and those of the normal fore limb (Fig. 8.5) are precise mirror images for each corresponding phase of the body movement. If we resolve the movement again into its component muscular contractions, we note that at any one moment the combination of muscles active in the reversed limb is identically the same as the one that would be active at that particular moment if the limb were a normal unreversed one. Using the myochronogram as index of the central impulse pattern, we thus learn that the centers have continued to call up the individual muscles in the same rhythm, sequence and intensity as they had done when they were still operating normal legs with unreversed musculature. In doing this, however, they lead to peripheral effects which are exactly the opposite from what would serve the organism: instead of progression, they produce regression. This is explained in the diagram (Fig. 8.6).

In phase 1, the reversed limb on the right side has taken hold on the ground. During phases 2 and 3 the extensor (■) and adductor (●) muscles contract—the same muscles which are active during phases 2 and 3 in the normal animal (Fig. 8.5). This swings the body backwards (see arrow), while the arm on the left side reaches backward owing to the contraction of its elevator (△), flexor (□) and abductor (○). In phase 4, this free arm, in turn, takes hold on the ground, and the following contractions of its adductor (●) and extensor (■) bring the body still further backward through phases 4, 5, and 6. Thus, the muscles of the reversed limbs, while going through precisely the same cycle of innervation which their synonymous muscles would go through in the normal limbs, move the body backward instead of forward.

Actual regression occurs only if other means of progression, such as the tail and hind limbs, have been removed or paralyzed. If the hind limbs are present, however, the resultant effect is a constant struggle between the hind limbs and the fore limbs, the former striving to advance the body and the latter cancelling the effect by moving the body backwards by the same amount. The net result is that the animal swings back and forth without ever moving from the spot. It is almost pathetic to see how helpless the animals are about their predicament, and although some of them have been kept for more than a year, long beyond metamorphosis, their behavior has never changed.

From these results it must be concluded that the centers operate in terms of individual muscle calls which are combined into definite groupings so pre-arranged as to yield suitable effects in an animal with normal distribution and normal attachments of its muscles, and that the centers continue to operate according to the old scheme even when the peripheral anatomy is no longer normal and the central design no longer yields the desired peripheral effect. Paraphrasing the situation, one might say that the centers continue to act under the illusion that they are still operating a normal limb with consequential results.

In these experiments, the objection certainly no longer holds that the disturbance of behavior was not sufficiently crucial for the animal to attempt an adaptive change. If they could not improve under these conditions, then they surely cannot under any circumstances. There is one possible objection, however, that deserves some consideration. It might be submitted that the anatomical conditions in the reversed legs might have been such as to preclude, for purely mechanical reasons, an effective participation of these limbs in forward locomotion, in which case even the highest power of central re-education would have been able to do no good. To this one could simply reply that in that case the animal might, at least, have learned to suppress the activities of the useless for limbs altogether, which undoubtedly would have been of some help. However, there is more pertinent evidence on hand to invalidate the mechanical argument. It lies in the observation that animals with reversed fore legs can actually exert forward traction through these limbs. This happens whenever the animal as a whole tends to retreat.

Figure 8.7 explains the case. The upper half of the picture shows the fore limb coordination of a normal animal which tries to recede from a repulsive stimulus; for instance, strong ammonia vapor, or a moving object of threateningly large dimensions. The essential mechanism consists of adducting (●) and flexing (□) the elevated (△) arm, then setting it down on the ground (✕), and finally extending (■) and abducting (○) it, with the result that the body is thrust backward. Usually the right and the left arm alternate, as is shown in the myochronograms at the top and bottom of the figure. A comparison of these myochronograms with the records of forward locomotion in Fig. 8.5 reveals that the essential difference between the two types of movement is the change in the phases in which the abductor and adductor muscles come in. In both movements the

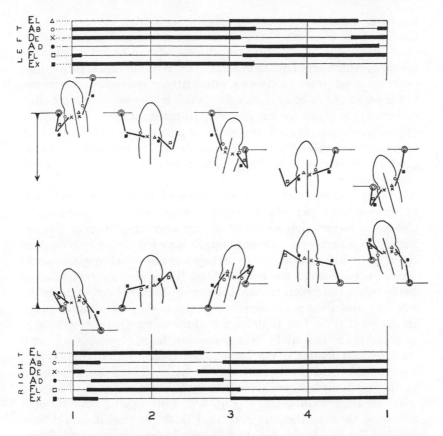

FIG. 8.7.   Myochronogram of fore limb action during "Retreat," executed by normal salamander (upper center) and salamander with reversed fore limbs (lower center).

elevator and flexor muscle, and likewise the depressor and extensor, operate approximately in phase, while the abductor works with the former group in the case of progression and with the latter group in the case of retreat, the reciprocal holding for the adductor. There are other minor differences, but this is the most conspicuous one. Incidentally, this alternative association of the shoulder muscles with either one or the other elbow muscle group is a good illustration of the diversity of muscle combinations possible on level O.

Now, if the myochronogram of retreat is projected into the musculature of an animal with reversed forelegs, a movement results such as the one illustrated in the lower half of the center strip of Fig. 8.7. As one can see, the effect is that the body is being pushed forward. This the animals have actually been seen to do in the face of a repelling stimulus, and, biologically speaking, the result is as absurd, if not even more so, as in the case of forward locomotion: In their attempts to recede, they bring themselves closer and closer to the stimulus which they tend to avoid. For us the observation proves that even reversed fore limbs can efficiently contribute to forward locomotion of the body if only their muscles are activated in a time pattern appropriate for the purpose. In purely anatomical regards, the reversed fore legs are, therefore, as adequate for forward as for backward motion; hence their persistent failure to cooperate in the total locomotion of the body cannot be ascribed to mechanical incompetence.

A comparison of the myochronograms of ambulation and retreat at the same time permits us to define precisely what changes in the pattern of locomotion would have been necessary in order that the animals with reversed fore limbs might have learned to employ their limbs more judiciously. There are two ways in which the functional incongruity between the normal hind limbs and the reversed fore limbs could have been removed. One would have been to make the adductor and abductor phases trade places in the central time score of progression at the fore limb level, and the other would have been to combine the hind limb fraction of the time score of progression with the fore limb fraction of the time score of retreat. Both changes would have led to essentially the same net results, namely, a transformation at the fore limb level exclusively of the myochronogram of Fig. 8.6 into the myochronogram of Fig. 8.7. This would have restored harmony between the fore and hind limbs in that it would have enabled the fore limbs, too, to take part in body propulsion (lower row of Fig. 8.7). In other words, it would not even have been necessary to rebuild the whole locomotor pattern de novo. Most of it could have been left unaltered, with a simple shift of the abductor innervation from the elevator-flexor phase to the depressor-extensor phase, and conversely, of the adductor from the depressor phase into the elevator-flexor phase. This would have involved the time schedule of one muscle pair only. Or the retreat pattern might have been divided into its fore limb and hind limb parts, and the fore limb part alone substituted for the part normally assigned to the fore limbs in progression.

These would seem to be relatively minor changes, and if the amphibian central nervous system had any tendency and power to take into account and to repair inadequate peripheral results, the emergency of the reversed fore limbs should have proved to be a minor problem. As it is, however, it proved to be insurmountable, and neither were corrections effected nor any tendencies at correction, however abortive, ever observed.

The conclusions to be drawn from the reported results are the following: *The chronological scores,* according to which muscles are called into action when a limb is supposed to move *are rigidly fixed.* The centers contain a definite repertoire of such fixed and discrete scores; for instance, one for ambulation, one for retreat, one for swimming, one for righting, one for turning, and so forth, each of which can be displayed only as a whole or not at all. The nervous system cannot recombine for simultaneous execution parts of one score with parts of another score, nor can it alter the sequence and associations among the individual muscles within a given score. In other words, coordination patterns from level S down are ingrained in the centers and are not "effect-determined."

Basic coordination is thus revealed to deal exclusively with the central representatives of muscles, regardless of what effects these dealings will entail. So far as the basic scores are concerned, the muscles might be non-existent. Amphibian coordination operates "blindly," reeling off available central scores evoked by the stimulus situation. In fact, it can be predicted that they would continue to do so even after the interruption of all motor nerves, or the amputation of all limbs. If it were technically feasible to direct each muscle free, fully protecting its nerve supply, and then to attach them individually to writing levers, we should expect to obtain a myochronogram reconstructed from the muscle play in a smoothly moving normal limb with all muscles in place. In fact, the result should not be essentially different if we cut all nerves and registered oscillographically the activity of all central stumps. Pieced together, the records should again present the myochronogram of one definite movement or another. This would be true not only of type reflexes, for which our statement is not likely to be questioned because it refers to a standard practice in reflex registration, but also for the much more complex and highly coordinated movements which form the locomotor repertoire of the species.*

It will be noted that in this description a possible determining influence of sensory innervation has been completely left out of consideration. This is fully justified by the facts. While a more detailed discussion of this problem will be presented below, we may already in this place point to the fact that in amphibians the basic

---

*Editor's footnote. In the recent literature on invertebrate neurobiology, there are numerous instances in which the entire nervous system is removed from the animal and kept in a dish. Recordings from the motor nerve-stumps of these isolated nervous systems show that the nervous system can continue to send out the complex pattern of commands that would produce, for example, feeding or locomotion in the intact animal.

patterns of coordination are not disturbed by the radical removal of sensory innervation from the muscles executing those patterns.

[Editor's note. Here I have omitted a lengthy discussion of evidence that the development of the central patterning mechanisms in amphibian locomotion owes very little to the effects of sensory input and/or the opportunity for motor activity. The passage is a fascinating one, and, in some ways, the major focus of Weiss's paper. However, my concern in this book is with the mechanisms of coordination, *not* the ontogeny of those mechanisms. We rejoin Weiss at the point where he returns to a discussion of the mechanism itself.]

How are we to visualize these patterns [of centrally generated motor commands]? It must be admitted that the prospect of identifying their material basis and dynamic properties is not yet very bright. It seems that all we can do at present, is to reconstruct them from their manifestations. We know that when we provide them with a system of detector muscles, they will produce a definite myochronogram for each particular act, such as exemplified in Figures 8.5–8.7. The myochronogram, therefore, may be regarded as a peripheral projection of the time schedule according to which the various modulated ganglion cell groups are being activated. If we could let all motor ganglion cells register their phases of activity in separate tracings, this would give us a direct record of their time schedule—a *"neurochronogram."* The neurochronogram, in turn, is only an expression of the time order in which the principle which activates the motor cells becomes effective, a record of what we have called the "central score." This is as far as our factual knowledge will take us, and unless we want to enter the field of hypothesis, the nature and localization of the agents in back of it all must at present remain unaccounted for. Even so, however, we can make certain definite statements about their reality, characteristics, development, behavior, and effects.

1. The central score remains constant amidst the reported experimental changes forced upon the periphery. The stability of organization, therefore, justifies the assumption of an underlying central state or process of correspondingly definite organization.
2.   The organization of the scores on level O (coordination within a limb; "intra-appendicular" coordination) is stable only for a given motor act. The fore limb score for ambulation, for instance, provides for the combination of the adductor, depressor and extensor in one team, and of the abductor, elevator and flexor in the other. The score of the same center, however, for the act of retreating combines the abductor, depressor and extensor in one phase, and the adductor, elevator and flexor in the other.

3. The intra-appendicular scores on level O are indissoluble in their composition within any given act. Even urgent biological necessity cannot modify the chronological patterns exemplified under (2).

4. The scores on level S (coordination among limbs; "inter-appendicular" coordination) for a given act (ambulation; retreat; etc.) operate through the subordinated intra-appendicular scores provided for those acts according to (2). But the time relations among the individual limb actions are more variable than the time relations of muscle actions within the limb (see p. 248).

5. In spite of greater temporal elasticity, the combination of partial scores of level O executing interappendicular coordination of level S is indissoluble within a given act. Fore limb scores of retreat cannot be combined with hind limb scores of progression even under the pressure of biological necessity.

6. The scores provided for the different basic biological acts appear to be discrete entities with no intergradations. Each one represents a ready mechanism to execute one vital function with great adequacy, provided the animal is equipped with just the kind of anatomical apparatus for which the score is designed, including proper nerve modulation.

7. The basic scores develop by self-differentiation within the centers, molded by the pre-functional agents of embryonic differentiation. Not all of them develop at the same time, and many are not completed until late in post-embryonic life. Some are permanently in operation (e.g., respiratory movements), others may remain latent under ordinary circumstances. The totality of preformed scores owned by a species may be called its *"motor repertoire."*

8. Since different scores are executed by the same muscles and ganglion cells, only in different assortments and sequences, it becomes impossible to view them in terms of rigidly established neurone connections after the fashion discussed on page (223ff). Consequently, the definiteness and constancy of their structure must be based upon definite dynamic properties (time parameters; chemical affinities; or the like) of the central agents, rather than on unique morphological connections.

According to these points, the amphibian central nervous system self-differentiates a definite and limited repertoire of discrete and strictly circumscribed scores upon which the animal must draw for all its perfomances. Animals of the type here discussed have never shown any ability of adding to this inherited repertoire in their later life by experience. *The elementary mechanisms of coordination are inherent in the centers,* and *the units of coordinated behavior are integrated complexes of the kind reflected in a myochronogram,* rather than indiviudal neurone activities. This is the basic fact which all theories of coordination will have to keep in view, and compatibility with which will be their test.

[Editor's note. I have omitted a section that argues for what Weiss termed the resonance theory. This was the theory that a complex signal from the central programs was sent simultaneously and continually to all motor neurons and that different motor neurons were sensitive to different aspects of that signal. The theory was an alternative to the connectionist theory, which holds that the central program sends signals over selected neural pathways to activate specific motor neurons at appropriate times. Evidence presently available favors the connectionist theory, at least at the spinal level.

I have also omitted several pages at the beginning of the next section. They contain a lengthy discussion of sensory deafferentation studies and what they do or do not prove about the viability of the chained reflex theory of locomotion. Since the literature around which this discussion turns has been superseded by more recent work, we skip the discussion of these now outdated studies and take up with Weiss's conclusion, which (in the editor's opinion) is essentially correct.]

Plainly there are differences between the movements of a fully sensitive and a de-afferented limb, as well as differences in the behavior of the whole animal, which become increasingly greater as the extent of de-afferentiation increases. The finer polish through which the movements become smooth and are kept in harmony with the changing topography of the environment disappears, and only the crude basic structure of the main patterns is left. But the difference between the polished behavior of the normal animal and the cruder performance of the de-afferented animal is so much smaller than the difference between the still highly coordinated function of the latter and a disorganized state of random contractions, which would mark the break-down of coordination, that it becomes practically negligible so far as the problem of basic locomotor coordination is concerned. The step from the irregular twitching of an uncontrolled muscle machine to the coordinated activities observed even in de-afferented animals is so immense, when compared with what sensory control has to add in the way of further accomplishment, that our sense of proportions should revolt against the recurrent attempts to give sensory control full credit for the whole achievement.

However, clarification of the whole issue will be greatly aided, if we abandon such inarticulate utterances about sensory control as that it is "of paramount importance," "dominant," "essential," "vital," or, on the other side of the picture, "irrelevant," "practically insignificant," and so on, and replace them by precise statements as to what phases of motor activity depend upon the integrity of sensory innervation, in what respect, and to what degree. Such a program would make no sense unless the hierarchical constitution of nervous functions is recognized. But if we admit that sensory influx may have different effects with regard to some levels of nervous activity than with regard to others, we realize the necessity of a more differentiated rating of those effects, than merely as a point on a scale from "unimportant" to "highly important." Without trying to be exhaustive, here is a brief list of known sensory functions as they affect motor behavior.

1. The afferent influx initiates responses by releasing central discharges of definite pattern.

2. It conditions the centers for subsequent excitations by residual effects on central excitability and excitatory state. The total afferent influx thus produces a continuously shifting background of central excitability, which explains much of the latitude of the stimulus-response relation.

3. It decides which response from among the plurality of latent discharge patterns composing the central "repertoire" is actually to go into effect. It also influences direction, intensity, speed and duration of the elicited response.

4. Afferent proprioceptive impulses control the degree of muscular tone, and hence, maintenance of posture against gravity.

5. They also contribute to the precision and smoothness of a movement through local stretch reflexes (myotatic reflexes) acting as "governors."

Since each major item of this list can be still further subdivided, it will be realized how complex the effects of sensory influx are, hence, how futile it is simply to assert their bearing on motor functions without further qualification. A toad with deafferented hind limbs moves perfectly well over rough ground; but when it happens to land from a jump with its limbs contorted, no postural correction will ensue until the next locomotor impulse automatically returns the limbs to their normal position. This exemplifies the kind of disturbances to be ascribed to lack of sensation. Other shortcomings are the cruder dosing of the muscular contractions, exaggeration of movements, abnormalities of the tonic background, and so on, none of them serious enough to mask the essential fact that the basic central scores through which locomotor coordination is effected survive the elimination of the sensory influx.*

COORDINATION IN MAMMALS

If central self-differentiation unguided by peripheral experience is so dominant in the establishment of motor coordination, how is it then possible that the recognition of this fact could so long have remained in doubt? Two reasons may be advanced: First, the lack of adequate experimentation; second, the anthropocentric factor, that is, the tendency, mentioned in the introductory chapter, to interpret animal behavior on the basis of human experience. The prominence of the volume of acquired habits in human coordination intimated that all basic coordination had originated in a similar way. By extrapolation from his own faculties, *man* conceded *experience* a role in the primary modelling of coordination, as well as a capacity to remodel such coordination once it had ceased to serve the needs of the body. In contrast to this view, we now learn of the great rigidity and unmodifiability of coordination patterns in the *lower vertebrates*.

Since it would be entirely unsatisfactory to let the matter rest with this obvious schism between lower and higher vertebrates, it seems desirable to indicate briefly how the gap can be bridged. In *amphibians* learning ability seems to be definitely confined to levels higher than S, with all partial acts below level S being firmly and irrevocably set. Thus an amphibian can be conditioned to exhibit a certain motor reaction, for example, alarm, preying, retreat, etc., in response to a certain set of sensory stimuli. Yet, in producing these responses, it is bound to use the existing repertoire of preformed motor mechanisms, such as they are.

Proceeding to a higher animal, and choosing the *rat* as representative of lower mammals, the experiments of Sperry (1940, 1941) have demonstrated that the basic central scores are strikingly rigid and unmodifiable even on this scale of organization. The tendons of the major dorsi-flexor and plantar-flexor of the foot were crossed so as to cause either muscle to produce an excursion of the ankle joint in the opposite direction from normal. In order to avoid

---

*Editor's footnote. A further discussion of the literature on sensory deprivation and the development of the mechanisms of coordination is omitted here. The conclusion drawn in the omitted passage, namely, that basic motor scores develop even when sensory input is absent from birth, holds for primates (Taub, 1976) as well as for amphibians.

possible compensatory adjustments through normal muscles, all muscles but the crossed ones were extirpated. After the operation, the rats first showed clear-cut reversal of foot movements, which was evident both in type reflexes and in complex postural and locomotor actions. If the central nervous system were to have re-integrated the ankle movements with those of the other joints, it would have had to retime the innervation of the crossed muscles so as to excite either of them at such moments when in normal coordination the other would have been activated. That such retiming would have led to mechanically and biologically satisfactory results, was shown by crossing the nerves to the crossed muscles. As we mentioned earlier, nerves transposed after their modulation has become immutable continue to operate according to the time schedule of their original muscles. Thus, a *plantar-flexor* muscle, provided with a firmly modulated *dorsi-flexor* nerve, acts in the *dorsi-flexor* phase of each movement (Sperry, 1941). Since in the animals with crossed tendons the effect of a former *plantar-flexor* is mechanically converted into *dorsi-flexion*, the nerve crossing rectifies the reversal produced by the tendon crossing, and movements are again correct. However, in no case did rats after simple tendon crossing (Sperry, 1940) or simple nerve crossing (Sperry, 1941) learn to adjust their foot movements. They persevered in operating the hind limb muscles according to the inherited coordination scores and failed to re-arrange the timing even under crucial training conditions. In conclusion, so far as plasiticity of basic coordination patterns is concerned, the rat possesses none in its *hind* limbs, and, therefore, lines up in this respect with the amphibians.

A repetition of the experiments on the *fore* limb, however, has suggested that there may be a significant difference between fore limb and hind limb coordination (Sperry, 1942). Tendon crossing in the fore limb again led to reversal of all standard movements and postures in the manner described for the hind limbs. However, some rats seem to have discovered an emergency solution, consisting of locking the extended elbow joint mechanically so that the stiff fore limb can be used as a brace for the support of the fore body. In this manner the animals can avert the caving in of the elbow joint which would otherwise accompany the supporting phase of all movements and postures because of the translocation of the extensor tendons to the flexor side of the joint. Even while this adjustment is in effect, the transposed muscles continue to contract in their original phases. The adjustment consists of an appropriate twisting of the whole arm by the shoulder muscles rather than a corrective retiming of the arm muscles. A point to be stressed in this connection is that the locked position is assumed and maintained only for the one specific act for which it has been acquired, namely, the support of the body, while in all other performances the elbow is still moved in reverse. Moreover, frequent relapses occur even during the supporting phase.

In other words, the basic patterns of coordination have not been remodeled, extensor and flexor muscles have not traded their phases of innervation as they would have had to do if the mechanical reversal were to have been compensated for, and in this respect the experiments on the fore limb merely duplicate those of the hind limb. However, in addition and on top of the immutable inherited pattern, a trick performance has been established, the locking reaction, through which the old automatic and inadequate response can be temporarily superseded in a manner profitable to the body as a whole. This new performance is neither a permanent substitute for, nor is it in itself a revised edition of, the old pattern. The old stereotyped automatism continues in existence, only intermittently covered up by the action of another nervous apparatus more responsive to the needs of the body.

The adjustment of the fore limb behavior is of a very crude and primitive nature. However, an adjustment it is, nevertheless, and possibly the first faint trace of that capacity for learned coordination, which has reached such high degree in man. Pending proof to the contrary, one would feel inclined to ascribe this incipient adjustive capacity to the beginning evolutionary efflorescence of the motor cortex. Accordingly, the cortico-spinal system would have to be considered as the mediator in these adjustments (see Tower, 1936), and the lack of secondary adjustments of the *hind* limb movements of the rat could be correlated with the fact that in this animal only a small fraction of the pyramidal system reaches the hind limb centers Ranson, 1913). Through its short-cut from the cortex to the spinal efferent neurones, this system is obviously enabled to deal with the muscles directly under circumvention of the whole hierarchy of lower centers. Whereas such motor acts as are produced through the mediation of lower centers will continue to exhibit the stereotyped inherited patterns, responses effected over the cortico-spinal system may engage the muscles in new temporal groupings of varying combinations, to be deleted or retained depending on their ultimate success for the body.

Whether these new patterns are established by a trial-and-error procedure, or by vitrue of some intrinsic self-regulatory capacity of the cortical system, is impossible to say and also wholly irrelevant from our present point of interest. The main thing is that this cortical activity, or to put it more cautiously, adjustive capacity of higher centers, is limited to setting up new secondary patterns without power to remodel or abolish the primary patterns. This would seem to imply that *the primary and secondary patterns are operated by different central mechanisms.*

As we go up in the scale of mammals, the wealth of secondary patterns—that is, of acquired performances, learned under the guidance of cortical activity—becomes so enormous that their preponderance tends to obscure the existence of the old primary patterns which dominated the amphibian picture. The presence of basic patterns of the primary unlearned type even in man, has of course been widely recognized. Studies on fetal behavior (Hooker, 1939) and child development (Gesell, 1929, Shirley, 1931) have been particularly suggestive. However, the distinction between primary and secondary patterns was usually based merely on differences of origin: autonomous central maturation of the former, as against peripheral acquisition of the latter by experience. There has been no intimation that the difference may also be one of plasticity. Hence, if we want to homologize the primary innate patterns of man with the basic coordination patterns of the lower vertebrates, we must first prove that they are equally unmodifiable. This is an empirical task which has not yet been accomplished thus far.

The problem is to separate those motor performances in which the chronological scores of muscular contractions are absolutely fixed, and remain so even when they lead to unsatisfactory results for the body, from those in which the muscles can be operated in freely variable combinations so as to yield aimful responses. The most valuable experimental material bearing on the problem is in the hands of orthopedic surgeons, who are studying the recuperation of useful coordination after muscle transplantation in partially paralyzed limbs. Some well analyzed cases have brought to light a real conflict between inherited and unmodifiable patterns on the one hand, and novel patterns learned by experience with the aid of physical therapy, on the other (Scherb, 1938). However, no more than the first step towards a really clearcut classification and distinction in these matters has been undertaken.

Another source of valuable evidence lies in the study of the comparatively rare cases of functional supernumerary appendages in man. One such case has been examined and has yielded some instructive data. A girl with three supernumerary fingers, which could be identified as a third, fourth, and fifth finger, when first tested, showed distinct "homologous response" between each extra finger and the corresponding normal finger of the same hand (P. Weiss, 1935). Thus, obviously, the principle of myotypic response is as valid in man as it is in lower vertebrates. Whenever homologous muscles operate in association, this may be taken to indicate that they were activated through the mediation of the spinal mechanism to which the neurones of synonymous muscles respond in unison. However, after continued training with conscious effort, the girl finally managed to produce a very clumsy, but, nevertheless, real dissociation between homologous muscles (P. Weiss and Ruch, 1936). She had apparently learned to innervate the extra fingers and the homologous normal fingers independently. This lasted, however, only so long as her attention was concentrated on the job. As soon as mental or physical fatigue or distraction of attention weakened the effort, the old associated movements of homologous fingers re-appeared immediately. Here, too, cortical efforts have been successful in temporarily superseding and circumventing lower mechanisms with the result of greater refinement of movement, but this has not entailed a permanent reorganization of the lower effector patterns in the direction of better adjustment. These results, moreover, suggest that the adjustive higher mechanism (hypothetically identified here with the cortex) does not necessarily operate according to the myotypic principle, as the lower mechanisms of coordination do.

Of course, this is only a single case, and the examination leaves much to be desired. Much valuable evidence is consistently being wasted by not giving natural occurrences, such as the one here described, the critical experimental study which their fundamental significance would warrant. It is hoped that the concrete and differentiated questions raised in this paper may lead to increased interest in phenomena of this kind and to a more articulate evaluation of the information which they present.

CONCLUSIONS

It would be needless repetition to review here the specific conclusions reached from our experiments and deliberations, which have already been summarized in their context throughout this paper.

However, we may briefly examine how the answers to some of the standard questions about coordination will look in the light of our results. The term "coordination," one will remember, is used here strictly in reference to the fact that the central nervous system engages the muscles in such a definite order that, in a normal animal, their combined activities result in orderly movements, which, in turn, yield acts of biological adequacy for the animal as a whole.

It will have become obvious that questions such as: *"Is coordination inherited or acquired?", "Is coordination rigid or plastic?", "Is coordination under sensory control?"* just cannot be answered in that generality. There are patterns of coordination, as we have seen, that are definitely inherited, of prefunctional and pre-experiential origin; there are others that are definitely "learned." The former are rigid in some regards, but show a certain latitude in other regards. The latter show greater plasticity, but even so within definite bounds. Sensory "control" is not vital for coordination; however, coordination may suffer from its absence, the degree varying from one class of animals to another. We have found it necessary to speak of different degrees of coordination; to distinguish levels of coordination; to separate coordination of muscles in moving a limb from coordination of limbs in moving the body, and the latter from coordination of body movements for the satisfaction of biological needs. These are not all the same thing. They cannot be treated all alike and squeezed into a single formula. What holds for one level or one animal, cannot be applied as a matter of course to all levels and all animals.

Failure to recognize this truth cannot but breed sterile controversies. In fact, if it were not too far a digression from our main subject, it would be an easy matter to trace many a heated dispute of the past back to the fact that two schools, starting from two sets of different but equally valid data, generalized far beyond the legitimate scope of those data, ending up with irreconcilable theories, all in the name of simplicity. We prefer to think of natural principles as of great uniformity and universality, and we are partial to doctrines which present them as such. Accordingly, we would have expected coordination to be either all plastic or all rigid; all preformed or all individually acquired. To learn that it is partly one way and partly the other, is disappointing. Nevertheless, this is precisely what the facts have revealed, and we must acknowledge their testimony. Let us briefly review the evidence.

Is Coordination Inherited or Acquired?

Undeniably, the *basic* patterns of coordination are inherited. That is, the nervous system of every vertebrate about which we have sufficient information, amphibian as well as mammal, develops a certain repertoire of patterns of coordination prefunctionally. These patterns differentiate by virtue of the developmental dynamics of the growing organism in forward reference to their future function, but without the benefit of exercising that function during their formative period. They are laid down in a hierarchy of functional levels, of which the lowest, i.e., the one dealing directly with the muscles, operates in terms of specific signals, one signal for each individual muscle ("myotypic" principle). That the centers should be able to differentiate such a variety of specific signals (specific biochemical processes or specific electric states) is no more surprising than that different glands should be able to produce different secretions.

Once in operation, these basic patterns of coordination act "blindly," unconcerned of whether or not their peripheral effects are of service to the animal. Achievement counts in neither their making nor maintenance. In normal animals they are serviceable by predesign—evolution has taken care of that. When disarrangement of the bodily machine for which they are pre-adapted abolishes their serviceability, they continue unaltered. This, better than any indirect evidence, proves their preformed stereotypism. To this extent the data confirm the *preformistic* concept.

However, there is a second side to the story of coordination that is distinctly *non-preformistic*. The preformed patterns are relatively crude, and only grossly speaking are they stereotyped. The inherited repertoire provides an animal only with what we may call an existential minimum of vital performances. Improvements are called for and occur in varying degrees.

In this connection it should be pointed out that the inherited patterns, of course, do not arise all at the same time, nor all in the embryonic phase. Not only does the metamorphosis of amphibians furnish many dramatic examples of comprehensive behavioral changes during the functional life span, but a progressive expansion of the motor repertoire is plainly observable even in non-metamorphotic animals. There is not the least doubt that this gradual enrichment has the same non-experiential origin as the earlier functional endowment, and is nothing but an external manifestation of the continuous progress in the elaboration of the central coordination systems by self-differentiation. The inability of amphibians to readjust primary coordination at any phase in life seems to dispose of the possibility that coordination patterns first exhibited in later life may, in contrast to earlier ones, have been molded by experience.

The inherent repertoire of an amphibian is fully adequate to carry the individual through life without major changes, and, qualitatively, the animal must get along with its limited repertoire of "scores." However, there is room left for improvement on the quantitative side: in the readiness with which a certain score is activated, the smoothness and speed with which it is executed, and in its competitive rating relative to other scores. That is to say, the behavior of an amphibian can become "conditioned" to the exigencies of its environment by selective facilitation or inhibition of existing motor patterns. Within these narrow limits actual experience with the environment then modifies the structure of behavior—although not the structure of its component scores—, and within these limits the *heuristic* concept finds support. So much for the amphibians.

Vertebrates higher on the evolutionary scale, of more complex organization and more specific in their requirements, face more complex tasks. The elasticity of the inherited scores is becoming increasingly insufficient to meet the accidents of the environment. It is on this level of the scale that a new method of coordination came into being: coordination by individual design and discovery, rather than by predesign and evolutionary tradition. This new develpment culminates in man. Man can operate his muscles in ever varying combinations, can discover and retain successful effects, eliminate wasteful ones, and thus force his motor apparatus into increasingly better adapted service. Here non-preformed, "invented," coordination patterns become so prominent that they obscure the more ancient stereotyped patterns with which they coexist and overlap. We have tentatively identified this plastic coordination with the activity of the cortex, but there is no definite proof that subcortical functions may not take part in it in higher mammals.

In the lower mammals, this type of coordination is, if present at all, still in a very rudimentary condition. While both the stock repertoire of the species and the ability of the individual to adapt the elastic stock performances to its needs seem to be considerably increased in the rat over what there is to be found in an amphibian, fundamentally the difference seems negligible as compared with the tremendous efflorescence of the ability to "invent" coordination patterns on the way from rat to man. On the other hand, the primitive trick adjustments of which the fore limbs of the rat are capable (p. 265f) may be a true trace of emergent "inventive" coordination.

Whether this type of coordination attains its effects by trial-and-error procedure or by more direct means, as suggested by adherents of a systemic concept (e.g., Goldstein), is entirely beyond the competence of the present article to decide. The only positive statement we can make is that, in contrast to preformed coordination, the adequacy of the effects is the guiding principle in it, and that it employs different mechanisms from the ones through which the preformed coordination patterns are put into effect. As we have indicated above (p. 268), it does not, for instance, operate through the myotypic principle, and sensory control, Exner's "senso-motility," seems to play a much more constructive role than it does in preformed coordination. For the rest, adequate elucidation of these problems will come from the admirable progress of primate neuropsychology.

The strictly preformistic concept must be qualified in still another respect. As it is usually presented, it is meant to imply preformation of function in form of a set neurone architecture: "anatomical" preformation. Because of this common connotation we have treated it above (p. 223f) under the double heading of "preformistic-structural." But it will have become obvious from our investigations that such an implication does not have to be accepted. An account of some reasons why minute and systematic anatomical preformation of central functions must be questioned, was presented above in the chapters dealing with the myotypic principle. While it is needless to repeat the whole argument, we may restate the case.

The function of each motor cell is variable, depending on its modulation. The central coordination scores, on the other hand, are invariable. Hence, their effect on the motor cells cannot be transmitted through fixed neurone connections. The existence of central states or processes of a high degree of specificity, a corollary of the myotypic principle, would explain the situation on a non-structural basis. In this view, "preformation" of a coordination pattern would mean that those hypothetic specific states or processes are activated in definite chronological sequences; much as in endocrine cycles, in which one gland activates another gland, which in turn activates a third organ, and so forth, likewise without special anatomical channels to pipe the effect along. To fill the picture with concrete sense, is a task of the future. But we had to stress the point that to acknowledge the preformation of coordination does not mean to acquiesce in the strictly structural interpretation of coordination. Preformation of dynamics is the alternative.

Is Coordination Plastic or Rigid?

After the foregoing remarks this question can be easily rectified. We must add: "Which type of coordination?" And, "Plasticity in what respect?"

If "plasticity" is understood in the sense of elasticity within a given qualitative performance, admitting of quantitative adaptation to what for the given species is a normal range of variability of the environment, both preformed and acquired coordination are "plastic." If, however, one defines plasticity as the ability of an organism to cope with emergency situations, lying beyond the normal range of elasticity, by creating new performances, previously not even latently in existence, the preformed type of coordination is definitely devoid of it. Since most of our experiments bear on this point, we need not labor it further.

Elasticity of performance is a different matter. As we mentioned before, there is latitude in the extent to which an animal draws on its motor repertoire, and in the rate at which it displays it. It may walk *or* swim, and do it either faster *or* more slowly. We also pointed out that the timing of the individual limbs in walking or swimming is not nearly as constant as the timing of the muscles in moving the limb (p. 248). But even so, the pattern according to which the limbs are moved will always be the same for all four—following either the "progression" score or the "retreat" score—without a trace of dissociability and "plastic" re-coordination.

That nervous integration bears all signs of being a *self-regulatory systemic* action, such as we know them from other organic systems, is not to be doubted. As a matter of fact, one of the earlier "organismic" attempts to interpret "animal behavior as the reaction of a system" came from the present author (P. Weiss, 1925). To discuss the merits of this view, is beyond the scope of this paper. It is strictly within our province, however, to stress that if the systemic concept is to be reconciled with the facts as they now have come to light, the nervous system will have to be viewed not as if it were *one monotonous whole*, in which what happens to any one part has a direct impact on all other parts, but rather as *a system of systems, each of which consists of subsystems*, and so on; in other words, as a *functional hierarchy* in which the competence, freedom of action, range of variability, etc., of each constituent member is strictly delimited by constitutional— and, on the higher levels, acquired—properties.

Thus, one might conceive, for instance, of the integrative complexes involved in progression or retreat as acting each as a single system, within which the actions of all component parts would be independent. However, the working units of these systems are in themselves systems of a lower order, in the present example elementary limb scores, and the integrative system is bound to operate through these subordinate systems as wholes. In other words, the systemic action of level S of the hierarchic scale (p. 236) might regulate the timing according to which the individual limbs are set in motion, but would be powerless to alter the limb scores themselves which operate on the lower level O. On this basis it would be understandable that after the amputation of a limb the timing of the remaining limbs can be aimfully revised for better service to the body

(Bethe, 1931), while retiming of the muscles within the limbs is yet impossible in all lower vertebrates thus far studies, up to and including the rat. The assumption that the progression system and the retreat system are each an entity, likewise explains the inability of our animals to piece together half of one with half of the other (p. 258). In a more general sense this view can be well reconciled, it seems, with the ideas of Lashley (1937, 1938a) on systemic action of the brain, and with the known facts concerning vicarious action and compensatory regulation in integrative function.

However, we do not propose to go into the subject here any further. We merely wanted to indicate that the negation for lower vertebrates of "plasticity" in the sense of an omnipotent faculty to invent novel coordination patterns to meet emergencies outside of the elasticity limits of the inherited repertoire, and the affirmation of systemic properties of the centers, implying free interplay of forces within the limits of the constitution of the central system, are not at variance. There will be no misunderstanding on this point so long as one keeps in mind that the higher integrative functions are bound to operate through the existing lower functional mechanisms and that the latter, qualitatively determined during the developmental, that is, pre-operational, phase, are inaccessible to reorganization. Only the higher mammals seem to have developed a new superstructure capable of setting up "plastic" coordination patterns by means which are not yet available on the lower levels of the animal scale.

SUMMARY

Experiments are described in which the method of transplantation of muscles and nerves was used to analyze the origin and, in certain regards, the operation of motor coordination in amphibians. The results support a preformistic concept of coordination in these forms. A basic repertoire of primary motor patterns develops during the developmental phase. These arise essentially by self-differentiation within the central nervous system, independent of the benefits of sensory control and guidance by experience. They are so predesigned that, when later projected into an anatomically normal peripheral effector system, they produce biologically adequate effects. If confronted, however, with an atomically disarranged periphery, they produce correspondingly distorted effects without signs of corrective adjustment. The relation of these facts to the phenomenon of "plastic" coordination observed in man and higher mammals, and their bearing on the theories of coordination is discussed.

DIAGRAMMING THE HIERARCHY

Weiss's outline of the six lowest levels in the hierarchy of action has never been improved upon. In one respect, however, the thirty some years that have passed since Weiss wrote have added to our perspective. We now can suggest plausible models for the processes that determine the coordinated actions of the higher levels in his hierarchy. Using these models, we can elaborate Weiss's hierarchical classification of coordinations into a hierarchically organized circuit diagram. In fact, we have already considered such models in some detail. The complex unit that controls the stepping of one leg of the roach (Fig. 5.4) operates at what Weiss called the fourth level of organization—the level at which units coordinate the musculature of an entire limb. The coupling circuitry (Fig. 5.5), by which oscillators for each leg maintain appropriate phase relationships among themselves, forms part of a unit at Weiss's fifth level of organization, the level that coordinates the musculature of all the limbs. The other part of this fifth-level unit is the command pathway (Fig. 5.6), the pathway that varies the nominal frequency of oscillation. The command pathway and the oscillator-coupling pathways coordinate the stepping cycles of the individual legs to produce gaits— interleg stepping patterns. Finally, the taxes, described in Chapter 6, are an example of Weiss's sixth level of coordination. The unit that coordinates locomotion operates together with a unit that controls orientation. The result of this coordinated functioning of a locomotory unit and an orienting unit is an act of the organism. Indeed, taxic acts are the kind psychologists are most used to considering—approach responses, as with a positive phototaxis, and avoidance response, as with negative phototaxis.

Now that Weiss has so ably argued the importance of hierarchical organization in behavior, the core ideas of this book are in place. The fact of hierarchical organization is one of the core ideas. In the next chapter, we will examine the innumerable manifestations and consequences of this organization. Another core idea is what Sherrington called the principle of the common path. I have called this principle the lattice hierarchy principle. (See Fig. 8.1 for a schematic rendering of this principle.) It cannot be emphasized too strongly that at every level of coordination, the same unit of coordination (the same neural circuitry) participates in—forms a component of—many different patterns of behavior. Thus, a unit of coordination is always subject to control by diverse and competing higher level units of coordination. At the neural level this means that any given neural pathway or connection may be functional (potentiated) under any of several disparate sets of circumstances and nonfunctional (depotentiated) under a number of other and equally disparate circumstances. The third core idea is the principle of selective potentiation and depotentiation. Higher level units of coordination achieve their ends not primarily by activating lower units but rather by potentiating some—increasing their potential for action—and depotentiating others.

To strengthen our grasp on these core ideas it will help to ascend Weiss's hierarchy. At each step we will see how units of organization at that level compete for control over a common pool of lower units—the lattice hierarchy principle. We will also see that at higher levels this control frequently takes the form of *permitting* certain lower circuits to function (potentiation) and not permitting others (depotentiation). The repeated illustration of intersecting lines of control and of control by potentiation and depotentiation will strengthen our understanding of these core ideas. The step by step ascent of the hierarchy will clarify what is meant by the claim that behavior—and the neural machinery that generates it—are hierarchically structured.

In ascending the hierarchy, I describe and portray neural circuitry in a schematic way for two reasons. Firstly, the details of the relevant circuitry in any organism are not known; only the general outline is known, and even large parts of the outline are conjectural. While I wish to illustrate the core ideas as particularly and concretely as possible, I do not wish to do so by means of neural circuit diagrams whose details are mostly conjecture. Those with a taste for detail—and the special and more refined insight that detailed analysis yields—may want to follow the work of Wine and Krasne and their collaborators on the control of escape behavior in the crayfish (see Krasne & Wine, 1978, for review). There are also a number of well written analyses of simple neural networks and the behavior they generate in Fentress (1976). Secondly, I do not want to commit myself to a particular organism. The illustrative purpose is better served if one has in mind a generalized and simplified four-footed mammal—a sort of warm-blooded salamander. The refusal to use a single actual organism to illustrate each and every level of organization precludes any detailed neural circuitry and forces one to adopt an approach that modern psychologists are in any event thoroughly at home with—box diagrams. On the other hand, one can find here and there in the neurobiological literature, particularly in the literature on invertebrates, many circuits that are known in some detail and that correspond to one or another of the boxes. So, one is operating in what follows at a level of analysis that is much closer to actual neural circuitry than is the case in most "boxological" analyses. To emphasize this, the illustrations deliberately combine standard neural symbols and the labeled boxes that are the mainstay of "boxology."

The lattice-hierarchy or common-path principle makes its first appearance when we consider the relation between level 1 (the level of the motor units) and level 2 (the level of whole muscle activation). Each motor neuron is a motor unit. It projects to a subset of the muscle fibers in a muscle. Each time the motor neuron fires, the muscle fibers it projects to give a twitch. If the motor neuron fires rapidly enough, the twitches of the muscle fibers fuse together to yield a steady contractile force. The force exerted by the muscle as a whole may be augmented by the graded recruitment of the motor neurons controlling other muscle fibers in the same muscle. In most behaviors, the motor units are activated by this kind of graded recruitment, because only graded recruitment effectively moves and/or stiffens a joint. But not all behavior utilizes graded motor-unit recruitment. The purpose of shivering is to increase muscular activity and thereby the heat from metabolism as much as possible while moving or stiffening the joints as little as possible. In shivering, motor units in all the muscles are excited to slow, independent, random firing. The result is the constant random twitching of subsets of muscle fibers, but very little contraction of muscles as a whole. The two alternative level 2 modes of activating the level 1 units are schematized in Fig. 8.8.

Moving up one level in Weiss's hierarchy brings us to the level Sherrington analyzed so thoroughly—the level of the simple reflex. Figure 8.9 portrays

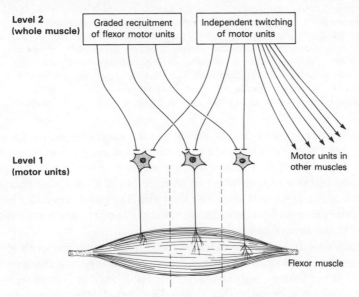

FIG. 8.8.   The motor units—sets of muscle fibers controlled by single motor neurons—may be activated in one of two basic patterns by the next level in the motor hierarchy. The motor units comprising a given muscle may be activated in a carefully patterned manner that produces a graded contraction of the muscle. The left hand box at level 2 represents the neural circuit that imposes such a pattern on the motor units of the flexor muscle. Alternatively, motor units in many different muscles may be activated in such a way that only a few units in any given muscle are twitching at any moment. The right hand box at level 2 represents the neural circuit that imposes this 'shivering' pattern on the motor units. This is an example of the lattice hierarchy principle operating at the lowest two levels of the hierarchy.

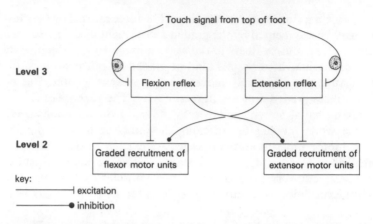

FIG. 8.9.   The boxes at level 2 represent neural circuits that generate graded contraction and relaxation of two different muscles. The boxes at level 3 represent reflex circuits that control the circuits at level 2. One circuit, the flexion-reflex circuit, excites the contraction of the flexor muscle while inhibiting the contraction of the extensor muscle. The other circuit, the extension-reflex circuit, does the opposite. This provides another instance of the lattice hierarchy principle, operating in this case between level 2 and level 3 of the hierarchy. Note that the two reflexes have the same adequate stimulus, that is, the same activating condition. They are not both activated under ordinary conditions because at any one time only one reflex is potentiated.

two opposing reflexes, a flexion reflex and an extension reflex. Opposing extension and flexion reflexes are the archetypical example of the common path or lattice hierarchy principle. The flexion reflex works by graded recruitment of the motor units to the muscles that flex a leg joint and graded inhibition of the muscles that extend the joint. The extension reflex imposes the opposite pattern of excitation and inhibition upon the graded recruitment circuits for the same two sets of muscles.

At Weiss's levels 3 and 4, which are, roughly speaking, the levels at which the elementary units of behavior are found, activating conditions enter the picture. The activating condition for a reflex is what Sherrington termed the adequate stimulus, the stimulus that triggers the reflex movement. The particular flexion and extension reflex that I have chosen for the present illustration have exactly the same adequate stimulus. Both of these reflexes are activated by a tap on the top or front of the animal's foot—the part of the foot that is most likely to strike against something that threatens to trip the animal or sweep its foot out from under it. Flexion and extension reflexes with this common adequate stimulus have been demonstrated in the cat by Forssberg, Grillner, and Rossignol (1975). The flexion reflex, which has the effect of lifting the swinging leg higher off the ground, is seen during the "swing" phase (lift and advance phase) of the stepping cycle. If one taps the leading edge of the cat's paw as the cat swings its leg forward, the tap elicits flexion of the leg joints—the toe, the ankle, the knee, and the hip. In a movie made of this experiment, one can see that the flexion has the effect of lifting the swinging leg up and over a stick that would otherwise have arrested the swing and tripped the cat. The extension reflex, on the other hand, is seen during the stance phase of the stepping cycle when the leg supports and propels the cat. If one taps the leading edge of the paw during this phase, the tap elicits extension of the leg joints. In the movie, one can see that this extension has the effect of hastening the completion of the stance phase, so that a moving object that would otherwise have swept the cat's foot out from under it does not do so.

Thus, the reflex effect of tapping the leading edge of the cat's paw undergoes "phase-dependent reversal": During one phase of the stepping cycle, the tap elicits flexion of the leg joints; during the other, it elicits extension. This is the archetypical example of the intelligent, highly adapted, flexible quality that behavior acquires from the interaction between potentiating and activating signals. Forssberg et al. (1975) assume, as do I, that the oscillator that generates the stepping cycle potentiates the circuitry for the flexion reflex during the swing phase and depotentiates it during the stance phase. The reverse applies to the extension reflex. Thus, a unit at a higher level of organization (level 4—the whole-limb level) *permits* the flexion reflex (a level 3 unit) to be active only at certain times, only when the leg is not supporting the cat. Notice that the form of control is permissive rather than commanding. The level 4 unit does not activate the level 3 unit; only the activating condition—the tap—does that. On 999 out of every 1000 swings the potentiated flexion reflex is not in fact activated. But, very occasionally, the swinging leg strikes something and then the flexion reflex produces one of those last minute adjustments that leads us to marvel at the intelligent manner in which animal action adapts itself to fluctuating circumstances.

The intelligence of the reaction is traceable to the integrating effects of selective potentiation. The action is intelligent because it furthers the general pattern of action—the swing—which prevails at the moment. In the absence of selective potentiation and depotentiation the impact of the tripping obstacle could elicit both flexion and extension. Flexion is consonant with what is happening during the swing phase; extension is consonant with what is happening during the stance phase. By potentiating the flexion reflex during the swing pahse and the extension reflex during the stance phase the oscillator sees to it that only the consonant reaction may occur. Selective potentiation is the agent of behavioral harmony.

We can, by the way, be sure that the phase-dependent governance of the flexion and extension reflexes is actually mediated at this lowest possible level of organization—the level of whole limb control. Forssberg et al.'s observations were made on the hind limbs of cats whose spinal cords were cut at a level that separated hind-limb circuitry from all higher control.

Shifting our attention to the fourth level of organization, we encounter another example of the lattice hierarchy principle. As Weiss emphasized, the same six muscles—the abductor, flexor, elevator, depressor, adductor, and extensor—are employed in both forward and backward locomotion. What varies is the pattern of coactivation, that is, which muscles contract and relax together.

In walking forward, the abductor, the flexor and the elevator are coactive. They contract together during the swing phase. The elevator raises the limb, the flexor bends it at the knee, and the abductor pulls it forward. During the stance phase the other three muscles contract: The depressor pulls the limb down so that it contacts the ground, the adductor pulls the limb backward and in toward the body, and the extensor extends the knee joint to offset the inward component of the adductor's action.

In walking backward, the phase of activation reverses for four of the six muscles types. During the swing phase the elevator contracts together with the adductor and extensor, so the foot is lifted and pulled back rather than lifted and pulled forward. During the stance phase, the depressor presses the foot to the ground, while the abductor and flexor pull the leg forward. This propels the animal backward.

We now know, as Weiss did not, that the timing of muscle contraction in stepping is controlled by an oscillator. It is reasonable to assume that the same oscillator times contraction in both forward and backward locomotion. There must, however, be two distinct circuits for distributing the timing signals to the muscles. In forward locomotion, the signal for the swing phase must excite the elevator, abductor and flexor; whereas in backward locomotion the same signal must excite the elevator, adductor, and extensor (Fig. 8.10).

In Fig. 8.10 we see the same principles at work as in Fig. 8.9. There is a common signal source—the oscillator in Fig. 8.10 and the tap stimulus in Fig. 8.9. Circuits exist for channeling the signal to the same group of muscles in either of two opposing ways. Which circuit is potentiated (allowed to conduct) is determined by signals that descend from a still higher level of organization. In Fig. 8.9, signals coming down from above determine whether the flexion or the extension reflex is potentiated at any given moment. In Fig. 8.10, signals coming down from above determine whether the F distributor or the B distributor is potentiated. If the F distribution network is potentiated the limb steps so as to propel the animal forward; if the B network is potentiated the stepping propels the animal backward. In other words, diverse and opposing higher-level units of coordination utilize the same set of lower-level units (the lattice hierarchy principle) to different effect by controlling the paths of signal flow (the principle of selective potentiation and depotentiation).

Moving up now to Weiss's fifth level, we reach the level of the central programs for forward and backward locomotion. As we saw in Chapter 5, the oscillator-dominated units that control the stepping of individual legs are the building blocks in this central program. To produce forward locomotion,

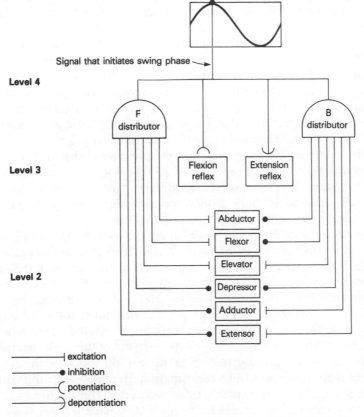

FIG. 8.10. Schematic rendering of the circuitry that controls the whole limb during walking. The oscillator supplies a timing signal that periodically initiates the swing phase. Whether the leg swings forward or backward depends upon how the signal from the oscillator is fed to the muscles. The neural circuitry representd by the F distributor feeds the signal to the muscles in such a way as to swing the limb forward. The circuitry represented by the B distributor feeds the same signal to the same muscles, but in such a way as to swing the limb backwards. This is another instance of the lattice-hierarchy or common path principle. The signal that initiates the swing phase also potentiates the flexion reflex and depotentiates the extension reflex. It does not activate (excite) these reflexes, it merely governs them. This is a low level instance of the principle of hierarchical control by potentiation and depotentiation.

these oscillators are coordinated in accord with the rules laid down by Wilson. The stepping is metachronal, that is, the swing phase of each successive leg progresses along the animal's body in the direction of locomotion. If the animal is moving forward, the rear leg swings first, followed by the front leg. The reverse sequence is observed when the animal moves backward. Stated in terms of phase relationships, the stepping cycle of the front leg lags the stepping cycle of the rear leg when the animal moves forward, and vice versa when the animal moves backward. In either case contralateral legs step 180° out of phase.

The phase-relationship between legs is maintained by coupling signals that pass between the oscillators. Here again the flow of coupling signals must be altered depending upon whether the front oscillator is to lag the rear or vice versa. We must imagine that the central program for forward locomotion potentiates one interoscillator coupling network; whereas the central program for backward locomotion potentiates a different coupling network (Fig. 8.11). Of course, the two networks may have many elements in common. That is, the lattice hierarchy principle, the principle of shared elements, may extend down to a level of neuronal detail that eludes any one-one mapping into behavior. What we regard as distinct circuits from a functional/ behavioral standpoint may exhibit considerable overlap at the neuro-anatomical/ neurophysiological level of analysis.

One attraction of the hierarchically organized coupled-oscillator scheme as it has been portrayed up to this level (Weiss's level 5) is that it explains both the variability seen in normally coordinated walking and the striking stereotypy of basic coordination brought out by Weiss's limb reversal experiments. Weiss notes in passing (p. 248) that in normal locomotion the limbs usually maintain constant phase relations but that it is by no means uncommon for the phase relations between front and rear limbs to be momentarily disrupted by one limb "stepping out of turn." He mentions this variable interlimb coordination as a further difficulty in the way of a connectionistic account of limb coordination. It is, however, a difficulty only so long as one adheres to purely reflex accounts. This relative rather than absolute coordination between limbs (or fins) is what led von Holst to the discovery of the role of coupled oscillations in the genesis of repetitive movement sequences. Stepping out of turn, that is, *phase drift* or *relative coordination*, occurs whenever the driving oscillators are not sufficiently strongly coupled. One can readily construct connectionistic mechanical or electronic models that display this phenomenon (for an example, see von Holst, 1973, p. 135). Von Holst regarded the existence of phase drift in the leg movement sequences of mammals as evidence that locomotion also depended on a system of coupled oscillators. From film strips of a sheepdog walking, von Holst (1973) made a detailed analysis of a sequence in which the dog's hind legs made 25 steps whilst the forelegs made only 20. The variation in step

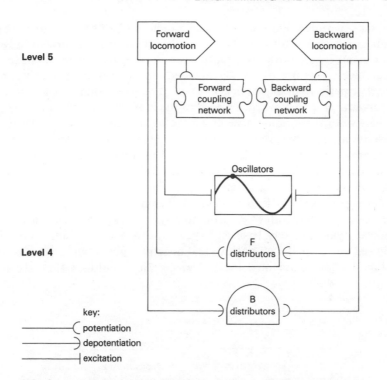

FIG. 8.11. Schematic rendering of the circuitry underlying the units that coordinate forward and backward locomotion. The unit for forward locomotion potentiates the coupling network that mediates the phasing appropriate to forward locomotion (front oscillators lag rear oscillators), excites the oscillators to cycle at a frequency proportional to the strength of the command, potentiates the F distributors, and depotentiates the B distributors. The unit for backward locomotion controls the same set of elements but to different effect, a further illustration of the lattice hierarchy principle.

amplitudes at various points in the drift were strikingly similar to the amplitude variations seen in the partially coupled fins of von Holst's decerebrate fish.

While normal walking manifests considerable variation in the relative timing of different limb movements, the *basic* schemes of forward and backward progression are indissoluble, at least in the salamander. The forward progression scheme at level 5 in the motor hierarchy of the salamander is truly a *unit*. It cannot be dissolved by a higher level of the hierarchy. A higher level, if it wants forward progression, must call up this scheme in its entirety. Even if this scheme cannot produce forward locomotion, the scheme must be activated in its entirety or not at all. The salamander cannot simultaneously activate half of its forward locomotion scheme and half of its backward locomotion scheme, even when a forelimb reversal experiment has rendered such a half-and-half combination the only combination that will work. This is the beauty of Weiss's forelimb reversal experiment. It demonstrates in the most compelling fashion the limits that the hierarchical structure of the salamander's motor system places upon the *realizable* patterns of muscular activation. If only the salamander could make his forward progression scheme control the movements of its hindlegs while his backward progression scheme controlled the movements of its rotated forelimbs it would progress forward. Nothing in the mechanics of its reversed limbs prevents this; nor does any aspect of its motor hierarchy at level 4 or below. Only the lack of a suitable patterning unit at level 5 prevents it. But this lack is decisive: Structure is fate.

Moving up one more level brings us to the final level of Weiss's hierarchy—level 6. Level 6 integrates the locomotor system with other systems so as to produce organismic acts. In order to portray this level of organization, I have endowed our animal with positive and negative light-orienting mechanisms. In Fig. 8.12, it is assumed that under certain conditions the animal will

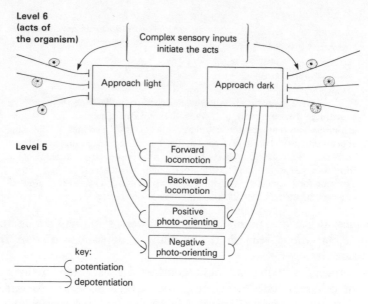

FIG. 8.12. Schematic rendering of the circuits underlying positive and negative phototaxes. Each taxis is realized by potentiating the unit that implements forward locomotion and one or the other light-orienting circuit. Note again the lattice hierarchy principle at work. The units at level 6 are themselves subject to potentiation, which integrates these acts into complex behavior sequences. The circuitry at level 6 receives complex sensory inputs that serve to activate the act when certain conditions are met. Note that *activating* the circuitry for the act as a whole *potentiates* the circuitry for the components of the act. In order for the activated act to occur other lower-level activating conditions will also have to be met (cf. Fig. 8.1).

approach the darkest region of its visual environment and, under others, it will approach the lightest region. These conditions, represented by the laterally impinging sensory neurons in Fig. 8.12, are high level activating conditions. The first act—approaching the light—involves potentiating the forward locomotion system and the positive light orienting system, while depotentiating the negative light orienting system and the backward locomotion system. The second act—approaching the dark—involves potentiating the forward locomotion system and the negative light-orienting mechanism, while depotentiating the positive orienting mechanism and backward locomotion. Note that the two different acts are realized by imposing different patterns of potentiation and depotentiation on the same set of lower-level units—a final illustration of potentiation and depotentiation in a lattice hierarchy.

In the discussion of taxic orienting mechanisms (Chapter 6), little was said about the actual muscular mechanisms for turning. This is because the mechanisms are extremely diverse. For the sake of concreteness, however, it seems appropriate to say something here about the actual muscular manifestations of activity on the part of the orienting units in Fig. 8.12. A principal aspect of the light orienting activity, at least during locomotion, may be very simple. The error signal deriving from the visual system determines the curvature of the animal's trunk. Thus the sixth level integrates a system that controls trunk curvature with a system that controls limb movements.

Trunk curvature is probably not, however, the sole muscular manifestation of the orienting circuits. The orienting mechanisms may also modulate stride length and/or the periods of the oscillators on opposite sides of the animal's body. Some such mechanism is clearly required in order to explain the stepping movements the animal uses to orient toward or away from light when, as sometimes happens, this orienting is not accompanied by locomotion.

In Fig. 8.12, the level 6 units are activated by a complex configuration of sensory factors. The sensory inputs were included to stress the fact that *every level of the action hierarchy from level 3 on up receives sensory input.* The sensory inputs at intermediate levels (Fig. 8.10 and 8.11) were omitted for the sake of diagrammatic simplicity. The nature and role of the sensory inputs to these levels are discussed in Chapter 4 and 5. Weiss (p. 262) is certainly correct in stressing the fact that such vague pronouncements about sensory input as that it is *"vitally involved in"* locomotion are not going to advance our understanding. The essential questions to be answered about the role of a particular input in the control of action is what level of the hierarchy receives the input and what effect does the input have on the signals that that level sends to lower units. Our understanding of the role played by sensory factors will progress hand in hand with our articulation of the structure and functioning of the action hierarchy.

As a rule of thumb, the higher the level receiving a sensory input, the more global and diverse will be the possible effect of that stimulus on the animal's action. As one ascends the hierarchy, stimuli play more and more of a role in determining the *general course* of action and less and less of a role in determining the *particular pattern* of muscular activity used to pursue that course at a given moment. A corollary of this principle is that the higher one goes in the hierarchy the more elaborate the sensory/perceptual analysis of sensory signals; or, what is almost but not quite the same thing, the more global the sensory factors that serve as inputs. The generals determine where the armies are to be deployed. In doing so they must respond to the geography of the country and the deployment of the opposing armies. The lieutenants determine where the trenches are to be dug. In doing so, they must respond to the local topography and the disposition of opposing forces in their locales. The sergeants determine where the latrines are to be dug. In doing so, they respond to the distribution of bushes in their immediate vicinities.

Weiss's level 6 is not the highest level of motor organization. An animal's individual acts must be integrated into behavior sequences. And behavior sequences must be integrated into the pursuit of long term goals such as the homeostatic regulation of the *milieu interne* and the production of offspring. Tinbergen (1951, Chapter 5) takes over where Weiss left off. He traces out the hierarchical organization of the behavior sequences that comprise the reproductive behavior of the stickleback. The reader who consults Tinbergen's elegant "Attempt at an Integration" will realize that the study of motivation, at least as the ethologists conceive of it, is continuous with the study of motor coordination. The drive concept in ethology and physiological psychology refers to internal states ("central motive states") that determine which stimuli will be effective (Deutsch, 1960; Lashley, 1938; Lorenz, 1937; Morgan, 1957; Stellar, 1960; Tinbergen, 1951). The concept is necessary for the elementary but often overlooked reason that a stimulus that is effective on one occasion at eliciting some response will often not be effective on another occasion. This variation in stimulus effectiveness is not random noise. When the mating drive is strong, whole classes of stimuli, namely, those stimuli that play an important role in mating, become effective elicitors of components of mating behavior. When the mating drive is weak, the same stimuli have no effect on the animal's behavior (Tinbergen, 1951). When the hunger drive is strong in the blowfly, diverse food-related stimuli become capable of eliciting or guiding diverse food-seeking or ingesting responses. When the fly is not hungry, these responses cannot be elicited: their "adequate stimuli" are no longer adequate (Dethier, 1976). Drives, in other words, are neural and hormonal signals originating high in the hierarchy that potentiate complementary acts, acts that serve a common purpose. But this selective potentiation of functionally coherent subsets of lower units is, as we have just seen, a central principle of motor coordination. It may be observed to operate

QUANTITY | CHECK WITH ORDER AUTHOR AND SHORT TITLE | | |

1 GALLISTEL ACTION   V   0937 1512C   29.95
   SBN* 047026912X

PACKING

LIST

NET WEIGHT   1LBS 13OZS
              NET AMOUNT
              SHIPPING AND HANDLING CHARGE

1 ← TOTAL
     QUANTITY R 20957 PLEASE ADVISE WITHIN 30 DAYS
     SHIPPED   OF ANY DISCREPANCY

JOHN WILEY & SONS, INC.
ONE WILEY DRIVE, SOMERSET, N. J. 08873

at the bottom of the behavioral hierarchical and at every intermediate level. Therefore, one may reasonably say that *the problem of motor coordination becomes the problem of motivation as one ascends the action hierarchy.*

If one had to say where in the action hierarchy one passed from the study of motor coordination to the study of motivation, one might draw the line at level 6. Tinbergen (1951, Chapter 5) observes that below this level, hierarchical integration is at least partially coordinative: it involves the simultaneous potentiation of two or more subordinate units with complementary actions. Above level 6 the units of organization determine acts or behavior sequences on the part of the whole organism. Since organisms can generally only be doing one thing at a time, the units at these higher levels can seldom have complementary organizing roles. Therefore, argues Tinbergen, above level 6, intralevel interactions are generally of a reciprocally inhibitory nature.

If one must draw a line between the problem of motor coordination and the problem of motivation, then Tinbergen's argument may provide the only rationale for determining the locus of that line. However, if we allow the intrusion of introspective observations, most of us will acknowledge that we often act from mixed motives. We do what we do out of a variety of complementary and sometimes not so complementary motives. Each motive has some influence on the exact manner in which we do what we do. Indeed, the fine art of character analysis lies in the dissecting out of the various motives that shaped the behavior we have observed. It would seem that even at the highest levels of the action hierarchy there is room for the simultaneous functioning of more or less complementary organizing processes. It may not be necessary or even possible to draw a clear line separating the problem of coordination from the problem of motivation.

In any event, the hierarchical structure of the mechanism that generates behavior is an inescapable reality. Equally inescapable, but often overlooked, is the fact that a unit that coordinates an action almost always plays a role in diverse behaviors. In order that the unit play its role at suitable moments, it is subjected to control by potentiation and potentiation. The following chapter traces some of the innumerable manifestations of these principles of behavioral organization.

9 Manifestations of Hierarchical Organization in Action

REVIEW OF PRINCIPLES

The concept of hierarchy is a central concept in many disciplines and in diverse discussions (*levels of analysis* in the philosophy of science; *how to organize animal care* in the drudgery of academic committeework). Not surprisingly, it means different things in different contexts. This chapter examines the salient aspects of the hierarchical concept as it pertains to the organization of action.

We will see in this chapter that manifestations of hierarchical organization may be found in phenomena as diverse as the reflexes of an upside down cockroach, rage in cats with transected nervous systems, the reactions of chickens and cats to electrical stimulation of the brain, nest-building in hybrid lovebirds, classical conditioning in humans, operant conditioning in the pigeon, the development of feeding in infant rats, and the recovery of voluntary behavior in brain-injured adults. In short, the salient features of hierarchical organization are manifest everywhere one looks, if only one knows to look for them. What, then, is one looking for when trying to perceive the hierarchical organization underlying some behavioral phenomena?

Intermediate Units of Organization

Above all, one is looking for intermediate units of organization. Between components of the system that organize the complete behavior and the elements out of which all actions are constructed there must be intermediate components that organize limited combinations of the basic elements of action. The intermediate components are controlled by the higher (or highest) level circuits: The highest levels seldom directly control the basic elements of action. They control the elements of action by way of the control they exert over intermediate units of organization.

Chained reflex accounts of behavior, at least in their simplest form, assume that the system underlying behavior is *not* hierarchically organized. Complex actions are regarded as the net result of the separate reflexes that occur in response to changing external and internal conditions (cf. Sherrrington's preface pp. 64–66). Behavior is simply the sum of its elements. Little mention is made of intermediate units of organization (cf. Hull, 1943). Between the elements (reflexes) and complete behaviors, these accounts do not recognize coherent combinations of reflexes that *behave as units*; by this I mean that the combinations tend to appear and disappear together under a variety of circumstances. And, combinations cannot readily be decomposed into their constituents, even when some new combination of their constituents may be called for. One gets the particular combination of components; or, one gets nothing.

A player piano provides a nonbiological instance of a system that generates complex outputs without benefit of intermediate units of organization. The strikings of the individual hammers against the strings are the elements out of which all outputs are constructed. The sequence in which these elements are activated is determined by the pattern of holes punched in the role of paper. Between the roles of paper, which organize entire outputs, and the individual hammer mechanisms, there are no intermediate units of organization. (The tune itself, of course, has intermediate units of organization—melodies, phrases, etc.—but here we are concerned with the player piano, not the tune.)

Weiss's work with salamanders (Chapter 8) is important to the hierarchical conception of how action is organized in part because it provides such striking evidence for the existence of fixed intermediate units of organization. When the salamander's forelimbs are reversed, they continue to move as if they were still oriented forwards rather than backwards. The muscles of the reversed limb are activated in the pattern that is functional in the normally oriented forelimb. In the reversed limb these patterns are no longer functional. Not because they no longer move the limb effectively! They do move it effectively; but they move it in the wrong way at the wrong time. When the salamander attempts to move forward his hindlimbs propel him forward, but his forelimbs propel him backward. When the salamander attempts to back-up, his hindlimbs propel him backward, but his forelimbs propel him forward. Clearly the salamander's nervous system contains two circuits that constitute intermediate units of organization—one circuit for forward progression, one circuit for backward progression. Each circuit coordinates a specific (but by no means stereotyped) pattern of activation of the muscles in all four limbs.

When forward or backward progression is required as part of some more complex behavior (food seeking, predator avoidance) circuits higher in the hierarchy activate the limb musculature via the two intermediate units of organization. When Weiss reversed the salamander's front limbs he rendered both locomotion programs nonfunctional. When the salamander's back limbs walked forward, its front limbs walked backward, and vice versa. In order for Weiss's salamander to successfully walk forward it would have to step its hind limbs in the normal manner for forward walking while its reversed forelimbs stepped in the normal manner for backward walking. This novel coordination of the level 4 units that control the stepping of each leg would function nicely. But the salamander does not have a level 5 circuit capable of producing the required coordination between the level 4 units. The salamander's persistent use of the normal but no longer functional patterns of interlimb coordination highlights the fact that these patterns are intermediate units in the salamander's action hierarchy. These units are not functionally dissoluble.

Sometimes the problems posed by the lack of suitable intermediate units of organization can be circumvented by activating another intermediate unit. When Sperry reversed the tendons in the forelimbs of rats (Chapter 8, p. 264–266) the intermediate units that control the pattern of muscle activation in a given limb during locomotion now produced maladaptive movements. The rats eventually minimized the resulting discoordination by substituting another intermediate unit of coordination that was not disturbed by the tendon crossing. The rats simultaneously contracted all the muscles of the forelimb, making it into a sort of pole, which was then moved by shoulder muscles.

Tendon reversal experiments on primates and man suggest that in these species the higher brain levels have more direct programming access to individual muscles and are therefore less constrained by the intermediate units of organization. This should not lead us to think, however, that intermediate units of organization play no role in organizing primate motor output. They are just as important in primates as in lower anaimals (cf. Schiller, 1952; Taub & Berman, 1968). However, they are less fixed by inheritance and more subject to modification through experience.

Later parts of this chapter survey some diverse manifestations of intermediate units of organization in motor output. The intermediate units in the organization of action may be seen in experiments as different as the behavioral genetics of nest-building and the operant conditioning of keypecking.

Potentiation and Depotentiation

A second manifestation of hierarchical organization is the selective and appropriately timed enabling and disabling of lower units of organization by higher units. Higher units do not, in general, actually trigger (set into action) or guide (steer) the action of lower units; rather they potentiate these units (increase their potential for action) or depotentiate them (decrease their potential for action).

The work of Camhi and his collaborators provides several lovely examples of the role of selective potentiation and depotentiation in the construction of coordinated units of behavior. For example, the flying locust has a yaw-correction mechanism. When a puff of air causes a sudden turning aside from its flight path (a yaw), the abdomen bends like a rudder, returning the body axis to the original orientation. Recordings from the abdominal motor neurons show that sensory signals from "puff-detecting" sensory hairs on the animal's head activate the abdominal motor neurons only when the locust's "flight motor" is running. The flight motor is an oscillator that sets the pace for the wings. In other words, the flight motor potentiates the yaw-correction circuit (Camhi & Hinkle, 1972).

More recently, Camhi (1977) has shown that there is an ensemble of functionally interrelated tactile reflexes in a large Madagascar cockroach that is switched off (depotentiated) when the cockroach is turned upside down. In its place, a new ensemble of tactile reflexes is switched on (potentiated). As with the phototaxes in *littorina*, and the stumble reflexes in the cat, the exact same stimuli can elicit different, indeed opposing actions. Which action the stimuli in fact elicit depends upon the pattern of selective potentiation and depotentiation imposed on the lower level units of action by circuits that mediate more complex, higher level patterns of action. When the circuit that controls righting behavior is activated (by sensory signals indicating that the roach's feet have lost contact with the ground), it depotentiates one set of tactile reflexes and potentiates a new set. This effect of the righting circuit upon tactile reflexes is but one component of its action. The same circuit controls a number of complex leg and body movements designed to right the roach (see below).

The Lattice or Common Path Principle

The third salient feature of hierarchical organization in animal action is what Sherrington termed the principle of the common path and I have called the principle of the lattice hierarchy. Under whatever name, the principle is that one and the same unit of coordination be utilized by diverse higher level units of organization. In addition to the many illustrations of this principle given in the preceding chapter, one may cite the recent work of Sherman, Novotny, and Camhi (1977). They showed that the leg movements the Madagascar roach makes in attempting to right itself differ from walking leg movements in one respect: Two muscles that contract together during walking contract alternately during righting movements. In most other respects, however, the leg movements made while righting are strikingly similar to those made while walking: The same motor neurons appear to be active; the cycle frequencies are the same; the lengths of the bursts of impulses sent to the extensor vary as a function of the period of the cyclical leg movement, as in walking; and, finally, the interleg coordination is the same. Sherman et al. conclude that the circuit that controls righting behavior employs the same oscillators and the same interoscillator coupling network as the circuit that controls walking.

Over and over again, at every level of organization, we see the same principle: A given unit of coordination is employed at one time or another in many different patterns of action. Lines of authority in the nervous system are like lines of authority in an extended family: More than one senior member tries to tell you what you can and cannot do; and they frequently do not agree.

Summary

In summary, the hierarchical organization of action has at least three salient aspects. First, there are intermediate units of organization: The basic elements of action do not combine indiscriminately. Rather, coherent integrations of basic elements appear and disappear as wholes. Second, higher levels control lower levels by selective potentiation and depotentiation. Lower units receive external stimuli directly and may have endogenous patterning mechanisms. But, higher units determine when the lower unit is free to respond, or to impose its endogenously generated pattern of commands on the units below it. Thus, activation of a unit of coordination is usually a joint function of higher level potentiating inputs and lower level activating inputs. Third, the vertical organization assumes the form of a lattice, with lower units subservient to diverse and competing higher units. We turn now to survey the domains in which these principles of hierarchical organization are manifest.

TRANSECTION STUDIES

The hierarchical organization of action is more than a heuristic way of analyzing action; it is a reflection of the organization of the underlying neurophysiology and neuroanatomy. The neurophysiological and neuroanatomical reality of hierarchical organization emerges from studies on the behavior of cats after cuts have been made through one or another level of their nervous system. These "transections" separate the part of the nervous system below the cut from control by the part above the cut, enabling one to see what the part below the cut can do on its own.

When the brain of a vertebrate is examined and dissected certain gross neuroanatomical divisions or levels are obvious (Fig. 9.1). Just after entering the head, the spinal cord enlarges into an elongated bulbous structure known

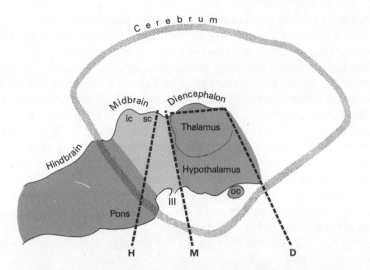

fig. 9-1

FIG. 9.1.   The brain of the cat showing various transections (heavy lines). The transection labeled H creates the "hindbrain cat" (or "pontile cat"). The transection labeled M creates the "midbrain cat." The transection labeled D creates the "diencephalic cat." In all of the transections except D the cerebrum (dashed outline) is completely removed. Transection D (actually an ablation) left some deep portions of the cerebrum adjacent to the diencephalon intact— for details, see Bard and Rioch (1937, Fig. 25). This figure is based on one by Wetzel and Stuart (1976, Fig. 12), who carefully review both transection studies and brain stimulation studies that bear on the neural control of locomotion and posture. Abbreviations: ic—inferior colliculus; oc—optic chiasm; sc—superior colliculus; III—third nerve.

as the *hindbrain*. Immediately in front of the bulge of the hindbrain is a short stretch of brain that is constricted on the bottom and sides but has two small bulges on top (known as the superior and inferior colliculi). This short stretch is called the *midbrain*. In front of the midbrain constriction is a downward bulge, called the hypothalamus (under-thalamus), on top of which, but completely enfolded in the *cerebrum*, is a large bulge called the *thalamus* (chamber). Together the hypothalamus and thalamus are known as the *diencephalon* (between-brain). The cerebrum is the most forward lobe of the brain in lower vertebrates (fish). In mammals, this lobe is massively enlarged: It engulfs the diencephalon and midbrain, and dominates the outward appearance of the brain as a whole.

Transection studies (Bard & Macht, 1958; Bard & Mountcastle, 1948; Bard & Rioch, 1937; Hinsey, Ranson, & McNattin, 1930) show that there is a rough correspondence between levels of organization in behavior and the first three subdivisions of the brain: The hindbrain integrates complex movements of the body as a whole (Weiss's level 5) but cannot produce complete acts

(Weiss's level 6). The midbrain integrates complex movements into simple acts, for example, walking. The diencephalon (and immediately adjacent portions of the cerebrum) integrate acts into motivated behavioral sequences.

When the brain is transected so as to separate the hindbrain and spinal cord from control by higher levels (cut H in Fig. 9.1), the sensory and motor pathways for simple acts such as righting and walking are left intact. In their reactions to various stimuli, these hindbrain cats display most if not all of the complex movements that comprise these simple acts but they are literally unable to get their acts together. They cannot coordinate the components of standing up so as to actually stand up. They cannot coordinate the components of walking and posture maintenance so as to actually walk, although nearly all of the necessary neural machinery lies below the cut (Bard & Macht; 1958; Wetzel & Stuart, 1976). They cannot crouch to defecate, like an ordinary cat, although if a probe is inserted up the rectum, they will, while lying on their side, extend their forelimbs and flex their hindlimbs as if to crouch.

If we move the level of transection up a bit so as to leave nearly all of the midbrain intact below the cut (cut M in Fig. 9.1), we have an animal that can perform complete acts, such as standing up, walking, crouching to defecate, shivering, panting, chewing, swallowing, growling, raising its fur, grooming itself, and so on. But these simple acts are not organized into motivated behavioral sequences. The midbrain cat does not walk to any purpose, for example, to search for food, or a warmer environment. It does not maintain its weight or body temperature; it looks angry or afraid in response to a painful stimulus or a loud police whistle, but neither attacks nor escapes effectively. In short, transection M separates the level where simple acts are organized from the level that integrates these acts into motivated behavioral sequences.

If we move our transection up another level, so as to leave intact below the cut most of the diencephalon and some adjacent parts of the cerebrum, we produce a cat whose behavior manifests "motivational" levels of functional integration.

From the standpoint of basic organization in behavior, this "diencephalic" cat differs little from the cat with its brain intact (Bard & Mountcastle, 1947; Bard & Rioch, 1937). With occasional experimenter encouragement, it eats enough to maintain its weight. It seems to search for food when hungry; bristles with rage and attacks or escapes when harmed; and so on. This is motivated behavior: It combines various simple acts—locomotion, bending and biting, chewing and swallowing—into integrated behavior sequences that appear purposeful and serve the cat's well being. The diencephalic cat also defends its body temperature. It shivers when cold and pants when hot. In the cold it will also walk around, seemingly in search of an environment with a warmer temperature. Note again that various simple acts—shivering, panting, locomotion—are called upon to promote the same general aspect of cat's well being. The coherence in function between separate acts is what leads us to speak of the ensemble as motivated behavior.

Note, also, that the same simple act of locomotion is used by two distinct motivational systems—the system that regulates nutrition and the system that regulates body temperature. Indeed, the act of walking is obviously employed in an immense variety of distinct and often competing patterns of behavior. If one defines the importance of an intermediate unit of organization in terms of the number and diversity of higher level units that make use of it, then locomotion is among the most important units of organization at the sixth level of functional integration, the level of simple acts.

That the diencephalic cat, which, be it remembered, is missing 75% of its brain, differs but little from the normal cat in the basic organization of its behavior is a startling claim. It calls for some elaboration. In reading the following descriptions of the behavior of diencephalic cats, one must bear in mind that the major sensory systems have been destroyed or severely damaged. The cats are blind and in some cases anosmic (lacking a sense of smell). Their hearing is severely impaired. These cats lack all of the cortical tissue whose job it is to analyze sensory input. The result is what one would expect of a large corporation if one left its chain of command intact but deprived it of its accounting, inventorying, and market researching departments. The basic organization is obviously present, but the performance is inept and poorly adjusted to external circumstances. So it is with the diencephalic cat, as the following passages from Bard and Rioch (1937) illustrate:

Hunger

Describing the behavior of a diencephalic cat with the input from its nose intact:

> Correlated with the anatomical integrity of a large part of the central olfactory mechanism was a definite response to certain odors. Most striking was the sniffing, licking, and moving about with mouth close to the floor when an odoriferous food (e.g., fish) was placed nearby. After a hearty meal this behavior could not be evoked and it was most intense when food had been withheld for some time. There was apparently no ability to locate the source of odors, and unless food was placed directly in front of the animal it was reached only by chance. The postprandial chop- and nose-licking with dorsiflexion of the head, which is seen in normal cats, was greatly exaggerated and prolonged in this animal [p. 79].

And, describing the behavior of another cat in which the transection was similar to the one in the cat discussed above except that it severed the neural input from the nose as well:

[the] main difference between this brain and the brain of cat 103 was that in the former the olfactory stalks had been severed. This condition accounts for the only definite difference observed in the behavior of the two animals. At no time did cat 313 show any response to olfactory stimuli. When mouth and tongue were placed in contact with a sapid food substance, she ate of her own accord, and so long as the food was kept within immediate reach of the mouth, she continued to eat until a large meal had been consumed. After food had been withheld for some time, and in the absence of any specific olfactory stimulus, this animal invariably began to lick the floor and to move about restlessly. The longer the food was withheld, the more intense was this activity; it never occurred during the hours following a meal. In short, a state which may be called hunger induced in this anosmic animal behavior very similar to that shown by cat 103 under the same circumstances. But the sniffing, so characteristic of 103, did not occur [p. 84].

Sexual Behavior

This same disoriented type of motivated behavior was also seen in the sexual domain:

On the twenty-ninth day following the final cerebral ablation it was discovered by chance that insertion of a clinical thermometer into the distal vagina immediately induced loud growling, lowering of chest and head, elevation of pelvis and tail and treading movements of the hindlegs. After removal of the stimulus the cat executed vigorous squirming movements on her side and playfully rubbed her cheek and occiput against the floor. Some experience with cats which had entered into "heat" in the laboratory made it impossible to mistake the nature of this performance. It was at once apparent that she was exhibiting one phase of the typical feline oestrual behavior. Crouching and treading occurred at this time whenever a gentle mechanical stimulus, such as rubbing or tapping, was applied to the vulva or to the skin area immediately surrounding it. This specific response to genital stimulation lasted from the twenty-ninth day to the fifty-eighth postoperative day and recurred for a few days during the eighth month. At all other times it could not be obtained. Vaginal smears showed the cellular picture characteristic of feline oestrus only when the behavior described above was evocable. Also it was solely at this time that she attracted males. On becoming the object of the attentions of a sexually excited male she exhibited oestrual behavior, but only in response to stimulation of her genital region. To such preliminary advances as vocalization and licking of her head she appeared entirely indifferent. Even when the male mounted and executed treading movements of the legs, she showed no actual oestrual response. Squatting flat on the floor she licked vigorously in response to incidental cutaneous stimulation. When he grasped her too violently by the nape of the neck or pulled her about, she spat, growled and lashed her tail. If, however, he pressed against her external genital region she immediately assumed the full oestrual crouch and treaded with tail elevated and laterally deflected. Intromission, signalled by typical vocalization on the part of the female and confirmed by finding spermatozoa in vaginal smears, occurred three times. On each of these occasions, after the male had dismounted, she turned onto her side, rolled and playfully rubbed her head with her forepaws. Such is the "after-reaction" shown by normal females after coitus. When in dioestrus, 103 showed no trace of this behavior in response to genital stimulation [pp. 80–81].

Rage

Also when the cat was enraged:

[Pinching the cat's tail] evoked a stereotyped reaction consisting of: lowering the head and forepart of the body into a crouch, raising the back, drawing back the ears, loud angry growling, frequent hissing, biting, vigorous alternate striking movements of forelegs with unsheathed claws, turning (almost always to the left), erection of the hair of tail and back, pupillo-dilation, retraction of nictitating membranes and widening of the palpebral fissures .

.... This behavior lacked no item of the activity exhibited by a normal cat when enraged and aggressive. It varied from the display of rage seen in normal cats mainly in being undirected and stationary [pp. 94–95].

And of a second cat:

During the last two months of her survival she shared a room with a number of normal cats. It was frequently observed that the more quarrelsome of these made a practice of striking at 244 whenever she came within range. Their blows usually landed on her face or on the sides or top of her head. We were very much surprised to observe that 244 responded by holding her ground, raising the forepart of her body and striking out with one or both forefeet. After such an attack she was sometimes observed to keep one forefoot raised with claws protruded apparently ready to strike again as soon as the combat was renewed. The striking was accompanied by retraction of ears, growling, spitting, erection of hair and the ocular signs of sympathetic discharge. Her blows were, of course, not directed, and they were easily avoided by her more resourceful opponent, but when the latter pressed the attack, she invariably struck harder and more frequently. It was discovered that gently tapping her on the nose or face evoked this same response and its quality made it advisable that the observer wear gloves. She never ran away or retreated during one of these bouts [p. 97].

Fear

Fearful behavior, like other motivated behaviors, comprises several distinct acts. Under appropriate circumstances, these appear as an ensemble in the behavior of the diencephalic cat. Their execution, however, is badly hampered by lack of relevant information:

> On the eleventh postoperative day while cat 103 was being observed in a large open space, it happened that the exhaust of an autoclave situated in an adjoining room was opened. The moment the loud noise of escaping steam was heard, the animal suddenly retracted and lowered her head, crouched, mewed and then dashed off, running rapidly in a slinking manner with head, chest, belly and tail close to the floor. After blindly colliding with several objects in her path she came to rest in a corner where she crouched, mewing plaintively. During this activity and for some time afterwards the eyes were widely opened, the pupils were maximally dilated and there was some erection of hair on the back and tail.
>
> When normal cats were subject to the blast of a bugle or the sound of escaping steam they reacted in very much the same way as did decorticate cats 103, 313 and 244. A few merely crouched with head retracted, eyes wide, and mewed as if frightened and bewildered. Some followed this maneuver by creeping away to hide in a far corner. Others at once dashed off precipitately and made wild attempts to escape from the room as if possessed by the most profound terror. Such observations lead to the conviction that it is entirely correct to describe the similar behavior of the decorticate animals as an exhibition of fear or terror. It is a very specific form of activity that cannot possibly be confused with any other mode of response. The element of escape which was completely lacking in the rage responses of these same animals was a most prominent feature of their fear reactions. Conversely, the element of attack which characterized their exhibitions of anger formed no part of the fear response [pp. 91–92].

The Doctrine of Anatomical Centers

In arguing that there is a reasonable correspondence between levels of functional organization in behavior and the anatomical levels of the nervous system, I am not arguing for the doctrine of anatomical centers. This doctrine naively assumes that we can take the box that we draw around "Forward Locomotion" in a functional diagram, draw a similar box around some structure in the nervous system and say, "That is the center for forward locomotion." What is naive about this approach is the belief that the neural circuitry that realizes some functional integration can be confined to a small area of the nervous system. This cannot be the case. The neural circuitry that realizes the functional integration we call forward locomotion must have ramifications in many parts of the spinal cord and brain stem in order to potentiate and depotentiate the appropriate local circuitry. The finding that hindbrain cats cannot walk, whereas midbrain cats can, does not mean that the walking center is in the midbrain. Rather it means that crucial elements of the neural circuit that integrates walking are located as high up as the midbrain. Cuts lower than this remove crucial elements, leaving the animal unable to walk. They do not, however, remove "the walking center." There is no such thing, anatomically speaking. There is a "walking circuit." But the circuit that coordinates walking is not located in a circumscribed area; hence it cannot constitute a center in the anatomical sense. It is a center only in the functional sense.

We quite reasonably speak of the sales department of a large corporation as a center of organization, because it constitutes a network of people and facilities that serve a distinct function and have their own executive structure. We do not thereby imagine that all of the people and facilities are grouped together physically in one building. In the very nature of sales work, the sales department must have branches that extend to wherever the company does business. The correspondence between levels in functional diagrams of hierarchical organization and the kind of behavior we see after transections at higher and higher levels of the nervous system means simply this: The neural circuits mediating relatively higher levels of functional integration have crucial elements located in relatively higher levels of the nervous system. Transection studies help to reveal intermediate units of organization at various levels of the action hierarchy, by rendering higher levels inoperative, not by removing all of the neural tissue mediating the higher function.

The transection studies indicate the following:

1. The neural circuitry mediating the fifth level of functional integration—interlimb coordinations such as the coordinated stepping of fore and hindlimbs—is left essentially intact in the hindbrain animal.
2. Neural circuitry mediating the next level—simple acts, such as locomotion—is left essentially intact in the midbrain animal.
3. Neural circuitry mediating the uppermost levels of integration—motivated behavior sequences—is left essentially intact in the diencephalic animal.

This implies that crucial elements of level 5 circuitry are to be found in the hindbrain, crucial elements of level 6 circuitry in the midbrain, and crucial elements of motivational circuits in the areas left intact in the diencephalic animal, most notably the hypothalamus.

BRAIN STIMULATION STUDIES

Experiments in which small areas of the brain are excited by electrical stimulation through fine wires called electrodes confirm the conclusions drawn from transection studies. Stimulation of localized areas in the hindbrain can elicit stepping; stimulation of localized areas in the midbrain elicits locomotion; and stimulation in the hypothalamus and ventral thalamus elicits motivated behavior. (For review of the transection and stimulation literature as it pertains to locomotion in the cat, see Wetzel & Stuart, 1976; for a review of the work on motivated behavior elicited by stimulation in and around the hypothalamus, see Jurgens, 1974; Mogenson & Huang, 1973.)

Stimulation studies have strikingly illustrated two other aspects of the hierarchical organization of action: (1) Higher level units generally control lower units by potentiation and depotentiation rather than by direct and immediate activation. (2) There is a latticework of higher-level pathways controlling the potentiation of any given lower unit.

The Selective Potentiation of Instinctive Behavior

The work of Flynn and his colleagues (see Flynn, 1972; Flynn, Edwards, & Bandler, 1971, for reviews) has laid particular stress on the concept of centrally arising potentiation of lower level sensorimotor units of coordination. Their work has focused primarily upon the predatory attack behavior induced by stimulating a variety of points in the midbrain and diencephalon of the cat. The phylogeny and ontogeny of the many distinct acts that come together in an integrated ensemble to form the predatory behavior of cats has been extensively analyzed by Leyhausen (1965). The picture Leyhausen paints of this complex behavior is in striking accord with the lattice hierarchy conception:

> The instinctive movements of predation (watching, crouching, stalking, pouncing, seizing, "angling") are performed independently of one another by the playing cat, in varied combinations with each other and with activities derived from instinctive systems other than predation. Only when and if the appetites for killing and/or eating dominate may the other instinctive acts be linked into an appetitive sequence resembling what Tinbergen (1951) describes as a "major instinct" [p. 482].

Stimulation of certain points in the diencephalon induces behavior that closely resembles spontaneous predation (Berntson, Hughes, & Beattie, 1976). Thus, the experimenter can arouse a "major instinct" at will and study the resulting changes at lower levels of sensorimotor integration. This is precisely Flynn's strategy.

MacDonnell and Flynn (1966a; 1966b) found that predation-inducing stimulation of the lateral hypothalamus selectively potentiates the reflexes that subserve predation. For example: During stimulation, a touch to the muzzle of the cat elicits a turn of the head toward the side touched; a touch to the snout causes the jaws to snap open in preparation for a lethal bite. The central stimulation does not itself elicit these reflex movements. Only the touches—the "adequate stimuli" for these reflexes—can activate the movements. The central stimulation potentiates the reflexes. In the absence of the central stimulation "adequate" stimuli are inadequate: A touch to the muzzle elicits nothing, or, if strengthened, a turn of the head *away* from the side touched. A touch to the snout elicits pursing of the lips, not opening of the jaws. In the absence of an appropriate, centrally arising motivational potentiation, these reflexes are in a state of depotentiation; they cannot be activated. The touch stimuli that would trigger these reflexes trigger opposing reflexes instead.

Bandler and Flynn (1972) found a similar story for visually triggered predatory reflexes. In the presence of the central stimulation, cats would lunge at an anaesthetized mouse when the experimenters moved it to within 2.5 inches of the cat. In the absence of the central stimulation, the cat's only reaction was to draw back its head somewhat when the experimenter waved the mouse in its face. One and the same visual stimulus activates different reflex movements, depending on the pattern of selective potentiation passed down to the reflex level of organization from higher levels.

Flynn's studies are remarkable for what they show about the find patterning of the reflex potentiation that derives from electrical stimulation of certain points in the hypothalamus. At moderate or weak levels of central stimulation the touch-elicited head turning and biting and the visually elicited lunging occur only when the adequate stimuli are presented to one side of the cat. In other words, stimulation on one side of the brain favors sensorimotor units on one side of the body. Thus, the potentiating effect of the hypothalamic stimulation is clearly not the indirect consequence of some stimulation-induced change in the general disposition of the cat.

The one-sided potentiation produced by moderate levels of central stimulation is, however, not the most striking example of how selectively patterned the potentiation from a given stimulation site can be. MacDonnell and Flynn (1966b; see also Flynn et al., 1971) showed that there were two distinct jaw-opening reflexes in predatory behavior. The adequate stimulus for one of these was a touch to the snout. The adequate stimulus for the other jaw-opening reflex was the visual input the cat received as it lowered its head to the rat, preparatory to biting. Stimulation from some electrodes potentiated both of these reflexes. Stimulation from other electrodes potentiated only the tactile jaw-opening reflex, not the visual jaw-opening reflex!

This subtle difference in the patterns of potentiation from different predation-inducing electrodes was brought out by experiments in which the sensory input from the snout was cut. After this operation, the predatory attack induced by stimulation from some electrodes bogged down at the last moment. The cat stalked, pounced, and pinned the rat, then lowered its head for the fatal bite, but failed to bite! The touch on the snout the cat received when it lowered its head to the rat could not elicit the jaw-opening movement, because the sensory pathway for the reflex had been cut. As already noted, however, cats possess another jaw-opening reflex whose adequate stimulus is visual. The sensory path for the visual reflex was not cut. But, some electrodes did not potentiate the visual reflex; they only potentiated the tactile reflex. Predatory attack induced by these electrodes bogged down when it came to the jaw-opening part of the behavior sequence, because the sensory pathway for the tactile reflex was cut and the visual reflex was not potentiated. Predatory attack induced *in the same cats* by stimulation at other points did not bog down, because stimulation at these other points potentiated the visual as well as the tactile reflex.

This last finding emphasizes the subtle differences in the patterns of selective potentiation produced by stimulating slightly different sites in the diencephalon. If different pathways high up in the hierarchy can, when electrically stimulated, produce such finely differentiated patterns of selective potentiation at the reflex level, then any given lower unit must receive an extremely rich and variegated set of potentiating and depotentiating inputs descending to it from a richly varied collection of higher level units of organization. The latticework of the lattice hierarchy is extremely intricate.

Multiplicity of Sites

The intricacy of the latticework explains one of the earliest and most salient findings from research on electrical stimulation at diencephalic and midbrain sites. Ever since the pioneering work of Hess (1954), it has been obvious that any given act, for example, locomotion, could be induced by stimulating at a great many different points in the brain. This has been something of an embarrassment for those who wanted to explain the behavioral effects of stimulation by saying that one was stimulating a locomotion center, or sex center, or hunger center, and so forth. For that reason, there has been some tendency, particularly in secondary sources, to play down the multiplicity of effective stimulation sites. This multiplicity of effective sites is, however, the universal finding, no matter what stimulation-induced behavior one looks at. (See Valenstein, Cox, & Kakolewski, 1970, for a review that emphasizes this.)

However embarrassing this multiplicity of sites may be for the doctrine of anatomical centers, it is what one expects if one assumes that the functional organization of behavior is a lattice hierarchy. In a lattice hierarchy, the unit that organizes a given act receives potentiating inputs from all those different higher level units that employ that act. Therefore, as von Holst and von St. Paul (1963) point out, one expects to find a variety of separate and distinct pathways that potentiate any given component of behavior. One expects a multiplicity of effective sites on the simple hypothesis that the different "pathways" in a functional diagram (such as Fig. 8.1) are represented by different neural pathways in the brain. The act represented by a node in Fig. 8.1 will be potentiated whenever one stimulates a neural pathway mediating the potentiating effect from any one of the several higher units of organization that utilize that act.

One might object that this last contention cannot be true for units at the highest level of organization. However, in Chapter 10 it will be pointed out that there probably is no fixed highest level of organization. At the higher levels of organization, the order of subordination—who utilizes whom—is dependent on circumstance. The lattice hierarchy becomes what Leyhausen (1965) termed a relative hierarchy. Thus, even the highest levels of behavioral organization receive a variety of potentiating inputs.

Multiplicity of Effects

The lattice-hierarchy concept was central to von Holts and von St. Paul's penetrating analysis of the behaviors induced by electrical stimulation of the brain in the domestic chicken. When they stimulated some sites in the chicken's brain, they induced simple acts, for example, standing up, sitting down, walking around, clucking, head bobbing ("aiming"), cackling, and so on. At those sites where stimulation induced only a simple act, the act was performed as if by an automaton—over and over again, more or less regardless of what external stimuli were present. This testifies to the neurophysiological reality of the notion of intermediate units of organization in motor behavior, in this case units that organize simple acts. When von Holst and von St. Paul stimulated other sites they obtained complex circumstance-dependent behavior sequences composed of varied combinations of the elemental acts. One site, for example, induced the complete spectrum of behavior that the chicken displays when threatened by a ground enemy. This spectrum includes many of the simple acts listed above. Such observations naturally led to a lattice hierarchy conception.

Von Holst and von St. Paul point out that the lattice hierarchy concept not only predicts the multiplicity of effective sites, but it also predicts that stimulation at one and the same site may induce now one behavior, now another, and now no behavior at all. Secondary sources tend to play down this last finding, namely, that the behavioral consequences of stimulating a given point are not fixed. It would seem to suggest that there is no lawful relation between brain structure and brain function! Such a view would mean that the physiological psychologist is wasting his time. Von Holst and von St. Paul point out that such pessimism is unwarranted. The variable behavioral expression of the potentiation produced by stimulating a given point is the natural consequence of the fact that the stimulated pathways are part of a lattice hierarchy. The behavioral consequences of stimulation are constant *"only so long as the internal central situation remains constant, in which every action is, as it were, embedded"* (von Holst & von St. Paul, 1963, p. 7).

Since diencephalic stimulation excites points high in the hierarchy it is bound to potentiate several different and sometimes mutually exclusive acts that may or may not be parts of a coherent whole. These same acts receive potentiating and depotentiating influences from other nodes in the hierarchy. These other nodes are not excited by the stimulation, but their degree of excitation is subject to natural variation. The degree of excitation in these other nodes will vary from occasion to occasion, depending on a variety of internal and external circumstances. Which of the acts potentiated by stimulating a given site actually appears is determined by the overall pattern of potentiation. The stimulated pathway is only one among many contributors to this pattern. Which act appears will depend also on whatever activating stimuli the environment provides. Potentiation merely potentiates acts, it does not trigger them or guide them. " . . . it then necessarily follows that the decision as to which behavior must become visible is made not in the stimulus field but *somewhere* else, by the total dynamic situation prevailing at the moment" (von Holst & von St. Paul, 1963, p. 19).

Some examples may illustrate this point. Chickens, like most smaller animals subject to heavy predation, have a behavior called "playing dead" (Gallup, 1974). They become motionless, semi-limp in a "waxy" way, and do not respond to most stimuli, even very painful ones. The behavior occurs when they are captured and pinned down. It demonstrably increases their chances of survival once they have fallen into the clutches of a predator, since the final acts in the predatory sequence are triggered by the struggles of the prey. If the prey doesn't struggle, it does not provide stimuli to trigger the final fatal bite. Not infrequently, the predator abandons its limp prey, without killing it.

It cannot be too strongly emphasized that playing dead is a behavior! The bird is not in a "trance" or "coma" but is monitoring the situation. The duration of playing dead, once it has been induced, is heavily influenced by the presence or absence of a pair of eyes looking at the animal. If a pair of eyes—even eyes from a taxidermy shop, mounted on dowels—is nearby and "staring at" the bird, it will continue to play dead. If the eyes are turned somewhat so that they are not looking at the bird, the duration of playing dead is shortened. If the eyes are removed altogether from the bird's view, the duration of playing dead is even shorter (Gallup, Nash, & Ellison, 1971). Playing dead is, in other words, a behavior that involves strongly *de*potentiating the entire motor system in response to capture.

An experimenter who does not take care to sooth the chicken before beginning the experiment can induce this behavior, or else induce "freezing"—another behavior that occurs in reaction to overwhelming threat. In such cases, electrical stimulation delivered to some previously effective site will now be ineffective. It will not induce whatever behavior it previously induced. The potentiation deriving from the stimulation cannot overcome the powerful and general depotentiation originating from other nodes in the lattice hierarchy. This provides one illustration of why a previously effective site may later prove ineffective.

Consider now a more interesting case: Stimulation at a given site sometimes induces attack behavior; at other times, the same stimulation induces fleeing and screeching. Has a pathway for potentiating attack suddenly become a pathway for potentiating fleeing or screeching? No! Our perplexity is a consequence of our ignorance of behavioral sequences in the chicken. Von Holst and von St. Paul—working closely with Baeumer, an expert on the ethology of the chicken—note that attack, fleeing and screeching are all elements of the behavior that a chicken may display when threatened by a ground enemy, such as a polecat. Whether the chicken attacks or flees screeching depends on how threatened it feels. Therefore stimulation that potentiates ground enemy behavior will result in either attack or fleeing depending on how threatened the chicken feels. How threatend the chicken feels depends not only on the stimulus objects present at the moment but also on the general context and on the chicken's recent history. Has the chicken, for example, recently been attacked? The effect of stimulating a given node or pathway in a lattice hierarchy depends upon the overall pattern of activity within the hierarchy. That pattern is determined by a multitude of past and present circumstances. *The functional role of the stimulated pathway does not by itself determine the behavior that the stimulation will induce; hence, stimulation of a pathway with a fixed functional role may induce different behaviors on different occasions.*

The brain stimulation experiments conducted by Flynn and his collaborators and by von Holst and von St. Paul are direct demonstrations of the neurophysiological reality of the drive theory of motivation that has long been favored by many ethologists and physiological psychologists. This theory was given its clearest formulation by Tinbergen (1951, Chap. 5). He postulated that "motivational impulses" descending from higher levels in the nervous system organize the coherent behavioral sequences that comprise instinctive behavior by selectively lowering the threshold of elicitation for the component acts. MacDonnell and Flynn produced predatory motivational impulses experimentally by electrically stimulating appropriate points in the diencephalon and directly demonstrated the selective lowering of threshold (potentiation) for a group of reflexes that subserve predation. So selective is this effect that a cat stimulated on only one side of the diencephalon may display the predatory reflexes only to stimuli delivered on one side of its body!

The Selective Potentiation of a Learned Behavior

A recent, extremely ingenious experiment by Beagley and Holley (1977) extends this result to the motivational control of a learned behavior. Their experimental animals were rats implanted with electrodes, through which the experimenter could stimulate points in the diencephalon that potentiate eating. The rats were deprived of food and trained to press a lever that delivered small pellets of food. Next, it was arranged that the lever would produce pellets only when a pair of lights was turned on. Training under this arrangement made the pair of lights a discriminative stimulus. That is, the lights activated the learned lever-pressing response: the hungry rat pressed the level only if the lights were on.

The ingenuity of the Beagley and Holley experiment lies in the positioning of the pair of lights. The lights were tiny bulbs attached to thin stalks mounted on the rat's head. The stalks were bent to position each bulb so that only one eye could see it.

When the rat was made hungry in the normal way—by deprivation of food—illuminating either bulb activated lever pressing. But, when food-seeking was potentiated experimentally by stimulating electrically an appropriate site on one side of the diencephalon, only the light seen by one of the eyes was effective. The rat paid no attention to the light seen by the other eye. It is as if the rat looked at its world on one side through the eye of a hungry rat, while on the other side, it looked through the eye of a satiated rat indifferent to food.

The Beagley and Holley experiment directly generalizes the drive or instinct concept of motivation to learned behavior. Whether the response to an activating condition is innate ("self-differentiated") or learned, the response is made to serve the animal's more general needs and purposes through the agency of motivating signals. Motivating signals originate in the diencephalon and cerebrum and descend to lower levels of the nervous system, where they selectively potentiate coherent subsets of possible acts.

THE BEHAVIOR OF HYBRIDS

The lattice-hierarchy concept has always been congenial to the ethologist. The ethological analysis of diverse behaviors into the elements (simple movements) of which they are composed highlights the fact that the same patterns of movement appear as components of diverse behavioral sequences (see, for example, Baeumer, 1955; von Holst & von St. Paul, 1963; Leyhausen, 1973; Lorenz, 1965; Tinbergen, 1951; Wiley, 1975). This leads naturally to the view that these simple patterns of movement constitute intermediate units. This view is strengthened when the ethologist compares across related species the components in a category of behavior such as predation, or courtship, or nest-building. These comparisons show that the behavioral differences between related species derive from the disappearance or diminution of certain components and the appearance of new components. This indicates that the intermediate units of organization in behavior are encoded at the genetic level and are thereby subject to natural selection.

The work of Dilger (1960, 1962) on nest-building behavior in lovebirds highlights the genetic basis for the intermediate units of organization and the significance of this in the evolution of behavior.

On a variety of morphological and behavioral grounds, it appears that the nine species of lovebird may be regarded as representatives of three distinctive evolutionary generations. Three species represent, the "first generation," that closest to the ancestral parrots. Two species represent an intermediate generation—the "second generation"; and four species represent the most recent—the "third generation." All nine species build nests. In this respect, they differ from their parrot ancestors, which simply lay their eggs in empty cavities. The differences, however, trace out a characteristic process of evolution by small steps. The nest-building of the species from the first generation involves little more than carpeting the floor of the cavity with small bits chewed from leaves and bark. The species of the third generation, on the other hand, chew-off strips of material and weave them into elaborately shaped nests; while the second generation species use strips but weave simple nests.

Dilger focuses his analysis of nest-building on the behavior by which species in each of the three generations carry the bits or strips from the place where they chew them off to the place where they are building their nest. The third generation do what it seems any sensible bird would—they hold a strip in their bill and fly to the nest. The grandparent species, who are, so to speak, first generation nest builders, have yet to hit upon this simple solution to the transport problem. They carry their bits to the nest by sticking them into their body-feathers. The second generation also carry nesting material in this unusual way.

For the grandparent generation, this way of carrying works fine, since 6 to 8 small bits may be carried in one flight with fair success. For the second generation it is a good deal less satisfactory. Strips are harder to insert than bits and do not stay put as well. The second generation loses about half its cargo on every trip. A glimmer of innovations to come in the third generation may occassionally be seen in the behavior of the second generation: On about 3% of their transport flights, they carry material in their bill!

These observations already provide a startling illustration of the importance of intermediate units of organization. The efficient transport behavior of the third generation consists of the combination of two acts common to all three generations: (1) "holding-material-in-the-bill," and (2) "flying-to-the-nest." The second generation repeatedly performs both of these acts, but seldom at the same time. *It lacks a well developed higher level unit that simultaneously potentiates these two acts in order to create a new method of transport.* Having the components of a behavior does not insure the emergence of the behavior. There must be a higher-level unit that welds the components together.

The transport behavior of the first generation arose from combining elements in the behavior of the non-nest-building great-grandparents. The elements were three, drawn from different "major instincts," and from different levels of the hierarchy: (1) Chewing on bark and leaves. This is done by most species in the parrot family. Its apparent function is to keep the beak sharp and properly worn down (analogous to gnawing in rodents). (2) Preening the body feathers with the bill. This is done by all members of the parrot family; indeed, by all birds. It seves to keep the plummage clean and combed out. In parrots that do not build nests, it may be observed that, when the act of preening happens to follow immediately the act of bill sharpening, bits of material are sometimes left in the plummage. (3) Flying to the egg cavity; an element of parental behavior (and many other lovebird behaviors). This last act is, of course, much more complex than the previous two. In the first generation of lovebirds, a superordinate unit came into being that forged these three disparate and functionally independent acts into the essential component of nest-building, namely, transporting chewed material to the cavity where eggs are to be laid.

The fact that the transport behavior of the second generation shows glimmers of the improved transport behavior of the third generation encouraged Dilger to conduct a breeding experiment that would highlight the genetic basis for improvement. Dilger bred a species from the second generation with a species from the third generation. The off-spring of this union were awkward and maladapted. They made repeated attempts to tuck the strips they chewed off into their tail feathers. They frequently did not succeed. When they did, the strips always fell out during the flight to the nest. Despite the fact that this transport behavior never worked, it persisted for months and even years. Repeated practice over the years made the hybrids considerably more adept at tucking the strips into their tail feathers, but since the strips never failed to fall out en route to the nest, the overall sequence remained nonfunctional. In their initial attempts at nest building, the hybrids got material to the nest only when they carried it in their bills, which they did only 6 percent of the time. Over the years, this functional sequence became much more frequent; but it was often performed only after the birds had made some attempt to tuck the strip in their feathers.

In summary, Dilger's hybrids demonstrate that the hierarchical structure of the neural circuitry mediating particular intermediate units of organizations has a genetic basis. Hence, the behaviors forged by these mechanisms are subject to evolution through selection. Dilger's experiment is the genetic equivalent of Weiss's experiment. Dilger created birds that had a completely nonfunctional intermediate unit of behavioral organization.

The latticelike hierarchical structure of animal behavior is a necessary consequence of the evolutionary process. It could be deduced *a priori*, from evolutionary first principles. In a beautifully argued recent paper entitled "Evolution and Tinkering" the French molecular geneticist Francois Jacob (1977) reminds us that in evolution: "*Novelties come from previously unseen association of old material. To create is to recombine*" (p. 1163, italics mine). Natural selection, like the tinkerer, must operate on the material at hand, forging new and more complex behavior out of behavioral components that were not developed to serve the use that the tinkerer eventually puts them to. These components must, at least originally, have some independent function, must that is, be units in their own right. The preening movements, which first and second generation lovebirds use to insert nest material in their feathers, have an independent function as grooming behavior. The complex behavior of nest building is created by combining several such units. *Other complex behaviors evolve as other combinations of the same materials.* Evolution must work in this way because it must procede in small steps. To quote Jacob (1977) again: "Evolution does not produce novelties from scratch. It works on what already exists, either transforming a system to give it new functions or combining several systems to produce a more elaborate one" (p. 1164).

Taken together, the transection studies, the stimulation studies, and the breeding studies show that the lattice hierarchy is not just an heuristic analytic concept; rather, it reflects structural realities in the causative mechanisms of behavior.

WICKENS REVISITED

The opening pages of Chapter 5 pointed out a variety of instances in which behavioral analysis must deal with a classic taxonomical problem: what appears unitary at one level of analysis has a variety of manifestations if we shift our attention to a lower level of analysis. The phenomena of response generalization in learning theory are an instance of this very general problem. Wicken's studies on response generalization in classically conditioned finger withdrawal received particular mention: Wicken's subjects had one hand strapped palm downward on a table, with the index finger resting on an electrode. Whenever a buzzer sounded, the electrode delivered a painful shock. Soon, the subjects jerked their finger up off the electrode whenever they heard the buzzer. When analyzed at the level of simple acts, the subjects had apparently learned a "finger-withdrawal-response." When analyzed at the level of joint movement or neuromuscular activity, the subjects had apparently learned a "finger-extension-movement" involving "extensor-excitation" and "flexor-inhibition."

The problem is that the two different descriptions of what was learned are not two different ways of describing the same thing. It is not simply a matter of taste which description one uses. If one turns the subjects' hands over so that the palm faces upward and the back of the index finger now rests on the electrode, the two descriptions of the learned response make opposite predictions about what will happen when the buzzer sounds. The "finger withdrawal" description predicts the finger will be lifted from the electrode ("withdrawn") when the buzzer sounds; the "extensor-excitation-flexor-inhibition" description predicts the finger will be pressed down against the electrode when the buzzer sounds. As it happens, the first prediction was correct for most of the subjects; *but the second prediction was correct for one of his subjects*!

The bipartite results of Wicken's response generalization test suggest that the distinction between the various levels at which a behavioral event may be described is of more than philosophical interest. Different levels of behavioral description would appear to correspond to different levels of organization in the causative mechanisms of behavior. The level of the mechanism whose structure was altered by the buzzer-shock pairing varied from one subject to the next. Consequently, the behavioral manifestations of this learning varied in the response generalization test.

Wicken's results emphasized a fourth aspect of hierarchical organization in action: The higher the level of an organizing unit, the more varied the expression of its effects at the level of neuromuscular activity. In one of Wicken's subjects, the buzzer-shock experience affected a low level unit of organization. It affected the reflex level—the level at which simple joint movements are organized. The unit that *extends* the finger joint came to be activated by a previously neutral stimulus, the buzzer. The neuromuscular expression of this unit's activity is always the same; no matter which way the hand lies upon the table, this unit produces extensor excitation and flexor inhibition. The activity of this unit either withdraws the finger from the electrode or presses it down upon it, depending on how the hand lies upon the table.

In the rest of Wicken's subjects, the buzzer-shock experience produced its changes at a higher level of organization—a level that potentiates now one reflex, now the other depending on how the hand lies. The unit that *withdraws* the finger came to be activated by the previously neutral buzzer. The mode of action of this unit is closely analogous to what we have already seen in the obstacle avoidance movements in the hind limb of the cat. Recall that the unit that controls the motion of a hind limb potentiates a flexion reflex during a swing phase and an extension reflex during the stance phase of a step. Similarly, in Wicken's subjects, an extension reflex was potentiated when the hand lay palm downward, a flexion reflex when the hand lay palm upward. In both of these examples, the action of a higher level unit has a varied expression at the level of neuromuscular activity. In both cases, this is because the higher level units operate through circumstance-dependent selective potentiation of alternative lower level units.

The structure of the lattice-hierarchy in a given animal ought to be a central concern of behavioristic learning theory. And so should the question: At what level did a given learning experience alter the structure of the hierarchy? As Wicken's experiment indicates, one needs to know the answer to both of these questions before one can predict the behavioral consequences of a learning experience. And one certainly needs to know the answers before looking for neural changes that mediate learning.

Learning experiments seldom look for changes in performance in situations other than the training situation. This failure to explore the full range of the alterations in behavior consequent upon a given learning experience has blinded theorists to the central importance of the structure of the response hierarchy in predicting learned behavior. Traditional transfer studies do not focus on the different levels at which a response may be described, hence they shed little light on the structure of the system generating the "learned" response. Let us assume, as Weiss suggests (p. 238), that learning operates for the most part on the upper levels of the hierarchy. Then, the behavioral consequences of a given learning experience will be as diverse and circumstance-dependent as are the behavioral consequences of activating an upper level pathway by electrical stimulation. To recast von Holst's observation to suit the present context: The behavioral consequences of a learning experience are constant only so long as the internal central situation remains constant, in which the structural alterations produced by experience are, as it were, embedded. Anything that alters this internal central situation, even when it occurs long after the learning experience, may alter the behavioral expression of the learning experience.

OPERANT CONDITIONING

While it may be true that "a rose is a rose, is a rose," recent work on the operantly conditioned keypeck in the pigeon has clearly shown that a peck is not a peck, is not a peck. There is one peck for food and another peck of distinctly different topography for water. Indeed, "peck" is probably a misnomer for the water response; "dip" would be more appropriate. The unfortunate fact that a peck and a dip can both depress the key in a Skinner box sufficiently to close the microswitch behind the key has blinded Skinnerian theorists to the importance of natural units in the construction of conditioned behavior. The theorists and experimentalists were until recently busy watching the cummulative recorder rather than the pigeon. They failed to perceive that the learned response was not so arbitrarily related to the reinforcement as was commonly supposed. We now know that, when a pigeon pecks a key that produces food, the pigeon employs precisely that coordination that it would employ to peck at the food itself. When the same pigeon pecks the same key, now wired to produce water, the pigeon employs the dipping motion that it would employ to drink water (Hearst & Jenkins, 1975; Jenkins & Moore, 1973). In both cases, the conditioned behavior is constructed out of the intermediate units of coordination that ordinarily come into play vis-a-vis the particular reward. The apparent effect of the conditioning is to redirect these actions toward a previously neutral stimulus.

When a particular type of reinforcer does not naturally tend to activate an intermediate unit of coordination that can, if redirected, depress a key, then it is difficult to condition key-pecking for that reinforcement. Hineline and Rachlin (1969), for example, spent several years trying to condition pigeons to peck a key in order to escape or avoid footshock. It is difficult to know what sorts of coordinations pigeons would naturally employ in coping with footshock, since it is a stimulus rarely encountered in nature. Flying, however, seems an intuitively appealing first guess. Since none of the components of flying is at all well suited to depressing the key in a Skinner box, it is not surprising that Hineline and Rachlin found it difficult to get pigeons to peck a key in order to escape footshock. Nor is it surprising that some of those birds that did eventually learn to depress the key to terminate shock did so by beating their wings against it (Rachlin, personal communication)!

The attempts to condition key pecking to escape shock serve to emphasize the extent to which conditioned behavior is synthesized out of the intermediate units of coordination that tend to appear in the unconditioned behavior elicited by and/or directed toward obtaining the reinforcer. Hineline and Rachlin unwittingly demonstrated how difficult it is to obtain conditioned behavior that is not synthesized out of such components.

The Hineline and Rachlin demonstration was unwitting in that the experiments were inspired by the *tabula rasa* school of behaviorism. This school operates on the premise that conditioned response are (or at least ought to be) arbitrarily related to the reinforcement that sustains them. This premise is diametrically opposed to the premise advanced here, namely, that the conditioned behavior is ordinarily synthesized out of response elements in the unconditioned behavior pertinent to the reinforcement. Keller and Marian Breland, early students of Skinner, who made a good living operantly conditioning a variety of species to produce entertaining animal acts, had a similarly unexpected encounter with the importance of instinctive response elements in conditioned behavior. In their case, however, the encounter led them to abandon the *tabula rasa* viewpoint. To quote from the opening passages of the paper that announced this abandonment (Breland & Breland, 1961):

> ... the ethologists Lorenz (1950, p. 233) and Tinbergen (1951, p. 6) have warned that if psychologists are to understand and predict the behavior of organisms, it is essential that they become thoroughly familiar with the instinctive behavior patterns of each new species they essay to study. Of course, the Watsonian, or neobehavioristically oriented experimenter is apt to consider "instinct" an ugly word. He tends to class it with Hebb's (1960) other "seditious notions" which were discarded in the behavioristic revolution, and he may have some premonition that he will encounter this *bête noire* in extending the range of species studied.
>
> We can assure him that his apprehension is well grounded [p. 681].

The Brelands go on to report a number of cases showing that conditioned behavior is synthesized out of instinctive acts, and that these instinctive building blocks of conditioned behavior often contain elements that interfere with the performance the behavioral engineer is attempting to establish. For example, the Brelands attempted to condition a racoon to deposit coins in a money box in order to obtain food. The racoon's conditioned behavior employed as a central component the food washing motions that form part of the racoon's unconditioned food oriented behavior. When the Brelands tried to get the racoon to deposit two coins for every one food reward, the racoon spent so much time "washing" the coins before finally dropping them in the box that the Brelands had to abandon the project.

The same point that neobehaviorists came to reluctantly has long been embraced in ethologically oriented research on learning. Thorpe (1963) and Vince (1956, 1958, 1961) studied the ability of various species of bird to learn to draw within reach otherwise inaccessible food by pulling on a string to which the food was attached. It has been known for centuries that some species of birds are remarkably adept at this seemingly intelligent "tool-using" behavior. In the sixteenth century, this behavior on the part of goldfinches was a drawing-room curiosity sufficiently wide spread to give rise to the name 'draw-water' or its equivalent in two or three European languages (Thorpe, 1963). The finches were kept in special cages that required them to obtain all of their food and water by drawing up little carts. The carts containing food or water were held on incline planes by a string. The bird could draw the cart up the incline plane by pulling in the string with its beak and holding it with its foot. When the string was released, the cart rolled down the incline plane.

Experimental studies of how readily this behavior was learned by birds of different species led Thorpe to the conclusion that species such as the robin and the wren, which do not use the feet in feeding, are unable to learn the task. The more highly developed the use of the feet in natural feeding, the more readily a species or individual will learn the required behavior. In species, such as the greenfinch, that do not ordinarily employ the feet in feeding, a successful solution was frequently synthesized out of other naturally occurring coordinations. Juvenile greenfinches, for example, frequently obtained the food not by pulling up a length of string and holding it with their foot, but rather by "nibbling along it," using a coordination that Marler suggests is ordinarily used to husk seeds (Marler & Hamilton, 1966, p. 883). Within species, there were marked individual differences, apparently correlated with the strength of the individual's disposition to keep trying until it synthesized a successful solution.

Shettleworth (1973, 1975) studied the effect of food reinforcement on six naturally occurring elements of golden hamster behavior—digging, scrabbling at the wall, rearing, face-washing, scratching with the hindfoot, and scent-marking. Food reinforcement greatly increased the frequency of the first three elements, digging, scrabbling and rearing, while having little or no effect on the frequency of the second three elements, face-washing, scratching, and scent-marking. Her findings deliberately illustrate the point that was inadvertently illustrated by the work of Hineline and Rachlin: In a given conditioning context only certain elements in the lattice hierarchy are available for synthesis into a conditioned performance. Shettleworth's work eliminates the possibility that the failure of a given response to be conditioned by a given reinforcer may be due simply to the failure of that response to occur. One might object that keypecking did not easily become a conditioned escape response in Hineline and Rachlin's experiments because it rarely or never occurred and hence could not be reinforced. All of the behavioral elements that Shettleworth studied occurred with some frequency. Yet reinforcing some of them with food led to the increase in frequency predicted by the "law of effect"; whereas reinforcing others with food did not.

A similar point is made by Sevenster's (1973) studies on conditioning elements of behavior in the ethologists' favorite fish, the three-spined stickleback. Sevenster found that the male stickleback could be conditioned to swim through a ring by reinforcing it with either: (a) the opportunity to fight with another male; (b) the opportunity to court a female. When he attempted to condition the stickleback to bite the tip of a rod, he found that only the first of these two reinforcers was effective. Sevenster's results are particularly important in that they show, first, that both reinforcers could be used to condition at least one response element and, conversely, that both response elements were conditionable by at least one of the reinforcers. Thus one cannot argue either that: (a) one of the reinforcers simply was not a reinforcer; or that (b) one of the responses was simply not conditionable.

One is forced to recognize that the use of a particular reinforcement establishes a context in which some elements of the response hierarchy are available for synthesis into a conditioned performance, while other response elements are unavailable. Elements may be unavailable for synthesis in a given reinforcement context even though they occur spontaneously in that context and even though they are available in other reinforcement contexts. The structure of the lattice hierarchy places important constraints on the kinds of new performance that will emerge from a conditioning experience.

Learning theorists have from time to time called attention to the similarity between the law of natural selection in evolutionary biology and the law of effect in the theory of operant or instrumental conditioning. The law of natural selection is appealed to in order to explain the selective preservation within a species' gene pool of favorable results from the random process of genetic mutation. The law of effect is appealed to in order to explain the selective retention within an individual's response repertoire of favorable results from the supposedly random process of trial and error responding. If this analogy had only been taken more seriously, it should long since have led to the acknowledgement of an important principle: The evolutionary biologist recognizes that the preexisting genetic structure of a species is a very important part of the context within which the law of natural selection operates. Natural selection favors mutations that produce useful syntheses of preexisting elements of behavior. Therefore, preexisting response elements determine the avenues along which natural selection may propel the evolution of behavior, as we saw when we considered the evolution of nest-building in lovebirds. This section makes much of the same point with regard to conditioning. The preexisting response elements and the constraints placed on their operation by their position in the lattice hierarchy determine the avenues along which conditioning experiences may propel the development of an individual's behavior. The structure of the lattice hierarchy generates the biological "boundaries of" or "constraints on" learning (cf. Seligman & Hager, 1972, and Hinde & Stevenson-Hinde, 1973).

Before leaving this point, the significance of the term *preexisting* needs clarification. Despite what may seem to have been implied by earlier references to instinctive behavior, the term preexisting is not synonomous with innate. Except in precocial species—species whose behavior is well-formed at birth—most behavior in most species is clearly not innate in the literal sense of the word. Even that favorite of instinct theorists, the courtship behavior of birds, is almost never present at birth, no matter how species specific the pattern of courtship may be. The ontogeny of any behavior, whether or not that behavior is regarded as "entirely instinctive" or "entirely learned," is always and necessarily the consequence of an interplay between genetic and experiential factors.

Some of the experiential factors may make only very general contributions to any given behavior. The presence of sufficient oxygen is an extreme example of an experiential factor that makes a very general contribution. Some of the experiential factors may make a very specific contribution.

Imprinting experiences are an example of experiential factors that may make a very specific contribution to the ontogeny of courtship behavior. Imprinting experiences may determine the objects toward which the courtship behavior will be oriented.

Exactly the same point applies to the contributions of genetic factors. Some contribute only very generally to the ontogeny of any given behavior, some contribute very specifically. Insofar as the form of a given behavior is homogeneous within a species, heterogeneous across species, and appears even after highly aberrant early experience, we assume that most of the factors that *differentiate* that form are genetic. We term such *differentiations* instinctive. Insofar as the forms of a given behavior are heterogeneous within a species and strongly dependent on particular kinds of experience, we assume that the factors that differentiate those forms one from another are largely experiential. We call such differentiations learned. This conception allows language, for example, to be called instinctive with regard to those aspects of its form that are homogeneous across members of the human race, absent in large part from other species, and present even after such aberrant experiences as rearing in institutions. Language, on the other hand, may be called learned with regard to those aspects of its form that differ from one human to another and are strongly dependent on a particular experience, such as hearing Chinese rather than English while growing up.

This digression into the entrails of the nature–nurture debate was necessary to forestall the possibility that someone might fail to appreciate the role of the preexisting structure of the lattice hierarchy in shaping learned behavior for fear that it implied too great a commitment to nativism. To say that the animal comes to any learning experience with a structured response hierarchy is not to say that the structure of that hierarchy is innate or determined by genetic factors. The ontogeny of the pre-existing structure is irrelevant. Whatever its ontogeny, it is there; and it constrains the outcome of the conditioning. One cannot predict the outcome of conditioning without knowing the constraints imposed by that structure.

DEVELOPMENT AND RECOVERY

The development of behavior from birth to adulthood may be one of the best windows we have through which to examine the structure and functioning of the lattice-hierarchy. One of the central themes in the development of behavior is the progressive assertion of control by higher level units over lower levels. Early in development we may observe a lower unit in the hierarchy functioning in the absence of higher control. Later, we observe the unit come under the potentiating and depotentiating influence of a higher level. We may also observe how this selective potentiation is used to integrate the unit's actions with that of other units, so as to produce more flexible, adaptive and intelligent behavior. Development, in other words, allows us to observe the emergence of the synthesizing effects of higher levels.

Both aspects of this thesis may be seen in recent work by Hall, Cramer, and Blass (1975; 1977) on the developmental history of the rooting and suckling reflexes in infant rats. The newborn rat pup has three low-level units of coordination that together constitute its feeding behavior. When placed near a warm furry object, it roots, that is, pokes its head here and there in the fur. When its snout comes in contact with a saliva coated nipple, it grasps at the nipple with its mouth. When the grasping has brought the nipple into the mouth, it sucks. These three units of coordination—rooting, grasping, sucking—appear to be coordinated simply by the chained reflex principle. Rooting produces the stimulus for grasping, which produces the stimulus for sucking. Once sucking is initiated, the pup stays on the nipple whether or not the nipple is producing any milk and whether the pup is well fed or 22 hours food deprived. Thus sucking is prepotent among the three reflexes. In the newborn pup, sucking is not subject to potentiation or depotentiation by a level of the hierarchy that monitors the pups' nutritional requirements, nor by a level that monitors whether or not the sucking is actually producing milk. Up to 8 days of age, a well nourished pup will suck vigorously on a "dry" nipple for up to 2 hours!

Between 8 and 10 days of age, a level of the hierarchy that monitors nutritional requirements abruptly asserts control over the feeding behavior. Whereas, before 8 days of age, well nourished pups find and attach themselves to the nipple, if anything, more rapidly than pups deprived of nourishment; after 10 days of age, well-nourished pups are slow to attach while deprived pups are fast. A level that monitors nourishment is depotentiating the feeding reflexes when the pup is well nourished and potentiating them when the pup is deprived.

The 10 day old pups, however, still suck steadily at a nipple that is not letting down any milk. The feeding reflexes are not yet coordinated by a level of the hierarchy that monitors whether or not the sucking is producing milk. Between 14 and 16 days of age this changes abruptly. The pup that attaches to a dry nipple, sucks it for a few moments, then rejects it and roots around again until it grasps and sucks another nipple. The components of feeding behavior are now coordinated by a higher level unit that monitors whether or not sucking is producing milk. When sucking does not produce milk, this higher level unit depotentiates sucking and grasping, thereby allowing renewed control of output by the rooting unit. Renewed rooting may in turn lead to contact with a nipple that is producing milk. Thus the milk-sensitive higher level unit uses selective, transient depotentiation to coordinate the elements of feeding so as to produce more flexible and intelligent feeding behavior.

Teitelbaum (1971; 1977) has borrowed the term "encephalization" from the 19th century neurologist Hughlings-Jackson to describe the gradual assertion of hierarchical control over lower units of coordination. The term encephalization reflects the facts with which this chapter began, namely, that there is a correlation between functional levels in behavior and the anatomical levels of the central nervous system. Higher levels of functional integration in behavior generally have crucial components of their mediating neural circuitry located in higher levels of the nervous system. For this reason, the emergence of higher level control in behavior is generally correlated with the assertion of control by higher levels of the nervous system over the course of events at lower levels. Higher levels of the brain begin to assert patterned potentiating and depotentiating influences on lower levels, thereby "opening" some pathways and "closing" others, depending on circumstances. Teitelbaum argues that a closely parallel reassertion of hierarchical control occurs during recovery from an injury to the higher levels of the nervous system. Thus, the study of the recovery of behavioral function following brain injury opens another window through which to observe the structure and functioning of the lattice hierarchy underlying organized action.

One line of evidence in favor of Teitelbaum's thesis is the reappearance of infantile reflexes in brain injured adults. Infantile reflexes such as the rooting reflex (turning the mouth toward a touch on the cheek), the Babinski (an upward deflection of the toes in response to stroking of the sole of the foot) and the grasp reflexes of the hand "disappear" (can no longer be elicited) during the course of normal development. Pediatric neurologists may test for their presence or absence to assess whether or not an infant's sensorimotor development is proceding normally. Teitelbaum (1967; 1977) points out that these reflexes reappear in adult patients who have suffered an injury to the frontmost portions of the brain. Not only do the reflexes reappear after frontal injury, the order in which they disappear during recovery parallels the order in which they disappear during normal development. This suggests that "in the course of normal development the frontal cortex exerts over these reflexes an inhibitory influence which, in some manner, integrates them into voluntary behavior" (Teitelbaum, 1967, p. 561). In other words, these reflexes do not really disappear from behavior. Like other low level units, they become subject to higher level depotentiation (inhibition) and potentiation (facilitation), whereby they are coordinated with other units.

In the case of infantile reflexes, the influence of the descending control inputs is such as to make the reflexes unelicitable *under the standard clinical testing circumstances*. Presumably there are, however, behavioral circumstances under which these reflexes become elicitable. The situation may be analogous to the extension reflexes recently demonstrated by Forssberg, et al. (1975): Under standard testing conditions, a stimulus on the upper side of a cat's hind paw elicits only leg flexion. But, if one tests during the stance phase in a walking cat, one discovers that the same stimulus now elicits not flexion but extension!

In summary, the disappearance of an infantile reflex during normal development marks the assertion of coordinative hierarchical control over that unit of action. The reappearance of the reflex after brain injury betokens the dissolution of hierarchical control by the injury. The disappearance of the infantile reaction during the recovery from brain injury marks the reassertion of hierarchical control. Teitelbaum has applied this conception to the development and recovery of feeding behavior in rats (1971) and to a variety of development and recovery phonomena in other species (1977).

In this chapter, I have deliberately surveyed a diverse range of phenomena. My purpose has been to show the widespread manifestations of the latticework of hierarchical controls underlying the functional organization of behavior. The elucidation of the structure of this hierarchy and the principles governing the interactions between units within the hierarchy is or should be a central concern of behavioral research, whether that research focusses primarily on development or learning or cognition or evolution or brain-behavior correlation. Each specialty can offer its own angle of illumination on what should become a central conceptual edifice in psychology, occupying a position similar to that occupied by the fusion of Darwinian selection and Mendelian genetics in biology.

10 Central Motive States

SELECTIVE POTENTIATION
AND THE DRIVE CONCEPT

The conceptual link between muscles and motivation has now been forged. In analyzing the hierarchical arrangement of the mechanisms of sensorimotor coordination I noted the central importance of selective potentiation, which permits a unit of coordination to operate only when its operation will be functional. If we allow for a moment functional units to be personified as actors, then we may say that potentiation and depotentiation determine who may act and when, in order that the animal may produce a show and not a circus. Whether a potentiated actor actually performs depends upon whether the stage contains the props for his act and/or upon whether the actors already on stage produce his entrance cue.

The principle of selective potentiation has been repeatedly recognized by physiological psychologists (von Holst & von St. Paul, 1963; Lashley, 1938b; Morgan; 1943; Stellar, 1960) and by ethologists (Leyhausen, 1965; Lorenz, 1937; Tinbergen, 1951) as central to their understanding of the closely related concepts of drive and instinct. Lashley (1938b) speaks of drives as processes in the central nervous system that selectively facilitate specific sensorimotor patterns. This facilitation lowers the threshold for the elicitation of those patterns by external stimuli, and it broadens the class of stimuli that will elicit a specific reaction. Morgan (1943, p. 461) speaks of *central motive states* as establishing "a *set* or potentiality for presenting various patterns of behavior when the appropriate stimulus conditions in the external environment are available." Stellar (1960, p. 1502) speaks of drives determining "whether or not external stimuli will be effective." Lorenz (1937; 1950) speaks of action specific energy that renders the actions to which it is specific more readily elicitable. His concept of action specific energy is essentially the same as Lashley's action-specific facilitation. Tinbergen's (1951) "motivational impulses" are action-specific energy dressed up in more physiological language. The motivational impulses render specific actions more readily releasable.

Tinbergen (1951) pictures hierarchically arranged neural centers. The neural centers (corresponding to the nodes in Fig. 3.1 and 8.1) mediate specific actions or assemblages of actions. The neural centers also serve as focal points for the streams of motivational impulses that render actions more elicitable. The reader will recognize the strong similarity between Tinbergen's scheme and the one elaborated in Chapters 8 and 9. This same scheme, in which the principle of selective potentiation figures so strongly, was also central to von Holst and von St. Paul's interpretation of the motivating effects of electrical stimulation of the brain in chickens (see p. 302–305).

Thus, physiological psychologists and ethologists have long been accustomed to think of drives in terms of selective potentiation. But, as we saw in Chapters 8 and 9, the principle of selective potentiation appears already in the analysis of very simple and basic processes of sensorimotor coordination. The cat's ability to walk over rough ground is aided by the alternating potentiation of joint-flexing reflexes during the swing phase and joint-extension reflexes during the stance phase. As this simple example illustrates, the principle of selective potentiation is central to an understanding of how different levels of sensorimotor organization interact, regardless of how high up or low down one looks in the hierarchical structure of action. For this reason, it is not useful to distinguish sharply between the study of sensorimotor coordination and the study of motivation.

Motivation, as I use the term here, refers to those processes in the central nervous system that organize behavior so that, in the aggregate, the animal's separate acts tend toward some culminating point, or action, or state of affairs. Motivation refers, in other words, to those processes that impart to behavior the characteristics that make us speak of purposes and goals. When, however, we analyze the principles that govern these motivational processes we encounter the same principles underlying the coordinative mechanisms that generate the simple acts. The difference between "purposive," "goal-oriented," "motivated" behavior and "automatic," "machinelike" "sensorimotor" behavior does not reflect differing principles in the underlying mechanisms; rather it reflects the fact that the organization of simple acts is traceable to relatively low levels of the motor hierarchy, while the organization of "motivated" behavior is traceable to higher levels. The behavioral manifestations of selective potentiation are readily perceived at the sensorimotor level. The flexibility and adaptability of the behavior that flows from selective potentiations at higher levels dazzles us, hindering our perception that much the same principles are at work. The intelligence of the behavior defeats the analytic faculty in our own intelligence, leaving us to argue endlessly about voluntary versus involuntary and the like.

The behavior controlled by the higher, "motivational" levels of the sensorimotor hierarchy is flexible, adaptable, puposive, and intelligent precisely because of the hierarchical arrangement. The higher levels lay down a *frame* or *general direction* for behavior by selectively potentiating coherent sets of behavioral options. The flexibility of the behavior, its variability from occasion to occasion, and its suitability to momentary and unforseeable circumstances reflect the fact that what higher levels establish are options not requirements. The higher levels do not directly command muscles. They do not determine which muscles shall contract and when. They determine the set of general patterns or integrated sequences of simple acts that *may* be observed when a particular motivational state is in force. The imposition of a general plan by means of selective potentiation gives behavior its purposive quality, its long-term functional coherence. Each lower level in the hierarchy specifies more narrowly which of the many variations, sub-variations, and sub-sub-variations of the general plan will actually appear at a particular moment. Lower levels fill in or determine *details* within the general pattern.

The lower level filling-in of details, in accord with the stimuli arising as the pattern unfolds, gives behavior its flexibility, its ready adaptation to momentary circumstance. The principle of selective potentiation makes this last minute filling-in of adaptive detail possible. The *exact* set of muscular actions by which the walking cat swings its hind leg forward on a particular step is still being determined while the swing itself is in progress. If the leg touches an obstacle during its swing, that stimulus triggers a selectively potentiated flexion reflex that adaptively alters the muscle commands while the swing is in progress.

The flexible filling-in of detail is central to many hierarchically arranged command structures, when those command structures are functioning well and properly. Suppose we let the camera of our imagination zoom in on an American footsoldier on some foreign battle field and ask Weiss's basic question of coordination: What determines what that soldier is doing at a given moment and how has this determination been put into effect? Well: The President and Congress determined that we should be fighting a war in that country at this point in history. The draft board determined that this particular man should belong to the Army. The generals determined that his division should be attempting to move up that peninsula at that time. The sergeant determined that they could interrupt their march for a little rest, and the footsoldier himself determined that he would be smoking a cigarette during the break.

When we ask why the footsoldier is doing what he is doing, the answer depends on the perspective we take. Different perspectives lead us to focus on different levels of the hierarchy. Why is he in this country? Ask the President, the Congress, and his draft board? Why is he resting? Ask the sergeant. Why is he smoking a cigarette? Ask him. Every level of the hierarchy must be taken into account in giving a complete causal analysis of why he is, where he is, doing what it he, when he is. The same necessity to consider all levels of the command hierarchy arises when we ask why a given motor unit (a footsoldier in the neuromuscular hierarchy) is doing what it is when it is.

This layering of decision processes is what creates the seemingly immense gap between the central motive states and the actual neuromuscular expression of motivated behavior. The gap between the policy deliberations of the President and Congress and the ultimate expression of these policies in the activity of individual soldiers and civil servants is similarly immense. Yet the connections are there and may be traced. The command structure exists and may be diagrammed. And it does, however awkwardly, account for the general pattern of activity within the civil and military bureaucracies. Similarly, we now have some grasp of the neuromuscular command structure. We can to some extent diagram it (cf. Chapters 5, 7, and 8). And we can thereby perceive how central motive states find expression in appropriately patterned neuromuscular activity.

THE ORIGINS OF CENTRAL MOTIVE STATES

It remains to consider how central motive states arise. What causes them? What principles govern their waxing and waning? How do diverse motivational states interact? This, as Bolles (1967) acknowledges, is the familiar province of a large segment of physiological psychology. A detailed account of the physiological, neural, and hormonal variables that determine hunger, thirst, and concupiscence may be found in any modern textbook of physiological psychology. In this chapter, I confine myself to some very general observations about these questions.

Reflex, Oscillatory, and Servomechanistic Processes

When we step back from an examination of the details—which sex hormone does what, which receptor site in the brain responds to which thirst stimulus, and so on—when we step back and ask what *kinds of processes* determine the central motive states, we find the same kinds of processes we are already familiar with: releasing processes, oscillatory processes, and cybernetic processes. Let me briefly illustrate:

In humans, erotic stimuli may release a state of sexual arousal, much as the adequate stimulus for a reflex releases muscular contraction. As with all central motive states, the behavior that actually appears when an erotic stimulus releases sexual arousal depends upon the context. Very frequently, the context is such that there are no or only very subtle outward behavioral manifestations of the sexual arousal released by some casual incident. When the releasing principle functions at the upper levels of the hierarchy, what is released is a *disposition*—a pattern of selective potentiation—*not* a pattern of muscular activity. A disposition may come and go without eventuating in any overt behavior.

The principle of release by specific stimuli plays an important role in controlling sexual arousal in many species other than man. It is central to an understanding of reproductive behavior in some birds (Lehrman, 1965), the function of many pieces of reproductive behavior being to release a suitable central state in the partner.

On the other hand, the state of sexual arousal in the female rat and in the females of many other species is not released by external stimuli. Sexual arousal in the female rat fluctuates under complex cyclical timing processes within the central nervous system and the endocrine system (Adler, 1978). The waxing and waning of sexual arousal in the female rat is governed in other words by central oscillators.

The waxing and waning of still other central motive states, particularly the "homeostatic" drives of thirst, hunger and thermoreguation, must be understood in servomechanistic terms. These central motive states are error signals reflecting the discrepancy, if any, between some reference signal (the so-called "set-point") and a sensory signal indicating the actual momentary value of some important variable, for example, body temperature. The ensuing complex of behavioral and physiological responses serves to reduce the discrepancy that gave rise to the central motive state in the first place. The animal's behavior ensures that the actual body temperature never departs far from the temperature that corresponds to the set point signal; hence the term homeostasis—stable or constant state.

The above categorization of central motive states into *released, oscillatory,* and *homeostatic* is an oversimplification. When any one central motive state is closely examined, all three sorts of processes may be seen to have some effect. A rat's disposition to eat is only partly a reflection of the homeostatic processes that maintain the rat's weight at a nearly constant value. Oscillatory processes also influence the rat's eating. The central clock, which imparts a daily rhythm to all the rat's behaviors, has a pronounced influence on feeding behavior, an influence that overrides purely homeostatic considerations. During the daylight hours the rat, who is a nocturnally active animal, is not much disposed to eat, despite the fact that it is in "negative energy balance" during these hours (Le Magnen, 1971). During this phase of its day, the rat uses up more chemical energy than it takes in; hence it draws on its nutritional reserves by breaking down its body fat. Conversely, during the night hours, the rat eats every two or three hours, despite the fact that it is in positive energy balance. During this phase of its day, the rat takes in more chemical energy than it needs and converts the excess to body fat. The clock that regulates the daily pattern of activity patterns the bouts of food seeking and eating in a way that cannot be predicted from purely homeostatic considerations. Hence, feeding behavior is not governed solely by the servomechanistic (i.e., homeostatic) principle.

Social releasing stimuli exert some control over the rat's disposition to eat. Young rats, at least, are more disposed to eat when and where they see other rats eating (Galef & Clark, 1971). The importance of social releasing stimuli in the etiology of hunger has probably been underestimated, because the homeostatic conception of the problem so dominates the thinking and the experimentation of most investigators. In any event, all three principles— servomechanistic, oscillatory, and stimulus-released—play a role in the complex etiology of most central motive states.

The Autonomous Buildup of Specific Potentiation

There appears to be a further principle that plays an important role in the origin of drive states. As Lorenz (1950) was the first to stress, the disposition to perform certain acts often becomes stronger as a function of the time since the act was last performed, *whether or not* the renewed performance of the act serves any obvious purpose or helps to satisfy any objective biological need. Take, for example, the starling which Lorenz had confined to its cage for some weeks. When released, it went through the entire sequence of acts in its insect-hunting behavior, even though there were no insects flying about and the bird was fully fed (Lorenz, 1937). Lorenz termed the performance of an act in the absence of objective need and appropriate activating conditions *vacuum behavior*. Lorenz pointed out that vacuum behavior was an extreme manifestation of a principle that applies to many higher level units of behavior: If a unit is not activated in the ordinary course of events, it becomes more and more potentiated until practically any kind of stimulus will set it off.

In Lorenz's thinking, the concept of potentiation was spoken of as a kind of energy that accumulates in the neural circuitry coordinating some act and is "discharged" when the act is performed. The more energy has accumulated, the more easily the act may be elicited, until eventually the act may occur in the absence of any eliciting stimulus whatsoever. This concept of "action specific energy" has inspired a great deal of criticism, much of which rests on a more literal reading of the energy metaphor than Lorenz may have intended. Lorenz's important principle—the autonomous build up of a potentiated condition in a unit that coordinates some long uncalled upon act—has been lost sight of in the swirl of controversy over energy theories of motivation. Numerous ethological observations confirm Lorenz's point that an act may be in a high state of potentiation for no other reason than that it has been unperformable for some while. The only thing that reduces this state of potentiation is the occurrence of the potentiated act.

In other words, many acts do not always remain subservient to some more general behavior, whose purposes they supposedly serve. This functional semi-independence of supposedly subordinate actions is strikingly apparent in all careful field studies on the behavior of predators. Predation is widely supposed to be functionally subordinate to hunger. The writers of popular nature documentaries reassure us that the lioness only kills to satisfy her need for food (and only after selecting the weak and the sick to be her meal). However appealing to both reason and sentiment, the reassurance is false. When prey are plentiful or when some prey animal unwittingly comes within easy striking distance, the lion and the tiger and every other predator whose behavior in the wild has been carefully observed appear to kill "for the sport of it," leaving the prey uneaten (Kruuk, 1972; Leyhausen, 1965; Schaller, 1972).

In the drive-around wild-animal parks now common in the United States the lions and tigers are kept well fed; yet it would be foolish to get out of one's car in their vicinity. Though well fed, the animals have no chance to hunt. Lorenz's principle of the accumulation of action specific energy applies with some force. The animals are ready to hunt for hunting's sake. Indeed, Premack's methods (see below) would probably show that these animals will eat *in order* to hunt!

A study by Tinbergen (1965) of the behavior of two foxes with burrows near a large colony of breeding sea birds provides a chilling example of the functional autonomy of predation. The foxes—like some hunting gentlemen of the last century—killed dozens of birds every night and left them lying on the dunes.

In his comparative and developmental study of feline predation, Leyhausen (1965) found that simpler acts that form components of the predatory sequence also lead a life of their own. These simple acts —stalking and pouncing, for example—are frequently performed in isolation. A large part of the play of felines consists of pieces of predatory behavior performed either in isolation or in unusual sequence. Just as predation is not strictly subservient to hunger, "pouncing" and "stalking" are not strictly subservient to predation. Cats frequently stalk for stalking's sake and not as part of some predatory sequence. Similarly in Lorenz's pet starling, the neural machinery coordinating the act of catching insects became so potentiated that, when released to fly about the room, the starling repeatedly went through the motions of catching nonexistent insects. While there is little doubt that the act of catching insects may and often does become potentiated because the bird is "hungry," one is forced to recognize that the potentiation of an unperformed "food-seeking" act grows over time, even when no nutritional deficit exists. One is forced to recognize, in other words, a fourth principle in the etiology of central motive states: the autonomous accumulation of specific potentiation, and this may help explain the periodic nature of most motivated actions in humans (cf., Toman, 1960).

LABILE VERSUS FIXED HIERARCHIES

The principle of autonomous accumulation has an impact on one's conception of the hierarchical organization. It introduces the notion of a relative or labile hierarchy as opposed to the absolute or fixed hierarchical structure we have so far considered. So far the relation *superordinate–subordinate* has been assumed to be an immutable property of the relation between two functional units. The flexion and extension reflexes triggered by a touch on the leading edge of the cat's hind leg are subordinate to the stepping oscillator, and not vice versa. The oscillator selectively potentiates and depotentiates these reflexes to insure that these reflex movements fit the rest of the cat's locomotory movements. The reflexes do not potentiate and depotentiate the oscillator so as to make the oscillator's action fit or serve the purpose of the reflex action. The relation between the higher level represented by the oscillator and the lower level represented by the reflex is as fixed as the ranks in the army. The principle of action specific energy moved Lorenz to suggest that a more labile ranking obtains between functional units near the top of the action hierarchy, at least in birds and mammals. Lorenz (1950) coined the term *relative hierarchy* for hierarchies in which the order of subordination was labile rather than fixed. Relative alludes to the fact that which action serves which is context dependent. In some contexts X serves Y; in others Y serves X.

This principle of a relative or labile order of subordination was strikingly illustrated by the early work of Premack (see Premack, 1965, for review). When a rat's opportunity to drink is restricted, the rat will run in a running wheel in order to drink. That surprises no one. It agrees with our rationalist common sense about the functional organization of behavior and with the common assumption that all actions must ultimately serve some biologically *obvious* need, such as reproduction or the maintenance of a water/salt balance in the body. It surprised many people, however, when Premack (1962) showed that the relation between running and drinking was reversible: When the rat's opportunity to run in the running wheel was restricted, the rat drank in order to run!

Wheel running (which is probably an outlet for daily exploratory activity—Kavanau & Rischer, 1968) provides an excellent illustration of the principle of action specific energy. The biological need to *repeatedly* explore one's environs or run in a wheel is far from obvious. Indeed, it may be gratuitous to postulate such a need; but whether or not the need exists, the neural circuitry that organizes this activity is a focus for the autonomous accumulation of potentiation. The disposition to engage in exploration grows stronger when an animal is deprived of the opportunity, even if the environs are already well known to the animal. This autonomously arising potentiation may then spread to other actions, for example, drinking. Only the performance of exploratory locomotion can quench the potentiation at its source. The rat drinks in order to run when the *source* of the potentiation organizing this behavioral sequence is in the circuitry for running; it runs in order to drink, when the source of the potentiation is in the drinking circuitry.

Premack (1965) and Kavanau (1969) between them have repeatedly demonstrated the importance of the principle of autonomous accumulation of action-specific potentiation, at least in mammals. The disposition to engage in almost any activity, whether innate (shredding paper for nest building) or seemingly artificial (manipulating an experimenter-provided lever, or plunger, or a hinged door), fluctuates to some extent independently of the larger functional context in which these actions may occasionally play a role. When the animal's free engagement in any one of these activities is impeded, the animal will mobilize other acts that remove the impediment.

Figure 10.1 schematizes the labile hierarchy demonstrated by Premack's experiments. In one context, where access to water is restricted, the potentiating signals that organize the rat's behavior originate in the "thirst" circuit, the circuit that integrates the rat's actions in such a way as to maintain an appropriate amount and distribution of water and salt in the body. The signals spread from this source (Fig. 10.1a) to potentiate running behavior, probably by way of a higher level circuit that organizes exploratory activity. There is no negative feedback from running to the source of the potentiating signal, hence running cannot be the culminating act in this context; only drinking can. In the other context (Fig. 10.1b), where all outlets for exploratory action are limited, the potentiating signal originates in the circuit that organizes exploratory activity—an instance of the autonomous accumulation of potentiation. The signal flows to the circuit that integrates drinking, perhaps by way of the more general circuitry for thirst, perhaps not. There is no negative feedback from drinking to the source of the potentiating signal, so drinking cannot be the culminating act; only running can. In the first context, the function of running is to permit drinking. In the second context, the function of drinking is to permit running. Which act serves which is context dependent.

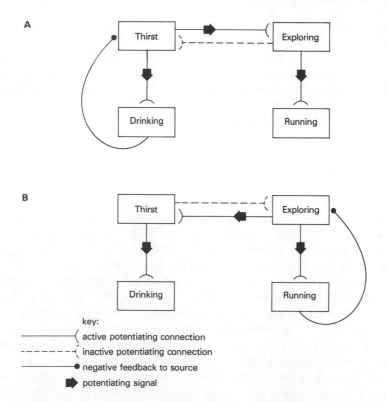

FIG. 10.1. Schematic interpretation of the context-dependent order of subordination demonstrated by Premack (1962). (*a*) When access to water is limited, the thirst circuit becomes the source of signals that potentiate both drinking and running. However, only drinking can terminate the behavioral sequence. (*b*) When exploratory activities, such as wheel running, are restricted, the circuit that organizes these activities becomes the source of potentiating signals. Now, only running can terminate the behavioral sequence.

THE ROLE OF LEARNING

The existence of a path along which potentiation may flow from running to drinking may depend on the animal's earlier experience. It may derive in other words from a process of learning. The concept of motivation as the patterned flow of potentiating signals along the pathways that form the latticework of a lattice hierarchy does not commit one to the nativist assumption that the pattern of interconnections is determined by the genes. At least in mammals, the structure of the hierarchy—which units connect to which—will depend upon an interplay between genetic and experiential factors. No doubt much of the structure at any one time reflects learning. However, much of this learning is of a kind undreamed of by learning theorists! Many kinds of experience other than favorable outcomes (the reinforcements of traditional learning theory) result in structural alterations in the hierarchy (Gallistel, 1978).

Which *kinds* of experience cause which *kinds* of structural alterations is a question that remains largely unanswered. In the context of traditional learning theory the question made no sense. Everyone "knew" that learning phenomena were of one or at the most two kinds—classical and instrumental. Now, however, this dogma is crumbling. As more and more investigators take an ethological approach to learning phenomena, the question of which kind of experience is required for a given kind of structural alteration begins to receive some preliminary answers (see Hinde & Stevenson-Hinde, 1973; Rozin & Kalat, 1971; Seligman & Hager, 1972).

Insofar as learning alters the structure of the lattice hierarchy, that is insofar as experience determines which functional units connect to which, learning shapes motivated behavior. The possible forms of behavior potentiated by a central motive state are determined by the structure of the lattice hierarchy. This structure *is* the latticework of interconnecting pathways, by which the potentiation is distributed to certain functional units and not others. Changes in this structure necessarily alter the extent to which various functional units are or are not potentiated by a central motive state arising at a given node in the latticework. Thus, structural changes wrought by experience alter the likelihood that a given activity will or will not be performed in the presence of a given central motive state.

Allowing experience to play a hand in fashioning the structure of the latticework within which potentiating signals are constrained to flow is one approach to specifying the relation between learning and motivation. In this approach, those aspects of the latticework that derive from experience constitute the animal's acquired knowledge of the world. The animal's "memories" are simply the structural alterations wrought by experience in the latticework of the action hierarchy. These memories alter behavior insofar as they alter the flow of potentiating signals. I think that such an approach may be appropriate to many kinds of early or *critical period* learning phenomena and to many kinds of motor or skill-learning (Schiller, 1952; 1957); I do not think it provides a satisfactory view of some kinds of learning.

It seems to me undeniable that much learning, even in lower organisms such as the digger wasp, involves the formation of representations of the world. The animal lays down in memory coded representations of signficant points in the environment or states of the world. It also lays down coded representations of the relations between points or between states. In other words, animals lay down in memory maps of the environment and propositions of the form: "digging at X produces Y." The problem then becomes: How can a map or a series of propositions in memory control the course of an animal's actions? The next chapter ventures some suggestions about this long-standing puzzle.

SUMMARY

Before going on to wrestle with the problem of memory and action, let us take stock of what we can say about motivation and action. Motivational states are potentiating and depotentiating signals arising at or near the top of the lattice hierarchy. The nodes of this lattice hierarchy are neural circuits mediating different patterns of organization in action. Although these circuits are symbolized by nodes in functional diagrams, they of course have no sharply circumscribed physical locus in the nervous system. The pathways between nodes conduct potentiating signals from one node to another, that is, from one neural circuit to another. A node receiving a potentiating signal represents a neural circuit prepared to be active. Whether or not it actually is active depends upon whether or not the external or internal environments provide appropriate stimuli (activating conditions). A node receiving a depotentiating signal represents a neural circuit that is not prepared to be active. Even if the external and internal environment provide appropriate stimuli, a depotentiated neural circuit does not function. Through selective potentiation and depotentiation, motivational states establish coherent, functionally interrelated sets of behavioral options. Other, nonmotivational factors—the activating conditions—determine which options are actually exercised. Hence, the behavioral consequences of motivational states are necessarily highly variable. This variability in the behavioral expression of a central motive state has deceived some behaviorists into arguing that such states have no objective existence. But they demonstrably do exist. Their existence has now been extensively documented at both the behavioral and physiological levels.

When the flow of potention is asymmetric—when it can flow from node A to node B but not from node B to node A, we have a fixed hierarchy. The circuit represented by node A controls where and when the circuit represented by node B may be active, and not the reverse. When the direction in which the potentiating signal flows depends on the behavioral context, then one has a labile rather than a fixed hierarchy; one has a "relative hierarchy" or context-dependent hierarchy. Whether A is subordinate to B, or vice versa, depends on whether the potentiation is flowing from A to B, or vice versa. Under this arrangement, the action mediated by circuit A may not be part of a more general scheme mediated by circuit B. Indeed, the action mediated by or patterned by circuit B may be more circumscribed and stereotyped (e.g., "pouncing") than the action mediated by circuit A (e.g., "searching"). One says that A is subordinate to B in the sense that the action mediated by A forms part of a sequence that can only be terminated by the action of B. Thus, whenever the principle of relative hierarchy prevails, the sense in which one unit is subordinate to another is not the same sense in which a unit in a fixed hierarchy is subordinate to a higher unit.

In mammals and perhaps to a lesser extent in birds, the principle of relative hierarchy is widespread near the top of the lattice hierarchy, that is, at motivational levels of the hierarchy. The "lateral" flow of potentiating signals between units at the higher levels is closely analogous to what Sherrington, speaking of lower units, called the facilitation of agonistic reflexes.

The principles governing the waxing and waning of potentiation at motivational levels of the hierarchy are much the same as those one encounters at lower levels: The potentiation may be released by some external stimulus; or, the potentiation may oscillate under the influence of some endogenous oscillatory process; or, the potentiation may constitute the "error signal" in a servomechanistic process. However, there appears to be a fourth important principle governing the waxing and waning of the potentiating signals we call motivation. This is Lorenz's principle of autonomous accumulation. Some neural circuits become potentiated whenever they have been inactive for some while. Activating them reduces (discharges) the potentiation. This autonomously arising potentiation must take the form of a signal, because it can be transmitted to other circuits, just as can potentiation arising from other causes. This principle of autonomous accumulation seems to go hand in hand with the principle of relative hierarchy. The fact that potentiation can flow either from A to B or from B to A seems intimately related to the fact that either A or B may be the source of a potentiating signal. When potentiation arises in circuit A because A has been inactive, then only the performance of the culminating act peculiar to A can quench the potentiation at its source. Similarly, when B has been the focal point for the autonomous growth of a potentiating signal, then only B's culminating act can eliminate the potentiating signal and terminate the behavioral sequence organized by that signal.

The allied principles of autonomous accumulation and relative or labile hierarchy relieve one of the embarrassing necessity of trying to compile a list of the major drives or major instincts á la Tinbergen (1951, pp. 112–113). If one imagines a hierarchy in which there is a fixed order of subordination and superordination all the way from the bottom to the top, then one is forced to try to identify the (presumably) relatively few nodes at the very top that are the major drives or major instincts. This necessity always leads to embarassment when one contemplates the behavior of the more advanced animals. The effort to make the extreme variety of behaviors displayed by such organisms entirely subordinate to a few major instincts or drives always seems artificial and forced. One ends up postulating such dubious and vague "major instincts" as curiosity, exploration, social well being, and the like. The recognition of a labile order of subordination, and of the general tendency for potentiation to grow up around individual acts in a quasi-autonomous fashion, removes the felt necessity for identifying the oligarchs that supposedly rule the instinctual oligarchy. The concept of an oligarchy is replaced by the concept of a parliament.

Within this parliament of acts that constitute the upper levels of the action hierarchy not all acts are equal. As in human parliaments, some members are a good deal more equal than others. That is, some upper level nodes have very extensive connections to other nodes; hence, potentiating signals emanating from these nodes commonly organize extensive and complex patterns of action. On the other hand, some upper level nodes have only limited connections to other nodes. Potentiating signals emanating from these less influential nodes do not ordinarily organize extensive patterns of behavior. However, as in a human parliament, a humble node with a connection to one of the plenipotentiary nodes can be the *source* of a potentiating signal that mobilizes the organizing power of the more influential node. When this happens, the organism may perform elaborate appetitive chains of behavior merely to enable some humble act to occur. The cat may pursue for some while and with considerable resourcefulness a pattern of action that finally yields something for it to pounce upon. Not, mind you, something of obvious biological significance such as food; just something to pounce upon, pouncing itself being the culminating act in the entire behavior pattern. Similarly, a monkey may work resourcefully and at length merely to gain access to an "intesting" manipulandum. Observers of human parliaments are frequently bemused or angered by the analogous situation, in which the parliament carries out some lengthy and complicated legislative maneuver to gratify some humble member "with the right connections."

Schiller's (1957) observations on the experiential and maturational factors in the development of a chimpanzee's ability to solve the kind of stick and box problems that Köhler (1927) studied, strongly suggest a biological rationale for the tendency toward autonomous potentiation in the circuitry controlling simple acts. The tendency results in the aimless mixing of behavioral fragments—the seemingly purposeless play that is so salient in the behavior of higher animals. Schiller's (1957) observations suggest that this jumbling of acts creates novel combinations, which "can be stabilized in more or less comprehensive units by reenforcement" (p. 179).

In summary, the analysis of motivation is the study of what acts are selectively potentiated in what combinations and under what circumstances. This is the approach to motivation that Bolles recognized as typical of physiological psychologists (see Preface). However, the approach achieves its full power only when one also has a detailed analysis of the movements and combinations of movements by which the elementary acts are realized. One must have an understanding of the functional organization of the sensorimotor hierarchy from the level of acts on down—in short, an analysis of coordination—and an understanding from the level of acts on up—in short, an analysis of motivation. Then, the gap between the central motive states and behavior is bridged.

If we can now make some suggestions as to how central motive states combine with empirically derived representations in memory, so as to generate actions whose patterning reflects the information gained from experience, then our theory of motivation becomes quite general. The next chapter addresses itself to the interplay between central motive states and acquired knowledge of the world.

11

Representation of the World and the Organization of Action

KNOWLEDGE AND ACTION

The brains of many animals store records of the information conveyed to the brain by the sensory-perceptual side of the nervous system. These records constitute representations of the world: Someone who understood the memory code and who had the technical means to examine the memory could reconstruct those aspects of the external world represented in the records. When a representation of some aspect of the world has been laid down in memory, it may help to guide and control the animal's subsequent actions. The question is: How does the brain system that controls the generation of signals to motor mechanisms interact with the brain systems that form and store coded representations of the world? Or, to strip the question of neuropsychological jargon: How can knowledge control action?

In the S-R learning theories that were fashionable up until a decade ago, this question did not arise in any serious or independent way. The system that stored up knowledge and the system that generated action were conceived of as one and the same. The term knowledge was thought to mean or refer to changes that experience had wrought in the structure of the mechanism that generated action. To know about something was simply to have a motor system that was disposed to respond in a certain way in the presence of that something, because previous experience with that something had altered the structure of the motor system. This premise was asserted in the title of an early, influential paper by one of the central figures in this school of thought, Clark L. Hull. Hull's "Knowledge and Purpose as Habit Mechanisms" (1930) argues that to acquire knowledge is to acquire habits. Hull (1943) subsequently spelled out what he believed habits meant at the neural level. He believed, as did Sherrington, that the reflex arc was *the* basic building block out of which actions were constructed. The acquisition of a habit was simply the creation of new reflex arcs by experience. Thus, Hull's theory of knowledge was interwoven with his theory of action. If knowing something is simply having certain reflexes instilled by experience, then there is no question as to how one's knowledge gets translated into action. One's knowledge is embedded in the structure of the reflex units that generate action.

Skinner, another central figure of the S–R schoool, has scrupulously avoided any theoretical mention of neural mechanisms or other physiological concepts, but he has insisted that all of the "mentalistic" notions invoked to explain action—knowledge, purpose, intention, mental representation, etc.—have meaning *only* insofar as they refer to alterations in the probability of emitting certain responses. In Skinner's view, "knowing calculus" is nothing other than "having a high probability of giving correct answers when confronted with problems in calculus." And, "having an accurate mental representation of Boston Commons" is nothing other than "having a low probability of going astray while walking near central Boston." In this view, the question of how knowledge controls action is meaningless. Knowledge is regarded as a concept that has no meaning apart from certain patterns and probabilities of action.

A substantial fraction of Skinner's writing has been devoted to ridiculing the "homunculi" that seem to play a central role in cognitive theories. Cognitive theories, unlike S–R theories, treat perception and knowledge as separable from action. Homunculi are little imaginary men in the head whose services are surreptitiously invoked, claims Skinner, to explain how a mental representation of Boston Commons gets translated into a specific pattern of movement through central Boston. The little man reads the map and pushes the right buttons on the console that controls the motor system. The point of this satire is that when we imagine there exist in the brain representations of the world, then the question arises, how do these representations influence action. As Skinner's satire suggests, there have been very few explicit theories of how representations could govern the course of action. The problem of how an action-system could make use of a representation of the world to pattern commands to the motor apparatus has been widely ignored. Cognitive theorists, who conceive of knowledge in terms of representations stored in memory, have let imaginary little men inside the head solve the problem of making such knowledge enter into the control of action.

In the last decade, cognitive theories have enjoyed a considerable resurgence, at the expense of the S–R theories. This resurgence has been facilitated by the advent of the computer, which has been a rich, if overworked, source of analogy in theorizing about higher brain function. The existence of machines that form and make use of representations removed the stigma of mentalism from the concept of representation. For thirty years, the word representation had been all but banned from respectable discourse within scientific psychology, because it was associated with those nonphysical principles whose explanatory services were resolutely dispensed with in the first chapter. These days, however, we have terrain-recognizing guided missiles that store in memory representations of the terrain en route to their target and that make use of these representations to steer themselves to the target. In the face of such indubitably physical objects making unblushing use of representations, it is no longer possible to regard the concept of a representation of the world as an inherently vague, meaningless, mentalistic concept that could not control action in any physically explicable way.

Another and ultimately more significant reason for the return of representations of the world as central concepts in the explanation of behavior is that much of behavior cannot be explained in any other way. When knowledge enters into the control of action is such a way as to produce sequences that are uniquely suited to the particular circumstances in which the animal finds itself at that moment—sequences that the animal has never generated before and will probably never generate again—then it is exceedingly difficult to conceptualize knowledge in terms of "habits" or "altered response probabilities." Yet knowledge often does enter into the control of action in just this way.

The use of knowledge to generate novel but appropriate behavior is clearly seen in studies of the paths animals take when traversing familiar territory toward some goal. These studies strongly imply that the animals form a representation of the territory they have surveyed and that the system that generates action makes use of this representation to produce actions that are suited to whatever circumstance or location the animal finds itself in at a given moment. Before considering explicitly specified and physically realizable action-systems that can utilize representations in this way, let us consider two classic studies demonstrating the sort of behavior one must attempt to explain.

INSIGHTFUL DETOUR BEHAVIOR IN THE RAT

In the late 1920's, N. R. F. Maier ran small groups of thoroughly tamed rats on a series of maze problems that tested the rats' ability to synthesize two separately acquired sets of information into an overall representation of an environment. Because the tests required the rat to synthesize the information gained from separate experiences, Maier's data are usually discussed in connection with the rat's capacity for reasoning. Equally interesting, however, is the rat's use of the synthesized representation to direct a lengthy detour around a screen that prevented direct access to food. The rat's detours provided the evidence that the rat had indeed synthesized an overall representation of the environment from separate experiences with different portions of the detour.

Maier's experiments provide compelling evidence that a representation of the environment may be used by the rat to generate a novel, but purposeful course of action. The rat's performance defies explanation in terms of habits or differential response probabilities. The performances must derive from a biological machine with two distinct subsystems—a cognitive system that forms representations of the environment and an action system that employs the representation to control the path the machine takes in locomoting through the environment. After examining this performance of the rat and a similar performance by the digger wasp, in the hope of convincing the reader that this claim must be correct for a wide range of organisms, I will turn to a consideration of an explicit proposal as to how the cognitive and the action system interact.

The first of the two sets of information Maier's rats had to synthesize was acquired during the rats' unfettered exploration of the room portrayed in Fig. 11.1. The rats were free to run around in this room all day, every day, except

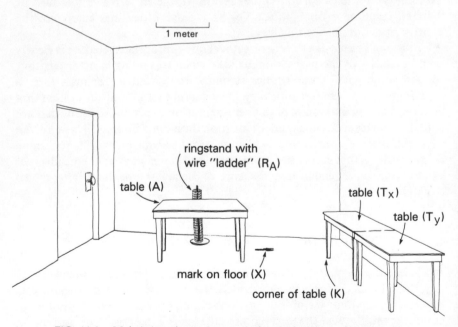

FIG. 11.1. Maier's experimental room during the lengthy period when the rats were free to explore. The rats could climb up and down the ringstand (R_A) to get on and off the table (A). K marks a point on the floor; X marks another point between K and the base of the ringstand. (This perspective drawing is based on Maier, 1929, Fig. 5a, and the accompanying narrative, pp. 22–25.)

during the periods when the experimenter was in the room testing their detour-taking behavior. The room had three tables, two of which (T_x and T_y) served only as landmarks. There was no way for the rats to climb onto these two tables. Table A, on the other hand, had a ringstand (Ringstand A) near it, which the rats could and did climb up and down to reach the table from the floor and vice versa—a maneuver at which these rats had become expert in the course of earlier experiments in other rooms.[1]

The second set of information was acquired just before the detour-taking test. The experimenter entered the room, confined the rats to a cage, and set up four elevated pathways and Table C, as shown in Fig. 11.2. From previous experiments, the rats were accustomed to running along such elevated boards and to climbing the supporting ringstands to get on and off them. When the set-up was in place, each rat was taught to run from a point on the floor near one of the ringstands, up the ringstand, and along the path to the new table, Table C, thence along the path to the food, F, on a corner of Table A that was screened off from the remainder of the table by a wire mesh screen. The training was minimal. The following is the protocol of the training received by one rat (based on Maier, 1929, p. 25).

1. Placed on Table C and allowed to run along the elevated path from Table C to the food on the screened off corner of Table A
2. Placed on Pathway 1 and allowed to run down it to Table C, thence to the food on Table A
3. Placed at the base of the Ringstand 1 and allowed to run up it to Pathway 1, thence to C and thence to the food on A
4. Placed at the point marked K, underneath a corner of the landmark, T_x, a little distance from Ringstand 1 and allowed to run to R1, up it, and thence to C and the food on A. The purpose of this fourth learning trial was to allow the rat to note the position of Ringstand 1 relative to a landmark (corner of T_x) that one might assume would be part of the representation of the room constructed during the periods of free exploration. This was presumed to be a crucial element in the rat's synthesis of the information gained from its two separate exploratory experiences—exploration of the room, and exploration of the set-up.

These four training trials constituted the second information gathering experience. Immediately after the fourth trial, the rat was placed on Table A, *on the other side of the wire mesh screen from the food.* It did the following (for illustration, see dashed route on Fig. 11.2):

---

[1] I am assuming from context that Table A and the Ringstand A were present during these periods. The published description does not make clear how much of the eventual "set up" was present during the periods of free exploration.

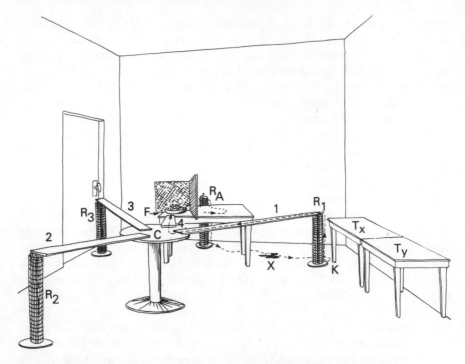

FIG. 11.2.   Maier's experimental room during the detour test and the brief period of training preceding the detour test. Food has been placed on a corner of A screened off from the rest of A. Table C has been set up and is the focus of three elevated pathways (1, 2, & 3), supported at their other ends by climbable ringstands (R_1, R_2 R_3). A path (4) leads from C to the food on the corner of A. The dashed trajectory is the route taken by the rat when it knew both the room and the path from K up R_1 to C and thence to food. (Based on Maier, 1929, p. 25.)

1. For 45 seconds it ran around the top of Table A in the vicinity of the screen that prevented its reaching the food directly.[2]
2. At the end of 45 seconds it began descending Ringstand A, reaching the floor when 52 seconds had elapsed since its initial placement on the table.
3. Ten seconds later (62 seconds elapsed time) it was under Table T_x and two seconds later (64 seconds elapsed time) it had begun to climb Ringstand 1.

[2]The rat had repeatedly experienced this dilemma in earlier experiments, which is part of the reason it did not persist much longer in its attempts to solve the problem by finding a way directly over, under, or around the screen. As we shall see, the rat's knowledge of an alternative route is the other part.

4. It reached the food 75 seconds after being placed on Table A, having descended Ringstand A, made a beeline across the floor in the direction of the Ringstand 1 (which it "knew" led up to a pathway to food), and completed its detour by climbing R1 and running along the previously taken elevated route to food.

The part of this performance that presents the most challenge to a theory of action is the beeline across the floor from Ringstand A to Ringstand 1. Twice during the four training trials the rat had been rewarded with food for climbing Ringstand 1 and running along the elevated path to food; hence, one could regard this segment of the detour performance as simply the performance of a (rapidly acquired!) "habit." One could make a similar argument for the segment of the detour involving the descent from Table A to the floor. The rat had been tested in a large number of detour problems, almost all of which had required it to use a ringstand to descend from the starting table. From problem to problem the rats stopped sooner and sooner trying to get at the food directly, in favor of descending the ringstand to the floor in search of a detour. One could therefore argue that this segment of the rat's test performance was a manifestation of a habit that had developed over successive detour problems. Thus, the first and last segments of the detour performance could be viewed as manifestations of acquired habits. One could imagine that previous experience had altered the structure of the system that generates action in such a way that the probability of generating these patterns of action in response to these stimuli was high. Insofar as one can explain the detour performance as a sequence of habits, one need not concede that the performance was based on or controlled by a representation of the environment. However, the middle segment of the detour performance, the beeline across the floor from the base of Ringstand A to the base of Ringstand 1, cannot be regarded as the performance of a habit. The rat in all probability never previously followed that course. Certainly, it never followed that course any more often than the numerous alternative courses it may pursue on departing from Ringstgand A.

That the beeline across the floor was based on the rat's representation of the environment traversed by this beeline is not yet evident, because I have not yet described Maier's control experiment. At this point, one might think that the explanation for this crucial middle segment of the detour performance trivial. Cannot we assume that upon reaching the floor the rat catches sight of R_1— the ringstand that when climbed has led to food? If so, then the beeline may be nothing more than an approach to a stimulus associated with food. And one could argue that such approach responses are at the core of most acquired habits (Spence, 1956). Alternatively, can we not imagine that during the two last training trials the rat left some distinctive odor mark at the base of R_1. If so, then the beeline may be nothing more than the following of some odor "beacon" to its source. We could use either of these alternative explanations were it not for Maier's control experiment, which rules them both out.

In the control experiment, Maier used exactly the same set-up. And this particular rat received six rather than four training trials. On the last three of these six training trials, the rat was placed at some point on the floor near the base of R_1 and allowed to climb R_1 and proceed along the elevated route to food on Table A. However, the set-up was in a room the rat was unfamiliar with! (See Fig. 11.3.) The rat *had no opportunity to form a representation of the relation between the points near the base of Ringstand 1 and the points near the base of Ringstand A*. Put another way, the rat had no opportunity to form a representation of the sequence of points that had to be traversed in making a beeline across the floor from Ringstand A to Ringstand 1.

If the middle segment of the rats detour, the beeline from R_A to R_1, were simply an approach to R_1 steered by visual or olfactory information emanating from R_1, then a lack of familiarity with intervening points should make no difference in the performance.[3] However, the protocol of the rat's performance in this control test shows that this lack of information about intervening points was decisive (For illustration, see dashed route in Fig. 11.3):

1. (Rat placed on Table A on other side of screen from food.) Rat spent the first 200 seconds alternatively running around top of Table A, trying to clamber over, under, or around the screen that separated it from the food, and looking down at floor from top of Table A.
2. At 200 seconds elapsed time it began descending Ringstand A, reaching the floor at 205 seconds, elapsed time.
3. For the next 40 seconds after reaching the floor it ran very rapidly in a zig-zag, here and there on the floor, *coming at one point within 1 meter of Ringstand 1*. (Note that whatever information about Ringstand 1 may or may not have been conveyed to the rat's senses by some kind of stimulus beacon—light, chemical, etc.—originating at Ringstand 1, it did not steer the rat's behavior even at a distance of 1 meter.)
4. At 245 seconds elapsed time, the rat arrived at Ringstand 2 and began climbing it. (Note that this is *not* Ringstand 1, the ringstand the rat climbed to reach the food on the training trials.)
5. Having climbed Ringstand 2, the rat ran down the unfamiliar Path 2 to Table C (familiar from the training trials), made a short side excursion down the unfamiliar Path 3, retraced its steps to Table C and thence to the food on the corner of A, reaching the food after 280 seconds elapsed time.

---

[3]Unless we assume a general unwillingness to traverse unfamiliar territory. However, the protocol of the performance in the control experiment will show that the rat was more than willing to rapidly traverse unfamiliar territory in search of a detour.

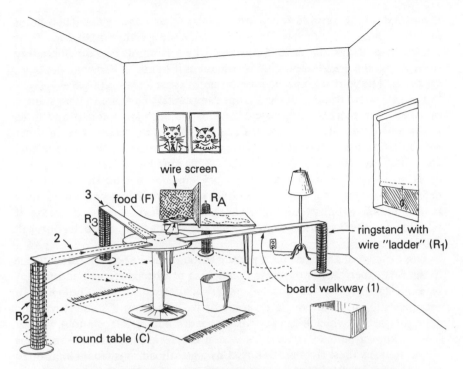

FIG. 11.3.   Maier's control experiment. The set-up is the same as in Fig. 11.2, but placed in a new room, a room the rat was unfamiliar with. The rat was trained to run to the food from a point near the base of R_1. However, it had not been allowed to explore the room prior to the setting up of the elevated pathways; hence it did not know how to get from R_4 to R_1. Notice that in its wanderings on the floor, the rat passed within 1 meter of R_1, without being attracted to it. (Based on Maier, 1929, p. 28.)

This control experiment, in which the rat was unfamiliar with points in the environment between the base of the Ringstand A and the base of Ringstand 1, shows that familiarity with these points was crucial to the rat's ability to steer a beeline from Ringstand A across the floor to Ringstand 1 in the preceding experiment. This performance cannot be conceived of as a habit, because it is in essence novel or unique. In exploring the floor during the first phase of Experiment 1 the rat will either:

(a) Never have steered that particular course away from Ringstand A

or

(b) Steered that course no more or less often than any of the numerous other courses the rat could take upon departing from Ringstand A.

In either case, the rat's behavior during the period of free exploration will not have given any occasion for forming the habit of running a beeline from

Ringstand A to Ringstand 1, or the habit of approaching any particular point on this beeline. Nor is the beeline explicable on the assumption that the rat is steered from Ringstand A to Ringstand 1 by a stimulus beacon emanating from Ringstand 1 and impinging on the rat as it stands at Ringstand A (e.g., an odor). The control experiment eliminates those explanations.

The rat's behavior as it departs from Ringstand A en route to Ringstand 1 must be controlled by a representation of the path from Ringstand A to Ringstand 1, to Path 1, to Table C, to the food. The behavior is, in other words, controlled by the rat's *knowledge* of the points lying between the goal and where the rat now is. The behavior, at the moment of leaving Ringstand A, is not dependent only on the sensory input acting on the rat at that moment. It depends also, somehow, on information contained in a representation—a map, of the environment—information that makes it possible for the behavior to anticipate the inputs that the behavior will produce.

This element of anticipation is present throughout the behavioral sequence in the first experiment, not just in the making of a beeline from Ringstand A to Ringstand 1. In the control experiment, the rat does not have a representation of the points intervening between Ringstand A and Ringstand 1, on the basis of which it can anticipate that descending Ringstand A will put it on a known path to food. This lacuna in the rat's representation of the situation is manifest right at the outset by a greatly diminished inclination to embark on a detour. In the first experiment, when there was no such lacuna in the rat's knowledge, it reached the food by means of a detour in 75 seconds. In the second experiment, when there was a lacuna, the rat spent over 200 seconds trying to get the food directly, before descending Ringstand A to search for an alternate route. Thus representational knowledge of the complete detour (or the lack of such knowledge) affects behavior at the outset.

If we grant that the rat, as it explores an environment, constructs a representation of that environment (a cognitive map), there is nothing mysterious about its being able to anticipate that following course x will bring it to point y. If you are driving across Arizona following a roadmap indicating that the highway you are on leads to Phoenix, you are not surprised when you eventually see a sign saying "Welcome to Phoenix." Nor would an observer of your behavior—an observer who believed you were using a map—be perplexed by the fact that your choosing that highway in the first place seemed to anticipate that it would bring you to Phoenix, even though nothing could be seen or heard (or smelled) of Phoenix when you first turned onto the highway. The mystery of this performance, once we grant your ability to have a map, lies in you, the map reader. The problem for the theory of action is to dispense with the little you, the homunculus that we seemingly place inside the rat's head when we say that the rat determines what course to follow by "reading" its map.

The rat's map, just like your roadmap, must contain representations of innumerable points in the environment and routes between them. How is it that only that part of the rat's representation lying between its goal and where it now is exerts control over its behavior? What is the process by which the rat's motivation (hunger) combines with its representation of the environment in order to control the rat's actions with respect to that part of the environment that the rat can perceive in the moment of acting?

This central problem in the theory of action arises even when we analyze the actions of much simpler creatures than the rat. It arises whenever the behavior of an organism seems clearly to make use of a representation of the environment, a cognitive map. And the behavior of at least some insects does just that! There is a substantial body of literature (Beusekom, 1948; van Iersel & van den Assem, 1965; Tinbergen, 1951, pp. 97-100) showing that bees, ants, and wasps make use of cognitive maps in moving back and forth between their nests and food sources. One of the most compelling studies was reported in a short paper by Thorpe (1950). That this study, showing so unequivocally that the digger wasp uses a cognitive map, should remain all but unknown to psychologists is a testimony to the power of perceptual defense. The study was reported in an era when the habit theory of knowledge reigned supreme. To suggest that creatures as lowly as the rat made and utilized cognitive maps was enough to earn one a reputation for soft-headedness. To publish in such an era observations showing that the digger wasp made and used so dubious an article was to publish what psychologists were simply not willing to hear or see. And so, they did not.

COGNITIVE MAPS IN THE DIGGER WASP

The female digger wasp digs a small burrow in the ground, in which she lays her eggs. She then covers the burrow over, rendering it all but invisible to the human eye (and to her eye as well, as we will see). She then makes a stereotyped reconnaissance flight in the vicinity of the burrow, and departs on a hunting flight that may carry her more than one hundred meters away. She is hunting other insects. When she catches one, she immobilizes it with her sting, carries it back to her burrow, reopens the burrow, and stuffs the immobile prey inside. When the eggs hatch, the larvae have the still living prey to feed on.

In an earlier study, Tinbergen and Kruyt (1938) showed that the wasp made a representation of landmarks in the vicinity of the burrow during her predeparture reconnaissance flight. She used this representation to steer herself to her burrow when she returned from the hunt. While wasps were away hunting, Tinbergen and Kruyt displaced the configuration of twigs and pine cones surrounding the burrow. When the wasps returned they went to where the hole "should have been" in relation to the configuration of twigs

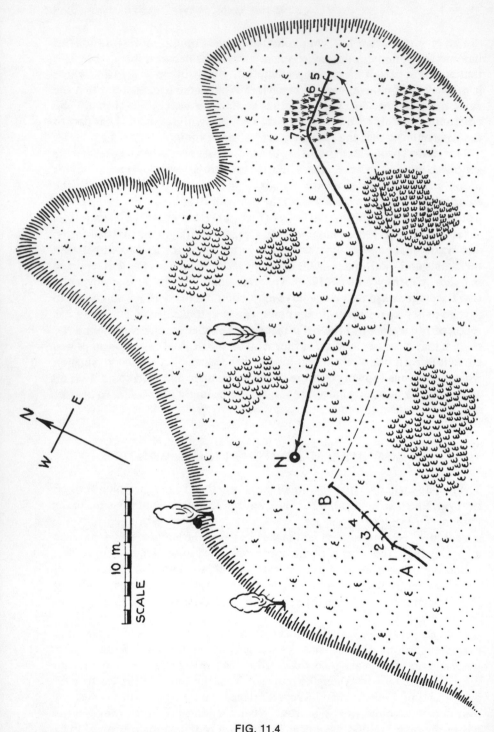

FIG. 11.4

and pine cones. Upon not finding the hole at the point where her cognitive map indicated it should be, the wasp became disoriented, wandered around more or less at random, and often failed to locate the burrow, even though the configuration of twigs and cones had been displaced by less than a meter. This study and a similar one by van Iersel and van den Assem (1965) show that the female wasp forms representations of visual configurations, and uses these to orient herself in the final stages of her approach to her burrow, much as a terrain-recognizing missile uses a representation of the terrain surrounding its target to steer itself in the final stages of its approach. These studies also pretty well rule out the possibility that the female uses some sort of scent mark in order to find her way home again. Such odor beacons ought to be most effective close to the burrow.

Since the female wasp is guided by representations of the terrain in the final stages of her approach, it seems likely that her entire flight home is steered by her representation of the terrain. It is, however, difficult to be sure, because one cannot readily follow a wasp in flight. The difficulty was overcome by Thorpe (1950). He studied a species that captures prey too large and heavy to be carried home in flight. Instead, these wasps drag their prey home.

Thorpe's original interest was in whether these wasps, busy dragging their prey home across the stony ground, would readily detour around novel obstacles placed in their path by the experimenter. The answer was a clear "yes." When confronted by a metal screen placed in their path, the wasps unhesitatingly either walked round or flew over the screen and immediately resumed their course. Encouraged by this result, Thorpe captured homeward bound wasps and rapidly transported them inside a dark box to release points as much as fifty meters away from the capture point, in a different direction from the nest the wasp was trying to reach. As can be seen from Fig. 11.4 and 11.5, the wasps made their way home from the release points with astonishing directness.

FIG. 11.4.   *(Opposite page.)* Diagram to show the route taken during detour and displacement experiments by an individual of A. pubescens engaged in dragging its prey towards the nest. Heavy line indicates course of insect. A = point at which first observed. Numbers 1–4 indicate points at which metal screen placed in its path for detour tests. B = point at which insect captured. Broken line indicates transfer of insect in box to release point C. Numbers 5–7 indicate further detour experiments. N = nest. The shading indicates a slight depression in an area of gravelly heath land with small patches and scattered plants of Erica and Calluna indicated by the symbol 'E' and with small birch trees (Betula) about 4–6 feet high indicated by the conventional tree symbol. The remaining symbol indicates tussocks of *juncus,* etc. Conditions: Bright sunshine. Noon, 27 July, 1947. Eversley Heath. Berkshire. Time taken by insect approximatley 15 minutes. (From Thorpe, 1950, by permission of E. J. Brill, publisher, and the author.)

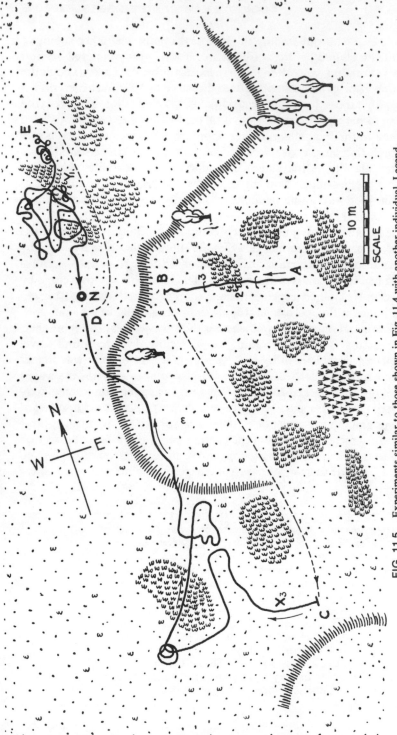

FIG. 11.5. Experiments similar to those shown in Fig. 11.4 with another individual. Legend and symbols as in Fig. 11.4. Capture points B & D. Release points C & E. Numbers 1-3 indicate points of detour tests. X_3 = site of a group of three short survey flights. Y_1 = site of a single survey flight. Conditions: Bright sunshine. Time 13.30. 27 July, 1947. Eversley Health, Berkshire. Time taken by insect on its routes—A to D, 20 minutes, E to N, 15 minutes. (From Thorpe, 1950, by permission of E. J. Brill, publisher, and the author.)

One of the attractions of studying the navigational abilities of animals is that there are a limited number of ways in which it is in principle possible to generate a given performance. The logic and limits of the possible methods have been subjected to intense study for centuries. Thus, one can conclude with some confidence that in order to find her way home the wasp consults a map (a representation of burrow location in relation to an earthbound set of stimulus sources or stimulus gradients). The three classes of alternative explanations are: (1) The use of a stimulus beacon emanating from home, for example, an odor. (2) Celestial navigation, that is, computing by reference to the sun's position one's latitude and longitude and then steering so as to reduce the discrepancy between momentary latitude and longitude and the latitude and longitude of the homesite. (The wasp's probable ability to use the sun and/or the earth's magnetic field as a compass reference will not solve the wasp's problem. It does not help to know which way is north unless you know whether you are north or south of where you wish to go![4]) (3) Double integrating the acceleration vector on the outward flight, *and* again while being displaced by the experimenter, to obtain one's displacement vector; then, steering on the homeward journey so as to reduce the displacement vector to zero.

The first class of explanation is pretty well ruled out by the earlier work of Tinbergen and Kruyt (1938). Any beacon emanating from the burrow site should be most effective at close range. But even at a range of a few meters the wasp cannot find a burrow when its relation to local landmarks has been perturbed (van Iersel & van den Assem, 1965). These findings argue against a beacon theory, of which odor theories are simply the most obvious subcategory. The second class, the celestial navigation explanation, would require the wasp to resolve the angular position of the sun to an accuracy of a fraction of a second of arc (a second is one 3600th of a degree!) *and* to have a clock as accurate as a good modern quartz-oscillator wrist watch (the kind that lose less than 15 seconds in a month). In short, celestial navigation on a scale of meters would require angle measurements and time measurements that would severely tax modern technology. A similar objection applies to the third alternative—inertial navigation by the double integration of the acceleration vector: The wasp would have to have an accelerometer and an integrator of dazzling precision. In short, we can be reasonably sure that wasps, like rats, make cognitive maps and use them to orient their movements. They either do that or they do something even more remarkable (e.g., perfect double-integration of acceleration).

---

[4]Although a compass is not sufficient, it may be used to maintain orientation, once the direction to be moved in has been determined.

GETTING RID OF THE HOMUNCULUS

I have belabored the wasp's homing abilities in order to emphasize that the use of cognitive maps is not some exotic characteristic of only the highest organisms. It is a widespread principle in the biology of action, one that may be profitably studied in a relatively simple organism such as the wasp. Psychology, however, has produced very few explicit theories as to how a cognitive map could control an animal's actions. Until recently, psychology refused to entertain such speculations, because the suggestion that some such process was at work was rejected out of hand by proponents of the habit theory of knowledge. They argued that theories involving representations of the world were inherently "mentalistic" (not physically realizable) and inevitably presupposed an homunculus. The existence of terrain-recognizing guided missles lays such metaphysical objections permanently to rest. Such missiles are beyond doubt physically realized entities and there is no little man inside them to make them work. So we can turn without embarrassment to a consideration of one of the few explicit theories psychology has produced concerning the process by which a cognitive map can control an organism's actions.

THE DEUTSCH MODEL

Deutsch (1960) proposes that the rat makes purely topological maps of its environment. These maps have but two kinds of elements: (1) Representations of points in the environment, and (2) connections between such representations. For the sake of concreteness one may think of the representations as snapshots, although modern perceptual studies show that this is too simpleminded. (Here, as elsewhere, I am deliberately ignoring many perplexing perceptual problems.) We will regard these snapshots as nodes in a cognitive map. Recognizing a point in a familiar environment is the operation of comparing the sensory input from a point in that environment to the snapshots (nodes) in memory until one finds the snapshot corresponding to the point.

The connections between snapshots may be thought of as signal transmitting wires that link together the nodes of the cognitive map. Two snapshots (two representations) are wired together if the rat has encountered the corresponding points in the environment in immediate succession. If the rat has encountered Point A in the environment and immediately afterward point B, then shapshots a and b are wired together in memory. If immediately after B, the rat encountered C, then snapshot c will be wired to snapshot b, etc. If the points A, B, C in the environment form a triangular configuration, so that the rat has encountered A immediatley after C (or vice versa), then c will be connected to *a*; hence *a* will now have direct connections to both *b* and *c*. There is no limit on the number of other snapshots to which a given snapshot may be connected. However, in all cases two snapshots (nodes on the map) are directly connected only if the animal may progress directly from one corresponding point to the other corresponding point in the environment. Thus, the pattern of connectivity between nodes in memory captures the topology of the points in the environment represented by those nodes.

So far I have described what the two kinds of elements on a Deutschian cognitive map represent. The nodal elements represent points in the environment. The connections between these nodes represent the fact that the point represented by a node may be reached directly from the point represented by another node, and vice versa. *Neither the nodes nor the connections between nodes encode instructions for action!* The rat's representation of the environment specifies which points may be reached from which, just as does a roadmap. It does not specify which way the rat should go any more than does a roadmap. One motorist may be using a roadmap to drive from New York to Detroit, while another uses the same map to drive from Philadelphia to Boston. Clearly, the map the motorists are using does not by itself specify which way to drive. Similarly, the kind of cognitive map Deutsch posits does not in and of itself give any suggestions as to how a rat possessing such a map will act. The map is what the rat knows. Knowing what an organism knows does not enable us to predict what that organism will do (although the habit theory of knowledge would have us think so). Yet, just as clearly, the animal's knowledge is *an* important determinant of what it does. So how can one conceptualize the relation between its knowledge and what it does? How, in other words, can a cognitive map enter into the control action?

In order, to answer this question we again have to consider the organism's motivation. If we know both what an organism wants and what it knows, then we feel intuitively that we can predict what the organism will do. If one knows the motorist in Pennsylvania wants to get to Pittsburgh and one knows the roadmap he is using, then one can predict where he will turn off the turnpike, and so on.

What I mean by motivation is the notion of motivation put forward in the preceding chapter. Motivation is a potentiating signal arising at a node in the upper levels of the motor hierarchy. It is conducted from node to node within the motor hierarchy by the connections between nodes. Nodes are potentiated in proportion to the strength of the potentiating signal they receive. The selective potentiation of the coordinations controlled by these nodes imparts to behavior its overall cohesiveness, its goal-directedness.

In Deutsch's theory, motivation is likewise a signal arising high in the action hierarchy. The signal is conducted through the cognitive map from node to node along the connecting elements. And, the strength of the signal reaching a given node in the cognitive map plays a role analogous to that of selective potentiation. In other words, the flow of a motivational signal through the cognitive map serves to organize an action sequence, just as does the flow of a motivating signal from node to node within the action-hierarchy. The difference is that "nodes" in the action hierarchy are circuits controlling a pattern of action, whereas "nodes" on a cognitive map are representations of points in an environment.

There are four central assumptions in Deutsch's suggestion as to how motivation and the cognitive map combine to control action: (1) The assumption that certain nodes in a cognitive map are automatically connected to particular sources of motivational signals. (2) The assumption that the motivational signal spreads decrementally through a map from a point of entry. (3) The assumption that a telotaxis is the type of response unit generating the action. (4) And, finally, an assumption as to how the relative strengths of the motivating signals reaching nodal elements in the map determine which point in the external environment will be the focal stimulus for the telotaxis. We consider them in order:

1. If the animal perceives a point in the environment having certain characteristics relevant to the function of an upper-level node in the action hierarchy, then the representation of that point on the cognitive map is automatically connected to that upper-level node. For example, if the rat perceives food, the node representing that food is automatically connected to the hunger center in the action hierarchy. The hunger center in the action hierarchy is where potentiating signals arise when the animal is undernourished. The connections emanating from this are such that these signals selectively potentiate food-producing behavior. The assumption that food nodes on the animal's cognitive maps are likewise connected to this hunger center means that a potentiating signal from the hunger center is automatically conducted to nodes representing food. If a node representing food is in turn connected to a node representing a point in a mapped environment, then the hunger signal will pass from the food node into the cognitive map.

2. Once a motivational signal enters a map it is conducted *decrementally* from node to node by way of the connections between nodes. The signals exiting from a node are always weaker than the signals entering a node. The nodes connected to the food node receive a weaker signal than does that food node itself. The nodes connected to these nodes receive a still weaker signal; and so on, for ever more remote nodes. The more remote a node is from the node where a motivational signal enters, the weaker the potentiating signal it receives. Put another way, the entry of a motivational signal into a map sets up a motivational gradient on the map: Nodes near the node of entry receive a

strong signal; nodes far away receive a weaker signal. The remoteness of a node is determined solely by the number of intervening nodes that a potentiating signal must traverse.[5]

3. The third assumption concerns the unit of action, the unit that generates commands to the muscles during sequences controlled by the cognitive map. Deutsch assumes that the unit is always the same, namely a telotaxis. A telotaxis, remember, has two basic subunits, a unit controlling the animal's orientation and a unit generating forward locomotion. The unit controlling orientation is a servomechanistic unit. It computes the deviation between the animal's body axis and an imaginary line leading from the animal to a point in the external environment (the telos). If there is any deviation, the output from this unit commands the turning musculature, inducing a turn that reduces the deviation. Hence, the orienting subunit keeps the animal pointed at the telos. The other subunit, the locomoting subunit, propels the animal forward. Together the two subunits generate an approach to the telos.

4. The fourth assumption specifies how the strengths of the potentiating signals reaching the nodes of the cognitive map determine which point in the environment will at a given moment be the telos (orienting point) for the telotaxis. First, one must remember that only currently perceived points in the external environment may function as the telos at any given moment! The animal cannot use a stimulus it does not perceive as a cue for orienting. No extrasensory perception is allowed! Hence, the question becomes this: Of the several points in the environment that the animal perceives at a given moment, which point will be the telos for the animal's telotaxis? Which point will serve as the perceptual reference point in the computations of the subunit that controls orientation? Deutsch assumes that this is determined by the relative strengths of the potentiating signals reaching the nodes that correspond to the currently perceived points. The animal is assumed to recognize the currently perceived points: It compares the sensory inputs from them to the representations (nodes) on its map, thereby establishing which points in the environment correspond to which nodes on the map. This recognition makes it possible to decide which point will serve as the momentary telos: The point whose corresponding node receives the strongest potentiating signal will serve as the telos.

If, in the course of approaching that point, the animal perceives a new point whose node receives an even stronger signal, the new point will take over the role of the telos, and so on. Hence, the rat always orients up the motivational gradient on its map. It orients toward the environmental point whose

---

[5]Actually, Deutsch's assumptions regarding what determines the strength of the motivational signal received by a node are more complex than this. I am deliberately simplifying.

representative on the map receives the strongest potentiating signal. As it moves toward that point it encounters points whose representatives are yet higher on the motivational gradient.

These four assumptions insure that whenever an animal is in a familiar environment, an environment for which it has a map, it will move from point to point in a sequence determined by the motivational gradient on the map. The rat always moves *up* the motivational gradient, toward points that are ever closer to the point represented by the node at which the potentiating signal enters the map. This, then, is a (considerably simplified) account of Deutsch's procedure for combining motivation and a representation of the world—the cognitive map—in order to generate a sequence of action that reflects the animal's knowledge. The theory accounts for the ability of the rat and the wasp to pursue direct paths across known environments to specific goals (the food in the rat's case, the burrow in the wasp's case), even though they have never before taken those particular routes to those particular goals. It explains, in other words, what habit theories of knowledge could not explain. And it gives theories of cognition an indication of at least one explicit process by which cognitions might enter into the control of action. To get a better feel for the theory, let us consider how it explains Maier's observations.

During the periods when Maier's rats were free to explore the room and Table A, they acquired a representation of this environment. This representation is illustrated in Fig. 11.6. During the second phase of training, when the elevated pathways are set up and the rat is shown a route to the food, the rat acquires a representation of a path from a familiar point in the room, point K, to food on the corner of Table A. The addition of this representation is illustrated in Fig. 11.7. Note that one node in this representation of the path to food is also a node in the rat's representation of the room: The node that represents the point K appears on both representations. During the free exploration phase of the experiment, this node has become connected to nodes representing adjacent points in the room, as illustrated in Fig. 11.6. During the second phase, the path-to-food training, this same node is connected to the node representing the ringstand R_1, as illustrated in Fig. 11.7. This node interconnects representations of the world derived from two separate experiences. It is the interconnection at node K that synthesizes the knowledge gained from the separate experiences into a single map. This map controls the rat's detour behavior. Finally, note that the nodes representing points on Table A near the ringstand (R_A) are no longer connected to the node representing the corner where the food is. The screen prevents travel from the food corner to other points on the table; hence these connections are broken.

If there were no motivational gradient imposed on the map, there would be nothing to organize and direct its use. Nothing about maps, qua maps, gives any direction to the system concerned with the generation of action. The rat's cognitive maps, like the roadmaps one gets from a filling station, specify what

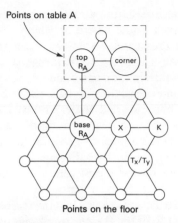

Points on table A

Points on the floor

FIG. 11.6. The rat's representation of Maiers experimental room at the end of the period of free exploration. Each circle is a node. A node represents a point in the environment. The circle labeled X is the rat's representation of the point X on the floor between the point K and the base of the ringstand, R_A. (For the actual environment see Fig. 11.1.) Note that the geometrical relations between points in the environment are not encoded. The lines connecting nodes represent only the fact that one point may be reached from another. The map is *topological*, that is, angles and distances on any drawing of the map are meaningless. Any other drawing that preserved the same pattern of internodal connections would be an equally good drawing of the rat's map.

FIG. 11.7. The rat's representation of the environment after the second phase of training, the phase in which it is shown a route to food from the point K, up the new ringstand (R_1), along the elevated pathway (1) to the new table (C) and thence along the pathway (4) to food on the screened off corner of the old Table A. The node representing the corner of Table A is no longer connected to the nodes representing the other points on Table A, because the screen prevents the rat from going to these other points from the corner, and vice versa.

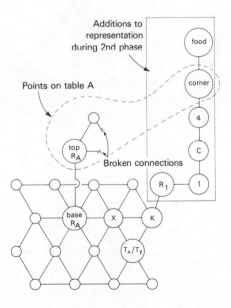

leads to what, *not* where one should go given where one is. A roadmap is no use to a man who doesn't know where he wants to go. He will perish by indecision at the first crossroads. Similarly, a cognitive map without a motivational gradient on it is of no consequence to a rat of action.

However, the representation of the food on the corner of Table A is connected to a source of potentiating signals, the hunger node in the action hierarchy. If the rat is hungry—and Maier's rat was—then the potentiating signal arising at the hunger node spreads into the cognitive map and is conducted decrementally from node to node, as illustrated in Fig. 11.8. This decremental conduction of the potentiating signal to ever more remote nodes on the cognitive map establishes a motivational gradient on the map. And, this gradient serves to direct the rat's action.

When the rat turns in frustration away from the screen that blocks its access to food, it perceives the top of the R_A, the ringstand that leads to the floor. Or perhaps it only perceives a point on the route across the table top to the top of R_A; the result will be the same in either case. The node representing the top of R_A, or the point en route to R_A, will be receiving a *stronger* potentiating signal than will the nodes representing other perceived points not lying directly on the route to food. All of the nodes, of course, will be receiving some signal. But, the signal reaching nodes that do not lie directly on the route to food will have had to pass through more intervening nodes than will the signal reaching the node that lies on the direct route. Hence, the signal reaching these off-the-route nodes will be weaker than the signal reaching the on-the-route nodes.

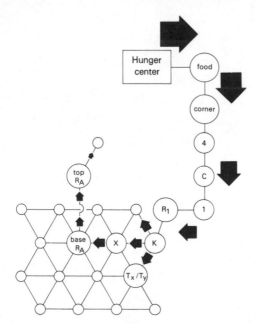

FIG. 11.8. The motivational gradient on the rat's map is indicated by the shrinking arrows emanating from the Hunger Center, to which the representation of food is connected. Upon reaching the node K, the potentiating signal spreads in all directions, but only its spread along the detour is shown.

The rat's telotaxic subunit is so constructed that it always uses as the telos the perceived point whose node receives the strongest potentiating signal. Hence, the rat will always orient toward the points lying on the most direct *known* route to food. (There may well be more direct routes in the environment, but not represented on the map, hence not known.)

In this manner the rat's telotaxic response unit, operating under the direction of the motivational gradient on the cognitive map, carries the rat down Ringstand A, toward the point represented by the node X, a point between K and the base of Ringstand A.

When the base of Ringstand 1 is perceived, it is immediately approached even though the rat thereby shortcuts the point K, whose node interconnected the maps. If the rat is standing at the point represented by the node X and perceiving the points represented by the nodes labelled R_1 and K, it will orient toward R_1, even though the potentiating signal to the node X, comes from the node K. The action system pays no heed to where signals come from, only to the relative strengths of the signals reaching the nodes that represent currently perceived points. Hence, the system automatically takes short cuts whenever they present themselves. Shortcuts, on the other hand, were always an embarrassment to habit theories of knowledge. The taking of novel shortcuts, which is a frequently observed aspect of animal behavior, illustrates in a simple way that the animal's actions are not bound by habit. Habit theories of knowledge always had difficulty explaining the appearance of nonhabitual but nonetheless intelligent responses, such as taking a shortcut.

When the rat's representation of the currently perceived space around him is not connected however remotely to a source of potentiating signals, then there can be no motivational gradient on the representation. Hence, there will be no coherent utilization of the representation. Such was the case in another control experiment (not previously mentioned). The rat was run in a familiar room without being shown a path from the floor to food (i.e., with no second phase). The behavior under these conditions was much like the behavior in the first control experiment, where the rat was unfamiliar with the room. In both control experiments, deliberately contrived gaps in the rat's representations of the world prevented potentiating signals from reaching the nodes representing intervening points on a detour. Gaps in the rat's knowledge stopped the flow of the signals, thus depriving the action system of the signals needed to determine the point toward which it must orient.

The explanation of these control experiments highlights a central feature of Deutsch's theory. It is the flow of a potentiating signal *by way of representations of points not yet perceived* to the representations of points currently perceived that gives behavior the property we term foresight. The flow of a potentiating signal through the map mediates the effect that knowledge of what lies ahead has on current behavior. Current behavior is steered by the strengths of the potentiating signals reaching the representations of what is currently perceived. In order to reach those representations, the potentiating signals must pass through rerpresentations of points not currently perceived, points that will be perceived only if a particular course of action is taken. The intervening representations help determine whether that particular course of action will be followed insofar as they block or do not block the propagation of the potentiating signal. The services of the homunculus are now no longer required! The function of looking ahead on the map has been realized by a potentiating signal that is conducted decrementally from element to element within a map.

I have presented this sketch of Deutsch's theory because it is one of the few explicit suggestions that have been made for getting rid of the homunculus in explaining actions whose direction seems clearly to derive from a cognitive representation. We have no idea what the neurophysiological embodiment of these ideas might be. It would be folly, however, to count that as a strike against the theory. The principal obstacle to constructing a plausible neurophysiological embodiment of this circle of ideas is that no one knows what the neurophysiological embodiment of a representation might look like. Indeed, we have only the vaguest notions of what the neurophysiological embodiment of any sort of genuine memory might be. That, however, is a problem for neurophysiologists and reductionistic physiological psychologists (like myself) not a problem for psychologists. The behavioral evidence that the brains of animals form and store representations of selected aspects of the world is overwhelming.

A close reading of Maier and other sources (e.g., Olton & Samuelson, 1976) suggests that the rat's representation of familiar spaces is more nearly Euclidean than topological, that is, the maps directly represent distance instead of representing it only secondarily (as the number of intervening points). It also appears that the rat uses perceived landmarks to chart a course through the represented space rather than approaching one adjacent point after the other, as Deutsch assumes. If true, these observations require considerable revision of the theory. This is not the place to embark on such a revision. Suffice it to say that the key notion of a potentiating signal spreading through the representation from an origin at the goal is still required.

This key notion may also be applied to other sorts of representations. One may imagine, for example, maps whose nodal elements represent states, and whose connective elements represent actions that bring about one state given another state. Thus, for example, one node could represent a Skinner box with no food in the hopper; another node could represent the same box with food in the hopper; and connecting these nodes will be an element representing the action of pressing the lever in the Skinner box. Such a representation might arise in a rat whose experience had shown that pressing the lever produced food. In order to explain how a representation of this sort can determine a course of action, it is again tempting to employ the notion of a potentiating signal that spreads decrementally from the representation of the goal state to the representations of sub-goal states (states en route to the goal state) by way of connective elements representing actions. This example is intended *only* to suggest the possible range of representations that Deutsch's basic notion might help translate into action. It would seem pointless to proceed further until experimental work has more sharply delineated the constraints a theory must satisfy. It is, however, reassuring to have at least one homunculus-free model of the manner in which cognition may organize action. Cognitive theorists have always rejected the accusation that they believed in homunculi. But, they have not always been able to suggest how the link between cognition and action could be achieved without the aid of Skinner's little button-pusher in the head.

12 Some Recent Trends

LINKS WITH COGNITIVE PSYCHOLOGY

During the Behaviorist epoch in psychology there was a prejudice against any sort of theorizing that imputed an elaborated structure to the processes that generate animal and human behavior. It was felt that such theorizing risked returning the science of behavioral analysis to some sort of prescientific mentalism. A welcome gust of fresh thinking swept into psychology when the cognitive approach supplanted the stimulus-response approach. The tendency to conceptualize perceptual and mnemonic processes by analogy to computerized information processing allowed one to talk about the structure of internal processes in a way that sounded sufficiently hardheaded. On the other hand, the dominance of the information processing viewpoint made the problem of action recede into the background. Computers are symbol manipulating machines. They take symbols as inputs and produce symbols as outputs. The structure of overt computer action bears little if any interesting resemblance to the structure of animal action. Hence, in modern psychology "theories of perception abound, [while] theories of action are conspicuous by their absence" (Turvey, 1977, p. 211).

One senses, however, a restlessness among cognitive psychologists about the absence of action. Their inattention to the problem has been a matter of oversight, not disdain. In trying to figure out how we figure things out they have not had time to wonder how we translate the results into action. Here and there the attention of cognitive psychologists has turned from the contemplation of ever more intricate associative structures in ever more numerous kinds of memory and toward the problem of organizing action. Cognitive psychologists who let their attention wander in this direction are likely to complain with Turvey that psychology has no theory of action (e.g., Weimer, 1977). This book was composed in the belief that this is not so. Some psychologists, mostly on the biologically oriented periphery of psychology, have a theory of action, a theory for which there is a great deal of detailed evidence. The preceding chapters articulate that theory and illustrate its major concepts with examples drawn from the ethological and neurobehavioral study of animal action. This final chapter links these concepts to some recent work in cognitively oriented human and animal psychology. Such linkages may encourage the rest of psychology to consider seriously what might be called the neuroethological theory of action (in recognition of its roots in behavioral neurobiology and ethology).

THE TURVEY THEORY

The most ambitious attempt to relate cognitive psychology to the organization of action appears in a recent chapter by Turvey (1977). Turvey draws heavily on a school of thought founded by Nicholas Bernstein, the Russian mathematician and behavioral biologist who devoted his life to the detailed analysis of human and animal movements. His work was little known abroad until the publication of a collection of his papers in English translation (Bernstein, 1967), but his influence on a large and active group of Russian behavioral physiologists was profound (cf. Gelfand, Gurfinkel, Tsetlin, & Shik, 1971). His ideas have been developed mathematically by Greene (1972), although it remains to be seen whether this largely schematic development can be fruitfully applied.

The other major source for Turvey's model of how action is organized is the concept of hierarchically structured reflex ensembles advanced by Easton (1972). Easton's treatment of action is strikingly similar to the one advanced in the preceding chapters of this book. The Turvey conceptualization also has much in common with the one presented here, but the overlap is not immediately apparent because of the mathematical metaphors through which the concepts are advanced. Turvey (1977), for example, formulates "... a most provocative and important hypothesis, namely, that tunings parameterize the equivalence classes of functions specified by executive procedures" (p. 239). Such formulations are enough to make anyone retreat to the restful contemplation of associative structures.

Major Themes

Degrees of Freedom. There are several major themes in Turvey's synthesis. First, he emphasizes the "degrees of freedom" problem. Bernstein used this phrase to refer to the mechanical latitude inherent in the skeletomuscular system. A ball joint like the shoulder, moved by elastic elements like the muscles, has very complex and unconstrained mechanical properties. It can move in lots of ways (cf. Weiss, Chapter 8). This poses a problem for the nervous system, whose job it is to make these mechanically unwieldy members move in orderly and functional ways. Turvey broadens the term to refer to the innumerable ways in which any action may be performed, whether the action is a single movement or a complex pattern of behavior. The cockroach, for example, never runs in quite the same way on two separate occasions. Every scamper it makes is made under conditions that vary in some detail from the conditions during any previous run. A careful analysis of the timing and magnitude of the signals sent to leg and trunk muscles during the course of each run will reveal corresponding differences in the details of these motor signals. The number of different ways of running—the degrees of freedom—is very large. The higher levels of the nervous system, the levels that decide whether it is advisable to run for it, cannot be charged with specifying the complete set of commands required to get the muscles to do just the right thing. The list of specifications would be too long and too many unforseeable lower-level aspects of the circumstances would have to be taken into account.

Hierarchical Structure.   Turvey's second theme is that the nervous system resolves the degrees of freedom problem by means of a hierarchical command structure. From higher levels of the hierarchy issue signals that specify the kind of action that is appropriate in the light of high-level, global analysis of sensory input. Each lower level elaborates on these signals in the light of specialized sensory information that it receives, sending to the level below a more richly patterned output, an output that contains more detail about how the action signaled from above is to be translated into neuromuscular activity. Every lower level adds still more detail. At the bottom of the hierarchy, there issues forth an immensely complex and elaborate flow of signals to the muscles. This complex and endlessly detailed flow of motor neuron signals governs the biomechanical realization of the action.

The modern understanding of the control of walking, presented in Chapter 5 and again in Chapter 8, illustrates Turvey's conception of how the hierarchical structure of command resolves the degrees of freedom problem. There are only two degrees of freedom in the signal by which the highest levels of the brain (the cerebrum or cerebral ganglion or diencephalon) command the lower levels of the nervous system to walk. All possible walking outputs are obtained by varying the strengths of two signals. One signal specifies direction of locomotion (forward or backward); the other specifies average speed (see Fig. 8.11). Chapters 5 and 8 explain how this command, with its two degrees of freedom, is elaborated by lower and lower levels of the action hierarchy to produce a motorneuron output that has as many degrees of freedom as there are motor neurons, which is to say a large number of degrees of freedom.

The Relative Autonomy of Lower Units of Organization. Turvey's third theme is that the hierarchical structure has several levels, with relatively autonomous units of organization at each level. These units receive commands from higher levels, commands that indicate what is desired, so to speak. The units of organization at any level are relatively autonomous in that it is left to them to determine the pattern of commands which must be issued to still lower levels in order to realize the desired action. The control of locomotion may again be used to illustrate this concept. The chicken running around with its head cut off is a barnyard manifestation of the autonomy of the neural system that generates locomotion. The system functions perfectly nicely, if also perfectly aimlessly, in the absence of any cerebral instruction.

The phenomenon of locomotion in the absence of any patterned set of commands from higher centers can also be produced in the laboratory with mammals. A cat or dog whose brain has been transected at high midbrain levels will show normally patterned, albeit awkward locomotion when appropriate sites in the lower midbrain are electrically stimulated (Shik & Orlovsky, 1976). In such cases, the electrical stimulation is the source of the command to walk. Only one parameter of the electrical stimulation—its strength—has any appreciable effect on the pattern of walking. The stronger the stimulation, the faster the animal attempts to walk. The circuit that organizes locomotion is autonomous to such an extent that it can translate a walk command that has only one dimension of variation (one degree of freedom) into the richly patterned set of commands that activate the animal's muscles.

Even the speed of walking is not really fixed by the strength of the electrical stimulation. If the cat walks upon a treadmill whose speed is independently varied, proprioceptive input overrides the speed specified by the electrical stimulation, preventing the animal from walking faster than the ground will move under it. The trigger-delaying reflex described in Chapter 5 is an even lower level instance of a subordinate unit asserting its judgment to override an instruction from above when conditions are not propitious for the execution of that instruction. So, lower units are autonomous in two senses: It is left to them to fill in the details. And, they may override an instruction in response to factors that were not taken account of by the higher unit in formulating the instruction.

Control by Parameter Adjustment ("Tuning"). The fourth theme in Turvey's paper is that higher units exert control over lower units largely by altering two kinds of parameters: parameters of the units themselves and parameters of the pathways by which the units interact. A parameter is something that determines the kind of output a system will give, without actually generating an output itself. Consider for example, a piano or guitar. Turning the tuning pegs to tighten or loosen the strings does not produce music, but it profoundly affects the music that is produced. The tightness of each string is a parameter of a piano or a guitar. Signals that adjust these parameters are called parameter adjusting or tuning inputs to distinguish them from activating inputs like the key-strikes and string-plucks. A signal from above that alters the strength or duration of a reflex response without actually triggering the response is said to tune the reflex. Eccles and Lundberg (1959) have demonstrated electrophysiologically that signals descending from the brain may tune a reflex by acting on the interneurons of the reflex arc. Similarly, a signal from above that shuts off one set of interoscillator coupling pathways and turns on another alters the interaction between leg-stepping units by changing the parameters of the coupling circuitry (see Fig. 8.11).

It should be obvious from the above two illustrations that the concept of control by parameter adjustment is the concept we are already familiar with under two headings: (1) control by selective potentiation and depotentiation; and (2), facilitation of agonistic units and inhibition of atagonistic units. Chapters 6, 8, 9, 10, and 11 provide a great many illustrations of control by potentiating and depotentiating selected neural pathways in lower level circuitry.

Potentiation is an increase in the ease with which a unit may be activated. Alternatively, potentiation is an increase in the activity seen in response to suprathreshold activation. Either way, potentiation is a change in a parameter (excitability) of a unit. Facilitation is also an increase in the excitability of a unit, in other words, a parameter change (Chapters 2 and 3). I have restricted the use of facilitation to parameter changes produced in one unit of organization by signals from another (agonistic) unit at roughly the same level (see also Easton, 1972; Pal'tsev, 1967). The effect, however, is the same as potentiation, and so, probably, is the neurophysiological mechanism (cf. Fig. 2.8 and 6.9 and accompanying text). The distinction between potentiating a subordinate unit and facilitating a peer unit is heuristic only and should be abandoned wherever and whenever it proves awkward. Turvey and Easton use the term "tuning" in both senses.

Turvey, drawing on a large body of work by the Russian school, calls attention to a third use of tuning—in the class of voluntary movements initiated directly from the highest levels of the brain rather than by low-level activating inputs. Experiments by Gurfinkel, et al. (1971) and Kots and Zhukov (1971) show that in a reaction-time experiment, where the human subject must make some simple limb movement immediately upon hearing some cue, the brain varies the parameters of a great many spinal reflexes *after* it hears the cue but *before* it sends down the signal that initiates muscle contraction. To speak metaphorically, before the President can tell a low level civil servant to do something he has to warn the man's superiors and coworkers. Otherwise, the abrupt intrusion of a command from the top upsets the routine and creates a muddle, as most Presidents learn to their sorrow. For electrophysiological evidence of such forewarnings, see Evarts (1973).

Coalition Heterarchy. Turvey also argues that action is heterarchically organized. By this he appears to mean partly that the control of higher units over lower units is gubernatorial rather than dictatorial: The higher domains "enter into 'negotiations' with lower domains in order to determine how the higher representation [of an action] shall be stated" (Turvey, 1977, p. 224). This notion is very similar to the concept of selective potentiation from above delimiting the subset of action options (introduction to Chapter 10).

Turvey also draws an analogy to the heterarchic concept in information processing (Falk, 1972; Minsky & Papert, 1972; Sutherland, 1973). The analogy implies that Turvey also understands under "coalition/heterarchy" something akin to the concept of a relative hierarchy, a hierarchy in which the organizing powers of a seemingly higher unit may be called upon by a seemingly lower unit to help that lower unit carry out its function (cf. Chapter 10).

Terminology and Metaphors

Turvey follows Easton in calling a unit of action, whether elementary or compound, a "coordinative structure." He also follows Easton in calling elementary units of action "reflexes." Easton and Turvey use the term reflex to refer to any kind of elementary unit of action, explicitly including what I have termed oscillators and servomechanisms. In fact Turvey regards the muscle spindle system as "the fundamental servomechanism (or, more aptly, the fundamental coordinative structure)" (1977, p. 232).

The muscle spindle system is a sensorimotor structure much studied by neurophysiologist, which, on the basis of its anatomy and electrophysiology, certainly appears to be a servomechanism of some kind. Merton (1973) describes it and argues that it functions as a feedback mechanism that adjusts the motor commands to the muscle in such a way that the muscle contracts at the desired rate or maintains a desired length in the face of varying loads (see also, von Holst & Mittelstaedt's treatment, p. 198–200).

In fact, however, it is unclear what the behavioral function of the muscle spindle system is. There is a fair amount of evidence that it often does not function in the traditional manner envisaged by Merton and Turvey (Crago, Houk, & Hasan, 1976; Goodwin & Luschei, 1974, 1975; Prochazka,

Westerman, & Zicone, 1977; Taylor & Cody, 1974; Vâllbo, 1974) and rather little evidence that it ever does (Granit, 1975). The muscle spindle system illustrates the frequently made point that one can know a very great deal about the anatomy and electrophysiology of a system and yet have a very poor understanding of its behavioral function.

In any event, we should probably not regard the muscle spindle system as *the* fundamental unit in the action hierarchy. Severing all of the sensory nerves at the point where they enter the spinal cord (deafferentation) destroys the muscle spindle system in every muscle below the neck, but leaves most basic patterns of action intact, even in primates (Taub, 1976). If the muscle spindle system were really the fundamental coordinative structure in the sense in which carbon is the fundamental element in biochemistry, then the findings from deafferentation studies would be tantamount to the discovery that the removal of carbon did not fundamentally alter the basic biochemicals!

Turvey (1977), again following Easton, calls the reflexes, that is, the elementary units of action, the "basis' of the set of all . . . functional groupings and hence of the infinitely large set of all acts," explaining that he means 'basis' in the sense in which it is used in the mathematical theory of vector spaces (p. 219). This mathematical metaphor is not used casually. It is the point of departure for much of the subsequent metaphorical development of Turvey's argument. The metaphor is unfortunate—opaque for those who do not know linear algebra and misleading for those who do.

A vector is an ordered string of numbers, each number representing a "dimension." Thus [3, 59, 7] is a three-dimensional vector. A vector space is a set of such vectors, frequently an infinite set. For example, the three-dimensional vector space of the integers is the set of all possible three-integer strings. A basis for such a space is a selection of vectors from which all other vectors in the space can be generated by addition (adding each number in one string to the corresponding number in another) and scalar multiplication (multiplying each number in a string by any constant number, the so-called scalar).

The process of obtaining a very large, even infinite number of vectors by the addition and scalar multiplication of the very few vectors required to form a basis seems at first blush somewhat like the process of building up a very large number of complex behaviors by combining elementary units of behavior. The problem is that the vectors produced by combining other vectors do not increase in complexity and do not incorporate in any real sense the vectors that were combined to produce them. The vector produced by adding two basic vectors is just another string of 3 numbers, no more nor less complex than the two strings that were added. In fact, one can always create a new basis for the space simply by replacing either of two supposedly basic vectors with the vector that is their sum. With one technical exception, any vector in the whole space is as eligible to be a member of "the" basic set as any other. If we took the vector space metaphor seriously, we would conclude that every act was as elementary as any other.

Turvey's subsequent mathematical metaphors, as for example the notion that "action concepts" are "operations defined over the set of coordinative structures," may be faulted on similar grounds. On the other hand, his sketch of how different aspects of the visual array enter into the genesis of action is important. Some aspects, for example, the form and identity of a moving object, are processed at the highest levels and enter into the decision to initiate a complex behavioral sequence, such as predation. Others, such as the pattern of point flow in the optic array—see Gibson (1958)—enter at lower levels and control the animal's orientation and gait from moment to moment.

SKILLS AND SCHEMAS

Hierarchical Organization

Studies of the acquisition of skilled action by telegraphers (Bryan & Harter, 1899), typists (Book, 1908), athletes, craftsmen, and industrial workers, (Bernstein, 1967), and experimental subjects controlling a moving target by pressing keys on a computer console (Pew, 1966) have repeatedly demonstrated that skilled action is hierarchically organized. The individual movements that comprise the skill are first perfected to the point where they can be made rapidly and accurately with little variation. Then they become welded together into "chunks." Chunks are larger units of action, as for example the typing of whole words rather than individual letters.

In other words, the process of skill acquisition parallels the process of behavioral evolution. First, a low level unit of action that has a function in its own right is acquired—striking the "a" key with one's left little finger, for example. Later this unit is brought under the control of higher units, units that sequence the activation of several key-striking motions to produce common words (e.g., *after*) or spelling units (e.g.,-*ation*).

Pew (1974) has recently given a thoughtful review of the human perceptual-motor performance literature, which emphasizes both hierarchical structure and the role of diverse kinds of feedback. The two topics—hierarchical structure and types of feedback control—go hand in hand, because different types of feedback control tend to correspond to different levels of hierarchical control. This point can be illustrated by the results of sine wave tracking experiments. In these tracking experiments, the subject tries to keep the tip of a stylus or other pointer on top of a sinusoidally undulating target, while the experimenter varies the frequency of undulation. Records of the subjects error-correcting movements show that at low frequencies the movements are the result of perceived discrepancies between the position of the pointer and the position of the target. At higher frequencies of undulation, subjects switched to a different mode of control: They generated their own sinusoidal movements and adjusted the parameters of their movements so as to match the trajectory of the pointer to the trajectory of the target. In this higher level mode of control, the error signal no longer derives from the discrepancy between the spatial positions of pointer and target. The error signal derives from the discrepancy between the phase, period, and amplitude of the target's trajectory and the phase, period and amplitude of the pointer's trajectory. Likewise, the error signal no longer adjusts position; rather it adjusts the phase, period and amplitude of the movement.

Schemas

When subjects adopt the second strategy in sine-wave tracking tasks they are making use of perceived regularities in the behavior of the target in order to extrapolate its future behavior. This extrapolation permits the construction in advance of a representation of a to-be-performed movement. Such representations are called *schemas*. One advantage of coming to the concept of a schema by way of the results from sine-wave tracking tasks is that one may avoid the air of mystery and vagueness that surrounds the term. The schema may be nothing more mysterious than a neural oscillator (cf. Fig. 4.24) whose phase, period and amplitude have been adjusted to correspond with the target's. Whether this is in fact the way the nervous system accomplishes the generation of a sinusoidal pointer movement that matches the sinusoidal target movement, no one knows. Assuming that it does, however, permits one to formulate certain ideas about schemas more sharply than if one makes no attempt to specify what the embodiment of a schema ("motor plan," "movement formula," etc.) might be.

For the sake of conceptual explicitness, let us therefore assume that subjects represent the trajectory of the target by means of a neural oscillator. The perceptual system adjusts the period, amplitude, and phase of electrical oscillation in a neuron or neurons until the oscillation matches the oscillatory perception produced by the target's motion. This type of perception is called *analysis by synthesis,* because the perceptual system determines the representation of an input (analyses an input) by constructing (synthesizing) a model of the input.

Let us further assume that when a representation of the perceived movement is stored in memory, the engram—neural embodiment of a memory—records the strengths of six signals: The value of the first element in the engram represents the strength of the signal required to make the period of the internal oscillator match the period of external oscillation. Thus, the first element in the engram represents period. The value of the second element in the engram represents amplitude.The value of the third represents the reference phase, that is, the phase relationship between this oscillation and any concurrent oscillation (see below). The values of the remaining three elements in the engram represent the plane in which the oscillation occurs. Is the target undulating up and down, or back and forth, or from side to side, and so on? Mathematically speaking, the engram of the target's trajectory is a six dimensional vector. That is, the engram may be represented mathematically by a string of six numbers. The first number specifies period, the second amplitude, and so on.

These explicit assumptions about how the brain might store in memory a record of some movement illustrate what it is Bernstein (1967) might have referred to when he wrote that underlying any rhythmic skilled human movement (walking, hammering, filing, piano-playing, etc.) "there exist in the central nervous system exact formulae of movement ... or their engrams, and these formulae or engrams contain in some form of brain trace the whole process of the movement in its entire course in time" (p. 37). A neural oscillator putting out a sinusoidal signal with the appropriate period, and so forth, together with these three signals specifying a plane in space, is a movement formula. It contains the information one needs to trace the movement "in its entire course in time." The record of the six signals that uniquely determine the oscillation constitute a "brain trace [of] the whole process of the movement."

The vector (the six signals) that characterizes a sinusoidal trajectory is all that the motor side of the nervous system needs to direct the generation of such a trajectory. Let us assume that an appropriately adjusted oscillator is not only the last stage of the perceptual process (the analysis-by-synthesis process), but also the first stage of the motor process. Assume that this oscillator sends to lower centers a sinusoidally oscillating signal whose period, amplitude, and phase specify the period, amplitude and phase of the desired trajectory. Accompanying this sinusoidal signal are three tonic signals, which specify the plane in which the oscillatory trajectory is to be traced out.

The assumption that the last stage of the perceptual process and the first stage of the motor process are one and the same is attractive because it solves the problem of imitation. That is, it explains how perceiving a movement enables the brain to formulate the commands that produce a corresponding movement. On the present hypothesis, the process of perceiving a sinusoidal movement culminates in the creation of precisely those neural signals that are needed to direct a corresponding voluntary movement. The present hypothesis also makes clear what Turvey (1977) may mean when he writes that "the notion of perceiving and acting as dual representations of common neural events may be a reasonable alternative to the sensory and motor views of mind" (p. 259). The signal vector (set of six signals) that specifies the period, amplitude, phase and plane of oscillation is, on the one hand, a representation of sensory experience, while, on the other hand, it directs the generation of a corresponding action.

If it were not for the Fourier theorem, this exposition of how the brain might perceive, record, and reproduce a simple sinusoidal trajectory would seem longer than such a special case would merit. The Fourier theorem, however, enables us to generalize directly from this special case to the perception, remembrance, and reproduction of any movement whatsoever. Any movement can be regarded as a set of trajectories for different points on the body. Furthermore, for most movements it is clear that achieving a certain trajectory for one or a very few points on the body is the aim of the movement. The trajectories of other points are subordinated to this aim. Thus, for example, the trajectory of the hand is crucial in handball; the trajectories of the elbow, shoulder, hips, etc. are subordinated to achieving the desired trajectory of the hand. Therefore, the governing code for any skilled movement need specify only a small number of crucial trajectories. The Fourier theorem says that any trajectory may be represented as the sum (superimposition) of a suitably chosen series of sinusoidal trajectories. The sinusoidal trajectories that must be superimposed are called the Fourier components of the movement. Since any trajectory may be created by superimposing a set of Fourier components, my interpretation of the concept of a schema as it applies to performance on sinusoidal tracking tasks could be the prototype for all motor schemas. In this view, knowing a skilled movement reduces to having the appropriate set of six-element engrams, each engram specifying a Fourier component of the movement.

The "Fourier" model of motor schemas is put forward to render the concept of a motor schema as concrete as possible, and, to suggest that the neural embodiment of the concept could make use of many of the same processes that are evident in the innate actions of organisms as lowly as the cockroach. Whether the model bears any relation to the truth is problematic, because there is very little relevant evidence. About all one can say is that the Fourier model of motor schemas has the requisite degree of abstraction from actual motor signals. That is, the schema for a skilled movement contains no elements that specify which groups of muscles are to be active, in what order, and for how long. That sort of detail is left to lower centers to fill in when the code is activated (see next section).

Many authors have contended that the code for skilled movements must specify the movement itself, not the neuromuscular activity required to realize that movement in any one case (Bernstein, 1967; Lashley, 1951; Pew, 1974; Turvey, 1977). The code cannot specify the pattern of neuromuscular activity, because, under differing circumstances a movement of the same form is generated by means of grossly differing patterns of neuromuscular activity. This point is usually illustrated by appeal to everyday observations about handwriting. One's signature preserves its basic form whether one writes at a desk or on a blackboard or traces it in the sand with the big toe. When writing at a desk, it is the muscles of the forearm that generate the required trajectory; when writing on a blackboard, it is the muscles of the shoulder; when tracing with the toe, it is the muscles of the upper leg and hip. Which muscles are involved and the required pattern of motor neuron activity vary greatly but the form of the signature remains nearly constant. Turvey (1977) calls this the problem of action constancy to emphasize the parallel between it and the problem of perceptual constancy. (Perceptual constancy is the constancy of percepts, such as the perceived size and shape of an object, despite variations in sensory input, such as changes in the size and form of the retinal image of the object.)

The phenomena of action constancy strongly imply that the representation of skilled movement in memory—the engram—specifies the form of the movement rather than the pattern of neuromuscular activity to be used in producing that form. The Fourier theory of the engram does precisely that; it encodes the required trajectory in terms of its Fourier components; it does not specify neuromuscular actvity. Whether or not the Fourier model bears any resemblance to underlying reality, it at least captures the idea of a code that specifies the form of movements rather than the motor signals required to generate movements. Also, the key concept of the model—the superimposition of sinusoidal commands whose phase relationship is controlled by interoscillator coupling—is a proven reality in the nervous system (Chapters 4 and 5). Finally, a number of transpositions of the movement, such as performing the movement in a different plane or inverting the movement, are easily realized by simple, mathematically describable variations of selected elements of the code. The model may help psychologists and neurobiologist discover a common ground for communication by bringing together two seemingly remote domains of discourse.

Relating Neuromuscular Space to Code Space

Because the code that governs the performance of a skilled movement does not specify the neuromuscular activity that implements the performance, one must have lower stages capable of translating trajectory-specifying signals into appropriate patterns of motor-neuron activity. The Fourier model of the code enables us to formulate this problem more sharply: Assume that the command-level sends to lower levels signals of the form envisioned by the Fourier model—a sinusoidally oscillating signal together with three signals that specify a plane of action. The task of the lower levels is to convert this command into an appropriate pattern of neuromuscular activity.

It would seem necessary for at least one lower stage to be concerned primarily with constantly tuning spinal circuitry so as to relate *neuromuscular space* to *code space*. By code space, I mean the representation of the space around the body in the code for skilled movement. We do not know what system of coordinates this representation implies. Since the only purpose in mentioning an explicit system of coordinates is to explicate the concept of code space, let us assume that the movement code represents space by reference to the planes that anatomists use—the saggital plane, the horizontal plane, and the transverse plane. A portrayal of this representation of body space may be found in most textbooks of physiological psychology (e.g., Carlson, 1977, p. 87). To say that the code for skilled movement represents space by reference to these planes is to say that the three signals that specify a plane of movement each specify an angle relative to one of these planes. One signal specifies an angle relative to the horizontal plane, one relative to the saggital, and one relative to the transverse. The stronger a given signal, the greater the angle of the movement relative to that plane.

By neuromuscular space, on the other hand, I mean the direction of the movement produced by a given pattern of neuromuscular activity. If one's hand lies upon a table palm down and one turns it palm up, one has rotated the neuromuscular space of the fingers by 180°. When Wickens turned the subject's hand over after conditioning a finger withdrawal response, he was testing whether the conditioning operated at a level above or below the level that relates neuromuscular space to code space (cf. Chapters 5 and 9). During the original conditioning, when the palm was down, extensor excitation and flexor inhibition moved the tip of the finger upwards. In the generalization test, with the hand turned over, the same pattern of neuromuscular activity moved the finger down. Without the intervention of a level that related neuromuscular space to code space, the subjects in the generalization test would all have pressed the tip of their finger down upon the electrode when they heard the buzzer signalling shock. One of them in fact did. But all the rest did not. A level that relates neuromuscular space to code space intervened. This level rechanneled the excitation triggered by the buzzer so as to excite the flexors of the finger and inhibit the extensors. This rechanneling related neuromuscular space to code space by varying the neuromuscular expression of the learned reaction in such a way as to preserve the direction of the movement within the space defined by body-anchored planes of reference.

The level that relates neuromuscular space to code space varies the manner in which movement signals from the command or engram level are channeled into the motor neurons. Presumably, it does this by potentiating and depotentiating (tuning) appropriate interneurons on the basis of proprioceptive signals and efference copy signals. To make this as explicit as possible, imagine that there is a neural pathway descending from the brain to spinal levels which carries a signal specifying the strength and speed of upward movement of the fingertip. This signal may excite either of two populations of interneurons. One population excites extensor motor neurons and inhibits flexor motor neurons. The other population does the opposite. Sensory signals (and efference copy signals) that give information about the actual (or presumed) orientation of the hand potentiate and depotentiate these two populations of interneurons. By this means they channel the "up" command to the muscles of the finger in such a way as to produce an upward movement of the fingertip regardless of the orientation of the hand.

Linearizing the Relation Between Command and Movement

If the system that converted movement codes into neuromuscular activity were linear, then the movement produced by a given command would be the same regardless of which other movements preceded, accompanied or followed it. A command to wave the tip of the finger sinusoidally in the saggital plane with 2° amplitude and a period of 2 seconds would produce that movement whether or not the hand were simultaneously swinging back and forth in the horizontal plane. One of the major themes of Bernstein's writing was that there is no linear relation between neuromuscular activity and the resulting movement because the biomechanics of the limbs and muscles are strongly nonlinear. In other words, the last stage is strongly nonlinear.

The nervous system's problem is beautifully captured in an analogy given by Pew (1974).

> Early in the space program the National Aeronautics and Space Administration was interested in studying the effects of very high intensity noise on the fatigue strength of the materials used to construct large boosters. To examine these effects they commissioned a study to expose these materials to pure sinusoidal vibrations at 160 dB, a very loud sound indeed. The engineering problem was how to produce pure sinusoidal wave forms at this intensity. Everyone knew that if they started with a sine wave signal, any sound transmission or loudspeaker system would severely distort it, and the actual sound produced would hardly be a high-fidelity pure tone. The solution was obtained by working backwards. The engineers asked, in effect, what kind of a wave shape must we put in such that the distortions introduced by the system will leave us with a pure sine wave at the output [p. 21]?

The stages that translate the movement code into appropriate neuromuscular activity must do just what the engineers did; they must translate the incoming sinusoidal commands into patterns of neuromuscular activity that are not themselves sinusoidal but that produce sinusoidal movement. They must distort the relation between the command and neuromuscular activity in order to linearize the relation between the command and movement.

The nervous system confronts the further problem that the (nonlinear) properties of the final stage vary as a function of many factors (limb position, speed, orientation, etc.). Therefore, the form of the offsetting distortion that intermediate stages must apply to the movement command is itself subject to constant change. In terms of Pew's analogy, it is as if the properties of the loudspeaker itself varied as a function of the inputs that preceded and accompanied a given input. In such circumstances, there is no single adjustment of an intervening stage—no single tuning—that will offset the distortions imposed by the final stage. The tuning of the intervening stage must itself be tuned whenever a single Fourier component (a single sinusoid) is to be accompanied by other components. The distortion of the relation between command and neuromuscular activity that linearizes the relation between a given command and the answering movement is itself a function of other movements in progress. Therefore, the required distortion of each component of the command is a function of the combination of components.

This last point, the need for tuning the tuning in order to implement a new combination of command components goes some way toward explaining the role of extensive practice in the mastery of a skilled movement. The general idea behind most skilled movements comes relatively quickly, at least to adults. A little observation, or a little shadow practice, enables almost anyone to encode the motion required by a tennis serve. But, implementing that motion while simultaneously adjusting the trajectory of the racket so that it intersects the trajectory of the ball at a propitious moment is quite another matter. The attempt to reorient the trajectory of the swing so as to compensate for variations in the trajectory of the ball reduces the serve of an unpracticed player from a thing of beauty to an awkward compromise. The trick is to implement the code for a proper swing while carrying out the necessary correcting movements at the same time. That, I suggest, involves learning through practice to send down from higher levels a complex set of signals that adjusts the parameters of the linearizing circuitry. The linearizing circuitry in turn adjusts the parameters of the network that translates command codes into motor neuron codes: Whence the phrase "tuning the tuning."

Recent work on the muscle spindle system suggests that sensory signals fed back to the central nervous system from the muscle spindle organs in the muscle play a role in linearizing the behavior of the neuromuscular system (Crago, Houk, & Hasan, 1976; Nichols & Houk, 1976). An active muscle does not behave like a spring when stretched. The elastic counterforce is not proportional to the stretch. This is one example of the biomechanical nonlinearity that Bernstein (1967) emphasized. If it is true that the muscle spindle system helps linearize the behavior of the neuromuscular system, then this system provides an excellent model for studying the phenomenon of tuning the tuning. Descending signals alter the parameters of the sensory side of the muscle spindle system. They do this by way of a specialized set of motor neurons called the γ-efferent neurons (Emonet-Dénand, Laporte, Matthews, & Petit, 1977; Matthews, 1964). These neurons innervate a specialized muscle fiber within the muscle spindle. The sensory receptors of the muscle spindle system wrap around these specialized fibers and signal stretch. By means of the γ-efferent neurons the central nervous system controls the extent to which these signals reflect either stretch per se or the rate of stretching. If we assume that the signals fed back to the central nervous system from the muscle spindle tune the network that converts command signals into motor neuron signals, then the tuning of the spindle by γ-efferent signals is an instance of tuning the tuning.

DEVELOPMENTAL ANALYSIS OF HUMAN COORDINATION

Twitchell

It was suggested in Chapter 9 that developmental studies offer one of the best approaches we have for identifying the elementary units of coordinated action and specifying the manner in which these are integrated into more complex units of action. Developmental research is particularly important for understanding the structure of human coordination because lines of research that involve direct intervention in the nervous system are foreclosed. Twitchell's (1970) studies of the development of grasping in infants are an excellent example of what developmental research can reveal. Twitchell shows that one may spot the units that combine to form mature reaching and grasping as these units emerge one by one in the course of normal infant development. One may also see how the assertion of control by higher levels keeps these units from getting in each other's way.

Among the units that will be integrated to form mature reaching and grasping, the first to emerge is what Twitchell calls the traction response. The response involves a powerful contraction of the muscles that flex the finger, wrist, and elbow joints. It is activated by any pull on the arm that stretches the flexor and adductor muscles of the shoulder. It is seen in its purest form from birth to 2 weeks of age. From 2 to 8 weeks of age one sees this unit begin to interact with another unit, which Twitchell calls the grasp reflex. The grasp reflex involves flexion and adduction of the fingers and thumb in response to a pressure stimulus that moves outward from the base of the palm. The adequate stimulus for the grasp reflex—outward moving pressure on the palm—facilitates the traction response. This is a fine example of what Turvey might call within-level tuning, or, in Sherrington's terms, facilitation of an agonistic unit.

In the period from 8 to 20 weeks one sees the assertion of a hierarhical control that potentiates and depotentiates the reflex circuitry whose presence was manifest at an earlier age. For example, a pull on the arm no longer elicits the full traction response or does so only weakly. The fingers do not flex. However, if the grasp reflex has been activated, if, that is, flexion of the fingers has already been activated by the appropriate stimulus to the palm of the hand, then a pull on the arm strengthens this finger flexion. In other words, the circuitry for the full traction response is still present, but it can only be activated under more differentiated conditions. Under ordinary circumstances, a higher level unit depotentiates all aspects of the traction response, particularly the finger flexion. If, however, the grasp reflex is activated, this removes the depotentiation of the traction response, insuring that the traction response is ready to come to the aid of the grasp response. response.

Twitchell goes on to describe the fractionation of the grasp reflex, the emergence of hand orienting reactions, groping movements, trap reactions, and avoidance reactions. The avoidance reactions and the grasping reactions are, like the flexion and extension reflexes in the hind limb of the cat, mutually exclusive reactions to one and the same stimulus. In the early stages of development they often both occur in rapid alteration, which prevents either from functioning effectively. By the end of the first year, they have both been subjected to control by potentiating and depotentiating signals from higher level units of coordination. This control prevents the reflex conflict known as athetosis.

Bruner

Studies by Bruner and his collaborators take up more or less where Twitchell's studies leave off. They have studied the development of the movements by which babies aged 4–18 months take possession of an object, get an object out of a box with a sliding cover, and reach around an obstacle (Bruner, 1970). It would seem that the reflex units analyzed by Twitchell play some role in these acts. Bruner (1970, p. 70) asserts emphatically that they do not, but gives no justification for the assertion. Two observations seem pertinent: (1) The reflex circuits whose behavioral manifestations Twitchell describes are certainly present and capable of functioning in the adult, because the reactions reemerge in precisely their infantile form when neurological disease impairs higher control (Seyffarth and Denny-Brown, 1948). (2) Depotentiating and potentiating signals impinging on selected components of a circuit from above may make substantial modifications in the form of the movements which that circuit contributes to a complex behavior. Only a very careful *longitudinal* tracking of the development of the complex act may permit one to see the manner in which reflexes are incorporated into it. Bruner himself later recognizes the fact that the process of incorporating an action module into a more complex act may involve "a virtual decomposition and recomposition of the modular act." (1970, p. 72).

In a recent review, Bruner (1974) makes a number of general points that may be more readily appreciated by reference to examples we are now familiar with. Firstly, he distinguishes between three kinds of "feedback"— "*feedback proper,*" "*internal* feedback," and "*knowledge of results.*" By feedback proper Bruner means the kind of feedback we analyzed at some length in connection with the optokinetic reaction (Chapter 7). By internal feedback he means efference copy or corollary discharge, also described and analyzed in Chapter 7. By knowledge of results he means high level assessments of the form and consequences of an act, assessments made after the act has been completed. High level assessments of the form of an act may be used to adjust the tuning signals sent to lower levels the next time the act is essayed (cf. above discussions of Pew & Turvey). High level assessments of the consequences may also, to paraphrase Schiller, stabilize fortuitous but felicitous combinations of acts into higher level units of behavior (cf. end of Chapter 10).

Secondly, Bruner (1974) sees the development of skillful action in terms of the hierarchical incorporation of action units that have an innate (or prefunctional) foundation but are brought to more perfect functioning by exercise:

> ... the infant comes early to solve problems of high complexity and does so on the basis of encounters with the environment that are too few in number, too unrepresentative, or too erratic in consequence, to be accounted for either on the basis of concept attainment or by the shaping effects of reinforcement. Initial 'learning' has a large element of preadaptation that reflects species-typical genetic instructions ... The initial patterns of action that emerge through exercise then become constituents for new patterns of action directed at more remote or complex objectives. Here too the role of learning in the conventional sense is not clear. Indeed, what is striking about the opening year of life is how specialized and circumscribed the role of learning turns out to be [p. 168].

The concept of tuning the parameters of a neural circuitry in order to improve the action mediated by that circuitry suggests a rephrasing of Bruner's hypothesis about one of the circumscribed but important roles that experience plays in the early development of skilled action: Anyone who has ever watched a baby knows that babies spend a great deal of time practicing— doing the same simple thing over and over again for no apparent reason. In this sense a large part of the baby's experience is self-generated. Paraphrasing Bruner, one is led to suggest that the feedback from this practice plays an important role in tuning the underlying neural circuitry, that is, in adjusting the parameters of the circuitry so as to make the movement or act smoother, more effective and more reliable. In other words, the development of optimal parameters in the neural circuitry coordinating a unit of action underlies what Bruner and many others have called the automatization or modularization of lower units (or subroutines, in the metaphor of information processing).

The well known studies of Held and Hein (e.g., 1963) show that depriving infant mammals of important modes of sensory feedback during the early months can permanently prevent or seriously retard the development of the mature form of some behaviors. One does not, of course, conclude from such deprivation experiments that the form and pattern of early experience determine the form and pattern of mature behavior. The hierarchical view of skill development and the notion that the feedback from self-initiated practice modularizes units of action provide quite a different interpretation. Depriving the developing infant of important avenues for sensory feedback prevents the perfecting of the constituents of an act. The act itself, being assembled out of faulty and unreliable components, is not effective. It eventually drops out of the repertoire of acts that the animal uses, just as the ineffective pattern of carrying nesting material gradually disappears from the behavior of Dilger's hybrid lovebirds (Chapter 9). If the period of deprivation is lengthy, the development of the act may be permanently prevented for two reasons: First, the early ineffectiveness of the act has made it the last to be called on in most if not all contexts. Secondly, the tendency to practice the constituents over and over diminishes with age, so the animal past a certain age may no longer initiate the experience required to tune the constituents. The ensemble—that is the act—remains ineffective on the rare occasions when it is employed. In consequence, the tendency to employ it diminishes further, even when the animal is no longer deprived of the feedback.

A third theme of Bruner's (1974) review concerns a somewhat different role for experience in development. The play of babies, like the play of other young mammals, consists of the repetition of many acts, often from quite different levels, in jumbled sequence, to no particular end. Bruner, acknowledging his debt to Schiller's (1957, 1952) work with chimpanzees, suggests that this aspect of juvenile behavior provides the raw variation—the random mutations, to use an evolutionary metaphor—upon which mechanisms of reinforcement or act-outcome learning operate. Bruner calls this kind of play "mastery play," because it seems to enrich the child's knowledge of means-ends relations. Our understanding of this position may be enriched by realizing its close connection to Lorenz's important concepts: the autonomous accumulation of potentiation and the relative or labile hierarchy (Chapter 10). A child that runs up a hill for no other reason than that he has not run up a hill for a while exemplifies the kind of behavior that led Lorenz to formulate the concept of an autonomous or spontaneous build up of "action specific energy." And, when the child employs some other complex sequence of behavior simply in order to be able to run up a hill, the child exhibits the seeming reversal of means-ends relations in behavior that led Lorenz to speak of a relative as opposed to a fixed hierarchy (Chapter 10; and also the discussion of Turvey's heterarchical concept above).

A fourth theme in Bruner's (1974) review is the role of intention in skill development. Bruner argues that in the earliest stages objects arouse in infants the intention to deal with the object in some way. This intention to deal with the object in some way is evidenced by the loosely ordered performance of many of the constituent movements. The infant that intends to grasp an object and bring it to its mouth exhibits prolonged orientation toward the object, extension and flexion of the arm, finger flexion and extension, opening and closing of the mouth, tongue protrusions, etc. Anyone who has watched an infant will recognize the syndrome. These motions are consituents of the act of grasping the object and bringing it to the mouth to be tasted. But, the constituents are performed with so little finesse and so little coherence of order that the intention is not realized. The course of development lies in the perfecting of the constituents and the maturation of the intermediate units of action that coherently order the constituents. Bruner argues that it is the capacity of objects to arouse such intentions that sustains the course of development.

It may be remarked parenthetically that Gelman and Gallistel (1978) give a very similar analysis of the development of skill in counting in preschool children. They argue that the constituents of counting are perceptible in two year olds. In the course of development, these constituents are perfected and coherently ordered to produce mature enumeration. This development is, they argue, sustained by a scheme in the Piagetian sense, a high level system that directs and motivates the development of counting.

Bruner (1974) introduces the concept of intention with a nervous look over his shoulder at philosophers: "Intention viewed abstractly may be at issue philosphically. But it is a necessity for the biology of complex behaviour, by whatever label we wish to call it." (p. 168). But he goes on to define it in a way that accords with the concept of motivation as it has been elaborated in this book: "Intention, viewed behaviourally, has several measurable features: anticipation of the outcome of an act, selection among appropriate means for achieving an end state, sustained direction of behavior during deployment of means, a stop order defined by an end state, and finally some substitution rule whereby alternative means can be deployed for correction of deviation or to fit idiosyncratic conditions." (p. 169). In preceding chapters I have tried to explain how such properties are imparted to behavior and to base the explanation as closely as possible upon clearly demonstrable principles of behavioral neurobiology. Let us see how principles that have already been explicated and exemplified can clarify what it might mean to say that an object arouses in an infant the intention to grasp an object and bring it to its mouth to be tasted. The perception of a novel object, an object that does not match any representation in memory, arouses in the infant brain a central motive state. A central motive state is a signal that descends from cerebral levels of the brain and organizes a course of behavior by selectively potentiating the constituent acts. The signal potentiates a constituent act by reducing the threshold for the activation of crucial elements in the neural circuitry that coordinates the act.

The tonic organizing signal from the cerebrum explains the "sustained direction of behaviour during the deployment of means." The means are the individual acts that comprise a behavioral sequence. The sustained direction of a motivated behavioral sequence signifies that one does not observe just any sequence or combination of acts; one observes sequences and combinations that have a common tendency. Why? Because the organizing signal from the cerebrum does not potentiate just any collection of acts; it potentiates coherent subsets of acts. In other words, it specifies "appropriate means for achieving an end state."

Feedback of one kind or another from one or a few of the potentiated acts terminates the cerebral organizing signal. Thus, there is an end state that generates a stop order.

There is a provision for the deployment of alternative means "to fit idiosyncratic conditions," because the organizing signal from the cerebrum potentiates acts rather than initiates them. Which among the potentiated acts actually occurs depends upon the activating conditions of the moment.

The efference copy signals that nullify the reafference from a movement anticipate the outcome of the movement. At a much higher level, an animal's orientation in a known environment is governed not only by what the animal perceives at the moment, but also by the animal's representation of relations between what it now perceives and what it cannot yet perceive. Such phenomena, beautifully demonstrated by experiments on homing behavior in digger wasps and detour behavior in rats, are higher level instances of anticipating the outcome of acts. Deutsch's model, whether true or not, dispels any lingering belief as to whether it is possible for a purely physical system with no homunculus in it to anticipate an outcome of its own behavior. The quality of anticipation in map-directed behavior is mediated by the propagation of a drive signal through the map. The drive signal is, of course, the organizing signal from the cerebrum.

Why does the very young infant not make good on his intention to grasp an object and bring it to his mouth to be tasted? Because the circuitry mediating intermediate units of behavior is not fully formed. The circuitry mediating behavior is hierarchically structured. The organizing signal from the cerebrum does not act directly upon the most elementary units of behavior. It acts upon circuits that themselves organize the actions of still lower circuits. Each level of circuitry helps fill in the details of the pattern of motor neuron activity required to implement the general course of behavior specified by the signal from the cerebrum. The disorganized pattern of infant behavior, which displays the elements of the intended act but in no coherent order, means that the intermediate units are not doing their job. How do they come to do their job? Partly through maturation and partly through practice. What keeps them practicing? The tonic organizing signal from the cerebrum.

MAPS AND THE BRAIN

Euclidean versus Topological Representations of Space

Deutsch's (1960) model for the control of action by a cognitive map was described at some length in Chapter 11, because it is, so far as I know, the only model that explicitly specifies a physically realizable process by which a motivational signal may organize the use of a map. Most discussions of behavior that presume the use of an internal representation of the environment seem to imply the presence of an homunculus, a little man who examines the internal representation and decides on an appropriate course of action. If one believes that internal representations of the environment play an important role in directing the behavior of animals as lowly as the wasp, the bee and the ant, then it is important to prove that there need be no implicit postulation of an homunculus in such a view. Deutsch's model proves that. Furthermore, the principle by which Deutsch dispenses with the homunculus—having a potentiating (motivating) signal flow decrementally through the map—is both simple and ingenious.

It is clear, however, that in two important respects Deutsch's model is wrong: (1) The model assumes a purely topological representation of the environment (see p. 350). A close reading of Maier (1929) and of the extensive (*non-Hullian*) literature on spatial learning makes it appear that the internal representation must be more nearly Euclidean (see Woodworth & Schlosberg, 1954, Chapter 21, for review). That is, distance and angles must be represented as well as which points are adjacent to which. This appears to be true in animals as diverse as the chimpanzee (Tinkelpaugh, 1932), the rat (Maier, 1929), and the ant (Brun, 1914; Schneirla, 1929). (2) Deutsch's model assumes that the animal orients at any given moment by reference to some perceptible point that is more or less immediately in front of the animal and on the route to the animal's destination. Deutsch's model assumes, in other words, that the animal orients first toward one subgoal, then toward the next, and so on. Each subgoal corresponds to a node in the animal's internal representation of the environment, a mode that represents a point nearer to the goal. The literature just mentioned makes it clear that this is not the case. Rather, the animal appears to use a variety of landmarks, not necessarily nearer to or in the direction of the goal, in order to determine where on its map it now is. Having established where it is, it then sets a course and distance that will carry it to some subgoal (turning point, etc.). The animal may use other cues, for example, angle with respect to the sun, to hold the course while it travels the estimated distance. Having traveled a specified distance in a specified direction, the animal takes another "fix on its position." That is, it uses currently perceived points in its immediate environment to check its position and orientation relative to its internal representation of the environment.

One simple demonstration that rats running a thoroughly familiar maze are reeling off courses of predetermined length comes from old experiments by Carr and Watson (1908). Carr and Watson shortened or lengthened one or another arm in a maze the rats knew well. The rats ran full tilt into the end walls of the shortened arms. And, they stopped in confusion after running down a lengthened arm a distance corresponding to the old length of that arm. Similar phenomena are observed in ants (Brun, 1914; Cornetz, 1914; Piéron, 1904).

A simple demonstration that rats pursue courses through a space defined by reference to landmarks comes from recent experiments by Olton and Samuelson (1976). They ran rats in a radial maze with 8 arms, each of which was baited with food. The rats rapidly learned to avoid returning to arms they had already sampled, until they had sampled all 8 arms. The question is what defines a sampled arm for the rat? Is a sampled arm defined by a chain of stimuli specific to that arm and leading from its entrance to its end? The Deutsch model assumes that this kind of representation is the basis for the rat's map-controlled behavior. Alternatively, the arms may be represented as paths in a Euclidean space. That is, a sampled arm may be represented as a line that traverses a certain distance in a certain direction relative to some set of landmarks located beyond or away from the path itself.

Rotating the radial maze after a rat has sample a subset of the arms tests which kind of representation the rat is using. After the rotation, some arms that the rat has already sampled now point in an unsampled direction. Conversely, some of the directions (paths through space) that the rat has already sampled are now occupied by arms that it has not sampled.

The rat freely enters already sampled arms that traverse unsampled spatial loci and avoids unsampled arms that traverse sampled spatial loci. In other words, the rat is not sampling different point sequences on a topological map, a map that represents which points follow which. Rather the rat is sampling paths to the 'north,' 'southwest,' 'east,' and so on, where 'north,' 'east,' and so forth are defined relative to a set of extramaze landmarks.

The same conclusion follows from old experiments by Tinkelpaugh (1932). Tinkelpaugh set up pairs of boxes in a circle around a chimpanzee chained to a chair, and hid a banana under one member of each pair. When the chimpanzee was later returned to the room where it had watched the boxes being baited, it went to the baited member of each pair of boxes. By repositioning the baited boxes while the chimp was out of the room, Tinkelpaugh showed that the chimp coded the positions of the bananas in the space defined by the room and the circle of box pairs, rather than noting distinctive features of baited boxes. The chimp looked under boxes at the positions that had been baited rather than under the particular boxes that had been baited. This was true even when a baited box was obviously unlike any of the other boxes.

Maier (1929) found that rats could solve his detour problems (see Chapter 11) even when the familiar space through which they had to detour was in total darkness. Under these conditions, the rats could not be homing upon perceptible points lying between them and the goal, as Deutsch's model assumes they do. Rather, they had to orient themselves in space on the basis of the orientation of familiar objects, which the rats contacted with their vibrissae (the sensory whiskers on the rat's snout).

Humans are made consciously aware of doing the same thing—orienting in a space by means of contact with objects whose shape and position in that space are internally represented—whenever they wake up in the middle of the night in some room other than their own and must fumble their way to the light switch. Under these conditions, one first summons to mind, often with some effort, an 'image' of the room one went to sleep in. Marcel Proust gives a lovely description of this process in his *Remembrance of Things Passed*. The narrator, on waking in the middle of the night, first thinks himself in another room. But his perceptions of the glint from a mirror, the position of a streak of light under a door, the feel of the bed, do not jibe with this representation of where he is. Then his image of the other room is supplanted by an image of the room he in fact went to sleep in. Now his perceptions fall into place. He knows where he is and can use that knowledge to find his way about in the darkened room.

Any careful reading of the extensive experimental literature on the homing abilities of diverse animals is enough, I believe, to persuade a skeptic that many, many animals possess the capacity to form a quasi-Euclidean representation of how objects, scents, textures, are distributed within an experienced space. Such representations are then used to instruct the animal's orienting machinery on what cues to use for orienting and what orientation to adopt. The foraging ant has more in common with Proust's narrator than one might imagine.

Neurobiological Evidence

Those who share my commitment to a reductionist analysis of the organizing mechanisms in animal behavior often resist the notion that animals make and use internal representations of experienced space. The concept of a Euclidean representation of space seems awfully remote from anything one sees in examining the workings of the nervous system. However, recent work on the function of the hippocampus in rats goes some way toward diminishing the seemingly immense gap between the firing of neurons in the brain and the concept of an internal representation of space.

The hippocampus is a phylogenetically ancient cortex-like region of the cerebrum. In mammals, it more or less wraps around the structures known to play a crucial role in originating motivational signals. Damaging the upper (dorsal) part of the hippocampus selectively abolishes the rat's ability to learn to return to a particular point in space (O'Keefe, Nadel, Keightley, & Kill, 1975; Olton, 1968, 1977; Sinnamon, Freniere, & Kootz, 1978).

Lesion-based evidence for the localization of some higher function in a particular brain structure is notoriously inconclusive. However, the conclusion that the dorsal hippocampus plays a central role in spatial learning is buttressed by evidence of a different kind obtained by O'Keefe (1976). O'Keefe used very fine wires called microelectrodes to record the firing of individual neurons in the hippocampus of the rat while the rat moved around in a familiar space. O'Keefe found three types of neurons, which he calls *place* units, *misplace* units, and *displace* units.

Place units increase their firing frequency only when the rat is within some fairly small region of the environment. Different place units fire at different places in the same environment. The place at which a given unit responds does not usually have any special significance for the rat. But every time the rat moves through that place the neuron fires rapidly, regardless (usually) of which direction the rat is moving. The neuron's firing at that place is not due to any stimulus at that place, but rather to the relation between that place and a number of remote cues (landmarks?).

Misplace units also fire only at certain places in the environment, different places for different units. However, the rat's being at the required place is not a sufficient condition for these units to fire. Something must be amiss at that place. An object that used to be at that place must have been removed or an object that did not used to be there inserted. The firing of a misplace unit is closely associated with the appearance of the investigatory sniffing behavior a rat displays whenever it encounters an alteration in a familiar environment. The firing of a misplace unit is not, however, a simple consequence of sniffing, because, to repeat, different misplace units become active at different places.

Displace units fire whenever the rat moves through space. There is some indication that the rate of their firing is related to the velocity of movement.

It is difficult to know if an experimenter has related the firing of single neurons in the brain to a functionally appropriate description of the concomitant stimuli and behavior. It is too early to judge whether O'Keefe has characterized the conditions that excite these hippocampal neurons in a way that is truly indicative of their behavioral function. Nonetheless, his data, together with the data from lesion studies, strongly suggest that the hippocampus plays an important role in mediating the rat's ability to find its way through familiar spaces. These data should give an impetus to behavioral and neurobiological experiments designed to elucidate the nature of the nervous system's representation of space and the manner in which the system employs that representation to guide the animal's behavior.

ALIGNING THE MAP WITH THE PERCEIVED SPACE

If behavioral and neurobiological experiments are to shed light on the nervous system's representation of space, experimentalists must no longer be skittish about the notion of representation. They must acknowledge the necessity of the concept in the explanation of behavior and design experiments that place constraints on possible hypotheses about: (a), the form of the representation, and (b), the operations that translate the representation into action. Lynn Cooper and Roger Shepard have taken the lead in this enterprise (see Cooper & Shepard, 1979; Shepard, 1975, for review). Although their work treats the rotation of mental images in humans, it may have greater relevance to the biology of action than is immediately apparent.

Shepard and his collaborators, most notably Cooper, have studied the speed of human reactions in tasks that require the subject to determine whether a currently perceived object has the same shape as an object represented in memory. The subject is first shown some standard, a representation of which is to be stored in memory. The standard might be an alpha-numeric character, a two-dimensional polygon, a three-dimensional nonsense shape composed of cubicle blocks (such as are used on most IQ tests), or a drawing of the left or right human hand held in various positions. The standard is then removed. A moment later the subject is shown a test shape, which may or may not be identical to the standard he has just seen, but which in most cases has a different orientation. For example, if the standard is an upright capital L, the test shape might be an L reversed and rotated 180° so that it is presented upside down. The subject's task is to say as quickly as he can whether the test shape is a reversed or normal version of the standard shape.

In some experiments the subject is not told how great will be the rotational discrepancy between the standard and the test shape. In others the subject is told what rotation to expect shortly before the test shape appears. In others the subject is instructed to mentally rotate his representation of the standard in some direction. In still others, the subject is not actually shown a standard; rather the standard is described verbally (e.g., "an upright capital-W").

In these experiments the human nervous system operates upon its representations of shapes as if the representations were little reproductions.

The reaction time data are consistent with the naive, almost prescientific hypothesis that the nervous system rotates a little reproduction of the standard shape into alignment with the test shape and then compares the forms. Shepard summarizes the data as follows (1975):

> The time to determine that a spatially transformed object is of inherently the same shape as some comparison or standard object increases monotonically with the extent of the transformational difference between the two objects.
>
> Under appropriate conditions, the monotone increase in reaction time with extent of transformation is uniformly linear.
>
> When the subject is set to carry out the mental rotation in a particular (clockwise or counterclockwise) direction, reaction time continues its linear increase beyond 180° through the full 360° circle.
>
> The linear increase in reaction time with angle of rotation of a three-dimensional object has essentially the same slope whether the axis of rotation coincides with the line of sight, so that the transformation corresponds to a rigid rotation of the two-dimensional retinal image, or is orthogonal to the line of sight, so that the transformation corresponds to much more complex, topologically discontinuous deformation of the retinal image.
>
> For a given axis of rotation, the reaction time has a strong dependence only upon the angle of rotation in three-dimensional space; it is influenced relatively slightly by whether or not such a rotation entails topological discontinuities in the two-dimensional retinal image.
>
> When the subject is given sufficient advance information concerning both the object to be presented and the orientation in which it is to appear, the reaction time becomes uniformly fast (on the order of 400 msec) and independent of that orientation.
>
> The dependence of reaction time on the angle of rotation is approximately the same both for the time needed to prepare for such a rotated object and for the time needed to respond to such a rotated object in the absence of advance preparation.
>
> During mental preparation for a rotated object, the orientation of the object for which the subject is most prepared from moment-to-moment is actually rotating in physical space.
>
> Advance information giving merely the orientation of a to-be-presented object is not sufficient to enable subjects to prepare for it in this way; subjects must also have information as to which concrete object is to be presented in that orientation.
>
> The internal representations that are mentally transformed in these ways preserve rather complete structural information about the external objects to which they correspond.
>
> The structural information contained in a mentally transformed internal representation does not come into play solely upon the external presentation of a corresponding stimulus; it is accessible to the subject for further cognitive processing in the absence of such an external stimulus.

These findings place constraints on hypotheses about how the human nervous represents shape and how it operates upon such representations. The representation must be of a sort that can be operated on in a manner that is closely analogous to the rotation in Euclidean space of a Euclidean reproduction of the represented shape. Of course, no one imagines that the representation of a hand by the brain has the physical form of a little hand, nor that this little hand is literally rotated within the space occupied by the neural tissue. An example of a more neurophysiologically plausible model is elaborated below. But first let us pause to ask how these results may be related to the organization of action.

It seems to me likely that Shepard is exploring the operation in the human brain of a process that any system must perform in using a Euclidean representation of space to control its progression through space. The alignment of the internal representation of the world relative to the coordinate system of the body must correspond to the alignment of the body relative to the world. Two examples may help to make clear what is meant.

When people use an actual map while driving, hiking, or canoeing in unfamiliar country, they show a strong tendency to rotate the map until its alignment with respect to the body corresponds to the body's alignment with respect to the world. When driving from San Francisco to Los Angeles one holds the map of California so that San Francisco is in toward the body and Los Angeles out toward the windshield. When driving back, the map is rotated 180° relative to the body. In both cases, the alignment of the map relative to the body is made to correspond with the alignment of California relative to the body.

When one comes up out of the subway at an unfamiliar stop, the alignment of one's internal representation of the city relative to one's body coordinates may fail to correspond for a while to the alignment of one's body relative to the city. In grid city's at least, the error of relative aligment is usually 90° or 180°. One comes up out of the subway at 59th Street in New York and sets off walking toward what one takes to be north, only to arrive with some bewilderment at 58th Street rather than 60th. At such moments, I, at least, just stand there until I "feel" my representation of the city swing round 180°. Only then can I set off to where I want to go.

I suggest that the homeward bound digger wasps that Thorpe captured and transported to different points of the compass (see Chapter 11) must perform a similar operation. The wasp has a map that specifies the position of its burrow relative to a set of widely visible landmarks. In orienting by reference to the map the wasp must, of course, determine its current position on that map. It must also, I suggest, rotate its map so that the map is aligned with the environment it represents.

Map-based orienting requires the orienting mechanism to inter-relate three systems of coordinates—the body's system of coordinates, the system of coordinates established by the map, and the system of coordinates established by the presently perceived environment. I suggest that the orienting mechanism interrelates these systems of coordinates by rotating the map so that its alignment vis-á-vis the body coordinates corresponds to the alignment of the currently perceived environment vis-á-vis those same body coordinates.

At this point I fear I may have aroused the intense skepticism of those who approach the problem of action from a neurobiological perspective. I began this book by trumpeting my commitment to a physically realizable and neurobiologically comprehensible account of the principles that organize animal action. I end by babbling about my mental image of New York. Worse yet, I apply this obscure figure of speech to the behavior of the digger wasp. What, neurobiologically speaking, could rotating a Euclidean representation of the world possibly refer to? Well...

It was explained in the foregoing that the trajectory of a finger or hand moving through space could in principle be represented in memory by a set of six-dimensional vectors. That is, the trajectory could be represented in terms of sinusoidal oscillations that when superimposed—performed concurrently —would yield the trajectory. Each of the required oscillations can be encoded by the strength of six signals. The strength of one signal specifies the period of the oscillation; the strength of another, the amplitude; the strength of the third, the reference phase; and the strength of the remaining three, the angle of a plane in a system of body coordinates. By increasing the dimensionality of the vector, that is, by adding a few more signals, the representation can be made to specify not only the angle of a plane relative to the body but also the distance of that plane from the origin of the coordinate system.

Imagine now the world or some object in the world reduced to a three-dimensional outline, a wire model so to speak, with each wire being a contour or edge. It would be possible to run the tip of one's finger along these contours and edges until one had traced out the whole outline. In other words, an outline of an environment could always be considered to be the trajectory of a point in motion. This means that any such outline could be encoded by the same principles we used to encode the trajectories of skilled movements. In other words, a three dimensional outline may be represented by Fourier components.

It has been suggested that the visual system reconstructs the visible world by means of a process best described within the framework of Fourier analysis (Pollen, Lee, & Taylor, 1971). There is psychophysical evidence that the visual system treats well separated Fourier components of the retinal image as though they activated separate channels (Campbell & Robson, 1968; Graham & Nachmias, 1971). And, the responses of neurons in the visual cortex to complex patterns of light on the retina can best be predicted from the assumption that each neuron is activated by a particular Fourier component of the image (De Valois, Albrecht, & Thorell, 1979). However, these data and the speculations they inspire are only tangentially related to my suggestion that we think of the representation of the environemnt in terms of the Fourier components of a trajectory corresponding to its outline. First, the form of the Fourier analysis employed in describing retinal images differs from the form of the Fourier analysis I used to describe trajectories in three-dimensional space. Second, it is far from clear how a system can obtain an accurate three-dimensional representation of the environment from a Fourier analysis of the grossly distorted two-dimensional retinal image of the environment.

In suggesting that we imagine representations of the environment or individual objects in terms of the Fourier components of the outline I do not wish to advance a seriously intended hypothesis about the neurophysiological embodiment of the code for shape. My purpose is only to exhibit an example of the sort of thing one could be referring to in speaking of the rotation of a Euclidean representation.[1]

The example I have given is neurophysiologically plausible only in that it reduces Euclidean representations to signal vectors. Insofar as we presently understand it, the sensory and perceptual side of the nervous system must represent everything in terms of signal vectors. That is, so far as we now know, the sensory system represents different features of the input in terms of the rates of firing in different neurons. The firing of any neuron signifies something different from what is signified by the firing of any other neuron. The representation of the input thus reduces to a set of signals of differing strengths, where each signal has a different relation to the input and a different role to play in the subsequent operations of the system. The complete set of signals generated by an input is what one means by the signal vector that represents that input.

Imagining the representation of a spatial configuration in terms of the Fourier components of the outline gets us away from little images on some kind of movie screen in the head and into the kind of thing we can plausibly conceive of as a neural process. The brain's representation of the

---

[1]The idea of representing space by means of Fourier components *as I have presented it here* is highly artificial. The sketch builds on the crude introduction to 1-dimensional Fourier synthesis given in Chapter 4 and elaborated on earlier in the present chapter. If one were to take the notion of representation by Fourier components more seriously, one would probably abandon the outline-as-trajectory artifice. One would work directly from 3-dimensional Fourier components. Mathematically, the Fourier representation of the distribution of matter in a 3-dimensional space is a straightforward generalization of 1-dimensional Fourier representations. It is hard, however, to convey any intuitive feel for the physical embodiment of a 3-dimensional Fourier component. It is hard to convey a feeling for why it is that any 3-dimensional configuration of matter may be decomposed into macroscopic "matter waves," analogous to sound waves.

configuration reduces to patterns of firing in distinct subsets of neurons, each subset composed of functionally distinct individual neurons. A given subset of neurons represents one Fourier component. The signal carried by each neuron in a subset specifies a distinct parameter of the component. The signal in one neuron specifies period, the signal in another specifies amplitude, and so on.

Once one has reduced the representation of a spatial configuration to a set of signal vectors, it is not hard to envisage an operation that corresponds to rotating the representation. Suppose that one signal in each vector represents an angle of a Fourier component relative to a reference plane. Then, to rotate the representation, the system need only simultaneously increase or decrease the strength of the corresponding signal in each vector. In this way, all of the Fourier components are simultaneously rotated by the same amount. By this means, the brain could make the representation adopt any desired alignment relative to a fixed system of body coordinates.

I doubt that this Fourier fantasy bears any detailed resemblance to neurophysiological reality. I hope, however, that it will bring together discussions of internal representations in cognitive psychology, animal behavior, and neurobiology. Data derived from experiments that were conceived and analyzed in terms of intuitions about mental images need not and should not be viewed as hopelessly remote from any neurobiological analysis of action. If the concept of internal representation is in fact indispensable in the analysis of action, then refusing to come to grips with the concept can only postpone the dawn of understanding.

SUMMING UP

The literature of cognitive psychology, ethology, and behavioral neurobiology contains, at least implicitly, a more elaborate and interesting theory of action than is commonly realized. The salient concepts in this theory are as follows.

1. The system that generates animal action is hierarchically structured.

2. At the bottom of the hierarchy are a relatively few kinds of elementary units of action.

3. Among these elementary units are the reflex, the oscillator, and the servomechanism.

4. A reflex circuit activates a particular set of motor neurons upon receipt of a particular sensory signal. The strength and duration of the motor neuron activity vary as a function of the strength and duration of the input, but feedback from the reflex movement during the movement does not alter the motor neuron signal.

5. An oscillator triggers rhythmic bursts of motor neuron signals. The period of oscillation may depend upon the tonic level of various inputs but the rhythm itself is endogenous—a consequence of the oscillator's properties.

6. A servomechanism activates motor neurons in a way calculated to reduce the discrepancy between two inputs. Changes in the discrepancy during the course of a servomechanistic movement alter the strength of the ongoing motor signal.

7. Signals flowing back and forth between circuits that organize elementary units of action help coordinate one with another. Among the distinguishable principles of intralevel coordination are:

   a. The facilitation of an agonistic circuit

   b. The inhibition of an antagonistic cricuit

   c. Chaining, that is, the production by one action of the stimulus conditions that activate another action

   d. Phase adjusting signals that transiently accelerate or retard an oscillation, depending on the phase of the oscillation at the moment the signal arrives

   e. Corollary discharge or efference copy signals that inhibit or algebraically cancel unwanted disruptive reafference

8. An ensemble of oscillators, interacting through phase-adjusting signals, may display a bewildering variety of outputs. The different ouputs result from small changes in a few controlling signals. These properties of coupled oscillator systems together with the pervasive rhythmicity in many complex patterns of behavior make it likely that networks of coupled oscillators are at the heart of the complex units of behavior known as central programs. The central program for walking is an instance.

9. Ensembles of elementary units of action are controlled as ensembles by signals that descend from circuits that coordinate more complex patterns of action. These more complex patterns constitute complex units of behavior. Again, the system that coordinates locomotion is an instance.

10. The structure of these complex units of action and the structures that interconnect them delimit the animal's behavioral options. Among the many manifestations of these structural constraints are limits on the kinds of solutions an animal will come up with in a learning situation. Instances of such limits are:

   a. The inability of salamanders with reversed forelimbs to learn a functional pattern of locomotion

   b. Pronounced species differences in the ability of birds to master a string pulling task

   c. The inability of racoons to master a fixed ratio piggy-bank task

   d. The extreme slowness with which hybrid lovebirds adopt a functional mode of carrying nest building material

11. The higher level circuits often control lower level circuitry by selective potentiation and depotentiation rather than direct activation. Potentiating a circuit, or a neuron within a circuit, lowers its threshold for activation. Depotentiating it raises its threshold.

12. Control by way of selective potentiation and depotentiation specifies a range of permissible actions. The pattern of activating inputs to lower levels determines which of the permissible actions actually occur. This arrangement provides for the flexible implementation of general plans.

13. This mode of control is demonstrable at every level of the system. It appears in the control of stumble-preventing reflexes by the stepping oscillator. It appears in the control that electrical stimulation of the diencephalon exerts over predation-subserving reflexes in the cat and learned food-producing responses in the rat.

14. A general course of action is specified by a relatively few command signals originating in the upper levels of the hierarchy. Each lower level narrows the range of possible momentary expressions of this plan. Thus, the signals that translate the plan into neuromuscular activity become more and more elaborate and detailed as the potentiating signals descend from level to level within the action hierarchy.

15. The concept of behavioral control through selective potentiation of functionally coherent subsets of lower units of action corresponds to the concept of drive as developed by ethologists and physiological psychologists. It helps clarify what is meant by intention, at least as that concept is applied to infant behavior by Bruner.

16. The processes governing the waxing and waning of drives have much in common with the processes that determine the forms of action in elementary units of behavior:

    a. Drive signals may be triggered by external stimuli

    b. Drive signals may be driven by endogenous oscillators

    c. Drive signals may reflect a discrepancy between set point signals and signals that indicate the actual state of a variable.

Often, all three sorts of processes have some effect on the level of a given drive signal.

17. Drive signals and intention signals may also grow stronger solely as a function of time since the last performance of the act organized by the signal. This phenomenon may be termed the autonomous accumulation of potentiation.

18. The phenomena described under the head of autonomous accumulation of potentiation seem to go hand in hand with the relaxation of a fixed order of subordination at higher levels of the action hierarchy. In place of a fixed hierarchy one observes a labile hierarchy, also termed a relative hierarchy or heterarchy. In a relative hierarchy a unit that seemingly belongs to a subordinate level of organization may potentiate units that would seem to

belong to a higher level, thereby bringing complex and lengthy patterns of behavior into the service of seemingly inconsequential ends.

19. The seemingly purposeless activity engendered by the autonomous accumulation of potentiation may serve a developmental purpose. It may provide the feedback experience necessary to adjust the parameters of the action circuitry so as to produce faster more reliable modules for incorporation into more complex patterns.

20. The autonomous accumulation of potentiation in relative low units of behavior and the attendant relaxation of a fixed scheme of subordination also yield playful behavior. In playful behavior, there are frequent reversals of means-ends relations and considerable aimless jumbling of diverse actions. The function of this play may be to reveal new and felicitous combinations of actions, combinations whose effects may be recorded for later use.

21. Points 19 and 20 cover two kinds of plasiticity in the organization of action, parameter optimization ("tuning") through practice and the creation of new units of action by novel combinations of old units. Another kind of plasticity, which is highly developed in man and the primates, involves the mastery of more or less arbitrarily skilled motions. These motions seem to be represented at the mnemonic level by a code that specifies trajectories but not the pattern of neuromuscular activity.

22. Fourier analysis of diverse skilled motions shows that their trajectories may generally be duplicated by imagining the motion to be the result of superimposing (performing concurrently) a few simple sinusoidal motions. This suggests that the engram for skilled movements may code movements in terms of their Fourier components, that is, in terms of the periods, amplitudes, phase relationships, and orientations of the sinusoidal motions that must be superimposed to obtain the required trajectory.

23. Assuming that the mnemonic code for skilled motions represents complex motions as combinations of simple motions oriented with respect to body space, there must be a stage that translates this code into appropriate neuromuscular activity. The translation stage must constantly rechannel the flow of signals to the limb musculature so as to align neuromuscular space with body space. This rechanneling insures that a signal commanding upward motion of the finger trips produces extensor excitation when the hand is oriented palm down and flexor excitation when it is oriented palm up.

24. In translating the motion commands into neuromuscular activity, the neuromuscular activity must be deliberately distorted in such a way as to offset the unavoidable distortions produced by the non-linear mechanical properties of the skeletomuscular system. This counter distortion linearizes the relation between the motion commands and the resulting movement.

25. One role of practice in the mastery of skilled motion may be to develop appropriate tunings (parameter adjustments) of the circuits that in turn adjust

the parameters of the counter-distortion stage. This may be termed tuning the tuning.

26. A fourth kind of plasticity in the organization of action depends on an animal's ability to form and store internal representations of the environment, that is, to make maps. Data on homing behavior and detour behavior show that map-based navigation is a startlingly widespread ability in the animal world, an ability clearly possessed by organisms as lowly as the rat, the ant, and the digger wasp.

27. Deutsch's model for the map-referenced control of orientation during navigation shows one way of dispensing with the homunculus, or little map reader, whose services are implicitly invoked in some discussions of behavior based on cognitive maps. A central concept in Deutsch's model is that the direction of orientation relative to the map is determined by the propagation of a motivational signal through the map.

28. The representation of space by animals as diverse as the chimpanzee, the rat, and the ant appears to be approximately Euclidean, that is, it appears to encode not only adjacency between points (as assumed by Deutsch) but also approximate distances and angles between points.

29. Studies by Shepard and Cooper show that humans can transform their representations of spatial configurations in a way that is closely analogous to the rotation of a Euclidean representation. It is suggested that animals navigating by reference to a Euclidean representation of the environment must perform a similar operation. The operation makes the alignment of their representation in the coordinates of body space correspond to the alignment of the body with respect to the environment.

30. It is difficult to envisage the neurobiological form of an animal's representation of space. What we believe about how the brain works suggests that this representation must be done in terms of signal vectors. That is, the engram must encode the strengths of some finite set of neuronal signals—signals deriving from the sensory perceptual system. Thus, one should be on the conceptual look out for signal-vector representations of 3-dimensional configuration. One should pay particular attention to representations having the property that an operation equivalent to rotation may easily be performed. Fourier analysis provides one illustration of the kind of code we should be on the look out for.

Glossary

ABDUCTOR. The muscle that pulls a limb forward and out away from (abduction) the body.

ABLATION. The removal of neural tissue.

ABSOLUTE COORDINATION. The maintenance of a constant phase relationship between two or more oscillators. (See Chapter 4.)

ACTION CONSTANCY. The achievement of movements that have a constant form despite wide variation in the underlying pattern of neuromuscular activity, as, for example, when one writes one's signature either at a desk or on a blackboard.

ACTION SPECIFIC ENERGY. Lorenz's term for selective potentiation.

ACTIVATING CONDITIONS. The stimulus conditions that cause a potentiated unit to become active, that is, to send out, or relay signals that influence the flow of signals to the muscles. (See p. 212 & Figure 8.1.)

ADEQUATE STIMULUS. The stimulus that is best suited to activate a particular reflex.

ADDUCTOR. The muscle that pulls a limb backward and in toward (adduction) the body.

AFFERENCE. An incoming signal. Sensory signals.

AFFERENT. Conducting (or conducted) toward the central nervous system, or toward the structure under discussion.

AGONIST. A unit (muscle, reflex, complex behavior pattern, etc.) that works *with* another unit or produces roughly the same result as another unit.

AMPLIFICATION. Relation between strength of input and strength of output. The process of changing the strength of a signal.

AMPLITUDE (of an oscillation). The maximal deviation from the midpoint or average position (See Figure 4.1a.)

ANALYSIS BY SYNTHESIS. Determining the constituents of an input by constructing a model of the input.

ANGULAR VELOCITY. The speed of rotation, the number of degrees (radians, cycles, etc.) rotated through in each second.

ANIMA. The nonphysical soul or spirit whose activity was thought by Hellenic philosophers to explain the actions of animals.

ANTAGONIST. A unit (muscle, reflex, etc.) that works against another unit or promotes an opposing result.

ARTHROPODA. Animals with a stiff body wall rather than a skeleton (or a shell), for example, insects, crayfish, spiders.

AUTOMATISM. A process that runs autonomously, that is, whose pattern of output is not determined by its pattern of input (although, the level and timing of input signals may affect some parameters of the output). Example: a pacemaker neuron, that is, an oscillator.

AXON. An individual nerve fiber. The long tubelike protrusion of a neuron, specialized for conducting nerve impulses.

BELL–MAGENDIE LAW. The law that of the two roots into which each peripheral nerve divides as it joins the spinal cord, the dorsal (backmost) one carries only incoming (sensory) signals and the ventral (frontmost) one carries only outgoing signals.

BREAK SHOCK. The electric shock in the secondary coil of an inductor that occurs at the moment the current in the primary coil stops flowing.

CELL THEORY. The theory that the nervous system is not made up of continuous conducting tubes, but rather of cells, called neurons, between which there are gaps that neural signals must somehow get across.

CENTRAL MOTIVE STATE. See DRIVE.

CENTRAL NERVOUS SYSTEM. Brain and spinal cord.

CENTRAL PROGRAM. A complex unit of behavior, in which activity of a circuit in the central nervous system establishes a basic program, pattern, or framework of movements. Sensory signals arising during the execution of the program produce variations in many details but the limits of variation and which variations are permitted at any moment are determined by the central circuitry.

CEREBRUM. The last (front-most) of the four major subdivisions of the brain; the part that is greatly enlarged in more recently evolved vertebrates. [See Fig. 9.1].

CHAINING. A method of generating a sequence of movements, acts, and so on, in which the first movement (act, etc.) in the sequence gives rise to stimuli that elicit the next movement, and so on.

CNS. Central nervous system.

COGNITION. A representation of some aspect of the world stored in memory.

COGNITIVE MAPS. A record of the relations between stimuli that experience and the operation of analytic–synthetic processes in the sensory system have revealed to the brain.

COGNITIVE THEORIES. A vaguely delimited class of theories about the causation of behavior that have in common only the assumption that behavior is the consequence of a series of complex processes whose structure is to be inferred from cleverly conceived experiments that neutralize the contribution of most of the stages and enable one to examine the contribution made by one or a few stages in the processing of input (information).

COMMON MODE REJECTION. An arrangement whereby a signal or signal component that is common to two signal pathways is blocked, usually by inverting one signal and subtracting it from the other.

COMMON PATH, principle of. See LATTICE HIERARCHY.

COMPLEX UNIT OF BEHAVIOR. A complex combination of actions that enters into several different behaviors and that cannot readily be activated piecewise. A complex unit coordinates the activities of two or more lower (more elementary) units of behavior.

CONTRALATERAL. On the opposite side.

COORDINATIVE STRUCTURE. Easton and Turvey's term for a unit of behavior.

COROLLARY DISCHARGE. A neural signal that arises as a corollary of a motor signal and inhibits neural pathways that would otherwise be activated by the sensory consequences of the movement initiated by the motor signal.

COUPLED OSCILLATORS. Neural oscillators that have a signal pathway between them carrying signals that tend to force one oscillator into a particular phase relationship vis-a-vis the other.

CRANIAD. Toward the cranium (skull).

CUTANEOUS. In or from the skin.

DEAFFERENTATION. Severing sensory nerves, usually at the point where they enter the spinal cord.

DECEREBRATION. Transecting the brain below the cerebrum.

DEGREES OF FREEDOM. The number of independent ways in which something may vary. Often used somewhat loosely to refer to the number of different directions in which a limb may move, or the number of different patterns of activity that may be generated in the same neuromuscular apparatus.

DENDRITES. Short protrusions of neurons, upon which other neurons make synaptic contacts.

DEPOTENTIATION. Reducing the potential for activity in a neural circuit so that its influence on behavior is removed or reduced. The complement of potentiation.

DEPRESSOR. The muscle that pulls a limb down.

DIENCEPHALON. The third of four major divisions of the brain, comprising the hypothalamus and thalamus. The level at which motivated sequences of behavior are organized. [See Fig. 9.1]

DORSAL. Toward the back.

DORSAL NERVE CORD. Spinal cord.

DORSAL ROOTS. See Bell–Magendie Law.

DRIVE. A signal originating at a high level in the hierarchical structure underlying behavior, which potentiates one class of behaviors, for example, behaviors that contribute to the maintenance of body water (thirst behaviors), and depotentiates other classes of behavior.

EFFERENCE. An outgoing motor signal; or simply an outgoing signal.

EFFERENCE COPY. A signal that is a proportionate copy of an efferent (motor) signal and that is used to cancel algebraically the reafferent signals, that is, the sensory signals produced by the animal's own movement.

EFFERENT. Conducting or being conducted away from the central nervous system toward muscles or glands; outgoing.

ELEMENTARY UNIT OF BEHAVIOR (or action). A nerve and muscle circuit capable by itself of mediating a simple naturally occurring movement. It must have a component or components in which nerve signals arise, components that conduct the signals to muscle, and muscles whose contraction causes the movement.

ELEVATOR. The muscle that elevates a limb.

ENCEPHALIZATION. The evolutionary and ontogenetic process through which the higher levels of the central nervous system assert coordinative control over units at lower levels.

ENGRAM. Neural embodiment of a memory.

ERROR SIGNAL. The signal sent to the motor machinery in a servomechanism. The sign ($\pm$) and magnitude of this signal reflect the discrepancy, if any, between the two signals that serve as inputs to the servomechanism. The error signal affects the motor apparatus in such a way that the resulting movement (or, in the case of a higher-level servomechanism, the resulting complex behavior) tends to reduce the discrepancy between the two input signals, thereby reducing the error signal. This reduction is called negative feedback.

EUCLIDEAN REPRESENTATION. A representation of points in space that encodes information about the angles and distances between the represented points. A scale model of an object is a Euclidean representation of that object. A globe is a Euclidean representation of the world. A flat map (Mercator Projection) is not, because it accurately represents angles but not distances.

EUCLIDEAN SPACE. An assemblage of points with distances and angles between them that may be completely expressed in a mathematical system of three dimensions. Roughly speaking, that space in the mathematical sense of the word, that corresponds most closely to our everyday intuitions about what is meant by the word space.

EXAFFERENCE.   Any afference (sensory signal) caused by movement of the environment (as distinguished from movement of the animal). (See Chapter 7.)

EXPECTATION.   A model of forthcoming sensory experience.

FACILITATION.   Making it easier for a unit of action to produce an output. The phenomenon is traceable to the nonlinear character of summation at synapses. Inputs that are below the threshold for a conducted output (an impulse) produce no output but provide a higher baseline of excitation or excitability upon which other inputs build.

FEEDBACK.   The effect of a response *upon the inputs that caused the response* (as distinguished from reafference, which refers to any sensory consequence of a response).

FINAL COMMON PATH.   Sherrington's term for the motor neurons; used in order to emphasize the fact that the same motor neurons were employed in many different reflexes.

FOREBRAIN.   The diencephalon and cerebrum. [See Fig. 9.1]

FOURIER COMPONENT.   One of a set of sinusoidal trajectories that when summed together (superimposed) yield a given trajectory. See Figures 4.1 through 4.4 for illustrations of the process of superimposing Fourier components.

GANGLION.   An aggregation of nerve cell bodies, where nerve signals are passed from one neuron to another; hence a site of integrative activity in a nervous system, a brain or sub-brain. The lower parts of the central nervous system in invertebrates consist of a number of separate sub-brains (ganglia) connected by nerve cords.

GRAY MATTER.   Regions of the central nervous system rich in cell bodies and dendrites, where neurons make functional contacts (synapses). Hence, the region within which neural signals are transmitted from one cell to another, being transformed and integrated in the process.

HEMISECTION.   Cutting into halves, for example, cutting the axons that connect the two bilaterally identical halves of a ganglion (sub-brain) in an invertebrate.

HETERARCHY.   See relative hierarchy.

HIERARCHY.   A system in which some circuits ("higher circuits") control the flow of activity in other circuits ("lower circuits").

HINDBRAIN.   The first of four major subdivisions of the brain; the bulbous portion of the brain, representing the continuation and enlargement of the spinal cord after it enters the skull. [See Fig. 9.1]

HISTOLOGY.   The study of tissue under a microscope.

HOLISTIC.   Adjective applied to theories that maintain that the functioning of a system cannot be comprehended on the basis of (weak holism), or does not depend on (strong holism), the properties of its parts and the laws or principles governing interactions between those parts.

HOMEOSTASIS.   The constancy of the *milieu interne*. The behavioral and physiological processes that maintain this constancy.

HOMONYMOUS.   Of the same name, e.g., "right front."

HOMUNCULUS.   A "little man" inside the brain whose assistance is implicitly summoned by psychological theorists who are unable otherwise to explain some aspect of human (or animal) behavior; used satirically.

HUMERUS.   Bone between the shoulder and the elbow.

IMPRINTING.   The formation of strong attachments to an object, animal, etc., experienced during an early period of postnatal development.

INTERNEURONS.   Neurons that are neither sensory neurons nor motor neurons, but are interposed between these two classes of neurons.

INTERNUNCIAL.   SEE INTERNEURON.

INTERSEGMENTAL.   Passing from one segment to another of an animal whose body is segmented (e.g., insects). Frequently there is a ganglion (sub-brain) in each segment, so intersegmental means passing from one ganglion to another by way of the interganglionic nerve cord.

INTROMISSION.   Penetration of the penis into the vagina.

IPSILATERAL.   On the same side.

LABYRINTHS.   The labyrinth shaped sensory organs designed to detect gravitational and accelerational forces in vertebrates; located adjacent to auditory structures.

LATTICE HIERARCHY.   A hierarchical control structure in which a unit at a lower level is subject to control by several units at a higher level.

LESION.   Damage or destruction of tissue.

LINEAR.   Having the property that the output for two or more inputs that occur close together or simultaneously is simply the sum of the outputs to each input alone.

MAGNET EFFECT.   The coordinative effect of a rhythmic signal upon an oscillator. The signal slows the oscillation if it arrives during one phase and speeds the oscillation if arrives during the other phase. This phase-dependent acceleration/deceleration tends to bring the oscillation into a fixed phase relationship with the rhythmic signal. The rhythmic signal may come from outside the animal (i.e., from a rhythmic stimulus) or from another oscillator within the animal.

MAKE SHOCK.   The electric shock from the secondary coil of an inductor at the moment current begins to flow in the primary coil.

MESOTHORACIC.   Middle of the thorax (chest-like region of an animal). The middle pair of legs in insects, which have 3 pairs of legs.

METACHRONAL.   Progressing in the direction of movement; used to describe the wave-like succession of leg movements, which, in an animal moving forward, begin at the rear and progress forward, and, in an animal moving backward, begin at the front and progress backward.

METATHORACIC.   After (behind) the chest; the hind pair of legs in an insect.

MIDBRAIN.   The second of four major subdivisions of the brain, the midbrain lies between the hindbrain and the diencephalon. The level at which many simple acts—such as walking, chewing, swallowing, grooming, expressing fear, rage, etc—are organized. [See Fig. 9.1]

MILIEU INTERNE.   The internal environment of the body: the temperature, salinity, pH, nutrient content, and so on, of the fluid surrounding a cell within the body of an animal. Homeostatic behavior is behavior that maintains the constancy of crucial aspects of this internal environment.

MOTIVATION.   See DRIVE.

MOTOR GANGLION CELLS.   Motor neurons.

MOTOR NEURONS.   The neurons that carry nerve impulses from the spinal cord to the muscles (by way of the ventral roots).

MOTOR UNIT.   A motor neuron and the muscle fibers it innervates.

MUTUAL FACILITATION.   See RECIPROCAL FACILITATION.

MUTUAL INHIBITION.   See RECIPROCAL INHIBITION.

NEGATIVE FEEDBACK.   The tendency of the actions controlled by a servomechanism to reduce the discrepancy between the two inputs to the servomechanism, thereby reducing the error signal, the signal which gave rise to, or direction to, the movements in the first place.

NERVE CORD.   See VENTRAL NERVE CORD.

NERVE FIBER.   See AXON.

NERVE TRUNKS.   Bundles of axons (nerve fibers) without any synapses.

NERVOUS IMPULSE.   The electrical impulse that sweeps down a neuron—the irreducible unit in which all conducted nervous signals are expressed.

NEUROGLIA.   Cells in the nervous system that support neurons and regulate the immediate environment of neurons but do not participate, so far as we know, in the generation, conduction, or integration of neural signals.

NEUROMUSCULAR SPACE.   The direction of movement produced by a given pattern of neuromuscular activity.

NEURON. A cell within the nervous system that generates, and/or conducts, and/or integrates neural signals.

NONLINEAR. Having the property that the output for two inputs that occur close together or simultaneously is not simply the moment by moment sum of the outputs to each input alone.

NONLINEAR SUMMATION. Summation in which the whole is greater than or less than the sum of the parts.

NYSTAGMUS. A movement of the eyes in which slow scanning motions alternate with abrupt returning motions.

OLFACTORY. Pertaining to the sense of smell.

ONTOGENY. The course of development; the processes by and through which an organic entity assumes its adult form.

OPTOKINETIC REACTION. An animal's tendency to turn the eye, or head, or body in the direction in which the image of the world moves across the eye. (See Introduction to Chapter 7.)

OSCILLATOR. A neuron or neural circuit whose electrical activity varies rhythmically in the absence of, or independently of, any rhythm in the signals impinging on it. Also used to refer to a unit of behavior whose rhythmic pattern is controlled by such a neuron or neural circuit.

PACEMAKER. A neuron or group of neurons that produce the rhythmic signal that drives some rhythmic muscle action. An oscillator.

PARAMETER. A variable (adjustable aspect of a system) that helps determine what kind of output the system generates, without actually initiating output.

PERIOD. The duration of one complete cycle of an oscillation.

PERIODICITY. The interval at which some cyclical perturbation of an oscillation recurs. (See Introduction to Chapter 4.)

PERISTALTIC. Involving waves of compression and expansion along a tube-like structure, as, for example, the digestive motion of the stomach.

PHASE-DEPENDENT ACCELERATION/DECELERATION. See MAGNET EFFECT.

PHASE. (See Introduction to Chapter 4.)

PHASE RELATIONSHIP. The relative positions of two oscillations in time, or, equivalently, the pattern of coincidences between their momentary phases.

PHASIC. Short lasting; varying rapidly.

PHYLOGENY. The sequence of forms through which a species has passed in the course of its evolution. The evolutionary history of a species or an anatomical, physiological, or behavioral unit.

PINNA. Tip of the ear.

PLANTA. Bottom of the foot or paw.

POTENTIATION (selective). Increasing the potential for activity in a neural circuit without actually causing activity. The principal means by which higher units coordinate the activity of lower units so as to produce complex behavior patterns whose details are adapted to momentary circumstances.

PRECOCIAL. Species in which the behavior of newborns is precociously well developed, so that the newborn can get around on their own.

PRECURRENT RECIPROCAL INHIBITION. (See Figure 3.4.)

PROPRIOCEPTIVE. Coming from sensory receptors in the joints and muscles.

PROTHORACIC. In front of the chest; the front pair of legs in an insect.

PROTOPLASM. The gelatinous substance inside a cell.

PROTRACTION. Swinging forward (when speaking of a leg); or pulling forward (when speaking of the action of a muscle on a leg).

PUSH-PULL CIRCUIT. A circuit in which the *appropriate* input produces changes of opposite sign in two signal pathways, that is, excites ("pushes") one pathway and inhibits (pulls) another. If the signal in one of these pathways is then subtracted from the signal in the other, one obtains a high and selective sensitivity to appropriate inputs. Inappropriate inputs, inputs that excite both pathways, are filtered out (common-mode rejection).

PYRAMIDAL SYSTEM. A set of neurons with a characteristic form that project directly from the cortex of the cerebrum to low-level spinal circuitry and to motor neurons; much more extensively developed in man and the primates than in other mammals and vertebrates.

REAFFERENCE. Reafferent signals, that is, sensory signals produced by the animal's own action.

RECIPROCAL FACILITATION. When two neural circuits, for example, two reflex arcs, send weakly excitatory branches to each other so that activity in one circuit promotes or makes easier the occurrence of activity in the other.

RECIPROCAL INHIBITION. When two neural circuits, for example, two reflex arcs, send inhibitory branches to each other so that activity in one circuit inhibits activity in the other.

RECURRENT RECIPROCAL INHIBITION. (See Figure 3.6.)

REFLEX. An elementary unit of behavior, mediated by a reflex arc consisting of a receptor tuned to respond only to certain natural stimuli, a sensory neuron that conducts the signals from the receptor into the CNS, a set of interneurons (usually) that relay the signal to an appropriate set of motorneurons, a set of motor neurons (or a hormone) that convey the signal to one or more effectors, and a set of effectors that translate the signal into muscular contraction or glandular secretion. A purely reflex response rises to a single peak and dies away; the amplitude and duration of the response are determined by the strength of the initiating stimulus and the properties of the synapses in the reflex arc; the feedback from response to the initiating receptors is irrelevant.

RELATIVE COORDINATION. The phenomenon of phase drift, at a periodically varying rate, which is observed when two or more oscillators are so weakly coupled that the coordinating signals passing between them do not have an effect strong enough to maintain a fixed phase relationship. (See Chapter 4).

RELATIVE HIERARCHY. A hierarchy in which different acts may serve as the culminating act in a behavioral sequence, depending on the behavioral context; hence, a hierarchy in which the order of subordination (which act serves which) is labile. (See Chapter 10.)

REPRESENTATION. A coded message or record that has been obtained from the interaction between the real world and an encoding device, such as the sensory system of an animal, and that has in it information from which some other process may determine some properties of the real world.

RETRACTION. Swinging backward (when speaking of a leg) or pulling backward (when speaking of the action of a muscle on a leg).

SACCADE. An abrupt change in the orientation of the eyes to a precalculated new position; a ballistic (reflex) rather than servomechanistic movement of the eyes.

SAGITTAL. The vertical plane that cuts through the midline of any symmetrical animal, dividing one half from the other (symmetrical) half of the body.

SCHEMA. A representation of a to-be-performed movement; a plan.

SELF-DIFFERENTIATED. Developed independently of the intervention of function; roughly speaking, what people have in mind (or ought to have in mind) when they say something is inherited.

SERVOMECHANISM. A unit of behavior for which there are (a) two inputs, (b) an error signal that is a function of the discrepancy between the inputs and that activates a movement or pattern of movements, and (c) a feedback effect of the movement(s) upon one or both of the inputs.

SIGNAL VECTOR. A set of signals, each signal having some strength. For example, a set of neurons each firing at some rate: the firing rate of each neuron—the number of impulses the neuron conducts per second—is one signal. The set of numbers representing the firing rate of each neuron is a vector in the mathematical sense.

SPINAL ANIMAL. Animal whose central nervous system has been transected so as to isolate the spinal cord from the brain.

SPINAL CORD. The cord like extension of the brain that runs within a protective bony channel formed by the vertebrae (the bones that comprise the backbone).

SPINAL ROOT GANGLION. A clump of cell bodies on one of the two roots that each peripheral nerve divides into as it joins the spinal cord. The spinal root ganglion contains the cell bodies of all of the sensory neurons in the nerve, but there are no synapses in this ganglion. The sensory neurons synapse with other neurons in the gray matter of the spinal cord.

S-R THEORY. A very influential theory of learning, particularly in the years 1930–1960. Its chief tenet is that learned behavior can be thought of as a chain of events in which the occurrence of an initial stimulus either "elicits" (Hull) or "increases the probability of the emission of" (Skinner) a response, which generates a new stimulus, which in turn "elicits" ("increases . . . ") a second response, etc. The tendency of a stimulus to "elicit" ("increase . . . ") some response is assumed to be governed by the law of effect, which states that the tendency increases if making that response in the presence of that stimulus has been followed by a pleasant outcome (a reinforcer), and decreases otherwise.

STATOCYST. Organ for sensing direction of gravitational pull. (See Figure 6.4.)

STATOLITH. Stone within a statocyst, which is pulled this way or that by gravity and indicates the direction of gravitational pull by bending the sensory hairs on which it rests.

SUBLIMINAL SUMMATION. The summation of inputs in a system that has some sort of threshold (limin) such that there is no output until or unless the sum exceeds the threshold—a common type of nonlinear summation.

SUPERIMPOSITION. The moment by moment addition of two or more movements or processes; the concurrent performance of two oscillatory motions. (See Figures 4.1 through 4.4 for illustration).

SWING PHASE. The phase of the stepping cycle when the leg is lifted and advanced, that is, swung.

SYMPATHETIC GANGLIA. Small clusters of neuronal cell bodies outside the central nervous system, where synaptic contacts are made between neurons coming from the spinal cord and neurons going to smooth muscles (intestine, etc.) and glands.

SYNAPSE. An area where the membranes enclosing two different neurons are closely juxtaposed and across which neural signals are transmitted in one direction only.

TAXIS. A servomechanism that keeps the body oriented at some fixed angle with respect to some stimulus. A *photo*taxis, keeps the body oriented with respect to light, a *geo*taxis with respect to the earth's gravitational pull, etc.

TONIC. Long lasting; changing only slowly if at all.

TOPOLOGICAL. Representing only the property of adjacency between points, not distances or angles; a characteristic of the cognitive maps assumed by Deutsch (1960).

TUNING. Adjusting a parameter, that is, something that determines what output a system will give without actually generating an output (e.g., adjusting the strength and duration of a reflex response, a response that will actually occur only if and when an appropriate activating stimulus occurs).

UNIT OF BEHAVIOR (unit of action). See *Elementary unit of behavior* and *Complex unit of behavior* for definition.

VACUUM BEHAVIOR. An act performed in the absence of appropriate activating conditions and in the absence of any objective need for the act.

VECTOR. A string of numbers.

VENTRAL. Toward the stomach.

VENTRAL NERVE CORD. The cord like bundle of axons that passes ventrally in arthropods (millipedes, crayfish, insects), connecting one ganglion to another. Functionally analogous to the white matter of the vertebrate spinal cord.

VENTRAL ROOTS. See BELL–MAGENDIE LAW.

WHITE MATTER. Portions of the central nervous system that contain only axons, no cell bodies, dendrites, or synapses. Therefore, portions which conduct signals but do not integrate or combine them in any way.

References[1]

Adams, J. A. Feedback theory of how joint receptors regulate the timing and positioning of a limb. *Psychological Review*, 1977, *84*, 504–523.

Adler, N. T. On the mechanisms of sexual behavior and their evolutionary constraints. In J. B. Hutchinson (Ed.) *Biological determinants of sexual behaviour*. New York: Wiley, 1978.

Adrian, E. D. Discharges from vestibular receptors in the cat. *Journal of Physiology*, 1943, *101*, 389–407

Adrian, E. D. *The mechanism of nervous action: Electrical studies of the neurone*. Philadelphia: University of Pennsylvania Press, 1932.

Adrian, E. D. Potential changes in the isolated nervous system of Dytiscus marginalis. *Journal of Physiology*, 1931, *72*, 132–151.

Ayers, J. L. & Selverston, A. I. Synaptic control of an endogenous pacemaker network. *Journal de Physiologie*, 1977, *73*, 453–461.

Babuchin, A. Uebersicht der neuen untersuchungen über Entwickelung, Bau und physiologische Verhältnisse der elektrischen and pseudoëlektrischen Organe. *Archiv für Anatomie, Physiologie, und wissenschaftliche Medicin*, 1876.

Bandler, R. & Flynn, J. P. Visual patterned reflex present during hypothalamically elicited attack. *Journal of Comparative and Physiological Psychology*, 1972, *81*, 541–554.

Bard, P., & Macht, M. B. The behavior of chronically decerebrate cats. In G. E. W. Wolstenholme & C. M. O'Conner (Eds.) *Neurological basis of behavior*. Boston: Little Brown, 1958.

Bard, P., & Mountcastle, V. B. Some forebrain mechanisms involved in the expression of rage with special reference to suppression of angry behavior. *Research Publications of the Association for Research in Nervous and Mental Disease*, 1948, *27*, 362–404.

Bard, P., & Rioch, D. McK. A study of four cats deprived of neocortex and additional portions of the forebrain. *Bulletin of The Johns Hopkins Hospital*, 1937, *60*, 73–147.

Bartlett, F. C. *Thinking*. New York: Basic Books, 1958.

---

[1] I have tried to put all of the citations in APA form. In some cases, however, it was not possible to complete a citation. Such cases are marked with an asterisk.

Bayliss, W. M., & Starling, E. H. The movements of the small intestine. *Journal of Physiology*, 1899, *24*, 99–143.

Beagley, W. K., & Holley, T. L. Hypothalamic stimulation facilitates contralateral visual control of a learned response. *Science*, 1977, *196*, 321–322.

Baeumer, E. Lebensart des Haushuhns. *Zeitschrift für Tierpsychologie*, 1955, *12*, 387–401.

Bell, C. *Idea of a new anatomy of the brain*. London: Strahan & Preston (printers), 1811.

Benson, J. A., & Jacklet, J. W. Circadian rhythm of output from neurones in the eye of aplysia. I-IV. *Journal of Experimental Biology*, 1977, *70*, 151–212.

Bernhard, C. G., & Therman, P. O. Alternating facilitation and inhbition of the extensor muscle activity in decerebrate cats. *Acta Physiologica Scandinavica*, 1947, *14*, Suppl. 47, No. 3.

Bernstein, N. *The coordination and regulation of movements*. London: Pergammon, 1967.

Berntson, G. G., Hughes, H. C., & Beattie, M. S. A comparison of hypothalamically induced biting attack with natural predatory behavior in the cat. *Journal of Comparative and Physiological Psychology*, 1976, *2*, 167–178.

Bethe, A. Die biologischen Rhythmusphänomene als selbständige beziehungsweise erzwungene Kippvorgänge betrachtet. *Archiv für die gesamte Physiologie*, 1940, *244*, 1–42.

Bethe, A. Plastizität und Zentrenlehre. In A. Bethe & T. Julius (Eds.) *Handbuck der normalen und pathologischen Physiologie*. Vol. 15. Berlin: J. Springer, 1931.

Bethe, A. Studien über die Plastizität des Nervensystems. I. Arachnoideen und Crustaceen. *Archiv für die gesamte Physiologie*, 1930, *224*, 793–820.

Bethe, A. *Allgemeine Anatomie und Physiologie des Nervensystems*. Leipzig: Thieme, 1902. [Erroneously dated 1903 by Sherrington.]

Bethe, A. Das central Nervensystem von Carcinus Maenas. II. Das normale Funktioniren von Neuronen nach Fortnahme der zugehörigen Ganglienzellen. *Archiv für mikroskopische Anatomie*, 1897, *50*, 629–639. (a)

Bethe, A. Vergleichende Untersuchungen über die Funktionen des Centralnervensystems der Arthropoden. *Archiv für die gesamte Physiologie*, 1897, *68*, 449–545. (b)

Bethe, A., & Fischer, E. Die Anpassungsfähigkeit (Plastizität) des Nervensystems. In: A. Bethe & T. Julius (Eds.) *Handbuch der normalen und pathologischen Physiologie*. Vol. 15. Berlin: Springer, 1931.

Bethe, A., & Woitas, E. Studien über die Plastizität des Nervensystems. II. Coleopteren, Käfer. *Archiv für die gesamte Physiologie*, 1930, *224*, 821–835.

Beusekom, G. van. Some experiments on the optical orientation in *Philanthus Triangulum* Fabr. *Behaviour*, 1948, *1*, 195–225.

Bizzi, E., Kalil, R. E., & Tagliasco, V. Eye-head coordination in monkeys: evidence for centrally patterned organization. *Science*, 1971, *173*, 452–454.

Böhm, H. Vom lebendigen Rhythmus. *Studium Generale*, 1950, *4*, 28–41.

Bohn, G. Attractions et oscillations des animaux sous l'influence de la lumière. *Memoire de L'Institut Général Psychologique*, 1905, *1*, 1–111.

Bolles, R. C. *Theory of motivation*. New York: Harper & Row, 1967.

Book, W. F. *The psychology of skill*. Missoula: Montana Press, 1908.

Breland, K., & Breland, M. The misbehavior of organisms. *American Psychologist*, 1961, *16*, 681–684.

Brown, T. G. On the nature of the fundamental activity of the nervous centres; together with an analysis of the conditioning of rhythmic activity in progression, and a theory of evolution of function in the nervous system. *Journal of Physiology*, 1914, *48*, 18–46.

Brun, R. *Die Raumorientierung der Ameisen and das Orientierungsproblem im Allgemeinen*. Jena: Gustav Fischer, 1914.

Bruner, J. S. The organisation of early skilled action. In M. P. M. Richards (Ed.), *The integration of a child into a social world*. London: Cambridge University Press, 1974.

Bruner, J. S. The growth and structure of skill. In K. Connolly (Ed.) *Mechanisms of motor skill development*. New York: Academic, 1970.

Bryan, W. L., & Harter, N. Studies on the telegraphic language: The acquisition of a hierarchy of habits. *Psychological Review,* 1899, *6,* 345–375.

Buddenbrock, W. von. Physiologie der Sinnesorgane und des Nervensystems. In his: *Grundriss der vergleichenden Physiologie.* Vol. 1. Berlin: Borntraeger, 1937.

Buddenbrock, W. von. Der Rhythmus der Schreitbewegungen der Stabheuschrecke *Dyxippus. Biologisches Zentralblatt,* 1921, *41,* 41–48.

Bullock, T. H. Mechanisms of integration. In T. H. Bullock & G. A. Horridge (Eds.) *Structure and function in the nervous system of invertebrates.* Vol. 1. San Francisco: Freeman, 1965.

Bullock, T. H. The origins of patterned nervous discharge. *Behaviour,* 1961, *17,* 48–59.

Bullock, T. H., & Diecke, P. J. Properties of an infrared receptor. *Journal of Physiology,* 1956, *134,* 47–87.

Bullock, T. H., Orkand, R., & Grinnell, A. *Introduction to nervous systems.* San Francisco: Freeman, 1977.

Camhi, J. M. Behavioral switching in cockroaches: Transformation of tactile reflexes during righting behavior. *Journal of Comparative Physiology,* 1977, *113,* 283–301.

Camhi, J. M., & Hinkle, M. Attentiveness to sensory stimuli: Central control in locusts. *Science,* 1972, *175,* 550–553.

Campbell, F. W., & Robson, J. G. Application of Fourier analysis to the visibility of gratings. *Journal of Physiology,* 1968, *197,* 551–566.

Carlson, J. R., & Bentley, D. Ecdysis: Neural orchestration of a complex behavioral performance. *Science,* 1977, *195,* 1006–1008.

Carlson, N. R. *Physiology of behavior.* Boston: Allyn & Bacon, 1977.

Carr, H., & Watson, J. B. Orientation of the white rat. *Journal of Comparative Neurology and Psychology,* 1908, *18,* 27–44.

Chomsky, N. *Aspects of the theory of syntax.* Cambridge, Massachusetts: MIT Press, 1965.

Cooper, L. A., & Shepard, R. N. Transformations on representations of objects in space. In E. C. Carterette & M. Friedman (Eds.) *Handbook of perception. Volume VIII. Space and object perception.* New York: Academic, 1979 (in press).

Cornetz, V. *Les explorations et les voyages des fourmis.* Paris: E. Flammarion, 1914.

Crago, P. E., Houk, J. C., & Hasan, Z. Regulatory actions of human stretch reflex. *Journal of Neurophysiology,* 1976, *39,* 925–935.

Darwin, C. *The expression of the emotions in man and animals.* London: J. Murray, 1872.

Delcomyn, F. The locomotion of the cockroach periplaneta americana. *Journal of Experimental Biology,* 1971, *54,* 443–452. (a)

Delcomyn, F. The effect of limb amputation on locomotion in the cockroach, periplaneta americana. *Journal of Experimental Biology,* 1971, *54,* 453–470. (b)

Deliagina, T. G., Fel'dman, A. G., Gelfand, I. M., & Orlovsky, G. N. On the role of central program and afferent inflow in the control of scratching movements in the cat. *Brain Research,* 1975, *100,* 297–313.

Dethier, V. G. *The hungry fly.* Cambridge, Massachusetts: Harvard University Press, 1976.

Deutsch, J. A. *The structural basis of behavior.* Chicago: University of Chicago Press, 1960.

DeValois, K. K., Albrecht, D. G., & Thorell, L. G. Cortical cells: bar and edge detectors or spatial frequency filters. In S. Cool (Ed.) *Frontiers of visual science.* New York: Springer-Verlag, 1979.

Dilger, W. C. The comparative ethology of the African parrot genus agapornus. *Zeitschrift für Tierpsychologie,* 1960, *17,* 649–685.

Dilger, W. C. The behavior of lovebirds. *Scientific American,* 1962, *206* (No. 1), 88–99.

Doty, R. W., & Bosma, J. F. An electromyographic analysis of reflex deglutition. *Journal of Neurophysiology,* 1956, *19,* 44–61.

Dresden, D., & Nijenhuis, E. D. Fibre analysis of the nerves of the second thoracic leg in Periplaneta americana. *Proceedings of Koninklyke Nederlanske Akademie van Wetenshapen, Series C,* 1958, *61,* 213–223.

Dullemeijer, P. Some remarks on the feeding behavior of rattlesnakes. *Proceedings of Koninklyke Nederlandse Akademie van Wetenshapen, Series C,* 1961, *64,* 383–396.

Dusser de Barenne, J. G., & de Kleyn, A. Ueber vestibulaeren Nystagmus nach Exstirpation von allen sechs Augenmuskeln beim Kaninchen. Beitrag zur Wirkung und Innervation des Musculus retractor bulbi. *Archiv für die gesamte Physiologie,* 1929, *221,* 1–14.

Easton, T. A. On the normal use of reflexes. *American Scientist,* 1972, *60,* 591–599.

Eccles, R. M., & Lundberg, A. Supraspinal control of interneurones mediating spinal reflexes. *Journal of Physiology,* 1959, *147,* 565–584.

Edkins, J. S. On the chemical mechanism of gastric secretion. *Proceedings of the Royal Society, Series B,* 1905, *76,* 376.

Eisenstein, E. M., & Cohen, M. J. Learning in a single insect ganglion. *Physiologist,* 1964, *7,* 123.

Elsner, N. The central nervous control of courtship behavior in the grasshopper Gomphocerippus refus L. (Orthoptera, Acrididae). *Symposium on Invertebrate Neurobiology,* Tihany, Hungary, 1972.

Emonet-Dénand, F., Laporte, Y., Matthews, P. B. C., & Petit, J. On the subdivision of static and dynamic fusimotor actions on the primary ending of the cat muscle spindle. *Journal of Physiology,* 1977, *268,* 827–861.

Erlanger, J., & Gasser, H. S. *Electrical Signs of Nervous Activity.* Philadelphia: University of Pennsylvania Press, 1937.

Estartús, M., & Ponz, F. Sobre la fisiologia de la locomocion de Blatta orientalis (L). II. Importancia de las patas en la coordinacion nerviosa de la marcha. *Revista Espanola di Fisiologia,* 1951, *7,* 49–61.

Evarts, E. V. Brain mechanisms in movement. *Scientific American,* 1973, *229,* (No. 1), 96–103.

Evarts, E. V., Bizzi, E., Burke, R. E., DeLong, M. & Thach, W. T. (Eds.) Central control of movement. *Neurosciences Research Program Bulletin,* 1971, *9,* No. 1.

Exner, S. In welcher Weise tritt die negative Schwankung durch das Spinalganglion? *Anchiv für Anatomie und Physiologie: Physiologische Abteilung,* 1877, 567–570.

Falk, G. Interpretation of imperfect line data as three dimensional scene. *Artificial Intelligence,* 1972, *3,* 101–144.

Fentress, J. C. The development of grooming in mice with amputated forelimbs. *Science,* 1973, *179,* 704–705.

Fentress, J. C. *Simpler networks and behavior.* Sunderland, Massachusetts: Sinauer, 1976.

Fielden, A. The localization of function in the root of an insect segmental nerve. *Journal of Experimental Biology,* 1963, *40,* 553–561.

Fischer, M. H. Die Funktion des Vestibularapparates (der Bogengange und Otolithen) bei Fischen, Amphibien, Reptilien und Vogeln. In A. Bethe & T. Julius (Eds.): *Handbuch der normalen und pathologischen Physiologie.* Vol. II. Berlin: Springer, 1926.

Fischer, M. H., & Wodak, E. Experimentelle Untersuchungen über vestibularis Reaktionen. *Zeitschrift fur Hals-Nasen-und Ohrenheilkunde,* 1922, *3,* 198–215. [or perhaps the following article by Wodak & Fischer entitled: Uber die Arm-Tonus-Reaktion. (Pp. 215–219) is von Holst's intended ref.]

Flynn, J. P. Patterning mechanisms, patterned reflexes, and attack behavior in cats. *Nebraska Symposium on Motivation,* 1972, *20,* 125–153.

Flynn, J. P., Edwards, S. B., & Bandler, R. J. Changes in sensory and motor systems during centrally elicited attack. *Behavioral Science,* 1971, *16,* 1–19.

Foerster, O. *Either:*Motorische Felder und Bahnen (Vol. 6, 1–357); *or:* Sensible Corticale Felder (Vol. 6, 358–449); *or:* Symptomatologie der Erkranungen des Ruckenmarks und seiner Wurzeln (Vol. 5, 1–403) In: O. Bumke & O. Foerster (Eds.) *Handbuch der Neurologie.* Berlin: Springer, 1935–1936. [It is unclear which of these three articles is von Holst's intended reference.]

Forbes, A. Conduction in axon and synapse. *Cold Spring Harbor Symposia on Quantitative Biology,* 1936, *4,* 163–169.

Forssberg, H. S., Grillner, S., & Rossignol, S. Phase dependent reflex reversal during walking in chronic spinal cats. *Brain Research,* 1975, *85,* 103–107.

Foster, M., & Sherrington, C. S. *Text-book of Physiology, Part III.* London: Macmillan, 1897.

Fraenkel, G. S. Untersuchungen über die Koordination von Refexen und automatischnervösen Rhythmen bei Insekten. IV. Über die nervösen Zentren der Atmung und die Koordination ihrer Tätigkeit. *Zeitschrift für vergleichende Physiologie,* 1932, *16,* 444–461.

Fraenkel, G. S., & Gunn, D. L. *The orientation of animals.* New York: Dover, 1961.

Frey, M. von. Untersuchungen über die Sinnesfunktionen der menschlichen Haut; Druckempfindung und Schmerz. *Abhandlungen der königlicken sächsischen Gesellschaft der Wissenschaften. Mathematisch-physikalische classe,* 1897, *23,* 169–266.

Friedländer, B. Beiträge zur Physiologie des Zentralnervensystems und des Bewegungsmechanismus der Regenwurmer. *Archiv für die gesamte Physiologie,* 1894, *58,* 168–207.

Fulton, J. F. *Physiology of the nervous system* (2nd ed.) London: Oxford University Press, 1943.

*Gad, J. *Tageblatt der 66te Versammlung deutscher Naturforscher und Aertze,* 1884.

Gad, J. & Joseph, M. Ueber die Beziehungen der Nervenfasern zu den Nervenzellen in den Spinalganglion. *Archiv für Anatomie and Physiologie: Physiologische Abteilung,* 1889, 199–237.

Galef, B. G., Jr., & Clark, M. M. Social factors in the poison avoidance and feeding behavior of wild and domesticated rat pups. *Journal of Comparative and Physiological Psychology,* 1971, *75,* 341–357.

Gallistel, C. R. The irrelevance of past pleasure: Comments on D. Bindra's, "How adaptive behavior is produced: A perceptual-motivational alternative to response-reinforcement." *Behavioral and Brain Sciences,* 1978, *1,* 59–60.

Gallup, G. G., Jr. Animal hypnosis: Factual status of a fictional concept. *Psychological Bulletin,* 1974, *81,* 836–853.

Gallup, G. G., Jr., Nash, R. F., & Ellison, A. L., Jr. Tonic immobility as a reaction to predation: Artificial eyes as a fear stimulus for chickens. *Psychonomic Science,* 1971, *23,* 79–80.

Gasser, H. S. The control of excitation in the nervous system. *Harvey Lectures,* 1936–1937, 169–193.

Gaze, R. M. *The formation of nerve connections.* New York: Academic, 1970.

Gelfand, I. M., Gurfinkel, V. S., Tsetlin, M. L., & Shik, M. L. Some problems in the analysis of movements. In I. M. Gelfand, V. S. Gurfinkel, S. V. Fromin, & M. L. Tsetlin (Eds.) *Models of the structural-functional organization of certain biological systems.* Cambridge, Massachusetts: MIT Press, 1971.

Gelman, R., & Gallistel, C. R. *The child's understanding of number.* Cambridge, Massachusetts: Harvard University Press, 1978.

Gergens, E. Einige Versuche uber Reflexbewegung mit dem Influenz-Apparat. *Archiv für die gesamte Physiologie,* 1876, *13,* 61–71.

Gesell, A. Maturation and infant behavior patterns. *Psychological Review,* 1929, *36,* 307–319.

Gettrup, E. Control of forewing twisting by hind-wing receptors in flying insects. Paper presented at the *International Congress on Entomology, 12th,* London: 1964.

Gettrup, E. Phasic stimulation of a thoracic stretch receptor in locusts. *Journal of Experimental Biology,* 1963, *40,* 323–333.

Gettrup, E. Thoracic proprioceptors in the flight system of locusts. *Nature,* 1962, *193,* 498–499.

Geuze, J. J. Observation on the function and structure of the statocysts of *Lynnae Stagnalis. Netherlands Journal of Zoology,* 1968, *18,* 155–204.

Gibson, J. J. Visually controlled locomotion and visual orientation in animals. *British Journal of Psychology,* 1958, *49,* 182 194.

Goldscheider, A. *Die Bedeutung der Reize für Pathologie und Therapie im Lichte der Neuronlehre.* Leipsig: Barth, 1898.

Goldstein, K. *The organism. A holistic approach to biology derived from pathological data in man.* New York and Cincinnati: American Book Company, 1939.

Goldstein, K., & Riese, W. Über den Einfluss sensibler Hautreize auf die sogenannten vestibulären Reaktionsbewegungen. *Klinische Wochenschrift,* 1925, *4,* 1201–4 and 1250–4.

Goltz, F. *Beiträge zur Lehre von den Funktionen der Nervencentren des Frosches.* Berlin: Hirschwald, 1869.

Goltz, F. *Ueber die Verrichtungen des Grosshirns.* Bonn: Strauss, 1881.

Goodwin, G. M., & Luschei, E. S. Effects of destroying spindle afferents from jaw muscles on mastication in monkey. *Journal of Neurophysiology,* 1974, *37,* 967–981.

Goodwin, G. M., & Luschei, E. S. Discharge of spindle afferents from jaw closing muscles during chewing in alert monkeys. *Journal of Neurophysiology,* 1975, *38,* 560–570.

Graham, N., & Nachmias, J. Detection of grating patterns containing two spatial frequencies: A comparison of single-channel and multiple-channel models. *Vision Research,* 1971, *11,* 251–259.

Granit, R. The functional role of the muscle spindles—facts and hypothesis. *Brain,* 1975, *98,* 531–556.

Gray, J. The role of peripheral sense organs during locomotion in the vertebrates. *Symposia of the Society for Experimental Biology,* 1950, *4,* 112–126.

Gray, J., & Lissmann, H. W. Further observations on the effect of deafferentiation on the locomotory activity of amphibian limbs. *Journal of Experimental Biology,* 1946, *23,* 121–132.

Greene, P. H. Problems of organization of motor systems. *Progress in Theoretical Biology,* 1972, *2,* 303–338.

*Griesmann, B. Zur kalorischen Erregung des Ohrlabyrinths. *Zbl. Ohrenheilk.,* 1922, 19, 336–7. [Sic. The only journal corresponding approximately to this v. Holst abbrev. in the World List of Periodicals is *Zentral blatt für Hals-, Nasen-, und Ohrenheilkunde,* but the indicated article is not at the indicated pages in either Volume 1, 1922, or Volume 19, 1932.]

Grillner, S. Locomotion in vertebrates: Central mechanisms and reflex interaction. *Physiological Reviews,* 1975, *55,* 247–306.

Gurfinkel, V. S., Kots, Ya. M., Krinskiy, V. I., Pal'tsev, Ye. I., Fel'dman, A. G., Tsetlin, M. L., & Shik, M. L. Concerning tuning before movement. In J. M. Gelfand, V. S. Gurfinkel, S. V. Fromin, & M. L. Tsetlin (Eds.) *Models of structural-functional organization of certain biological systems.* Cambridge, Massachusetts: MIT Press, 1971.

Hagiwara, S. Nervous activities of the heart in Crustacea. *Ergebnisse der Biologie,* 1961, *24,* 287–311.

Hagiwara, S., & Watanabe, A. Discharges in motoneurons of cicada. *Journal of Cellular and Comparative Physiology,* 1956, *47,* 415–428.

Hall, M. *Synopsis of the diastaltic nervous system.* London: Mallet (printer), 1850.

Hall, W. G., Cramer, C. P., & Blass, E. M. Developmental changes in suckling of rat pups. *Nature,* 1975, *258,* 318–319.

Hall, W. G., Cramer, C. P., & Blass, E. M. Ontogeny of suckling in rats: Transition toward adult ingestion. *Journal of Comparative and Physiological Psychology,* 1977, *91,* 1141–1155.

Haller, A. von. *De partibus corporis humani sentientibus et nonsentientibus.* Göttingen: Royal Society, 1752.

Harcombe, E. S., & Wyman, R. J. Output pattern generation by *Drosophila* flight motoneurons. *Journal of Neurophysiology,* 1977, *40,* 1066–1077.

Harmon, L. D. Neuromimes: action of reciprocally inhibitory pair. *Science,* 1964, *146,* 1323–25.

Haseman, J. D. The rhythmical movements of *Littorina littorea* synchronous with ocean tides. *Biological Bulletin of the Marine Biology Laboratory,* 1911, *21,* 113–121.

Hastings, J. W., & Schweiger, H. G. (Eds.) *The molecular basis of circadian rhythms.* Berlin: Dahlem Konferenz, 1976.

Haycraft, J. Reflex spinal scratching movements in some vertebrates. *Brain*, 1890, *12*, 516–519.

Hearst, E., & Jenkins, H. M. *Sign tracking: The stimulus-reinforcer relation and directed action.* Austin, Texas: The Psychonomic Society, 1975.

Hebb, D. O. The American revolution. *American Psychologist*, 1960, *15*, 735–745.

Held, R., & Hein, A. Movement produced stimulation in the development of visually guided behavior. *Journal of Comparative and Physiological Psychology*, 1963, *56*, 872–876.

Herman, R. M., Grillner, S., Stein, P. S. G., & Stuart, D. G. (Eds.) *Neural control of locomotion.* New York: Plenum, 1976.

Herrick, C. J. Localization of function in the nervous system. *Proceedings of the National Academy of Sciences*, 1930, *16*, 643–650.

Hertz, M. Zur Physiologie des Formen- und Bewegungs- sehens. I. *Zeitschrift für vergleichende Physiologie*, 1934, *20*, 430–449.

Hess, W. R. *Das Zwischenhirn* (2nd ed.) Basel: Schwabe, 1954.

Hinde, R. A., & Stevenson-Hinde, J. (Eds.) *Constraints on learning.* New York: Academic, 1973.

Hineline, P. N., & Rachlin, H. Escape and avoidance of shock by pigeons pecking a key. *Journal of Experimental Analysis of Behavior*, 1969, *12*, 533–538.

Hinkle, M., & Camhi, J. M. Locust motoneurons: Bursting activity correlated with axon diameter. *Science*, 1972, *175*, 553–556.

Hinsey, J. V., Ranson, S. W., & McNattin, R. F. The role of the hypothalamus and mesencephalon in locomotion. *Archives of Neurology and Psychiatry*, 1930, *23*, 1–43.

Hoffmann, F. B. Augenbewegung und relative optische Lokalisation. *Zeitschrift für Biologie*, 1924, *80*, 81–90.

Holst, E. von. Relative coordination as a phenomenon and as a method of analysis of central nervous functions. In: *The behavioral physiology of animals and man. Selected papers of Eric von Holst.* Coral Gables, Florida: University of Miami Press, 1973.

Holst, E. von. Die Arbeitsweise des Statolithenapparates bei Fischen. *Zeitschrift für vergleichende Physiologie*, 1950, *32*, 60–120. (a)

Holst, E. von. Die Tätigkeit des Statolithenapparates im Wirbeltierlabyrinth. *Die Naturwissenschaften*, 1950, *37*, 265–272. (b)

Holst, E. von. Von der Mathematik der nervosen Ordnungsleistungen. *Experientia*, 1948, *4*, 374–381.

Holst, E. von. Über relative Koordination bei Arthropoden (mit Vergleichsversuchen am Regenwurm). *Archiv für die gesamte Physiologie*, 1943, *246*, 847–865.

Holst, E. von. Entwurf eines Systems der lokomotorischen Periodenbildung bei Fischen. *Zeitschrift für vergleichende Physiologie*, 1939, *26*, 481–528. (a)

Holst, E. von. Die relative Koordination als Phänomen und als Methode zentralnervöser Funktionsanalyse. *Ergebnisse der Physiologie*, 1939, *42*, 228–306. [For English translation see v. Holst, 1973] (b)

Holst, E. von. Über relative Koordination bei Säugern und beim Menschen. *Archiv für die gesamte Physiologie*, 1938, *240*, 44–49.

Holst, E. von. Vom Dualismus der motorischen und der automatisch rhythmischen Funktion im Rückenmark und vom Wesen des automatischen Rhythmus. *Archiv für die gesamte Physiologie*, 1936, *237*, 356–378.

Holst, E. von. Die Koordination der Bewegung bei den Arthropoden in Abhängigkeit von zentralen und peripheren Bedingungen. *Biological Reviews. Cambridge Philosophical Society*, 1935, *10*, 234–261. (a)

Holst, E. von. Über den Prozess der zentralnervösen Koordination. *Archiv für die gesamte Physiologie*, 1935, *236*, 149–158. (b)

Holst, E. von. Über die Ordnung und Umordnung der Beinbewegungen bei Hundertfüssern. *Archiv für die gesamte Physiologie*, 1934, *234*, 101–113. (a)

Holst, E. von. Über das Laufen der Hundertfüsser. *Zoologische Jahresberichte der Abteilung für allgemeine Zoologie und Physiologie der Tiere,* 1934, *54,* 157–179. (b)

Holst, E. von. Weitere Versuche zum nervösen Mechanismus der Bewegung beim Regenwurm. *Zoologische Jahresberichte der Abteilung für allgemeine Zoologie und Physiologie der Tiere,* 1933, *53,* 67–100.

Holst, E. von. Untersuchungen über die Funktionen des Zentralnervensystems beim Regenwurm. *Zoologische Jahresberichte der Abteilung für allgemeine Zoologie und Physiologie der Tiere,* 1932, *51,* 547–588.

Holst, E. von, & St. Paul, U. von. On the functional organisation of drives. *Animal Behaviour,* 1963, *11,* 1–20. [Reprinted in von Holst, 1973].

Hooker, D. Fetal behavior. *Research Publications of the Association for Research Nervous and Mental Disease,* 1939, *19,* 237–243.

Horridge, G. A. Arthropoda: Physiology of neurons and ganglia. In T. H. Bullock & G. A. Horridge (Eds.) *Structure and function in the nervous systems of invertebrates.* Vol. 2. San Francisco: Freeman, 1965.

Horridge, G. A. Learning of leg position by the ventral nerve cord in headless insects. *Proceedings of the Royal Society, Series B,* 1962, *157,* 33–52.

Hoyle, G. Neural control of skeletal muscle. In M. Rockstein (Ed.) *The physiology of insecta.* Vol. 2. New York: Academic Press, 1965.

Hoyle, G. Exploration of neuronal mechanisms underlying behavior in insects. In R. Reiss (Ed.) *Neural theory and modeling.* Stanford: Stanford University Press, 1964.

Huber, F. The role of the central nervous system in Orthoptera during the co-ordination and control of stridulation. In R. G. Busnel (Ed.) *Acoustic behavior of animals* (Amsterdam-Elsevier, 1963.

Huber, F. Lokalisation und Plastizität in Zentralnervensystem der Tiere. *Verhandlungen der Zoologisch-Botanischen Gesellschaft im Wien,* 1962, *16,* 429–442.

Huber, F. Central nervous control of sound production in crickets and some speculations on its evolution. *Evolution,* 1962, *16,* 429–442.

Huber, F. Experimentelle Untersuchungen zur nervösen Atmungsregulation der Orthopteren. *Zeitschrift für vergleichende Physiologie,* 1960, *43,* 359–391.

Hughes, G. M. Locomotion: Terrestrial. In M. Rockstein (Ed.) *The Physiology of Insecta.* Vol. 2. New York: Academic Press, 1965.

Hughes, G. M. The co-ordination of insect movements. III. The effects of limb amputation and the cutting of commissures in the cockroach (Blatta orientalis). *Journal of Experimental Biology,* 1957, *34,*306–333.

Hughes, G. M. The co-ordination of insect movements. I. The walking movements of insects. *Journal of Experimental Biology,* 1952, *29,* 267–284.

Hughes, G. M., & Wiersma, C. A. G. The co-ordination of swimmeret movements in the crayfish, *Procambarus clarkii* (Girard). *Journal of Experimental Biology,* 1960,*37,* 657–670.

Hull, C. L. *Principles of behavior.* New York: Appleton-Century-Crofts, 1943.

Hull, C. L. Knowledge and purpose as habit mechanisms. *Psychological Review,* 1930, *37,* 511–525.

Iersel, J. J. A. van, & Assem, J. van den. Aspects of orientation in the digger wasp *Bembix rostrata.* In "Learning and Associated Phenomena in Invertebrates." *Animal Behaviour.* Suppl. 1, 1965.

Ikeda, K., & Wiersma, C. A. G. Autogenic rhythmicity in the abdominal ganglia of the crayfish: The control of swimmeret movements. *Comparative Biochemistry and Physiology,* 1964,*12,* 107–115.

Issel, R. *Biologia marina: Manuali Hoepli.* Milano, 1918. p. 275.

Jacklet, J. W. Neuronal circadian rhythm. Phase shifting by a protein synthesis inhibitor. *Science,* 1977, *198,* 69–71.

Jacob, F. Evolution and tinkering. *Science,* 1977, *196,* 1161–1166.

Jahn, T. L., & Bovee, E. C. Protoplasmic movements and locomotion of protozoa. In S. H. Hutner (Ed.) *Biochemistry and physiology of protozoa.* Vol. 3 New York: Academic Press, 1964.

*James, W. *Bost. Soc. Nat. Hist.,* 1880. [Sic. Sherrington may be referring to an article by James in the *Boston Medical and Surgical Journal,* 1880, 102, 94ff.]

Jenkins, H. M., & Moore, B. R. The form of the autoshaped response with food or water reinforcers. *Journal of Experimental Analysis of Behavior,* 1973, *20,* 163–181.

Jennings, H. S. *Behavior of the lower organisms.* New York: Columbia University Press, 1931.

Jurgens, U. The hypothalamus and behavioral patterns. *Progress in Brain Research,* 1974, *41,* 445–464.

Kanda, S. Studies on the geotropism of the marine snail *Littorina littorea. Bulletin of the Marine Biology Laboratory,* 1916, *30,* 57–84.

Kater, S. B., & Rowell, C. H. F. Integration of sensory and centrally programmed components in generation of cyclical feeding activity of (*Helisoma trivolvis*). *Journal of Neurophysiology,* 1973, *36,* 142–155.

Katz, D. *Die Gestaltpsychologie* 2nd ed. Basel: Schwabe, 1948.

Kavanau, J. L. Behavior of captive white-footed mice. In E. R. Willems & H. L. Raush (Eds.), *Naturalistic viewpoints in psychology.* New York: Holt, Rinehart, Winston, 1969.

Kavanau, J. L., & Rischer, C. E. Program clocks in small mammals. *Science,* 1968, *161,* 1256–1259.

Kennedy, D., & Davis, W. S. Organization of invertebrate motor systems. In E. Kandel (Vol. Ed.) The cellular biology of neurons. Volume 1 of M. Brookhart & V. B. Mountcastle (Section Eds.), *The nervous system.* Section 1 of *The handbook of physiology.* Washington, D. C.: American Physiological Society, 1977.

Köhler, W. *The mentality of apes* (trans. by E. Winter). New York: Harcourt Brace, 1927.

Kornmüller, A. E. Eine experimentelle Anästhesie der äussen Augenmuskeln am Menschen und ihre Auswirkungen. *Journal für Psychologie und Neurologie,* 1932, *41,* 354–366.

Kots, Ya. M., & Zhukov, V. I. Suspraspinal control of the segmental centres of muscle antagonists in man. III. "Tuning" of the spinal apparatus of reciprocal inhibition in the period of organization of voluntary movement. *Biophysics,* 1971, *16,* 1129–1136.

Krasne, F. B., & Wine, J. J. Extrinsic modulation of crayfish escape behaviour. *Journal of Experimental Biology,* 1975, *63,* 433–450.

Krasne, F. B., & Wine, J. Control of crayfish escape behavior. In G. Hoyle (Ed.) *Identified neurons and the behavior of arthropods.* New York: Plenum, 1978.

Kruuk, H. *The spotted hyena: A study of predation and social behavior.* Chicago: University of Chicago Press, 1972.

Kuffler, S. W., & Nichols, J. G. *From neuron to brain.* Sunderland, Massachusetts: Sinauer, 1976.

La Greca, M. Su una particolare maniera di deambulazione di un Acridide: *Tropidopola cylindrica* (Marsch.), *Bolletino di Zoologia (Torino),* 1947, *14,* 83–104.

Langley, J. N. On the stimulation and paralysis of nerve cells and nerve endings. Part I. *Journal of Physiology,* 1901, *27,* 224–236.

Langley, J. N., & Anderson, H. K. On reflex action from sympathetic ganglia. *Journal of Physiology,* 1894, *16,* 410–440.

Lashley, K. S. The problem of serial order in behavior. In L. A. Jeffres (Ed.) *Cerebral mechanisms in behavior.* New York: Wiley, 1951.

Lashley, K. S. Factors limiting recovery after central nervous lesions. *Journal of Nervous and Mental Disease,* 1938, *88,* 733–755. (a)

Lashley, K. S. Experimental analysis of instinctive behavior. *Psychological Review,* 1938, *45,* 445–471. (b)

Lashley, K. S. Functional determinants of cerebral localization. *Archives of Neurology and Psychiatry,* 1937, *38,* 371–387.

Lehrman, D. S. Interaction between internal and external environments in the regulation of the reproductive cycle of the ring dove. In F. A. Beach (Ed.) *Sex and behavior.* New York: Wiley, 1965.

Le Magnen, J. Advances in studies on the physiological control and regulation of intake. In E. Stellar & J. M. Sprague (Eds.) *Advances in physiological psychology.* Vol. 4. New York: Academic, 1971.

Lever, J., & Geuze, J. J. Some effects of statocyst extirpation in *Lymnae stagnalis. Malacologia,* 1965, *2,* 275–280.

Leyhausen, P. Über die Funktion der relativen Stimmungs-hierarchie (Dargestellt am Beispiel der phylogenetischen und ontogenetischen Entwicklung des Beutefangs von Raubtieren). *Zeitschrift für Tierpsychologie,* 1965, *22,* 412–494.

Leyhausen, P. *Verhaltenstudien an Katzen* (3rd Ed.) Berlin: Paul Parey, 1973.

Lissmann, H. W. The neurological basis of the locomotory rhythm in the spinal dogfish (*Scyllum canicula, Acanthias vulgaris*). *Journal of Experimental Biology,* 1946, *23,* 162–176.

Lorenz, K. Über die Bildung des Instinkbegriffs. *Die Naturwissenschaften,* 1937, *25,* 289–300, 307–318, 324–331.

Lorenz, K. The comparative method of studying innate behavior patterns. *Symposia of the Society for Experimental Biology,* 1950, *4,* 221–268.

Lorenz, K. *Evolution and the modification of behavior.* Chicago: Chicago University Press, 1965.

Lowenstein, O. Labyrinth and Equilibrium. *Symposia of the Society for Experimental Biology,* 1950, *4,* 60–82.

Luco, J. V., & Aranda, L. C. An electrical correlate to the process of learning. *Acta Physiologica Latinoamericana,* 1964, *14,* 274–288.

MacDonald, J. S. The injury current of nerve. *Thompson Yates Laboratories Report.* (University of Liverpool), 1902, *4* (Pt. 2), 213–272.

MacDonnell, M. F., & Flynn, J. P. Sensory control of hypothalamic attack. *Animal Behaviour,* 1966, *14,* 399–405. (b)

MacDonnel, M. F., & Flynn, J. P. Sensory control of hypothalamic attack. *Animal Behaviour,* 1966, *14,* 399–405. (b)

Magendie, F. Experiences sur les functions des racines des nerfs rachidien. *Journal de Physiologie Expérimentale et Pathologigue,* 1822, *2,* 276–279.

Magnus, R. *Körperstellung.* Berlin: Springer, 1924.

Maier, N. R. F. Reasoning in white rats. *Comparative Psychology Monographs,* 1929, *6,* No. 29.

Manigk, W. Umstellung der Koordination nach Kreuzung der Achillessehnen des Frosches. *Archiv für die gesamte Physiologie.* 1934, *234,* 176–181.

Manton, S. M. Locomotory habits and the evolution of the larger arthropodan groups. *Symposia of the Society for Experimental Biology,* 1953, *7,* 339–376.

Marey, E. J. *La méthode graphique dans les sciences expérimentales.* Paris: Libraire de l'Académie de Médecine, 1885.

Marina, A. Die Theorien über den Mechanismus der assoziierten Konvergenz-und Seitwärtsbewegungen, studiert auf Grundlage experimenteller Forschungsergebnisse mittels Augenmuskeltransplantationen an Affen. *Deutsche Zeitschrift für Nervenheilkunde,* 1912, *44,* 138–162.

Marler, P., & Hamilton, W. J. *Mechanisms of animal behavior.* New York: Wiley, 1966.

Matthews, P. B. C. Muscle spindles and their motor control. *Physiological Reviews,* 1964, *44,* 219–288.

Matula, J. Untersuchungen über die Funktionen des Zentralnervensystems bei Insekten. *Archiv für die gesamte Physiologie,* 1911, *138,* 388–456.

Maynard, D. M. Circulation and heart function. In T. H. Waterman (Ed.) *The physiology of crustacea,* Vol. 1. New York: Academic Press, 1960.

Maynard, D. M. Activity in a crustacean ganglion: II. Pattern and interaction in burst formation. *Biological Bulletin,* 1955, *109,* 420–436.

Milburn, N. S. Sensitivity of cockroach companiform sensilla to adrenergic drugs. *American Zoologist,* 1963, *3,* 513–514.

Merton, P. A. How we control the contraction of our muscles. *Scientific American,* 1973, *288,* 30–37.

Miller, P. L. Respiration in the desert locust. I. The control of ventilation. *Journal of Experimental Biology,* 1960, *37,* 224–236.

Minsky, M., & Papert, S. Artificial intelligence. *Artificial Intelligence Memo, 252.* Artificial Intelligence Laboratory, MIT, Cambridge, Massachusetts, 1972.

*Mitsukuri, K. Negative phototaxis and other properties of *littorina* as factors in determining its habitat. *Ann. zool. jap.* [sic] 1901, *4,* Part I, 1–19. [Fraenkel citation—not in Union Serials nor World List of Scientific Periodicals]

Mittelstaedt, H. Telotaxis und Optomotorik von Eristalis bei Augeninversion. *Die Naturwissenschaftem* 1949, *36,* 90–91.

Mogenson, G. J., & Huang, Y. H. The neurobiology of motivated behavior. *Progress in Neurobiology,* 1973, *1,* 52–83.

Moore, B., & Reynolds, H. W. The rate of transmission of nerve impulses through the spinal ganglia. *Centralblatt für Physiologie,* 1898, *12,* 501.

Morgan, C. T. Physiological mechanisms of motivation. *Nebraska Symposium on Motivation,* 1957, *5,* 1–43.

Morgan, C. T. *Physiological psychology.* New York: McGraw Hill, 1943.

Morse, M. W. Alleged rhythm in phototaxis with ocean tides. *Proceedings of the Society for Experimental Biology and Medicine,* 1910, *7,* 145–146.

Murphy, R. K., & Phillips, R. E. Central patterning of a vocalization in fowl. *Nature,* 1967, *216,* 1125–1126.

Nichols, T. R., & Houk, J. C. Improvement in linearity and regulation of stiffness that results from actions of the stretch reflex. *Journal of Neurophysiology,* 1976, *39,* 119–142.

Nijenhuis, E. D., & Dresden, D. On the topographical anatomy of the nervous system of the mesothoracic leg of the American cockroach (Periplaneta americana). I and II. *Proceedings of Koninklyke Nederlanske Akademie van Wetenshapen. Series C,* 1955, *58,* 121–136.

Noble, G. K., & Schmidt, A. Structure and function of the facial and labial pits of snakes. *Proceedings of the American Philosophical Society,* 1937, *77,* 263–288.

O'Keefe, J. Place units in the hippocampus of freely moving rat. *Experimental Neurology,* 1976, *51,* 78–109.

O'Keefe, J., Nadel, L., Keightley, S., & Kill, D. Fornix lesions selectively abolish place learning in the rat. *Experimental Neurology,* 1975, *48,* 152–166.

Olmsted, J., Margutti, M., and Yanagisana, K. Adaptation to transposition of eye muscles. *American Journal of Physiology,* 1936, *116,* 245–251.

Olton, D. S. Spatial memory. *Scientific American,* 1977, *236* (No. 6), 82–98.

Olton, D. S. Discrimination reversal performance after hippocampal lesions: An enduring failure of reinforcement and non-reinforcement to direct behavior. *Physiology and Behavior,* 1968, *3,* 719–724.

Olton, D. S., & Samuelson, R. J. Remembrance of places passed: Spatial memory in rats *Journal of Experimental Psychology: Animal Behavior Processes,* 1976, *2,* 97–116.

Pal'tsev, Ye I. Functional reorganization of the interaction of the spinal structure in connexion with the execution of voluntary movement. *Biophysics,* 1967, *12,* 313–322.

Pavlov, I. P. *Conditioned reflexes. An investigation of the physiological activity of the cerebral cortex.* London: Oxford University Press, 1927.

Pearson, K. G. The control of walking. *Scientific American,* 1976, *235* (No. 6), 72–86.

Pearson, K. G., & Fourtner, C. R. Nonspiking interneurons in the walking system of the cockroach. *Journal of Neurophysiology,* 1975, *38,* 33–52.

Pearson, K. G., & Iles, J. F. Nervous mechanisms underlying intersegmental coordination of leg movements during walking in the cockroach. *Journal of Experimental Biology,* 1973, *58,* 725–744.

Peretz, B. Central neuron initiation of periodic gill movements. *Science,* 1969, *166,* 1167–1172.

Pew, R. W. Human perceptual motor performance, In B. H. Kantowitz (Ed.) *Human information processing: Tutorials in performance and cognition.* Hillsdale, New Jersey: Lawrence Earlbaum Associates, 1974.

Pew, R. W. Acquisition of hierarchical control over the temporal organization of a skill. *Journal of Experimental Psychology,* 1966, *71,* 764–771.

Piéron, M. H. Du role du sens musculaire dans l'orientation de quelques espèce de fourmis. *Bulletin de L'Institute générale de Psychologie,* 1904, *4,* 168–186.

Pinsker, H. M. *Aplysia* bursting neurons as endogenous oscillators. I-V. *Journal of Neurophysiology,* 1977, *40,* 527–556.

Pollen, D. H., Lee, J. R., & Taylor, J. H. How does the striate cortex begin the analysis of the visual world. *Science,* 1971, *173,* 74–77.

Ponz, F., & Estartús, M. Sobre la fisiología de la locomoción de Blatta orientalis (L). III. Importancia del sistema ganglionar torácico. *Revista Espanola de Fisiologia,* 1951, *7,* 99–142.

Premack, D. Reinforcement theory. *Nebraska Symposium on Motivation,* 1965, *13,* 123–179.

Premack, D. Reversibility of the reinforcement relation. *Science,* 1962, *136,* 255–257.

Pringle, J. W. S. Proprioception in arthropods. In J. A. Ramsay, & V. V. Wigglesworth (Eds.) *The cell and the organism.* Cambridge University Press, 1961.

Pringle, J. W. S. On the parallel between learning and evolution. *Behaviour,* 1951, *3,* 174–215.

Pringle, J. W. S. The reflex mechanism of the insect leg. *Journal of Experimental Biology,* 1940, *17,* 8–17.

Pringle, J. W. S. Proprioception in insects. III. The function of the hair sensilla at the joints. *Journal of Experimental Biology,* 1938, *15,* 467–473. (a)

Pringle, J. W. S. Proprioception in insects. II. The action of the companiform sensilla on the legs. *Journal of Experimental Biology,* 1938, *15,* 114–131. (b)

Prochazka, A., Westerman, R. A., & Ziconne, S. P. Ia afferent activity during a variety of voluntary movements in the cat. *Journal of Physiology,* 1977, *268,* 423–448.

Prosser, C. L. The nervous system of the earthworm. *Quarterly Review of Biology,* 1934, *9,* 181–200.

Pumphrey, R. J., & Young, J. Z. The rates of conduction of nerve fibers of various diameters in cephalopods. *Journal of Experimental Biology,* 1938, *15,* 453–466.

Ranson, S. W. The fasciculus cerebro-spinalis in the albino rat. *American Journal of Anatomy,* 1913, *14,* 411–424.

Reiss, R. F. A theory and simulation of rhythmic behavior due to reciprocal inhibition in small nerve nets. *Proceedings of the American Federation of Information Processing Societies (Spring Joint Computer Conference),* 1962, *21,* 171–194.

Richet, C. *Physiologie des muscles et des nerfs.* Paris: Baillière, 1882.

Richet, C. *Dictionaire de Physiologie.* Vol. 1. Paris: Baillière, 1895.

Richter, C. P. *Biological clocks in medicine and psychiatry.* Springfield: C. C. Thomas, 1965.

Rijlant, P. Les manifestations electriques du tonus et des contractions voluntaires et reflexes chez les Arthropodes. *Comptes Rendus. Societé de Biologie,* 1932, *3,* 631–635. (a)

Rijlant, P. Introduction à l'étude du fonctionnement des centres nerveux. *Comptes Rendus. Societé de Biologie,* 1932, *3,* 636–639. (b)

Roeder, K. D. Reflex activity and ganglion function. In K. D. Roeder (Ed.) *Insect physiology.* New York: Wiley, 1953.

Roeder, K. D. The control of tonus and locomotor activity in the praying mantis (*Mantis religiosa* L.). *Journal of Experimental Zoology*, 1937, *76*, 353–374.

Roeder, K. D., Tozian, L., & Weiant, E. A. Endogenous nerve activity and behavior in the mantis and cockroach. *Journal of Insect Physiology*, 1960, *4*, 45–62.

Romanes, G. J. Further observations on the locomotor system of medusae. *Philosophic Transactions of the Royal Society of London*, 1877, *167*, 659–752.

Rozin, P., & Kalat, J. W. Specific hungers and poison avoidance as adaptive specializations of learning. *Psychological Review*, 1971, *78*, 459–487.

Russell, D. F., & Hartline, D. K. Bursting neural networks: A reexamination. *Science*, 1978, *200*, 453–456.

Schaller, P. *The Serengheti lion: A study of predator-prey relations*. Chicago: University of Chicago Press, 1972.

Scherb, R. Zur Sehnentransplantation bei poliomyelitischen Lähmungen. *Schweizer medizinische Wochenschrift*, 1938, *68*, 354–360.

Schiller, P. H. Innate motor action as a basis of learning. In C. H. Schiller (Ed.) *Instinctive behavior*. New York: International Universities Press, 1957.

Schiller, P. H. Innate constituents of complex responses in primates. *Psychological Review*, 1952, *59*, 177–191.

Schneirla, T. C. Learning and orientation in ants. *Comparative Psychology Monographs*, 1929, *6*, No. 4.

Schoen, L. Quantitative Untersuchungen über die zentrale Kompensation. *Zeitschrift für vergleichende Physiologie*, 1949, *32*, 121–150.

Schöne, H. Die Augen als Gleichgewichtsorgane bei Wasserkäferlarven. *Die Naturwissenschaften*, 1950, *37*, 235–236.

Seligman, M. E. P., & Hager, J. L. *Biological boundaries of learning*. New York: Meredith Corporation, 1972.

Setschenow, J. *Physiologische Studien über den Hemmungsmechanismus für die Reflexthätigkeit des Rückenmarkes und Gehirnes der Froschen*. Berlin: Hirschwald, 1863.

Sevenster, P. Incompatability of response and reward. In R. A. Hinde & J. Stevenson-Hinde (Eds.) *Constraints on learning*. New York: Academic, 1973.

Seyffarth, H., & Denny-Brown, O. The grasp reflex and the instinctive grasp reaction. *Brain*, 1948, *71*, 109–183.

Shepard, R. N. Form, formation, and transformation of internal representations. In R. Solso (Ed.) *Information processing and cognition: The Loyola Symposium*. Hillsdale, New Jersey; Lawrence Erlbaum Associates, 1975.

Sherman, E., Novotny, M., & Camhi, J. M. Modified walking rhythm employed during righting behavior in the cockroach *Gromphadorhina portentosa*. *Journal of Comparative Physiology*, 1977, *113*, 303–316.

Sherrington, C. S. *The integrative action of the nervous system*. New Haven: Yale University Press, 1947. (1st Edition, 1906).

Sherrington, C. S. On the reciprocal innervation of antagonistic muscles—Eighth note. *Proceedings of the Royal Society, Series B*, 1905, *76*, 269–297. [And previous 'Notes': *76*, 161–163; *66*, 66–67; *64*, 120–121; *61*, 247–249; *60*, 414–417; *53*, 407–420; *52*, 556–564.]

Sherrington, C. S. Qualitative difference of spinal reflex corresponding with qualitative difference of cutaneous stimulus. *Journal of Physiology*, 1904, *30*, 39–46. (a)

Sherrington, C. S. Correlation of reflexes and the principle of the common path. *British Association Reports*, 1904, 728–741. (b)

Sherrington, C. S. The spinal cord. In E. A. Sharpey-Schafer's *Textbook of Physiology*. Vol. 2. London: Pentland, 1900.

Sherrington, C. S. On the spinal animal. *Medico-chirurgical Transactions*, 1899, *82*, 1–31.

Sherrington, C. S., & Laslett, E. E. Observations on some spinal reflexes and the interconnection of spinal segments. *Journal of Physiology*, 1903, *29*, 58–96.

Shettleworth, S. J. Food reinforcement and the organization of behaviour in golden hamsters. In R. S. Hinde & J. Stevenson-Hinde (Eds.) *Constraints on learning.* New York: Academic, 1973.

Shettleworth, S. J. Reinforcement and the organization of behavior in Golden Hamsters: Hunger, environment, and food reinforcement. *Journal of Experimental Psychology: Animal Behavior Processes*, 1975, *104*, 56–87.

Shik, M. L., & Orlovsky, G. N. Neurophysiology of locomotor automatism. *Physiological Reviews*, 1976, *56*, 465–501.

Shin-Schi, T., & Goris, R. C. Electrophysiology of snake infrared receptors. *Progress in Neurobiology*, 1974, *2*, 309–332.

Shirley, M. *The First Two Years. A Study of Twenty-five Babies.* Vol. 1. Minneapolis: Univ. Of Minnesota Press, 1931.

Sinnamon, H. M., Freniere, S., & Kootz, J. Rat hippocampus and memory for places of changing significance. *Journal of Comparative and Physiological Psychology*, 1978, *92*, 142–155.

Skinner, B. F. Pigeons in a pelican. *American Psychologist*, 1960, *15*, 28–37.

Skinner, B. F. *The behavior of organisms.* New York: Appleton-Century, 1938.

Spence, K. W. *Behavior theory and conditioning.* New Haven, Connecticut: Yale University Press, 1956.

Sperry, R. W. The problem of central nervous reorganization after nerve regeneration and muscle transposition: A critical review. *Quarterly Review of Biology*, 1945, *20*, 311–369.

Sperry, R. W. The functional results of muscle transposition in the hind limb of the rat. *Journal of Comparative Neurology*, 1940, *73*, 379–404.

Sperry, R. W. The effect of crossing nerves to antagonistic muscles in the hind limb of the rat. *Journal of Comparative Neurology*, 1941, *75*, 1–19.

Sperry, R. W. Transplantation of motor nerves and muscles in the fore limb of the rat. *Journal of Comparative Neurology*, 1942, *76*, 283–321.

Spiegel, E. A., & Sato, G. Experimentalstudien am Nervensystem. *Archiv für die gesamte Physiologie*, 1927, *215*, 106–132.

Stein, P. S. G. A comparative approach to the neural control of locomotion. In G. Hoyle (Ed.) *Identified neurones and the behavior of arthropods.* New York: Plenum, 1977.

Stein, P. S. G. Neural control of interappendage phase during locomotion. *American Zoologist*, 1974, *14*, 1003–1016.

Stein, P. S. G. Intersegmental coordination of swimmeret motorneuron activity in crayfish. *Journal of Neurophysiology*, 1971, *34*, 310–318.

Steinach, E. Ueber die centripetale Erregungsleitung im Bereiche des Spinalganglions. *Archiv für die gesamte Physiologie*, 1899, *78*, 291–314.

Stellar, E. Drive and motivation. In J. Field & V. E. Hall (Series Eds.), *Handbook of physiology.* Section 1, H. W. Magoun (Section Ed.), *Neurophysiology.* Vol. 3. Washington, D. C.: American Physiological Society, 1960.

*Stirling, W. Ludwigs Arbeiten, 1874, p. 245. Leipzig. [Sic. Journal also known as: *Arbeiten aus der physiologischen Anstalt zu Leipzig.* Not easily obtainable.]

Sutherland, N. S. Intelligent picture processing. Paper presented at *Conference on the Evolution of the Nervous System and Behavior,* Florida State University, Tallahassee, 1973.

Szekely, G. Developmental aspects of locomotion. In R. M. Herman, S. Grillner, P. S. G. Stein, & D. G. Stuart. *Neural control of locomotion.* New York: Plenum, 1976.

Taub, E. Motor behavior following deafferentation in the developing and motorically mature monkey. In R. M. Herman, S. Grillner, P. S. G. Stein, & D. G. Stuart (Eds.) *Neural control of locomotion.* New York: Plenum, 1976.

Taub, E., & Berman, A. J. Movement and learning in the absence of sensory feedback. In S. J. Freedman (Ed.) *The neuropsychology of spatially oriented behavior.* Homewood, Illinois: Dorsey Press, 1968.

Taylor, A., & Cody, F. W. J. Jaw muscle spindle activity in the cat during normal movements of eating and drinking. *Brain Research,* 1974, *71,* 523–530.

Taylor, F. W. The effect of transposition of the Achilles tendon on the walking and righting movements of the frog. *Journal of Comparative Physiology,* 1936, *21,* 241–273.

Teitelbaum, P. The biology of drive. In G. Quarton, T. Melnechuk, & F. D. Schmitt (Eds.) *The neurosciences: A study program.* New York: The Rockefeller Press, 1967.

Teitelbaum, P. The encephalization of hunger. *Progress in Physiological Psychology,* 1971, *4,* 319–350.

Teitelbaum, P. Levels of integration of the operant. In W. K. Honig & J. E. R. Staddon (Eds.) *Handbook of operant behavior.* Englewood Cliffs, New Jersey: Prentice-Hall, 1977.

Ten Cate, J. Quelques remarques a propos de l'innervation des mouvements locomotoires de la blatte (*Periplaneta americana*). *Archives Néerlandaises de Physiologee,* 1941, *25,* 401–409.

Ten Cate, J. Beiträge zur Innervation der Lokomotionsbewegung der Heuschrecke (*Locusia viridissima*). *Archives Néerlandaises de Physiologee,* 1936, *21,* 562–566.

Ten Cate, J. Physiologie der Ganglionsysteme der Wirbellosen. *Ergebnisse der Physiologie,* 1931, *33,* 137–336.

Ten Cate, J. Contribution à la physiologie des ganglions thoraciques des insectes. *Archives Néerlandaises de Physiologee,* 1928, *12,* 327–335.

Thorpe, W. H. A note on detour behaviour with *Ammophila pubescens* Curt. *Behaviour,* 1950, *2,* 257–264.

Thorpe, W. H. *Learning and instinct in animals.* Cambridge: Harvard University Press, 1963.

Thorson, J. Dynamics of motion perception in the desert locust. *Science,* 1964, *145,* 69–71.

Tinbergen, N. Von den Vorratskammern des Rotfuchses. *Zeitschrift für Tierpsychologie,* 1965, *22,* 119–149.

Tinbergen, N. *The study of instinct.* London: Oxford University Press, 1951.

Tinbergen, N., & Kruyt, W. Über die Orientierung des Bienenwolfes (*philanthus triangulum* Fabr.). III. Die Bevorzugung bestimmter Wegmarken. *Zeitschrift für vergleichende Physiologie,* 1938, *25,* 292–334.

Tinkelpaugh, O. L. Multiple delayed reactions with chimpanzees and monkeys. *Journal of Comparative Psychology,* 1932, *13,* 207–243.

Toman, W. On the periodicity of motivation. *Nebraska Symposium on Motivation,* 1960, *8,* 80–94.

Tönnies, J. F. Die Erregungssteuerung im Zentralnervensystem. *Archiv für Psychiatrie und Nervenkrankheit,* 1949, *182,* 478–535.

Tower, S. S. Extrapyramidal action from the cat's cerebral cortex: motor and inhibitory. *Brain,* 1936, *59,* 408–444.

Trendelenburg, W. *Der Gesichtssinn.* Berlin: Springer, 1943.

Trendelenburg, W. Zur Kenntnis des Tonus der Skelettmuskulatur. *Archiv fur Anatomie und Physiologie: Physiologische Abteilung,* 1907, 499–506.

Trendelenburg, W. Über die Bewegung der Vögel nach Durchschneidung hinterer Rückenmarkswurzeln. Ein Beitrag zur Physiologie des Zentralnervensysems der Vögel (Nach Untersuchungen an Columba domestica). *Archiv für Anatomie und Physiologie: Physiologische Abteilung,* 1906, 1–126.

Truman, J. W., Fallon, A. M., & Wyatt, G. R. Hormonal release of programmed behavior in silk moths: Probable mediation by cyclic AMP. *Science,* 1976, *194,* 1432–1433.

Turvey, M. T. preliminaries to a theory of action with reference to vision. In R. Shaw & J. Bransford (Eds.) *Perceiving, acting, and knowing.* Hillsdale, New Jersey: Lawrence Erlbaum Associates, 1977.

Twitchell, T. E. Reflex mechanisms and the development of prehension. In K. Connolly (Ed.) *Mechanisms of motor skill development.* New York: Academic, 1970.

Valenstein, E. S., Cox, V. C., & Kakolewski, J. W. Reexamination of the role of the hypothalamus in motivation. *Psychological Review,* 1970, *77,* 16–31.

Vállbo, A. B. Human muscle spindle discharge during isometric voluntary contractions: Amplitude relations between spindle frequency and torque. *Acta Physiologica Scandinavica,* 1974, *90,* 319–336.

Vince, M. A. "String-pulling" in birds. I. Individual differences in wild adult great tits. *British Journal of Animal Behaviour,* 1956, *4,* 111–116.

Vince, M. A. "String-pulling" in birds, II. Differences related to age in greenfinches, chaffinches and canaries. *British Journal of Animal Behaviour,* 1958, *6,* 53–59.

Vince, M. A. "String-pulling" in birds. III. The successful response in greenfinches and canaries. *Behaviour,* 1961, *17,* 103–129.

Wachholder, K. Untersachungen über die Innervation und Koordination der Bewegungen mit Hilfe der Aktions ströme. II. Mitteilung: Die Koordination der Agonisten und Antagonisten bei der menschlischen Bewegungen. *Archiv für die gesamte Physiologie,* 1923, *199,* 625–650.

Weevers, R. de G. Proprioceptive reflexes and the co-ordination of locomotion in the caterpillar of *Antherea pernyi.* In J. E. Treherne & J. W. L. Beament (Eds.) *The physiology of the insect central nervous system.* New York: Academic Press, 1965.

Weimer, W. B. A conceptual framework for cognitive psychology: Motor theories of mind. In R. Shaw & J. Bransford (Eds.). *Perceiving, acting, and knowing.* Hillsdale, New Jersey: Lawrence Erlbaum Associates, 1977.

Weisenfeld, Z., Halpern, B. P., & Tapper, D. N. Licking behavior: Evidence of hypoglossal oscillator. *Science,* 1977, *196,* 1122–1124.

Weiss, P. Self-differentiation of the basic patterns of coordination. *Comparative Psychology Monographs,* 1941, *17* (No. 4).

Weiss, P. *Principles of development.* New York: Henry Holt, 1939.

Weiss, P. Further experimental investigations on the phenomenon of homologous response in transplanted amphibian limbs. I. Functional observations. *Journal of Comparative Neurology,* 1937, *66,* 181–209. (a)

Weiss, P. Further experimental investigations on the phenomenon of homologous response in transplanted amphibian limbs. IV. Reverse locomotion after the interchange of right and left limbs. *Journal of Comparative Neurology,* 1937, *67,* 269–315. (b)

Weiss, P. Selectivity controlling the central-peripheral relations in the nervous system. *Biological Reviews,* 1936, *11,* 494–531.

Weiss, P. Homologous (resonance-like) function in supernumerary fingers in a human case. *Proceedings of the Society for Experimental Biology and Medicine,* 1935, *33,* 426–430.

Weiss, P. Tierisches Verhalten als "Systemreaktion." Die Orientierung der Ruhestellungen von Schmetterlingen (Vanessa) gegen Licht und Schwerkraft. *Biologia Generalis,* 1925, *1,* 167–248.

Weiss, P., & Ruch, T. C. Further observations on the function of supernumerary fingers in man. *Proceedings of the Society for Experimental Biology and Medicine,* 1936, *34,* 569–570.

Wells, G. P. Spontaneous activity cycles in marine polychaete worms. *Symposia of the Society for Experimental Biology,* 1950, *4,* 127–142.

Wendler, G. Laufen und Stehen der Stabheuschrecke Carausius morosus: Sinnesborstenfelder in den Beingelenken als Glieder von Regelkreisen. *Zeitschrift für vergleichende Physiologie,* 1964, *48,* 198–250. (a)

Wendler, G. Über die Fortbewegung der Larven von Catharis fusca. *Zeitschrift für vergleichende Physiologie,* 1964, *48,* 283–294. (b)

Wendler, G. Relative Koordination erlautert an Beispielen v. Holst's und einem neuen Lokomotionstyp. *Biologishes Jahresheft,* 1964, *4,* 157–166. (c)

Wendler, G. Die Regelung der Körperhaltung bei Stabheuschrecken (*Carausisus morosus*). *Naturwissenschaften*, 1961, *48*, 676–677.

Wetzel, M. C., & Stuart, D. G. Ensemble characteristics of cat locomotion and its neural control. *Progress in Neurobiology*, 1976, *7*, 1–98.

Wickens, D. D. The transference of conditioned excitation and conditioned inhibition from one muscle group to the antagonistic group. *Journal of Experimental Psychology*, 1938, *22*, 101–123.

Wickens, D. D. A study of voluntary and involuntary finger conditioning. *Journal of Experimental Psychology*, 1939, *25*, 127–140.

Wiersma, C. A. G., & van Harreveld, A. The influence of the frequency of stimulation on the slow and fast contraction in crustacean muscle. *Physiological Zoology*, 1938, *11*, 75–81.

Wiersma, C. A. G., & Ikeda, K. Interneurons commanding swimmeret movements in the crayfish, *Procambarus Clarkii* (Girard). *Comparative Biochemistry and Physiology*, 1964, *12*, 509–525.

Wiley, R. H. Multidimentional variation in an avian display: Implications for social communications. *Science*, 1975, *190*, 482–483.

Wilson, D. M. The central nervous control of flight in a locust. *Journal of Experimental Biology*, 1961, *38*, 471–490.

Wilson, D. M., & Gettrup, E. A stretch reflex controlling wingbeat frequency in grasshoppers. *Journal of Experimental Biology*, 1963, *40*, 171–185.

Wilson, D. M., & Wyman, R. J. Motor output patterns during random and rhythmic stimulation of locust thoracic ganglia. *Biophysics Journal*, 1965, *5*, 121–143.

Wine, J. J., & Krasne, F. B. Organization of escape behavior in the crayfish. *Journal of Experimental Biology*, 1972, *56*, 1–18.

Wine, J. J., Krasne, F. B., & Chen, L. Habituation and inhibition of the crayfish lateral giant fibre escape response. *Journal of Experimental Biology*, 1975, *62*, 771–782.

Winfree, A. T. Phase control of neural pacemakers. *Science*, 1977, *197*, 761–763.

Wolff, H. G. Statocysts and geotactic behavior in gastropod mollusks. *Fortschritte der Zoologie*, 1975, *23*, 63–84.

Wolff, H. G. Statocysten funktion bei einigen Landpulmoniten (Gastropoda). *Zeitschrift für vergleichende Physiologie*, 1970, *69*, 326–366.

Woodworth, R. S., & Schlosberg, H. *Experimental psychology*. 2nd Ed. New York: Holt, Rinehart, and Winston, 1954.

Wundt, W. *Untersuchungen zur Mechanik der Nerven und Nervencentren. Zweite Abteilung. Uber den Reflexvorgang und das Wesen der centralen Innervation.* Stuttgart: Enke, 1876.

Wyman, R. J. Neural generation of the breathing rhythm. *Annual Review of Physiology*, 1977, *39*, 417–448.

Young, J. Z. The functioning of the giant nerve fibres of the squid. *Journal of Experimental Biology*, 1938, *15*, 170–185.

Author Index

Numbers in italic indicate the page on which the complete reference appears.

421

Subject Index

A

Action specific energy, 325
Activating conditions, 212
Adequate stimulus, 24ff
Afference:
  roles of in coordination, 262f
  role at different levels of the hierarchy, 285f
  role in development of coordination, 378
After-discharge, 27, 34f
Agonists, facilitation of, 55ff, 68
Allied reflexes, 51
Analysis by synthesis, 368
AND gates, 42
Anima, 1
Antagonists, inhibition of, 55, 58, 68
Automata, 2
Automatisms (*see also* Oscillators), 94
Autonomous buildup of specific potentiation, 325f

B

Bi-conditional decisions, 164
Block diagrams, 168ff
Brain stimulation:
  in different subdivisions of the CNS, 299f
  and selective potentiation, 300ff
  multiplicity of sites, 302f
  multiplicity of effects, 303ff

C

Cell theory, 17ff
Centers, anatomical concept distinguished from functional concept, 298f
Central motive states (*see* Motivation)
Central nervous system, study of presents problems that are *sui generis* 218ff
Central programs, 12
  ubiquity of, 216
Cerebrum, 293
Coalition heterarchy (*see also* Relative hierarchy), 365
Cockroach walking (*see also* Gaits), 7ff
Cognition, 14
Cognitive maps:
  behavior indicative of in the rat, 337ff
  behavior indicative of in the digger wasp, 345ff
  Deutsch model of how behavior controlled by, 350ff
  Euclidean vs. topological, 381f
  electrophysiological evidence, 384
  aligning with perceived space, 385ff
Command signals, 140, 275
Common mode rejection, 59f
Common path, principle of (*see also* Lattice hierarchy principle), 51f
Connectionistic systems:
  holistic criticisms of, 136, 215
  rejoinders to holistic criticisms, 136, 215f
  Weiss' criticism of, 224ff